THE TIMES

Guide to the European Parliament 1989

Edited by
Alan Wood
Former Head of Parliamentary Staff, *The Times*

Times Books

Published by Times Books Limited
16 Golden Square
London W1R 4BN

Acknowledgement
In compiling this guide, the editor, *The Times* and Times Books
wish to acknowledge their indebtedness for the assistance and
cooperation given by the Directorate General of Information
and Public Relations of the European Parliament based in
Luxembourg, the staffs of the offices of the Parliament in the
member states (and particularly that in the United Kingdom),
the Secretariats and press officers of the Political Groups and
the offices of political parties in the United Kingdom.

AHW

Typesetting by
News International Newspapers Ltd.
1 Virginia Street
London, E1 9XS

Printed in the UK by
Richard Clay Limited
Bungay,
Suffolk

British Library Cataloguing in Publication Data

The Times Guide to the European Parliament
    1989
    1. European Parliament - Periodicals
    I. Wood, Alan   1919-
    341.24'22'05   JN36

ISBN 0-7230-0336-X

Contents

Foreword

By Señor Enrique Barón Crespo
President of the European Parliament, July 1989

Señor Enrique Barón Crespo was elected President of the European Parliament on Tuesday, July 25, 1989. He was elected on the first ballot by the largest majority ever seen in such an election. He had served as a Vice-President of the European Parliament from 1987 and prior to the 1989 Euro elections he had been chairman of the committee drawing up the common socialist manifesto presented to the electorate in June 1989. Since October 1987 he has also been President of the International European Movement. Born in Madrid in 1944, he is the youngest President the European Parliament has ever elected. From 1977 to 1987 he was a member of the Spanish Cortes Generales, being economic affairs spokesman of the Socialist Party from 1977 to 1982 and Minister of Transport, Tourism and Communications from 1982 to 1985. Previously he had been a lawyer, specialising in the defence of trade unionists. He has also been a professor of economic, political and legal matters in Spain and in France.

Over the next five years, major changes will be taking place in Europe which will affect the daily lives of all our citizens. The European Parliament has the principal functions of protecting and defending their interests and pushing forward the process of European integration.

The realisation of the Single European Market in 1992 has already set in train a dynamic process which in the view of the European Parliament should be continued through to the achievement of a political union.

The process by which this new dynamism was brought into the development of Europe began with the proposals of the European Parliament for European Union put forward in February 1984. We intend to make similar proposals over the next few years so that the pace of progress does not slow down.

Members of the European Parliament are becoming better known to the people of the Community and this is shown by the increased correspondence which they receive, the growth in the presentation of petitions and the thousands of visitors who attend our plenary sessions every month. I believe that *The Times Guide to the European Parliament* will continue to play an important role in helping our citizens to understand the workings of the Parliament and the activities of its individual Members.

Enrique Bar...

The fourteen Vice-Presidents of the Parliament are:

Mme Nicole Pery, France, Soc
Herr Siegbert Alber, Germany, EPP
Mr Georgios Anastassopoulos, Greece, EPP
Herr Johannes Wilhelm Peters, Germany, Soc
Mme Nicole Fontaine, France, EPP
Mr David Martin, United Kingdom, Soc
Mr Georgios Romeos, Greece, Soc

Signor Roberto Formigoni, Italy, EPP
Sir Fred Catherwood, United Kingdom, ED
Senhor João Cravinho, Portugal, Soc
M.Yves Galland, France, LDR
Senhor Antonio Capucho, Portugal, LDR
Señor Fernando Pérez Royo, Spain, European United Left
Herr Wilfried Telkämper, Germany, Verts

Voting and results made many turn green

The third direct elections in the twelve states of the European Community to send 518 members to the European Parliament were held on June 15 and June 18, 1989. While the Centre/Right politicians lost their narrow majority in the Parliament, the Socialists and other forces of the Left found themselves in a situation in which they had clearly failed to take overall command. Centre/Right and Centre/Left, in order to win the day, have to find some allies. However, headlines proclaiming 'Europe swings Left' were exaggerated.

Some sources calculated immediately after the voting that the Left had an overall majority of as low as one. But even that was arguable; there were too many imponderables, among them voting discipline which up to now has not been strong in the European Parliament. Put simply, there is a hung Parliament - the scenario for an interesting five years of European politics over the integration of the European Commmunity scheduled for 1992.

The environment undoubtedly emerged as a, if not the, major issue of the elections, nowhere more so than in the United Kingdom. An increase to a block of 30 in the number of Green MEPs - the Greens in the Rainbow Group of the previous Parliament moved out to join the newcomers and form a Green Group, Les Verts - puts them in a healthy position amid the wheeling and dealing that inevitably goes on in such a multinational and multi-political assembly. The Communists also some-what complicated matters by a split into two groups, one largely consisting of the somewhat moderate pro-Euro Italians, and the other comprising the hard-liners of France, Greece and Portugal plus Mr Proinsias de Rossa of the Irish Workers' Party.

In the United Kingdom, the Greens (with over two million votes) failed to get a seat under the first-past-the-post electoral system. Nothing remotely comparable occurred elsewhere in the European Community. Under a proportional representa-tional list system, they claimed they would have had 12 MEPs, and at the first session of the European Parliament in Strasbourg in July they demonstrated accordingly. The newly-merged Democrat Party had dismal results in Britain but with over 6 per cent of the total vote they, too, failed to get an MEP. Symbolically, the Green Group (Verts) opted to have a UK Green join their bureau.

Throughout the European Community, turnout was again disappointing, falling in many member states. Overall some 58.4 per cent of electorate voted. Over 140m cast their votes out of an electorate in 1989 of just over 244m so that while more people actually went to the polling booths, growth in electoral population resulted in lower participation. However, looked at worldwide, it was still a remarkable election for a legislature that is unique in so many ways. In 1984, by way of comparison, some 114.4m out of a European electorate of 200.5m went to the polls.

The UK figure, although still low, was actually an improvement on 1984. However, it still seems highly improbable that the Euromoney spent by the parties on their information campaigns contributed much to this fact; the key, rather, was the Labour Party decision to use the Euroelection as a mid-term referendum on the record of Mrs Thatcher's Government. The attack proved successful, aided and abetted by a disastrous and divisive Conservative Euro campaign. It was a political strategy pursued by other parties in other member states — there was little joy for incumbent governments. Holding a general election at the same time as the Euro elections hardly proved a wise decision.

There was a time when many in the Community attached little significance to the Euro elections. The 1989 elections were a case of third time unlucky, not only when general elections coincided. In the UK the Government led by Mrs Thatcher remained intact, but experienced a reverse unknown since she became Conservative Party leader, losing 13 Euro seats to Labour. It was a reverse which was also to a large degree self-inflicted and not long after led to a massive reshuffle in which Sir Geoffrey Howe, Foreign Secretary, was replaced by Mr John Major and Mrs Lynda Chalker,

5

the Minister of State responsible for European affairs was moved sideways to take on Overseas Development.

With general elections being held at the same time, the June 1989 voting resulted in the fall of the Greek Government, and in the failure of Mr Haughey, the Irish Prime Minister, to obtain a deeply desired overall majority. There was the revamping of the Luxembourg coalition Government, and in Italy, although there was no general election, the veteran politican Sgr Giulio Andreotti, just elected an MEP, succeeded in forming yet another Italian coalition Government.

In Denmark, the governing Conservative party lost two seats to Social Democrats and Liberals. In Spain the ruling Socialist Party lost a seat while, to everyone's surprise, enough people backed the party of Señor Ruiz-Mateos, a business magnate seeking to clear his name, for it to gain a seat for both him and a relative. In Germany, the Republicans emerged to gain six seats mainly from the CDU/CSU list and joined the French National Front in the European Parliament group Droites Européenes; the CDU/CSU lost nine seats altogether as the Free Democratic Party re-emerged at the European Parliament with four seats in the Liberal group. In Belgium, the Greens had the biggest increase in votes, thus raising their number of MEPs from two to three.

The 13 gains by the Labour Party in the United Kingdom made sure that the Socialist Group remained the largest in the European Parliament. The group elected M.Jeanne Pierre Cot as leader, although it was suggested that as they were the group's largest delegation, the UK Labour Party could have had the chairmanship. Apparently this was turned down because the Labour MEPs had collectively resolved that their main task was to help Labour win the next UK general election. Such a posture does actually make sense. Immediately after the Euro elections, the enlarged group of British Labour MEPs discarded the old guard and brought to office the new in the shape of assured backers of Mr Neil Kinnock. But the 45 strong Labour group was still not wholly united. In the first week at Strasbourg and on a Socialist Group resolution lauding economic and monetary union, five Labour MEPs voted against and another five abstained because it was simply 'contrary to Labour Party policy.'

While the Socialist Group increased it numbers from 165 to 180, the European People's (Christian Democrat) Party had a jump in membership of eight, from 113 to 121, largely because of the defection from the European Democratic (Conservative) Group of members of the Spanish Parti Popular. Before the Euro elections, they had indicated they could no longer stomach the 'anti-community invective' of Mrs Thatcher. The EPP group now has MEPs from each member state, the sole UK representative being the Official Ulster Unionist, Mr Jim Nicholson. The EPP re-elected Herr Egon Klepsch as leader, the RDE Group by re-appointed M.Christian de la Malene. The defection of the Spanish Parti Popular, plus the loss of 13 seats in Britain and two seats in Denmark, demoted the European Democratic (Conservative) Group from being the third largest group in the European Parliament to the fourth. That brought much more to the fore the long-established hope of Conservatives to link with the Christian Democrats.

The third largest group, the Liberal and Democratic Reformists, are 49 strong compared to 46 and have a new leader in the former French President, M. Valery Giscard d'Estaing, who headed the UDF-RPR list. Mme Simone Veil, former President of the European Party, who headed the Centre list in France, joined up with him, but five of the other six Centre list MEPs opted for the EPP Group.

In the outgoing Parliament, the Arc-en-Ciel (Rainbow) Group, with 20 MEPs, contained an assortment of Green, anti-EEC, regionalist and other MEPs. With the Greens departing, the group shrank from 20 to 13. It now includes Mrs Winifred Ewing, President of the Scottish National Party. She switched from the RDE (European Democratic Alliance) Group in response to some criticisms by SNP members. She has a constituency as large as Belgium with 24 MEPs.

If the two big groups, Socialist (180) and EPP (121) wish their views to prevail they will have plenty to court in the search for the combination of 260 votes on 1992 legislation. The strengths of other groups are: European United Left (Communist) 28, RDE (European Democratic Alliance) 20, Droites Européenes (French National Front and German Republicans) 17, Coalitions des Gauches (Communist) 14, and non-attached MEPs 12.

On leadership, the Green and Rainbow Groups opted for sex equality - one male, one female co-chairs - in, respectively, Alexander Langer and María Santos, and Jaak Vandemeulebroucke and Birgit Bjornvig.

Over half the members to the new European Parliament are newcomers, an unprecedentedly high proportion. The proportion of women members remains higher than in most national Parliaments. But they all have contact with those Ministers occupying the Presidencies of the various Councils of Ministers and with members of the European Commission.

Following on from Spain, the French hold the Presidency of the EC in the second half of 1989. In 1990 this passes to Ireland and Italy; in 1991 to Luxembourg and the Netherlands; in 1992 to Portugal and the United Kingdom. Thus the UK will be in the hot seat at the end of 1992 when Community internal trade barriers are due to disappear. Belgium and Denmark are due to hold the Presidency of the EC in 1993, and Germany and Greece in 1994 when the next Euro elections take place.

Political groups in European Parliament following June 1989 elections

	B	DK	F	G	GR	IRL	I	L	NL	P	S	UK	Total
Socialist	8	4	22	31	9	1	14	2	8	8	27	46	**180**
EPP	7	2	6	32	10	4	27	3	10	3	16	1	**121**
LDR	4	3	13	4	–	2	3	1	4	9	6	–	**49**
ED	–	2	–	–	–	–	–	–	–	–	–	32	**34**
Verts	3	–	8	8	–	–	7	–	2	1	1	–	**30**
EUL	–	1	–	–	1	–	22	–	–	–	4	–	**28**
RDE	–	–	13	–	1	6	–	–	–	–	–	–	**20**
DR	1	–	10	6	–	–	–	–	–	–	–	–	**17**
CG	–	–	7	–	3	1	–	–	–	3	–	–	**14**
ARC	1	4	1	–	–	1	3	–	–	–	2	1	**13**
NI	–	–	1	–	–	–	5	–	1	–	4	1	**12**
Total MEPs	**24**	**16**	**81**	**81**	**24**	**15**	**81**	**6**	**25**	**24**	**60**	**81**	**518**

Group membership before 1989 elections

	B	DK	F	G	GR	IRL	I	L	NL	P	S	UK	Total
Socialist	8	3	20	33	10	–	12	2	9	7	28	33	**165**
EPP	6	1	8	41	8	6	27	3	8	4	1	–	**113**
ED	–	4	–	–	–	–	–	–	–	–	17	45	**66**
Comm and Allies	–	2	10	–	4	–	26	–	–	3	3	–	**48**
LDR	5	2	14	–	–	1	6	1	5	10	2	–	**46**
RDE (EDA)	–	–	19	–	1	8	–	–	–	–	–	1	**29**
ARC	4	4	–	7	–	–	2	–	2	–	1	–	**20**
DR	–	–	9	–	1	–	5	–	–	–	–	1	**16**
NI	1	–	1	–	–	–	3	–	1	–	8	1	**15**
Total MEPs	**24**	**16**	**81**	**81**	**24**	**15**	**81**	**6**	**25**	**24**	**60**	**81**	**518**

1989-94 a colourful and crowded arena

By Lord Plumb
President of the European Parliament, 1987-1989

The European Parliament elected in June 1989 will see the European Community through to and beyond the crucial year of 1992. Although the establishment of the internal market is better understood as a continuous process than by reference to a completion date, there is no doubting the symbolic importance of the date itself in the development of European Community policies.

The Commission's policy of 'Completing the internal market' has galvanised the European Community from the disappointments of the early 1980s of 'Eurosceloris'. But the events of the past two or three years have not only relaunched the European Community's policies but have also added a new and dynamic element to the Community's structure and operations.

These developments have included an enhanced role for the European Parliament in certain important areas: a strengthening of the Parliament's ability to amend or even reject draft Community legislation through a cooperation procedure with the Council of Ministers, characterised principally by two readings in both bodies. The practical operation of this reform has been extremely successful: Community procedures, as a result, have run more smoothly, and the roles of the European Parliament and national Parliaments are increasingly defined and seen as complementary to each other. I am sure that the next five years will see significant new developments in cooperation between European Community and national decision-making procedures, especially at the Parliamentary level.

The procedures have worked particularly well where they have been accompanied by discussion and dialogue between the Community institutions, especially as characterised by adaptations and extensions of the conciliation procedure, first proposed as long ago as 1983 in Stuttgart, and only now being examined on their own considerable merits.

The European Community is much more than just the sum of discussions between Member State governments. The very presence of a directly-elected Parliament and an executive Commission in the decision-making structures would seem to indicate that the European Community constitutes a fundamentally different set of multinational institutions from, for example, the United Nations or the Council of Europe.

The Parliament's direct mandate generates a democratic legitimacy which is only partially fulfilled by the powers extended to the Parliament by the Single European Act of 1987. Although the Parliament was ungracious about the Single Act when it was passed, it revised this negative view shortly afterwards: the Single Act has made an important contribution to the political integration of the European Community and to the quality of the Parliament's contribution to this process.

The Parliament's Agenda for the 1989-1994 period is bound to be a colourful and crowded arena. But never again can the Parliament be marginalised. Under-rated perhaps, but never justifiably, the Parliament is sure to play an ever more effective role in the five years ahead.

The European elections were characterised by a deep concern for environmental issues. The new Parliament will, I am certain, be in the vanguard of political efforts to achieve a truly European dimension for environmental and consumer policies. The importance of such efforts is symptomatic of the growing conviction among European voters that certain areas of policy-making cannot be limited to the national framework alone.

In the next few years, it will become clear that many other issues merit a European dimension as well, from research and development to social policy and industrial relations.

A major characteristic of European politics in the next five years will be the elaboration of a Community framework for the further integration of economic and monetary policies. The Delors Committee report, presented to the Madrid Summit shortly after the European Elections, was an important first step in this process.

The European Parliament has already expressed the view that an implemented Single Market is tied to the achievement of economic and monetary union. Some of the Member State governments take issue with this analysis. Future debate about the issue will focus on the extent of the linkage between the two objectives.

Central to this question is the need for new Treaty amendments to enable the progress towards economic and monetary union. National governments know that any Treaty amendments are likely to transfer a measure of sovereignty from the national to the European level, as the Single Act undoubtedly did in 1987.

The Parliament is the only institution that can ensure that such a transfer of sovereignty takes place with no loss of political sovereignty from the citizens who it represents. The Parliament of the next mandate will be nothing if not exciting: I look forward with relish to the debates and decisions ahead.

Leaders of the political groups

Jean-Pierre Cot
France
Socialist

Egon Klepsch
Germany
European People's
Party

Christopher J Prout
United Kingdom
European Democratic
Group

Valéry Giscard d'Estaing
France
Liberal, Democratic and
Reformist Group

Maria Amélia Mota
Santos
Portugal
Greens

Alexander Langer
Italy
Greens

Luigi Colajanni
Italy
European United Left

Christain de la Malène
France
European Democratic
Alliance

Jean-Marie Le Pen
France
European Right

René-Emile Piquet
France
Coalition of the Left
and Progress

Birgit Bjornvig
Denmark
Rainbow Group

Jaak Vandemeulebroucke
Belgium
Rainbow Group

10

Members elected to the European Parliament

In this list of members elected to the European Parliament in the third direct elections of the European Community held on June 15-18 1989, a * denotes those who were members of the outgoing 1984-89 Parliament.

Abbreviations used to designate the political groups of the newly-elected European Parliament are: Soc - Socialist; EPP - European People's Party (Christian Democrats); LDR - Liberal and Democratic Reformist; ED - European Democratic (Conservative); Verts - Greens; EUL- European United Left (Grupo por la Izquierda Unitaria Europea); RDE - Rassemblement des democrates européens (European Democratic Alliance); DR - Droites Européennes (European Right); CG - Coalition des Gauches (Left Coalition); ARC - Arc-en-Ciel (Rainbow Group); NI - Non-attached (independents/others).

Abbreviations of member state political parties of MEPs are set out at the end of this list on Page 23.

Name	Member state	Political group	Party

A

Name	Member state	Political group	Party
*Adam, Gordon	UK (Northumbria)	Soc	Lab
Aglietta, Signora Maria Adelaide	Italy	Verts	Verdi Arcob
Ainardi, Mme Sylviane	France	CG	PCF
*Alavanos, Alexandros	Greece	CG	SAP/Comm
*Alber, Siegbert	Germany	EPP	CDU
Alemann, Frau Mechtild von	Germany	LDR	FDP
*Alexandre, Jean-Marie	France	Soc	PS
Allègre, Claude	France	Soc	PS
Alliot-Marie, Mme Michèle	France	RDE	RPR
*Alvarez de Paz, José	Spain	Soc	PSOE
*Amaral, Rui	Portugal	LDR	PSD
Amendola, Gianfranco	Italy	Verts	Verde
*Anastassopoulos, Georgios	Greece	EPP	ND
*d'Ancona, Mevr Hedy	Netherlands	Soc	PvdA
*Andrews, Niall	Ireland	RDE	FF
Anger, Didier	France	Verts	Verts
*Antony, Bernard	France	DR	FN
*Arbeloa Muru, Victor Manuel	Spain	Soc	PSOE
*Arias Cañete, Miguel	Spain	EPP	PP
Aulas, Mme Marie-Christine	France	Verts	Verts
Autant-Lara, Claude	France	DR	FN
*Avgerinos, Paraskevas	Greece	Soc	PASOK

B

Name	Member state	Political group	Party
*Baget Bozzo, Gianni	Italy	Soc	PSI
*Balfe, Richard	UK (London South Inner)	Soc	Lab
Bandres Molet, Juan María	Spain	Verts	IP
*Banotti, Mrs Mary	Ireland	EPP	FG
*Barón Crespo, Enrique	Spain	Soc	PSOE
*Barros Moura, José	Portugal	CG	PCP
Barton, Roger	UK (Sheffield)	Soc	Lab
Barzach, Mme Michèle	France	RDE	RPR
*Barzanti, Roberto	Italy	EUL	PCI
*Baur, Charles	France	LDR	UDF/RPR

Name	Member state	Political group	Party
*Beazley, Christopher	UK (Cornwall & Plymouth)	ED	C
*Beazley, Peter	UK (Bedfordshire South)	ED	C
Beirôco, Luis	Portugal	EPP	CDS
*Belo, Sra Maria	Portugal	Soc	PS
Benoit, Jean-Paul	France	Soc	PS
Bernard-Reymond, Pierre	France	EPP	Centre
Bertens, Jan-Willem	Netherlands	LDR	D'66
*Bethell, Lord	UK (London North West)	ED	C
*Bettiza, Vincenzo	Italy	Soc	PSI
*Beumer, Bouke	Netherlands	EPP	CDA
Bindi, Signora Rosario (Rosy)	Italy	EPP	DC
*Bird, John	UK (Midlands West)	Soc	Lab
*Bjornvig, Fru Birgit	Denmark	ARC	F mod EF
Blak, Freddy	Denmark	Soc	S
Blaney, Neil	Ireland	ARC	Ind
Blot, Yvan	France	DR	FN
*Bocklet, Reinhold	Germany	EPP	CSU
Böge, Reimer	Germany	EPP	CDU
Bofill Abeilhe, Pedro	Spain	Soc	PSOE
*Bombard, Alain	France	Soc	PS
*Bonde, Jens-Peter	Denmark	ARC	F mod EF
Bonetti, Andrea	Italy	EPP	DC
Bontempi, Rinaldo	Italy	EUL	PCI
*Borgo, Franco	Italy	EPP	DC
Borloo, Jean-Louis	France	NI	Centre
Bourlanges, Jean-Louis	France	EPP	Centre
Bowe, David	UK (Cleveland & Yorks N)	Soc	Lab
Breyer, Frau Hiltrud	Germany	Verts	Grüne
Briant, Yvon	France	RDE	CNI
*Brok, Elmar	Germany	EPP	CDU
*Bru Puron, Carlos María	Spain	Soc	PSOE
*Buchan, Mrs Janey	UK (Glasgow)	Soc	Lab
*Buron, Mme Martine	France	Soc	PS

C

Name	Member state	Political group	Party
*Cabanillas Gallas, Pio	Spain	EPP	PP
*Cabazón Alonso, Jesús	Spain	Soc	PSOE
*Calvo Ortega, Rafael	Spain	LDR	CDS
Cámara Martínez, Juan José de la	Spain	Soc	PSOE
Canavarro, Pedro	Portugal	Soc	PS
*Cano Pinto, Eusebio	Spain	Soc	PSOE
*Capucho, António	Portugal	LDR	PSD
Cariglia, Antonio	Italy	Soc	PSDI
Carniti, Pierre	Italy	Soc	PSI
Carvalhas, Carlos	Portugal	CG	PCP
*Carvalho Cardoso, José	Portugal	EPP	CDS
*Casini, Carlo	Italy	EPP	DC
Caso García, José Ramón	Spain	LDR	CDS
*Cassanmagnago Cerretti, Signora Maria Luisa	Italy	EPP	DC
*Cassidy, Bryan	UK (Dorset E/Hampshire W)	ED	C

Name	Member state	Political group	Party
*Castellina, Signora Luciana	Italy	EUL	PCI
Catasta, Anna	Italy	EUL	PCI
*Catherwood, Sir Fred	UK (Cambs and Beds N)	ED	C
Caudron, Gérard	France	Soc	PS
Ceci, Signora Adriana	Italy	EUL	PCI
Ceyrac, Pierre	France	DR	FN
Chabert, Henry	France	RDE	RPR
*Chanterie, Raphaël	Belgium	EPP	CVP
Cheysson, Claude	France	Soc	PS
*Chiabrando, Mauro	Italy	EPP	DC
Christensen, Frode Nor	Denmark	EPP	CD
*Christensen, Ib	Denmark	ARC	F mod EF
*Christiansen, Ejner	Denmark	Soc	S
*Christodoulou, Efthimios	Greece	EPP	ND
Clercq, Willy de	Belgium	LDR	PVV
Coates, Kenneth	UK (Nottingham)	Soc	Lab
Cochet, Yves	France	Verts	Verts
*Coimbra Martins, António	Portugal	Soc	PS
Colajanni, Luigi	Italy	EUL	PCI
*Colino Salamanca, Juan Luis	Spain	Soc	PSOE
*Collins, Kenneth	UK (Strathclyde East)	Soc	Lab
Colombo, Emilio	Italy	EPP	DC
*Colom i Naval, Joan	Spain	Soc	PSOE
Contu, Felicetto	Italy	EPP	DC
Cooney, Pat	Ireland	EPP	FG
†Corleone, Franco	Italy	Verts	Verdi Arcob
*Cornelissen, Petrus	Netherlands	EPP	CDA
*Cot, Jean-Pierre	France	Soc	PS
Cox, Pat	Ireland	LDR	Prog Dem
Cramon-Daiber, Frau Birgit	Germany	Verts	Grüne
Crampton, Peter	UK (Humberside)	Soc	Lab
Cravinho, João	Portugal	Soc	PS
*Crawley, Mrs Christine	UK (Birmingham East)	Soc	Lab
Craxi, Bettino	Italy	Soc	PSI
Cunha Oliveira, Artur	Portugal	Soc	PS
Cushnahan, John	Ireland	EPP	FG

D

Name	Member state	Political group	Party
*Dalsass, Joachim	Italy	EPP	SVP
*Daly, Mrs Margaret	UK (Somerset & Dorset W)	ED	C
*Dankert, Pieter	Netherlands	Soc	PvdA
David, Wayne	UK (Wales South)	Soc	Lab
Defraigne, Jean	Belgium	LDR	PRL
Denys, Mme Marie-Jo	France	Soc	PS
*Deprez, Gérard	Belgium	EPP	PSC
*Desama, Claude	Belgium	Soc	PS
Desmond, Barry	Ireland	Soc	Lab
*Desyllas, Dimitrios	Greece	CG	SAP/Comm
*Diez de Rivera Icaza, Sra Carmen	Spain	Soc	PSOE
*Dijk, Mevr P (Nel) van	Netherlands	Verts	CPN
Dillen, Karel	Belgium	DR	VB
Domingo Segarra, Sra Teresa	Spain	EUL	IU

† Due to be MEP only until end of October 1989 when replacement is to be Sgr Virginio Bettini.

13

Name	Member state	Political group	Party
Donnea, Francois-Xavier de	Belgium	LDR	PRL
Donnelly, Alan	UK (Tyne and Wear)	Soc	Lab
Douste-Blazy, Philippe	France	EPP	Centre
*Dührkop Dührkop, Sra Barbara	Spain	Soc	PSOE
*Dury, Mme Raymonde	Belgium	Soc	PS
Duverger, Maurice	Italy	EUL	PCI

E

Name	Member state	Political group	Party
*Elles, James	UK (Oxford & Bucks)	ED	C
*Elliott, Michael	UK (London West)	Soc	Lab
Elmalan, Mme Mireille	France	CG	PCF
*Ephremidis, Vassilis	Greece	CG	SAP/Comm
Ernst de la Graete, Mme Brigitte	Belgium	Verts	Ecolo
*Escuder Croft, Arturo	Spain	EPP	PP
*Estgen, Nicolas	Luxembourg	EPP	PCS
*Ewing, Mrs Winifred	UK (Highlands & Islands)	ARC	SNP

F

Name	Member state	Political group	Party
Fabius, Laurent	France	Soc	PS
*Falconer, Alexander	UK (Mid Scot & Fife)	Soc	Lab
Falqui, Enrico	Italy	Verts	Verde
Fantini, Antonio	Italy	EPP	DC
Fantuzzi, Giulio	Italy	EUL	PCI
Fayot, Ben	Luxembourg	Soc	POSL
Fernández Albor, Gerardo	Spain	EPP	PP
Fernex, Mme Solange	France	Verts	Verts
Ferrara, Giuliano	Italy	Soc	PSI
*Ferrer i Casals, Sra Concepció	Spain	EPP	CiU
Ferri, Enrico	Italy	Soc	PSDI
Fini, Gianfranco	Italy	NI	MSI-DN
*Fitzgerald, Gene	Ireland	RDE	FF
*Fitzsimons, James	Ireland	RDE	FF
Flesch, Mme Colette	Luxembourg	LDR	PD
Florenz, Karl-Heinz	Germany	EPP	CDU
*Fontaine, Mme Nicole	France	EPP	Centre
*Ford, Glyn	UK (Gtr Manchester East)	Soc	Lab
Forlani, Arnaldo	Italy	EPP	DC
*Formigoni, Roberto	Italy	EPP	DC
Forte, Mario	Italy	EPP	DC
*Friedrich, Ingo	Germany	EPP	CSU
Fuchs, Gérard	France	Soc	PS
Funck, Honor	Germany	EPP	CDU

G

Name	Member state	Political group	Party
*Gaibisso, Gerardo	Italy	EPP	DC
Galland, Yves	France	LDR	Radical
Galle, Mark	Belgium	Soc	SP
Gallenzi, Giulio	Italy	EPP	DC
*Gallo, Max	France	Soc	PS
Gangoiti Llaguno, Juan	Spain	NI	PNV
*Garaikoetxea Urriza, Juan Carlos	Spain	ARC	EA
*Garcia, Vasco	Portugal	LDR	PSD

Name	Member state	Political group	Party
*García Amigo, Manuel	Spain	EPP	PP
*García Arias, Sra Ludivina	Spain	Soc	PSOE
*Gasòliba i Böhm, Carles-Alfred	Spain	LDR	CiU
*Gawronski, Jas	Italy	LDR	PLI/PRI-Fed
*Giannakou-Koutsikou Ka Marietta	Greece	EPP	ND
Gil-Robles, José María	Spain	EPP	PP
Giovanni, Biagio de	Italy	EUL	PCI
Giscard d'Estaing, Valéry	France	LDR	UDF/PR
Giudice, Calogero Lo	Italy	EPP	DC
*Glinne, Ernest	Belgium	Soc	PS
Gollnisch, Bruno	France	DR	FN
*Gomes, Fernando Santos	Portugal	Soc	PS
Goria, Giovanni	Italy	EPP	DC
Görlach, Willi	Germany	Soc	SDP
Graefe zu Baringdorf, Friedrich-Wilhelm	Germany	Verts	Grüne
Green, Ms Pauline	UK (London North)	Soc	Lab
Gremetz, Maximé	France	CG	PCF
Gröner, Frau Lieselotte	Germany	Soc	SDP
Grund, Frau Johanna-Christina	Germany	DR	Repub
*Gucht, Karel de	Belgium	LDR	PVV
Guidolin, Francesco	Italy	EPP	DC
Guillaume, François	France	RDE	RPR
*Gutiérrez Díaz, Antoni	Spain	CG	IU

H

Name	Member state	Political group	Party
*Habsburg, Otto	Germany	EPP	CSU
*Hänsch, Klaus	Germany	Soc	SPD
*Happart, José	Belgium	Soc	PS
Harrison, Lyndon	UK (Cheshire West)	Soc	Lab
*Hemeldonck, Mevr Marijke van	Belgium	Soc	SP
*Herman, Fernand	Belgium	EPP	PSC
Hermans, Mevr Anna	Belgium	EPP	CVP-EVP
*Hersant, Robert	France	LDR	UDF
Herzog, Philippe	France	CG	PCF
*Hindley, Michael	UK (Lancashire East)	Soc	Lab
*Hoff, Frau Magdalene	Germany	Soc	SPD
Holzfuss, Martin	Germany	LDR	FDP
*Hoon, Geoffrey	UK (Derbyshire)	Soc	Lab
Hoppenstedt, Karsten	Germany	EPP	CDU
Hory, Jean-François	France	Soc	PS
*Howell, Paul	UK (Norfolk)	ED	C
*Hughes, Stephen	UK (Durham)	Soc	Lab
*Hume, John	UK (Northern Ireland)	Soc	SDLP

I

Name	Member state	Political group	Party
Iacono, Franco	Italy	Soc	PSI
Imbeni, Renzo	Italy	EUL	PCI
Inglewood, Lord	UK (Cumbria and Lancs North)	ED	C
*Iodice, Antonio	Italy	EPP	DC

15

Name	Member state	Political group	Party
*Iversen, John	Denmark	EUL	SF
Izquierdo Rojo, Sra María	Spain	Soc	PSOE

J

*Jackson, Mrs Caroline	UK (Wiltshire)	ED	C
*Jackson, Christopher	UK (Kent East)	ED	C
*Jacobsen, Erhard	Denmark	EPP	CD
*Janssen van Raay, James	Netherlands	EPP	CDA
Jensen, Fru Kirsten	Denmark	Soc	S
*Jepsen, Fru Marie	Denmark	ED	KF
Joanny-Schlecht, Mme Claire	France	Verts	Verts
Junker, Frau Karin	Germany	Soc	SDP
Juppé Alain	France	RDE	RPR

K

*Kellett-Bowman, Edward	UK (Hampshire Central)	ED	C
Keppelhoff-Wiechert, Frau Hedwig	Germany	EPP	CDU
*Killilea, Mark	Ireland	RDE	FF
*Klepsch, Egon Alfred	Germany	EPP	CDU
Köhler, Heinz	Germany	Soc	SDP
Köhler, Klaus-Peter	Germany	DR	Repub
Kofoed, Niels Anker	Denmark	LDR	V
Kostopoulis, Sotiris	Greece	Soc	PASOK
Krieps, Robert	Luxembourg	Soc	POSL

L

Lacaze, Jeannou	France	LDR	UDF/RPR
Lagakos, Efstathios	Greece	EPP	ND
Lagorio, Lelio	Italy	Soc	PSI
*Lalor, Patrick	Ireland	RDE	FF
Lamassoure, Alain	France	LDR	UDF
*Lambrias, Panayotis	Greece	EPP	ND
Lane, Patrick	Ireland	RDE	FF
Langer, Alexander	Italy	Verts	Verde
*Langes, Horst	Germany	EPP	CDU
Lannoye, Paul	Belgium	Verts	Ecolo
*Larive, Mevr Jessica	Netherlands	LDR	VVD
Laroni, Nereo	Italy	Soc	PSI
*Lataillade, Pierre	France	RDE	RPR
*Le Chevallier, Jean-Marie	France	DR	FN
*Lehideux, Mme Martine	France	DR	FN
*Lemmer, Gerd Ludwig	Germany	EPP	CDU
*Lenz, Frau Marlene	Germany	EPP	CDU
*Le Pen, Jean-Marie	France	DR	FN
*Lima, Salvatore	Italy	EPP	DC
*Linkohr, Rolf	Germany	Soc	SDP
Livanos, Dionyssios	Greece	Soc	PASOK
*Llorca Vilaplana, Sra Carmen	Spain	EPP	PP
*Lomas, Alfred	UK (London North East)	Soc	Lab
Lopes Porto, Manuel	Portugal	LDR	PSD
*Lucas Pires, Francisco	Portugal	EPP	CDS
Lulling, Mme Astrid	Luxembourg	EPP	PCS

Name	Member state	Political group	Party
*Luster, Rudolf	Germany	EPP	CDU
Lüttge, Günter	Germany	Soc	SDP

M

Name	Member state	Political group	Party
Madelin, Alain	France	LDR	UDF/PR
Magnani Noya, Signora Maria	Italy	Soc	PSI
*Maher, Thomas	Ireland	LDR	Ind
Maibaum, Frau Gepa	Germany	Soc	SDP
*Maij-Weggen, Mevr Johanna	Netherlands	EPP	CDA
*Malangré, Kurt	Germany	EPP	CDU
*Malène, Christian de la	France	RDE	RPR
Malfa, Giorgio La	Italy	LDR	PRI/PLI-Fed
Malhuret, Claude	France	LDR	UDF/RPR
*Marck, Pol	Belgium	EPP	CVP
*Marinho, Luis	Portugal	Soc	PS
*Marleix, Alain	France	RDE	RPR
*Marques Mendes, António	Portugal	LDR	PSD
*Martin, David	UK (Lothians)	Soc	Lab
*Martin, Mme Simone	France	LDR	UDF/RPR
*Mattina, Vincenzo	Italy	Soc	PSI
Mayer, Mme Sylvie	France	CG	PCF
Mazzone, Antonio	Italy	NI	MSI-DN
*McCartin, John Joseph	Ireland	EPP	FG
McCubbin, Henry	UK (Scotland North East)	Soc	Lab
*McGowan, Michael	UK (Leeds)	Soc	Lab
McIntosh, Miss Anne	UK (Essex North East)	ED	C
*McMahon, Hugh	UK (Strathclyde West)	Soc	Lab
*McMillan-Scott, Edward	UK (York)	ED	C
*Medina Ortega, Manuel	Spain	Soc	PSOE
*Megahy, Thomas	UK (Yorkshire SW)	Soc	Lab
Megret, Bruno	France	DR	FN
Melandri, Eugenio	Italy	Verts	DP
Melis, Mario	Italy	ARC	VV-PSDA
Mendes Bota, José	Portugal	LDR	PSD
Menrad, Winfried	Germany	EPP	CDU
Merz, Friedrich	Germany	EPP	CDU
*Metten, Alman	Netherlands	Soc	PvdA
*Michelini, Alberto	Italy	EPP	DC
*Mihr, Karl-Heinrich	Germany	Soc	SDP
*Miranda da Silva, Joaquim	Portugal	CG	PCP
*Miranda de Lage, Sra Ana	Spain	Soc	PSOE
Monnier-Besombes, Gérard	France	Verts	Verts
*Montero Zabala, José María	Spain	NI	HB
*Moorhouse, James	UK (London South & Surrey East)	ED	C
*Morán López, Fernando	Spain	Soc	PSOE
Moretti, Luigi	Italy	ARC	Lega L
*Morodo Leoncio, Raul	Spain	LDR	CDS
*Morris, David	UK (Mid and West Wales)	Soc	Lab
Mottola, Giuseppe	Italy	EPP	DC
Müller, Gerd	Germany	EPP	CSU
*Münch, Werner	Germany	EPP	CDU
*Muntingh, Hemmo	Netherlands	Soc	PvdA

Name	Member state	Political group	Party
Muscardini, Signora Christiana	Italy	NI	MSI-DN

N

Name	Member state	Political group	Party
Napoletano, Signora Pasqualina	Italy	EUL	PCI
Napolitano, Giorgio	Italy	EUL	PCI
*Navarro Velasco, Antonio	Spain	EPP	PP
Neubauer, Harald	Germany	DR	Repub
*Newens, Stanley	UK (London Central)	Soc	Lab
*Newman, Edward	UK (Gtr Manchester Central)	Soc	Lab
*Newton Dunn, William	UK (Lincolnshire)	ED	C
Nianias, Dimitrios	Greece	RDE	DI-ANA
Nicholson, James	UK (Northern Ireland)	EPP	OUP
*Nielsen, Fru Tove	Denmark	LDR	V
*Nordmann, Jean-Thomas	France	LDR	UDF-Rad

O

Name	Member state	Political group	Party
Occhetto, Achille	Italy	EUL	PCI
Oddy, Ms Christine	UK (Midlands Central)	Soc	Lab
*O'Hagan, Lord	UK (Devon)	ED	C
*Oliva García, Francisco	Spain	Soc	PSOE
Onur, Frau Leyla	Germany	Soc	SDP
Oomen-Ruijten, Mevr Maria	Netherlands	EPP	CDA
Oostlander, Arie	Netherlands	EPP	CDA
Oreja Aguirre, Marcelino	Spain	EPP	PP
Ortiz Climent, Leopoldo	Spain	EPP	PP
Outrive, Lode van	Belgium	Soc	SP

P

Name	Member state	Political group	Party
Pacheco Herrera, Pedro	Spain	ARC	PA
Pack, Frau Doris	Germany	EPP	CDU
Pagoropoulos, Dimitrios	Greece	Soc	PASOK
*Paisley, Rev Ian	UK (Northern Ireland)	NI	DUP
*Pannella, Marco	Italy	NI	PLI/PRI-Fed
Papayannakis, Mihail	Greece	EUL	SAP/Comm
*Papoutsis, Christos	Greece	Soc	PASOK
Partsch, Karl	Germany	Verts	Grüne
*Pasty, Jean-Claude	France	RDE	RPR
*Patterson, Ben	UK (Kent West)	ED	C
Pedersen, Klaus Riskaer	Denmark	LDR	V
Peijs, Mevr Karla	Netherlands	EPP	CDA
*Penders, Jean	Netherlands	EPP	CDA
*Pereira, Virgilio	Portugal	LDR	PSD
*Pérez Royo, Fernando	Spain	EUL	IU
Pergola, Antonino la	Italy	Soc	PSI
Perreau de Pinninck Domenech, Carlos	Spain	NI	R-Mateos
Perschau, Hartmut	Germany	EPP	CDU
*Pery, Mme Nicole	France	Soc	PS
Pesmazoglou, Ioannis	Greece	EPP	ND
Peter, Helwin	Germany	Soc	SDP
*Peters, Johannes Wilhelm	Germany	Soc	SDP

Name	Member state	Political group	Party
Piccoli, Cesare de	Italy	EUL	PCI
Piermont, Frau Dorothee	Germany	Verts	Grüne
Pierros, Filippos	Greece	EPP	ND
*Pimenta, Carlos	Portugal	LDR	PSD
Pinxten, Karel	Belgium	EPP	CVP-EVP
*Piquet, René-Emile	France	CG	PCF
*Pirkl, Fritz	Germany	EPP	CSU
*Pisoni, Ferruccio	Italy	EPP	DC
*Pisoni, Nino	Italy	EPP	DC
*Planas Puchades, Luis	Spain	Soc	PSOE
*Plumb, Lord	UK (The Cotswolds)	ED	C
*Poettering, Hans-Gert	Germany	EPP	CDU
Pollack, Ms Anita	UK (London South West)	Soc	Lab
Pompidou, Alain	France	RDE	RPR
*Pons Grau, Josep Enrique	Spain	Soc	PSOE
Porrazini, Giacomo	Italy	EUL	PCI
*Prag, Derek	UK (Hertfordshire)	ED	C
*Price, Peter	UK (London South East)	ED	C
*Prout, Christopher	UK (Shropshire & Stafford)	ED	C
*Puerta Gutiérrez, Alonso	Spain	CG	IU
*Punset i Casals, Eduardo	Spain	LDR	CDS
Putten, Mevr Maartje van	Netherlands	Soc	PvdA

Q

Name	Member state	Political group	Party
Quisthouot-Rowohl, Frau Godclieve	Germany	EPP	CDU
Quistorp, Frau Eva-Maria	Germany	Verts	Grüne

R

Name	Member state	Political group	Party
Raffarin, Jean-Pierre	France	LDR	UDF/RPR
*Raggio, Andrea	Italy	EUL	PCI
*Ramírez Heredia, Juan de Dios	Spain	Soc	PSOE
Randzio-Plath, Frau Christa	Germany	Soc	SDP
Rauti, Giuseppe	Italy	NI	MSI-DN
Rawlings, Miss Patricia	UK (Essex South West)	ED	C
Read, Ms Imelda (Mel)	UK (Leicester)	Soc	Lab
Réding, Mme Viviane	Luxembourg	EPP	PCS
Regge, Tullio	Italy	EUL	PCI
Reymann, Marc	France	EPP	UDF/RPR
*Rinsche, Günter	Germany	EPP	CDU
*Robles Piquer, Carlos	Spain	EPP	PP
*Rogalla, Dieter	Germany	Soc	SDP
*Romeos, Georgios	Greece	Soc	PASOK
*Romera i Alcázar, Domènec	Spain	EPP	PP
Ronn, Fru Joanna	Denmark	Soc	S
Rosmini, Frédéric	France	Soc	PS
*Rossetti Georgio	Italy	EUL	PCI
Rossa, Proinsias de	Ireland	CG	WP
Roth, Frau Claudia	Germany	Verts	Grüne
Roth-Behrendt, Frau Dagmar	Germany	Soc	SDP
Rothe, Frau Mechthild	Germany	Soc	SDP
*Rothley, Willi	Germany	Soc	SDP
Roumeliotis, Panayotis	Greece	Soc	PASOK

19

Name	Member state	Political group	Party
Rovsing, Christian	Denmark	ED	KF
*Rubert de Ventós, Xavier	Spain	Soc	PSOE
Ruffini, Mario	Italy	EPP	DC
Ruiz-Giménez Aguilar, Sra Guadalupe	Spain	LDR	CDS
Ruiz-Mateos, José María	Spain	NI	R-Mateos
Rupo, Elio di	Belgium	Soc	PS

S

Name	Member state	Political group	Party
*Saby, Henri	France	Soc	PS
Sainjon, André	France	Soc	PS
*Sakellariou, Jannis	Germany	Soc	SDP
Salema, Sra Maria Margarida	Portugal	LDR	PSD
*Sälzer, Bernhard	Germany	EPP	CDU
*Salisch, Frau Heinke	Germany	Soc	SDP
Samland, Detlev	Germany	Soc	SDP
Sandbaek, Fru Ulla	Denmark	ARC	F mod EF
Santos, Sra Maria	Portugal	Verts	Os Verdes
*Sanz Fernández, Francisco	Spain	Soc	PSOE
*Sapena Granell, Enrique	Spain	Soc	PSOE
*Saridakis, Georgios	Greece	EPP	ND
Sarlis, Pavlos	Greece	EPP	ND
Sboarina, Gabriele	Italy	EPP	DC
*Schinzel, Dieter	Germany	Soc	SDP
Schlee, Emil	Germany	DR	Repub
*Schleicher, Frau Ursula	Germany	EPP	CSU
*Schmid, Gerhard	Germany	Soc	SDP
*Schmidbauer, Frau Barbara	Germany	Soc	SDP
Schodruch, Hans-Günter	Germany	DR	Repub
Schönhuber, Franz	Germany	DR	Repub
Schwartzenberg, Léon	France	Soc	PS
*Scott-Hopkins, Sir James	UK (Hereford & Worcester)	ED	C
*Seal, Barry	UK (Yorkshire West)	Soc	Lab
*Seligman, Madron	UK (Sussex West)	ED	C
*Sierra Bardaji, Mateos	Spain	Soc	PSOE
Siméoni, Max	France	ARC	Verts/UPC
*Simmonds, Richard	UK (Wight & Hampshire E)	ED	C
*Simons, Frau Barbara	Germany	Soc	SDP
*Simpson, Anthony	UK (Northamptonshire)	ED	C
Simpson, Brian	UK (Cheshire East)	Soc	Lab
Siso Cruellas, Joaquin	Spain	EPP	PP
Smith, Alex (Sandy)	UK (Scotland South)	Soc	Lab
*Smith, Llewellyn	UK (South East Wales)	Soc	Lab
Sonneveld, Jan	Netherlands	EPP	CDA
Speciale, Roberto	Italy	EUL	PCI
Spencer, Tom	UK (Surrey West)	ED	C
Speroni, Francesco	Italy	ARC	Lega-L
*Staes, Paul	Belgium	Verts	Agalev
Stamoulis, Ioannis	Greece	Soc	PASOK
*Stauffenberg, Franz Ludwig Graf von	Germany	EPP	CSU
*Stavrou, Konstantinos	Greece	EPP	ND

Name	Member state	Political group	Party
Stevens, John	UK (Thames Valley)	ED	C
*Stevenson, George	UK (Staffordshire East)	Soc	Lab
*Stewart, Kenneth	UK (Merseyside West)	Soc	Lab
*Stewart-Clark, Sir Jack	UK (Sussex East)	ED	C
*Suarez González, Fernando	Spain	EPP	PP

T

Taradash, Marco	Italy	Verts	Anti-Pro
Tauran, Jacques	France	DR	FN
Tazdait, Mme Djida	France	Verts	Verts
*Telkämper, Wilfried	Germany	Verts	Grüne
*Thareau, Bernard	France	Soc	PS
*Theato, Frau Diemut	Germany	EPP	CDU
Tindemans, Leo	Belgium	EPP	CVP-EVP
Titley, Gary	UK (Gtr Manchester West)	Soc	Lab
*Tomlinson, John	UK (Birmingham West)	Soc	Lab
*Tongue, Ms Carole	UK (London East)	Soc	Lab
*Topmann, Günter	Germany	Soc	SDP
Torres Couto, José Manuel	Portugal	Soc	PS
Trautmann, Mme Catherine	France	Soc	PS
*Trivelli, Renzo	Italy	EUL	PCI
Tsimas, Konstantinos	Greece	Soc	PASOK
*Turner, Amédée	UK (Suffolk)	ED	C

U

Ukeiwé, Dick	France	RDE	RPR

V

Valent, Signora Dacia	Italy	EUL	PCI
*Valverde Lopez, José Luis	Spain	EPP	PP
*Vandemeulebroucke, Jaak	Belgium	ARC	VU
*Vayssade, Mme Marie-Claude	France	Soc	PS
*Vázquez Fouz, José	Spain	Soc	PSOE
Vecchi, Luciano	Italy	EUL	PCI
*Veil, Mme Simone	France	LDR	UDF
Velzen, Willem van	Netherlands	Soc	PvdA
Verbeek, Herman	Netherlands	ARC	CPN
*Verde i Aldea, Josep	Spain	Soc	PSOE
Verhagen, Maxime	Netherlands	EPP	CDA
*Vernier, Jacques	France	RDE	RPR
Vertemati, Luigi	Italy	Soc	PSI
Verwaerde, Yves	France	LDR	UDF/RPR
Visentini, Bruno	Italy	LDR	PLI/PRI-Fed
*Visser, Ben	Netherlands	Soc	PvdA
*Vittinghoff, Kurt	Germany	Soc	SDP
Vitto, Lorenzo de	Italy	EPP	DC
Vohrer, Manfred	Germany	LDR	FDP
*Vries, Gijs de	Netherlands	LDR	VVD
*Vring, Thomas von der	Germany	Soc	SDP

Name	Member state	Political group	Party

W

Name	Member state	Political group	Party
*Waal, Leen van der	Netherlands	NI	SGP
Waechter, Antoine	France	Verts	Verts
*Walter, Gerd	Germany	Soc	SDP
*Weber, Frau Beate	Germany	Soc	SDP
Wechmar, Rüdiger von	Germany	LDR	FDP
*Welsh, Michael	UK (Lancashire Central)	ED	C
*West, Norman	UK (Yorkshire South)	Soc	Lab
*Wettig, Klaus	Germany	Soc	SDP
White, Ian	UK (Bristol)	Soc	Lab
*Wijsenbeek, Florus	Netherlands	LDR	VVD
Wilson, Joseph	UK (Wales North)	Soc	Lab
*Wogau, Karl von	Germany	EPP	CDU
*Woltjer, Eisso	Netherlands	Soc	PvdA
*Wurtz, Francis	France	CG	PCF
Wynn, Terry	UK (Merseyside East)	Soc	Lab

Z

Name	Member state	Political group	Party
Zaidi, Mme Nora	France	Soc	PS
*Zarges, Axel	Germany	EPP	CDU
Zeller, Adrien	France	EPP	Centre

Women in the European Parliament

One hundred women MEPs were elected in the 1989 Euro elections: there were 85 towards the end of the previous Parliament and 75 at its beginning. Sixty-seven were elected in 1979 plus two in the Greek elections of 1981. Some 25 of West Germany's 81 MEPs are now women, as against 16 in the outgoing Parliament. France has two more (19) and Spain three (9) while the number of United Kingdom women members is the same - 12.

Female representation of other countries, with outgoing Parliament figures in brackets, is: Belgium 4 (4), Denmark 6 (7), Greece 1 (2), Ireland 1 (2), Italy 10 (8), Luxembourg 3 (2), Netherlands 7 (7) and Portugal 3 (2).

The proportion of women members has been slightly higher than in national Parliaments ever since the first Euro elections in 1979. They have played a prominent role in the affairs of the Parliament quite apart from the work of the Committee on Women's Rights. The French Socialist MEP, Mme Nicole Pery, was re-elected senior Vice-President of the Parliament.

Three women chair parliamentary committees in the new Parliament: Mevr Hedy d'Ancona, Social Affairs, Employment and Working Environment; Ms Christine Crawley, Women's Rights, and Mme Viviane Réding, Petitions. They also occupy nine vice-chairs. Sra Maria Santos, of Portugal, is co-president of Les Verts, the Green Gp, and co-vice-president is Frau Claudia Roth. Officers of this group have a mandate that lasts 15 months from the beginning of this Parliament. Fru Birgit Bjornvig is co-chair of the Arc-en-Ciel (Rainbow) Group.

Mevr Johanna Maij-Weggen of the Netherlands is one of the five vice-presidents of the EPP (Christian-Democrat Group) whose Italian and Greek delegations are led by women - Signora Maria Luisa Cassanmagnago Cerretti and Ka Marietta Giannakou-Koutsikou. Fru Kirsten Jensen is a vice-president of the Socialist Group.

Member state political parties

Belgium
Agalev ....Anders gaan leven
CVP.............Christelijke Volkspartij
PSC ....Parti social-Chretien
Ecolo-V ....Ecologistes confederes
pour l'organisation de luttes
originales - Verts European
pour des regions
transfrontalieres et
solidaires
PRL.............Parti reformateur liberal
PVV.............Partij voor vrijheid en
vooruitgang
SP ....Socialistische Partij
PS ....Parti Socialiste
VU-Eva ....Volksunie - Europese Vrije
Alliantie
VB...............Vlaams Blok

Denmark
CD...............Centrum-Demokraterne
F mod EF.....Folkebevaegelsen mod EF
KF ....Det Konservative
Folkeparti
S..................Socialdemokratiet
SF ....Socialistisk Folkeparti
V ....Venstre, Danmarks
Liberale Parti

France
Centre...........Centre Party (Mme Veil
list)
FN ....Front national
PCF ....Parti communiste français
PS ....Parti socialiste
RPR.............Rassemblement pour la
République
UDF.............Union pour la democratie
française
UDF/RPR   Giscard d'Estaing list
Verts.............Les Verts-Europe-Ecologie

Germany
CDU.............Christlich Demokratische
Union
CSU..............Christlich-Soziale Union
FDP..............Freie Demokratische Partei
GRÜNE.......Die Grünen
Repub...........Die Republikaner
SPD ....Sozialdemokratische Partei
Deutschlands

Greece
DI-ANA ......Dimogratiki Ananeossi
ND...............Nea Dimokratia
PASOK ....Panelliniko Socialistiko
Kinima
SAP..............Synaspismos Tis Aristeras Kai
Tis Proodou

Ireland (Eire)
FF................Fianna Fáil Party
FG ....Fine Gael Party
Ind...............Independent
Lab ....Labour Party
PD ....Progressive Democrats
WP...............Workers' Party

Italy
Anti-pro........Lega Antiproibizionisti Droga
Arcob............Verdi Arcobaleno
DC...............Democrazia cristiana
DP ....Democrazia proletaria
Lega-L ....Lega Lombarda
MSI-DN ....Movimento sociale
italiano-Destra nazionale
PCI ....Partito communista italiano
PRI/PLI-Fed Polo Laico (Liberali -
Repubblicani-Federalisti)
PLI ....Partito liberali italiano
PRI..............Partito repubblicano italiano
PSDI.............Partito socialista democratico
italiano
PSI...............Partito socialista italiano
SVP ....Sudtiroler Volkspartei (Partito
popolare sudtirolese)
UV-PSDA ....Unione Valdostana- Partito
sardo d'azione
Verdi ....Verdi Europa

Luxembourg
DP ....Demokratesch Partei
PCS..............Parti chretien social
POSL...........Parti ouvrier socialiste
luxembourgeois

Netherlands
CDA ....Christen Democratisch Appel
D'66.............Democraten 66
PVDA...........Partij van de Arbeid
CPN.............Communistische Partij
Nederland
SGP ....Staatkundig Gereformeerde
Partij
VVD.............Volkspartij voor Vrijheid en
Democratie

Portugal
CDS.............Partido do Centro
Democratico Social
CDU ....Coligacao Democratica
Unitaria
Os Verdes.....Verdes
PCP ....Partido Comunista Portugues
PS ....Partido Socialista
PSD ....Partido Social Democrata

Spain
CDS.............Centro Democrático y Social
CiU ....Convergència i Unió
CN ....Coalición nacionalista
EP ....Coalición por la Europa de
los Pueblos: Eusko
Alkartasuna (EA)
HB...............Herri Batasuna
IP..................Izquierda de los Pueblos
IU ....Izquierda Unida
PA................Partido Andalucista
PP.................Partido Popular
PSOE...........Partido Socialista Obrero
Español
R-Mateos .....Agrupacion de electores 'José
María Ruiz-Mateos'

United Kingdom
C ....Conservative Party
DUP..............Democratic Unionist
Party (NI)
Lab ....Labour Party
OUP ....Official Ulster Unionist
Party (NI)
SDLP............Social Democratic and
Labour Party (NI)
SNP ....Scottish National Party

EP committee memberships

The European Parliament decided after the 1989 elections to maintain its existing 18 committees although it made some alterations to titles and scope of activities, and also changed the number of members on the committees. Three - Political Affairs, Economic and Monetary Affairs and Industrial Policy, and Environment, Public Health and Consumer Protection - each have over 50 members.

The Committee on Agriculture, Fisheries and Food is now known as the Committee on Agriculture, Fisheries and Rural Development while the Committee on Transport had its title extended to include tourism. The Social Affairs and Employment Committee had its terms of reference and title changed to embrace the 'working environment.' Henceforth it will deal with health and safety legislation which used to be handled by the Environment Committee. The task of drawing up a draft uniform electoral system for the European Community has gone to the Committee on Institutional Affairs.

The Committee on Women's Rights was given two additional responsibilities, the first relating to the assessment of common policies from the point of view of women and the consequences for women of the completion of the internal market. The second concerns the situation of migrant women and the partners of migrant workers and the status of women who are both European citizens and nationals of non-European countries within the framework of European legislation relating to the single market.

Membership of the committees is as follows, with vice-chairmanships given in order of precedence:

Political Affairs Committee (56 members)

Chairman: Giovanni Goria (Italy, EPP).
Vice-chairmen: Peter Crampton (United Kingdom, Soc), Willem van Velzen (Netherlands, Soc), Jean Defraigne (Belgium, LDR).
Soc (19): Moran, Planas, Verde, Hansch, Walter, Sakellariou, Cheysson, Trautmann, Baget Bozzo, Cariglia, Romeos, Balfe, Coates, Crampton, Ford, White, van Velzen, Dury, Fayot.
EPP (14): Cassanmagnago Cerretti, Ferrer i Casals, Goria, von Habsburg, Klepsch, Lenz, Michelini, Penders, Pesmazoglou, Pirkl, Poettering, Reding, Robles Piquer, Tindemans.

LDR (6): Capucho, Defraigne, Gawronski, Lacaze, Malhuret, Morodo.
ED (4): Bethell, Jepsen, Newton Dunn, Welsh.
Verts (2): Langer, Piermont.
EUL (3): Castellina, Napolitano, Pérez Royo.
RDE (2): Alliot-Marie, Lalor.
DR (2): Dillen, Schonhuber.
CG (1): Ephremidis.
ARC (1): Christensen.
NI (2): Fini, Pannella.

Committee on Agriculture, Fisheries and Rural Development (47 members)

Chairman: Juan Colino Salamanca (Spain, Soc).
Vice-chairmen: Franco Borgo (Italy, EPP), Friedrich Graefe zu Baringdorf (Germany, Verts), Mark Killilea (Ireland, RDE).
Soc (13): Colino, Sierra, Vazquez, Rothe, Gorlach, Thareau, Livanos, Woltjer, Happart, Cunha, McCubbin, Newens, Stevenson.
EPP (14): Bocklet, Borgo, Bourlanges, Dalsass, Funck, Keppelhoff-Wiechert, McCartin, Marck, Mottola, Navarro Velasco, Ortiz Climent, Pisoni N, Saridakis, Sonneveld.

LDR (4): Garcia, Kofoed, Martin S, Vohrer.
ED (3): Howell, Plumb, Spencer.
Verts (3): Falqui, Graefe zu Baringdorf, Verbeek.
EUL (2): Domingo Segarra, Fantuzzi.
RDE (3): Guillaume, Killilea, Lane.
DR (1): Le Pen.
CG (2): Dessylas, Piquet.
ARC (1): Blaney.

Committee on Budgets (42 members)

Chairman: Thomas von der Vring (Germany, Soc).
Vice-chairs: Mme Colette Flesch (Luxembourg, LDR), Petrus Cornelissen (Netherlands, EPP), William Newton Dunn (United Kingdom, ED).
Soc (12): Arbeloa, Colom, von der Vring, Cot, Samland, Hory, Vertemati, Papoutsis, Dankert, Newman, Tomlinson and one other.
EPP (8): Arias Canete, Boge, Christodoulou, Cornelissen, Forte, Langes, Lo Giudice, Theato.

LDR (3): Flesch, Holzfuss, Lamassoure.
ED (3): Kellett-Bowman, Newton-Dunn, Simmonds.
Verts (1): Cochet.
EUL (1): Colajanni.
RDE (1): Pasty.
DR (1): Blot.
CG (1): Moranda da Silva.
NI (1): Perreau.

Committee on Economic and Monetary Affairs and Industrial Policy (52 members)

Chairman: Bouke Beumer (Netherlands, EPP).
Vice-chairmen: Barry Desmond (Ireland, Soc), Gerard Fuchs (France, Soc), Alain Madelin (France, LDR).
Soc (20): Bofill, Colom, Hoff, Mihr, Rogalla, Wettig, Fuchs, Caudron, Mattina, Roumeliotis, Metten, van Hemeldonck, Cravinho, Cheristiansen, Desmond, Read, Seal, Tongue, Barton, Donnelly.
EPP (13): Bernard-Reymond, Beumer, Friedrich, Gallenzi, Herman, Hoppenstedtm Iodice, Lulling, Merz, Pinxten, Sboarina, Siso Cruellas, von Wogau.

LDR (6): Cox De Donnea, Madelin, Pedersen K, Punset i /casals, Visentini.
ED (4): Beazley P, Cassidy, Patterson, Stevens.
Verts (1): Ernst de la Graete.
EUL (3): De Piccoli, Papayannakis, Speciale.
RDE (1): Lataillade.
DR (1): Megret.
CG (2): Carvalhas, Herzog.
NI (1): Ruiz-Mateos.

Committee on Energy, Research and Technology (35 members)

Chairman: Antonino la Pergola (Italy, Soc).
Vice-chairmen: Bernhard Saelzer (Germany, EPP),
Paul Lannoye (Belgium, Verts), Gordon Adam
(United Kingdom, Soc).
Soc (11): Garcia Arias, Sanz, Linkohr, Schinzel,
Allegre, La Pergola, Lagorio, Desama, Adam, Smith,
West.
EPP (8): Carvalho Cardoso, Chiabrando, Pierros,
Quisthoudt-Rowohl, Rinsche, Robles Piquer,
Ruffini, Salzer.

LDR (4): Capucho, Gasoliba i Bohm, Larive,
Verwaerde.
ED (2): Rovsing, Seligman.
Verts (4): Anger, Breyer, Corleone (due to be suc-
ceeded as MEP by Bettiza), Lannoye.
EUL (2): Porrazzini, Regge.
RDE (1): Pompidou.
DR (1): Schlee.
CG (1): Mayer.

Committee on External Economic Relations (29 members)

Chairman: Willy de Clercq (Belgium, LDR).
Vice-chairmen: Eusebio Cano Pinto (Spain, Soc),
Konstantinos Stavrou (Greece, EPP), James
Moorhouse (United Kingdom, ED).
Soc (11): Cano, Miranda, Junker, Randzio-Plath,
Sainjon, Benoit, Bettiza, Tsimas, Bird, Hindley,
Titley.
EPP (6): Colombo, Chiabrando, Lemmer, Peijs,
Stavrou, Zarges.

LDR (3): De Clercq, De Vries, Porto.
ED (2): Elles, Moorhouse.
Verts (1): Aglietta.
EUL (1): Rossetti.
RDE (1): Chabert.
DR (2): Ceyrac, Neubauer.
CG (1): Gremetz.
ARC (1): Moretti.

Committee on Legal Affairs and Citizens' Rights (34 members)

Chairman: Franz Stauffenberg (Germany, EPP).
Vice-chairmen: Mme Marie-Claude Vayssade
(France, Soc); Willi Rothley (Germany, Soc);
Francesco Speroni (Italy, ARC).
Soc (12): Bru, Medina, Ramirez, Rothley, Vayssade,
Ferrara, van Outrive, Marinho, Falconer, Hoon,
Oddy and one other.
EPP (9): Anastassopoulos, Cabanillas Gallas,
Casini, Cooney, Garcia Amigo, Janssen van Raay,
Malangre, Reymann, Stauffenberg.

LDR (2): De Gucht, Salema.
ED (2): Inglewood, Simpson.
Verts (2): Bandres, Tazdait.
EUL (2): Ceci, Valent.
RDE (1): Briant.
DR (2): Gollnisch, Grund.
ARC (1): Speroni.
NI (1): Mazzone.

Committee on Social Affairs, Employment and the Working Environment (42 members)

Chair: Mevr Hedy d'Ancona (Netherlands, Soc)
Vice-chairmen: Lorenzo de Vitto (Italy, EPP);
Mihail Papayannakis (Greece, EUL); Jose Barros
Moura (Portugal, CG).
Soc (16): Alvarez, Cabezon, Salisch, Peters, Peter,
Buron, Carniti, Pagoropoulos, d'Ancona, Glinne,
Torres Cuoto, Ronn, Hughes, McMahon, Megahy,
Wilson.
EPP (9): Brok, Deprez, de Vitto, Giannakou-
Koutsikou, Menrad, Oomen-Ruijten, Pisoni F,
Suarez Gonzalez, Zeller.

LDR (3): Von Alemann, Mendes, Nielson T.
ED (2): Catherwood, O'Hagan.
Verts (2): Cramon-Daiber, van Dijk.
EUL (3): Bontempi, Catasta, Papayannakis.
RDE (1): Nianias.
DR (1): Le Chevallier.
CG (2): Barros Moura, Elmalan.
ARC (1): Sandbaek.
NI (2): Paisley, Pannella.

Committee on Regional Policy and Regional Planning (38 members)

Chairman: Antoine Waechter (France, Verts).
Vice-chairmen: Tom Maher (Ireland, LDR),
Proinsias de Rossa (Ireland, CG), Jean-Marie Al-
exander (France, Soc).
Soc (13): Inquierdo, Oliva, Kohler, Onur, Maibaum,
Hume, Alexandre, Rosmini, Gomes, Martin, Smith
A, David, Harrison.
EPP (8): Contu, Cushnahan, Escuder Croft, Iodice,
Lambrias, Lucas Pires, Nicholson, Pack.

LDR (3): Calvo, Maher, Raffarin.
ED (1): Prout.
Verts (2): Staes, Waechter.
EUL (2): Gutierrez Diaz, Raggio.
RDE (2): Fitzgerald, Juppe.
DR (1): Antony.
CG (2): De Rossa, Ainardi.
ARC (2): Garaikoetxea, Melis.
NI (2): Borloo, Montero.

Committee on Transport and Tourism (30 members)

Chairman: Rui Amarel (Portugal, LDR).
Vice-chairmen: Gunter Topmann (Germany, Soc),
Christopher Beazley (United Kingdom, ED), Frode
No Christensen (Denmark, EPP).
Soc (9): Sapena, Topmann, Luttge, Denys, Iiacono,
Stamoulis, Visser, Simpson, Stewart.
EPP (6): Bonetti, Fantini, Muller, Nor Christensen,
Romera i Alcazar, Sarlis.

LDR (3): Von Alemann, Amaral, Wijsenbeek.
ED (3): Beazley C, McIntosh, McMillan-Scott.
Verts (2): Fernex, Schlecht-Joanny.
EUL (1): Porrazzini.
RDE (2): De la Malene, Marleix.
DR (2): Schodruch, Tauran.
ARC (1): Bonde.
NI (1): Vanderwaal.

Committee on Environment, Public Health and Consumer Protection (51 members)

Chairman: Ken Collins (United Kingdom, Soc).
Vice-chairs: Frau Ursula Schleicher (Germany,
EPP), Sir James Scott-Hopkins (United Kingdom,
ED), John Iversen (Denmark, EUL).
Soc (19): De la Camara, Diez, Weber, Schmid,
Vittinghoff, Roth-Behrendt, Bombard,
Schwarzenberg, Mattina, Avgerinos, Muntingh, Du
Rupo, Canavarro, Jensen, Pollack, Bowe, Crawley,
Green, Collins.
EPP (11): Alber, Banotti, Chanterie, Douste-Blazy,
Florenz, Gaibisso, Guidolin, Llorca Vilaplana, Maij-
Weggen, Schleicher, Valverde Lopez.

LDR (5): Bertens, Pereira, Pimenta, Veil, Vohrer.
ED (3): Caroline Jackson, Prag, Scott-Hopkins.
Verts (4): Amendola, Monnier-Besombes, Partsch,
Quistorp.
EUL (3): Imbeni, Iversen, Puerta Gutierrez.
RDE (2): Fitzsimons, Vernier.
DR (1): Kohler.
CG (1): Alavanos.
ARC (1): Bjornvig.
NI (1): Muscardini.

25

EP COMMITTEE MEMBERSHIP

Committee on Youth, Culture, Education, the Media and Sport (31 members)

Chairman: Roberto Barzanti (Italy, EUL).
Vice-chairs: Max Simeone (France, Verts), Robert Krieps (Luxembourg, Soc), Mrs Mary Banotti (Ireland, EPP).
Soc (11): Duhrkop, Groner, Galle, Zaidi, Laroni, Kostopoulos, Galle, Coimbra, Krieps, Buchan, Elliott.
EPP (7): Estgen, Fontaine, Banotti, Gil-Robles, Hermans, Munch, Oostlander.

LDR (2): Bertens, Larive.
ED (2): Rawlings, Stewart-Clark.
Verts (2): Roth, Taradash.
EUL (2): Barzanti, De Giovanni.
RDE (1): Barzach.
DR (1): Autant-Lara.
ARC (2): Simeoni, Vandemeulebroucke.
NI (1): Gangoiti.

Committee on Development and Cooperation (43 members)

Chairman: Henri Saby (France, Soc).
Vice-chairs: Signora Rosy Bindi (Italy, EPP), Mme Marie-Christine Aulas (France, Verts), Sra Maria Belo (Portugal, Soc).
Soc (14): Pons, Rubert, Simons, Schmidbauer, Saby, Pery, Magnani, van Putten, Belo, Lomas, McGowan, Morris, Wynn and one other.
EPP (8): Bindi, Borgo, Gernandez Albor, Lagakos, Luster, Perschau, Tindemans, Verhagen.
LDR (5): Flesch, Galland, Mendes Bota, Nordmann, Ruiz Gimenez Aguilar.

ED (3): Daly, Christopher Jackson, Turner.
Verts (4): Aulas, Melandri, Santos, Telkamper.
EUL (3): Napoletano, Trivelli, Vecchi.
RDE (2): Andrews, Ukeiwe.
DR (1): Lehideux.
CG (1): Wurtz.
ARC (1): Ewing.
NI (1): Rauti.

Committee on Budgetary Control (29 members)

Chairman: Peter Price (United Kingdom, ED).
Vice-chairmen: Terry Wynn (United Kingdom, Soc), Miguel Arias Canete (Spain, EPP), Freddy Blak (Denmark, Soc).
Soc (11): Colom, Wettig, Saby, Craxi, Papoutsis, Dankert, Blak, Wynn, Lomas, McMahan, Tomlinson.
EPP (8): Arias Canete, Chiabrando, Cornelissen, Langes, Lo Guidice, Marck, Christodoulou, Theato.

LDR (3): Flesch, Holzfuss, Lamassoure.
ED (2): Kellett-Bowman, Price.
Verts (1): Cochet.
EUL (1): Iversen.
RDE (1): Pasty.
DR (1): Schodruch.
CG (1): Mayer.

Committee on Institutional Affairs (38 members)

Chairman: Marcelino Oreja Aguirre (Spain, EPP).
Vice-chairmen: Derek Prag (United Kingdom, ED), Enrico Ferri (Italy, Soc), Carlos Bru Puron (Spain, Soc).
Soc (12): Bru, Hansch, Rothley, Fabius, Fuchs, Ferri, Avgerinos, Dury, Marinho, Balfe, Donnelly, Martin.
EPP (10): Alber, Beiroco, Bindi, Cassanmagnago Cerretti, Cooney, Ferrer I Casals, Herman, Luster, Oreja Aguirre, Valverde Lopez.

LDR (4): Caso Garcia, de Gucht, Pimenta, von Wechmar.
ED (2): Prag, Prout.
Verts (2): Aglietta, Bandres.
EUL (3): De Giovanni, Duverger, Puerta Gutierrez.
RDE (1): Juppe.
DR (1): Blot.
CG (1): Ephremidis.
ARC (1): Speroni.
NI (1): Pannella.

Committee on Rules of Procedure, the Verification of Credentials and Immunities (27 members)

Chairman: Marc Galle (Belgium, Soc).
Vice-chairmen: Adrien Zeller (France, EPP), Florus Wijsenbeek (Netherlands, LDR), Lyndon Harrison (United Kingdom, Soc).
Soc (8): Bru, Peters, Rogalla, Stamoulis, Galle, David, Ford, Harrison.
EPP (6): Janssen van Raay, Lima, Malangre, Rinsche, Stavrou, Zeller.
LDR (3): Defraigne, Salema, Wijsenbeek.

ED (2): McIntosh, Prout.
Verts (2): Langer, Taradash.
EUL (1): Vecchi.
RDE (1): Lalor.
DR (1): Gollnisch.
CG (1): Ephremidis.
ARC (1): Vandemeulebroucke.
NI (1): Mazzone.

Committee on Women's Rights (33 members)

Chair: Mrs Christine Crawley (United Kingdom, Soc).
Vice-chairs: Signora Carmen Llorca Vilaplana (Spain, EPP), Frau Dagmar Roth-Behrendt (Germany, Soc), Signora Teresa Domingo Segarra (Spain, EUL).
Soc (12): Duhrkop, Roth-Behrendt, Maibaum, Grober, Vayssade, Kostopoulos, d'Ancona, Dury, Belo, Crawley, Pollack, Read.
EPP (8): Bindi, Giannakou-Koutsikou, Hermans, Lenz, Llorca Vilaplana, Lulling, Maij-Weggen, Pack.

LDR (3): Ruiz-Gimenez Aguilar, Larive, Salema.
ED (2): Daly, Rawlings.
Verts (2): Van Dijk, Ernst de la Graete.
EUL (2): Domingo Segarra, Napoletano.
RDE (1): Killilea.
DR (1): Grund.
CG (1): Elmalan.
ARC (1): Bjornvig.

Committee on Petitions (25 members)

Chair: Mme Viviane Reding (Luxembourg, EPP).
Vice-chairmen: Dimitrios Pagoropoulos (Greece, Soc), Ingo Friedrich (Germany, EPP), Gerard Monnier-Besombes (France, Verts).
Soc (9): Miranda, Schmidbauer, Sakellariou, Pagoropoulos, Happart, Coimbra, Adam, Newman, Simpson.
EPP (6): De Vitto, Friedrich, Gil-Robles, Lambrias, Lucas Pires, Réding.

LDR (3): Gasoliba I Bohm, Mendes, Punset I Casals.
ED (2): Cassidy, Newton Dunn.
Verts (1): Monnier-Besombes.
EUL (1): Gutierrez Diaz.
RDE (1): Fitzsimons.
DR (1): Dillen.
NI (1): Perreau.

26

Review of the Campaign in Europe

Splinter groups mean uncertain majority for Left

By Michael Binyon
Brussels Correspondent of *The Times*

Apart from general elections in India, the 1989 elections to the European Parliament were the world's biggest test of democratic opinion. It was only the third direct election to the 518-member Parliament at Strasbourg, and the first time that all 12 members of the enlarged Europan Community had all voted together.

And with 240 million people entitled to vote, the election came at a crucial time in the development of the European Community: halfway through the ambitious programme for completion of the Single Market by 1992, and after the 1987 Single European Act had given increased power to the European Parliament enabling it to play a growing role in shaping the growing volume of legislation emanating from Brussels.

The only issue that swept the campaign trail from Edinburgh to Sicily, Lisbon to Copenhagen, was the environment. The election saw a tidal wave of support for the Greens, who have now become a trans-national European movement, blurring left-right distinctions and profoundly influencing older traditional parties.

The results were a victory for the left in the new Parliament, with the strong showing by the British Labour party and the Greens in several countries giving the left narrow overall control. But it was a narrow and uncertain majority, depending on many of the new Greens, regionalists and small parties voting with the socialists and Communists.

The Green parties did well throughout the Community. In France, the Green list headed by M. Antoine Waechter won nine seats - overtaking the longer-established German Greens to make it the biggest Green group from any country. Greens entered Parliament also for the first time from Italy.

But the elections also brought in several splinter parties, whose affiliation was not immediately clear, and who are expected to vote sometimes with the left and at others with the right. They included one new Greek candidate, two regional candidates from Spain, including a Basque representative, and two members of a party founded by the fugitive Spanish businessman Señor José María Ruiz-Mateos, former head of the sequestrated Rumasa empire. In addition there are two Irish independents, four regional candidates from Italy and another representing a party that campaigned against the prohibition on drugs, and a Calvinist from the Netherlands as well as one member of the Dutch 'Democrat 66' centrists.

One group that significantly improved its position was the far right, represented at Strasbourg until June mainly by supporters of M. Jean-Marie Le Pen, the leader of the French National Front. It was strengthened by the influx of six German Republicans from the new party started by Herr Franz Schönhuber, and gained a member from the Flemish Bloc in Belgium. However, the four members of the Italian MSI right-wing party left the group in protest at what they called the 'pan-German' aspirations of the Republicans (a quarrel dealing mainly with the German-speaking minority in the Italian Alps).

But despite these changes in the smaller groups, the overall balance in Parliament has changed little, with the two big blocs - the EPP and the Socialists - maintaining their dominance, and pledged to continue informal cooperation.

The reason for this is the system of proportional representation used for the elections in all countries except Britain. With only 518 seats at stake, there would have to be a massive Europe-wide landslide to make much difference. As it is, each MEP represents on average 700,000 constituents. And under proportional representation, a swing of four or five per cent does not produce the huge change in marginal seats it does in Britain. Indeed, one of the main differences in the new Parliament is the larger number of British Labour MEPs.

Proportional representation in some countries, such as France and Spain, consists of a straight party list for the whole country. Each party puts up its slate of candidates, and the numbers elected from each are in direct proportion to the percentage of votes gained. In others, such as Germany and Italy, the lists are regional. This means seat allocation is not quite as close as the overall tally of votes, but each MEP does have a constituency to which he is answerable.

Luxembourg, with only 380,000 inhabitants, can afford an even more complicated system, allowing each voter six votes, one for each of the tiny country's six seats, and ensuring a variety of permutations. In Ireland, there is a transferable vote system, which makes exit polls an unreliable way of forecasting results. In 1982 the European Parliament proposed a form of proportional representation on a regional basis in order to enhance the chances of all significant political parties in the Community being represented. But member governments failed to agree on this, and Britain therefore retained its first-past-the-post system. However, the three Northern Irish seats are allocated on a proportional representation basis.

In nearly all PR systems there is a five per cent hurdle which parties must clear if they are to win seats - though in countries such as Spain where the vote was splintered among many regional and minor parties, MEPs were elected from several very small groups.

Turn-out in the elections was down slightly, from 61 per cent in 1984 to 58.5 per cent. It fell most sharply in France, Spain and Portugal, where only just over half the electorate voted, and rose in those countries such as Greece and Ireland holding general elections on the same day. More people voted in Italy - 37.9 million - than in any other country, with West Germany coming second at 27.8 million and France third with 19.3 million. Italy's high turn-out is partly explained by the fact that voting there is compulsory, as it is also in Belgium and Luxembourg.

In Italy there was also a referendum on the same day on a motion to give the European Parliament a mandate to form a federal Europe, and 88 per cent voted in favour of this. The vote, reflecting the wish for a strong government in Europe, had little practical effect in Strasbourg, however.

In general the campaigns in the various were somewhat lacklustre, and fought almost entirely on domestic issues. This was especially the case in countries where a general election was approaching, or where, as in Germany, growing criticism of the government's performance had emboldened the opposition.

Crucial test for Kohl

For Chancellor Helmut Kohl, the election was a crucial test of his waning popularity in the Federal Republic. He needed to show that his coalition was stable and rebuff challenges to his leadership of the Christian Democratic Union before the general election in December 1990. At the same time, he needed a good result for the junior partner in the coalition, the Free Democrats, so as not to exacerbate the strains with Herr Hans-Dietrich Genscher, the Foreign Minister and leader of the Free Democrats.

The campaign barely touched on European issues, which was significant. West Germany had always been one of the most 'European' of the Community members, with widespread public support for the EC and identification with the Community serving almost as an ersatz patriotism. But in 1989 the mood had changed. German public opinion was restive, chafing at the heavy costs the country bore as a net financial contributor, anxious for a greater German assertiveness both in the Community and Nato. A certain disillusionment with the EC had been prompted by Community policies on beer purity, the environment, regional support, industrial policies and social legislation. There was also a worry that hard-won German stability would be frittered away by too many concessions to the poorer Southern member states with their high inflation rate. Trade unions feared that West German social legislation would not be copied around the Community, making their labour expensive.

In such an atmosphere, the newly founded Republicans, fresh from their success in the West Berlin elections, campaigned hard on the issues of foreign immigration, German national interest, law and order and a tough line over the lost territories in the East. The Social Democrats campaigned against unpopular reforms brought in by the coalition in health, pensions, taxation and the post office.

The result was bad for both the big parties. As expected, the turnout was down. The victory of the Republicans at national level was an embarrassing shock for Herr Kohl, and forced him to swing sharply to the right to recapture lost ground. It also gave rise to alarm among Germany's neighbours. At the same time the failure of the Social Democrats to do any better than last time was a blow to hopes that they were on course for a victory in the next general. Even the Greens did not do as well as they had hoped: their support remained level, suggesting that this pioneer among Europe's Greens had reached an electoral ceiling. Only the Free Democrats could find comfort in their return to Strasbourg.

French had 16 party lists

Next door in France there was a similar lack of enthusiasm for the elections - mainly because this was the seventh time the French had been asked to vote in 15 months. Unlike Germany, the election would have little influence on the government as national elections were not due for several years. But it could go a long way towards deciding the future of the divided right-wing parties.

On Europe, there was general pride that France, which would take over the presidency a month later, was one of the most influential voices in the Community. Only the old-style Communists on the left and the National Front on the right were fundamentally hostile to the idea of the EC and the Single Market. Among the Socialists and the Gaullists, only the nuances were different - the socialists putting much more emphasis on such aspects of European policy as the social charter, and the right on economic liberalism.

But for a number of senior politicians, the election offered an ideal chance of a comeback - especially for former President Giscard d'Estaing, and for M. Laurent Fabius, the former prime minister and then president of the National Assembly. Both were heading electoral lists. M. Giscard d'Estaing, leader of the non-Gaullist Union for French Democracy (UDF) and nursing his own ambitions to become the new president of the European Parliament, was hampered however by the bickering with M. Jacques Chirac, the leader of the Gaullist Rally for the Republic (RPR). There were various attempts to patch up a single list. But when the leaders finally agreed, the centrists, led by Mme Veil, went on to form a separate list of their own.

Altogether there were 16 party lists. Most attention was concentrated on the Greens, whose message until recently had been peculiarly unappealing to French voters, who have little quarrel with nuclear power or the independent nuclear deterrent. Indeed the French Greens were considerably to the right of their fellow Greens in other countries.

Italy was another country where the Greens were novices on the scene, but where the ecology message began to make a serious impact. But the Italian Greens were divided into three factions, one concerned mostly with the environment and two others which campaigned on rather different issues such as opposition to the government's harsh crack-down on drugs.

Indeed campaigning in Italy was altogether livelier and more bizarre than in most countries, as the Italians, alone among the Twelve, allowed candidates from other nations to stand for election. Several took advantage of this, to the amusement of their fellow citizens at home and the bemusement of many Italian voters. Mr David Steel, the former British Liberal leader, was adopted on the Italian liberal party's list for the central region of the country. He campaigned gallantly - though with precious few words of Italian. But the Westminster style on the hustings was clearly foreign to most voters. Others who stood included Herr Daniel Cohn Bendit, the West German student leader during the 1968 student revolt in France; and Mr Danny Morrison, the head of publicity for Sinn Fein, who stood for two separate regions - the north-east and southern mainland - and was sponsored by a Marxist splinter group.

But in few other member states of the Community is there such enthusiasm for a federally united Europe. Opinion polls showed that a majority favoured European coins and banknotes, and 75 per cent wanted a European government. People even favoured bringing in foreign airlines on domestic routes to compete with strike-bound Italian carriers.

Italy has done well out of Europe, economically and politically, and Italians see tangible benefits from EC membership. The referendum asking the electorate whether they want the Strasbourg Parliament to be empowered to draw up a constitution for Europe that will lead to political unity raised no questions

29

among Italian voters about sovereignty or 'identikit Europeans,' as in Britain. Attitudes to integration are also coloured by the history of weak central government: the country's 48th postwar government collapsed just a month before the election, and Signor Ciriaco De Mita, the former prime minister, remained in office only as a caretaker.

The European campaign therefore became confused with the usual manoeuvring over the composition of the next government. The Socialists, headed by Signor Bettino Craxi, were hoping to use a good result to increase their bargaining power. The Communists were trying to put further distance between themselves and traditional Communism to stem the steady loss of support for the party, and were badly affected by the crackdown in China, which preoccupied Italian public opinion. The smaller parties were alarmed they would be squeezed out, and so three of them - the Republicans, Liberals, and some of the Radicals - joined together to form a 'lay alliance.'

The outcome was not what this alliance hoped for: they suffered a drop in their vote, whereas the Communists registered a small gain, halting their steady slide. The Christian Democrats also lost support, while the Socialists made the gains they had hoped for. The Greens won seven seats, though might have done even better if the three factions had managed to unite.

Spanish drop in enthusiasm

Factions and splinter groups were also a problem in Spain, with votes going to leftist regional parties such as the Basque Nationalists and the pro-ETA coalition Herri Batasuna as well as the Andalusian Party and the Convergence and Union party which controls Catalonia. But Señor Felipe González, the prime minister, had reason to be grateful. His PSOE socialist party did far better than predicted, losing only one seat and maintaining its dominant position in the country. This was despite the loss of support from the trade unions, who had fiercely opposed the government's economic policies, and a spirited challenge from the conservative Partido Popular, which moved to the centre to try to recapture disaffected middle class voters.

The election was a setback however to Señor Manuel Fraga, the conservative leader, who failed to gain more than one seat. It was also a severe blow to the Centre party under Señor Adolfo Suárez, the first democratically-elected prime minister of the post-Franco era. His party's lunge to the right failed to garner votes, and it lost two of its seven deputies at Strasbourg, taking only slightly more than seven per cent of the vote.

Despite a lively campaign with often heated exchanges, the electorate in Spain showed a noticeable drop in enthusiasm over the vote compared with 1987 - the only previous occasion when the country chose members for the European Parliament in a special election soon after Spanish accession. Part of this was due to a cooling of initial ardour for Europe. But part was also due to a surprisingly swift adjustment to membership, especially during the successful Spanish presidency of the Community, and a lack of urgency in demonstrating European credentials to other EC partners.

In neighbouring Portugal there was a similar drop in the turn-out compared with 1987, when Portugal also held its first European election. The campaign did not turn much on European issues, as the benefits or drawbacks of membership after only three years were not very clear to voters. And despite government exhortations to vote to further 'construction of Europe,' many saw the ballot as a way of recording their feelings about the two-year old Social Democratic government - the conservatives in the Portugues political spectrum - headed by Senhor Anibal Cavaco Silva.

The government did its best to show the advantages it had procured from the EC for Portugal: fast growth in the economy and productivity, political stability and huge EC grants (about £650 million in 1989) for agriculture, regional development and job training. The opposition severely criticized dependence on this money, and also poor supervision of its expenditure, which had led to large amounts of this money being misappropriated.

Portugal, which unlike Spain has not yet held the presidency of the Community, has been slower to adapt to the changed conditions, and was still apprehensive of the difficulties the fierce competition unleashed by the Single Market would bring to its small and previously protected industries.

In the end the results were somewhat ambivalent. The government, despite its large majority in the national Parliament, lost one seat at Strasbourg, while the Socialists gained two. The hardline Communist party lost one seat, while the Greens, who have still to make much impact in Iberia, gained one. But the turn-out was 22 per cent down on 1987, when the European election coincided with a national poll.

A more decisive result was obtained in Greece, where the European election was entirely eclipsed by the general election in which the central issue was the moral and physical health of the prime minister, Mr Andreas Papandreou. His Pasok party's defeat in the national poll was reflected in the European results: the New Democracy party of Mr Constantine Mitsotakis emerged triumphant with 10 seats, compared with nine for Pasok. The two communist parties, divided between competing Eurocommunist and pro-Moscow factions, formed an unusual alliance, and took 14 per cent of the vote, winning four seats.

New Democracy, the party that negotiated Greece's accession to the EC, made much of its European credentials. But for most voters, the real issue was the prime minister's well-publicized affair with an air hostess, his poor health and the financial scandal that had rocked the government.

Further north in Denmark the elections ended with no clear winner, after a campaign in which, almost alone among the Twelve, the question of continued membership of the Community remained an issue. Despite predictions that the anti-EC parties would be routed, the Popular Movement Against Danish Membership of the European Community – a motley grouping of members from several parties – held on to its seats, and the Social Democrats, who are lukewarm about membership, retained four seats.

The campaign, as elsewhere, focussed on domestic issues, and voters used the election to rebuff the prime minister, Mr Poul Schlüter, whose Conservative party lost two of its four seats. This was seen as a negative response to the government's tax reform programme, designed to cut Denmark's high income taxes and sharply cut the country's welfare system. However the Liberals, one of the three parties in the coalition government, gained a seat. And the small Centre Democratic party which supported the coalition doubled its representation to two.

On the opposition, the marked swing to the left elsewhere in Europe failed to materialize, with the far left anti-EC Socialist People's party losing one of its two seats. But the results were hardly a convincing picture of public opinion, as only 46 per cent of the electorate voted.

Strengthened by poll

The prime minister of the Netherlands was one of the European leaders who could take comfort from the results. Mr Ruud Lubbers, who was heading a caretaker government after the collapse of his centre-right coalition, emerged strengthened from the poll. His Christian Democratic party gained two seats, whereas the Liberals, his coalition party, lost two. The result clearly suggested voters' unhappiness with the break-up of the coalition over the Netherlands' ambitious plan to clean up the environment, and their blaming the party that precipitated the collapse.

Domestic issues were particularly to the fore in the campaign, which was seen as a preliminary round in the general election, held on September 6. On Europe, there was virtual unanimity on the need for further integration, improved social legislation such as the social charter, and more power for the European Parliament. The only pending disagreement with Brussels was over plans for cross-border television broadcasting, which some Dutch parties, especially the Calvinists, feared could open the screens to pornography.

As expected, the environment was one of the principle issues. But the Dutch Greens were unable to reap much advantage, as virtually all parties were strongly in favour of tougher action, domestically and at EC level, to tackle pollution. The Rainbow Coalition of small left-wing and environmental parties collected 7 per cent of the vote, up 1.4 per cent, but not enough to add to their two seats.

The Socialists, hoping for a good result to challenge the popular Mr Lubbers in September, saw their vote drop three per cent to just over 30 per cent, with the loss of one seat. But they were able to take comfort from the drift to the fringe parties and the low turn-out – only 47 per cent – which they hoped would be reversed during the general election.

Next door in Belgium, another popular and long-serving prime minister, Mr Wilfried Martens, saw his Christian Social party and his prestige enhanced, confirming the stability of his eighth coalition government. As always, linguistic and inter-communal politics determined the election campaign, with the real focus of interest on simultaneous elections for the new regional executive for Brussels – the final third body to be set up under Belgium's new federal structure. The far right Vlaams Blok, the Flemish anti-immigration nationalists, did well and gained a seat at the expense of the less extreme Volksunie, thus putting pressure on the Volksunie to pull out of the coalition government.

As in the Netherlands, the environment in this densely populated country was a big issue. The Flemish-speaking Green party Agalev almost doubled its vote to 8.1 per cent, but could not add to its single seat in the last Parliament, while its French-speaking counterpart went up from 3.9 per cent to 5.5 per cent, doubling its Strasbourg representation from one to two. The Flemish-speaking Socialists however did poorly, dropping from 17 to 13 per cent of the vote and losing a seat, while French-speaking Liberals in Wallonia also did badly.

Belgium, with its weak central government and long history of communal tensions, has long been an enthusiastic supporter of closer European unity. The very presence of the European Commission in Brussels and the vast economic benefits the large number of international civil servants bring also colours attitudes. And as 1992 approaches, more and more businessmen are looking to Brussels as a new headquarters. Mr Leo Tindemans, Belgium's foreign minister, rode this wave of enthusiasm by resigning to head the Flemish Christian Democratic list. He made no secret of his ambition to become president of the European Parliament in succession to Lord Plumb – an ambition that was quickly dashed.

Like Belgium, Luxembourg also benefits enormously from the presence of many European institutions, including the European Court, the European Parliament's secretariat, the Court of Auditors and the Council of Ministers building, used three times a year. However, Luxembourg is alarmed by the growing pressure to concentrate European institutions in Brussels, and one theme of the election campaign was the need to fight to retain the European presence in the Grand Duchy.

Luxembourg was probably the only country in the Community where a general election, held on the same day, was overshadowed by the European election. The small country of 380,000 people sends only six MEPs to Strasbourg. But recent EC developments have worried the country, especially the proposed changes in banking legislation that could rob Luxembourg of its banking secrecy and prosperous loophole status.

The election brought few surprises. The parties divided up the seats in the same way as before: three for the Social Christians, two for the Socialists and one for the Liberals. But the Greens also captured a larger share of the vote, especially in the simultaneous general election, which saw the return to office of M. Jacques Santer, the Social Christian prime minister.

Common threads

Although home politics dominated the elections in all Twelve countries, there were common threads running through the results. One was the need to tackle some of the big problems - the environment especially, but also unemployment, transport and economic stability - at European level, not just at national level. The Greens campaigned explicitly on an international agenda, and were rewarded with a strong showing - though sometimes there were big differences in the Green groups, especially between France and Germany.

The other trend was the growth of hard right nationalist parties. Paradoxically, this was also an international development, even though the strong showing of nationalists in Northern Ireland and Belgium were exceptions. But the French National Front, the German Republicans and the Italian MSI did not just have isolated concerns about drugs, crime and race, but also shared fears raised by pan-European developments, especially the gradual erosion of national sovereignty.

The Socialists and Social Democrats did reasonably well, and in many countries rallied round the social charter as a more visionary ideal of Europe than the Single Market with its associations of unrestrained capitalism. The moderate right, though losing its overall majority, also remained a substantial presence and benefitted from the general enthusiasm for Europe and sense of momentum which the 1992 programme has generated.

Overall, the European elections showed that the barriers between national and European politics are steadily breaking down. MEPs were forced often to campaign on domestic themes. But conversely, most of the big parties, in the general elections taking place simultaneously and shortly afterwards, devoted much of their platform to their policies on Europe.

Tory divisions led to disastrous loss of 13 seats

By Robin Oakley
Political Editor of *The Times*

The third direct elections to the European Parliament represented a significant comeback for the Labour Party led by Mr Neil Kinnock and a severe setback for Mrs Margaret Thatcher. For the first time ever since she became party leader in 1975, Mrs Thatcher lost a national election to the Labour Party. Labour gained 13 seats at Conservative expense and the Conservative representation in Europe was wiped out completely in Scotland and in Wales.

In an election occurring at mid-term in the Westminster Parliament cycle, with the economy faltering and the government of the country not at stake, it was always likely that the Conservative Government would suffer from a high protest vote.

But obvious divisions within the Conservative ranks, a maladroit campaign widely criticised for its negative approach to the Community and Labour's presentation of its policy review, offering more moderate policies, before the European contest resulted in an 8.5 per cent swing from Conservatives to Labour. If that were to be repeated in a Westminster General Election, it would be sufficient to give Labour a working majority.

The momentum of Labour's recovery, already witnessed in the Vale of Glamorgan Parliamentary by-elections and the 1989 county council elections, was increased and the increased credibility gave Labour a further immediate bonus in national opinion polls on voting intention at the next General Election.

The European elections also saw a spectacular rise for the Green Party which had never even succeeded previously in saving a candidate's deposit in a Westminster contest. In the 1987 General Election Green candidates secured 1.4 per cent of the vote. In the local government elections in 1989 that increased to 8.6 per cent. But the party's gamble in hazarding £78,000 of deposit money on fighting every British mainland Euro seat paid off spectacularly. The Greens saved every deposit and gained almost 15 per cent of the vote , more than in any other EC country, though the British first-past-the post voting system denied them any representation in the European Parliament.

They relegated the Social and Liberal Democrats to fourth place, seized public attention and forced environmental issues to the top of the political agenda. Their first demand after the election was for the sacking of Mr Nicholas Ridley, the Environment Secretary, and in the Government reshuffle in July 1989, Mr Ridley was shifted sideways to another department to allow for the promotion of a more sympathetically "green" Environment Secretary in Mr Chris Patten.

The results of the contest, with voting in Britain on Thursday, June 15, when the last votes were counted on Monday, June 18, were that Labour won with 6,153,640 votes, the Conservatives took 5,331,077 in second place and the Green Party was third with 2,292,705.

In fourth place, with 986,292, came the Social and Liberal Democrats. There were 406,686 votes for the Scottish National Party and 115,062 for Plaid Cymru, the Welsh National Party. The claims of the rump SDP, lead by Dr David Owen, to being a national party were severely exposed. They managed to fight only 16 seats and gained just 75,886 votes nationwide.

Labour's share of the vote climbed over the psychologically important 40 per cent barrier to 40.1 per cent, compared with 36.5 in the previous European Parliament elections in 1984. It was the highest share for Labour at any national election since 1970.

The Conservative share dropped from 40.8 per cent then to 34.7 per cent and the Democrats took 6.2 per cent compared with the 19.5 per cent scored by the SDP/Liberal Alliance in 1984. The Owenite SDP share of the vote represented just 0.5 per cent.

Turnout once again was pitifully low at 35.9 per cent, despite a European Parliament election conducted much more than usual on European issues. But at least it was an improvement on the 1984 figure of 31.6 per cent and it went up in Britain while turnout declined in some other countries.

The thirteen seats lost by the Conservatives, who dropped from 45 to 32, all went to Labour, which therefore increased its Strasbourg representation from 32 to 45. The Scottish Nationalists held on to their single seat in the Highlands and Islands. Labour had been progressing in the national opinion polls before the European contest opened. The evidence of the polls was that Mr Kinnock's party was continuing to establish its credentials as an alternative government. But the fact that the Labour and Tory votes combined showed a fall rather than an increase, despite the poor showing of the former Alliance parties, indicated that there was a strong protest element in the European voting. Almost all of the Green advance seemed to have been made at the Democrats expense.

The British European elections campaign effectively opened in the first week of May with the Prime Minister telling MPs in the Commons that she was "deeply concerned at the number of EC proposals in the pipeline". She insisted "We need a very careful watch on the tendency of the Commission to get an increasing competence about many matters which are not necessarily for the single market of 1992".

Tough role

Downing Street revealed that ministers and officials had been instructed to take a much tougher role in Brussels in seeking to restrict the role of the European Commission, particularly efforts at bureaucratic "tidying up". The message was that British sovereignty was to be jealously defended at every turn.

At every opportunity, Mrs Thatcher and her ministers and officials made it plain that they were opposed to the package of social legislation on union rights and worker participation - the "Social Charter" - being urged by M.Jacques Delors, the Commission president, as a counterweight to the business package of 1992 and to any further harmonization of taxes.

It represented an intensification of the themes first set out by Mrs Thatcher in her controversial speech in Bruges the previous autumn, when she declared: "We have not successfully rolled back the frontiers of the state in Britain only to see them reimposed at a European level with a European super-state exercising a new dominance from Brussels".

That had led to the polarising of attitudes within the Conservative Party, with the formation of a "Bruges Group" of Conservatives sceptical about moves to further European integration and counter claims from more pro-Market Conservatives. The evidence of a party divided on one of the central issues of the day continued to accumulate, with former premier Mr Edward Heath and Mr Michael Heseltine leading the chorus of those who wanted closer co-operation with Europe than that implied by Government rhetoric.

With the Chancellor having had to make a string of interest rate increases in the battle to contain inflation, a further sub-strand of argument was the constant debate about whether Britain should join the exchange rate mechanism of the European Monetary System. The tensions extended inside the Cabinet, with both Mr Nigel Lawson, the Chancellor of the Exchequer and Sir Geoffrey Howe, the Foreign Secretary, in favour of Britain joining and Mrs Thatcher's formula that she would do so "when the time was right" looking more and more like an excuse for permanent delay.

The arguments went on through the European elections contest and up to the European Council meeting in Madrid the next month and it was said to be the concerted tactics adopted by Mr Lawson and Sir Geoffrey in forcing Mrs Thatcher to take a more conciliatory attitude there to European monetary co-operation which determined her to move Sir Geoffrey from the Foreign Office in her subsequent Cabinet reshuffle.

As Labour prepared to slip on its more moderate clothes with publication of the policy review, designed as part of a three month campaign drive including the parliamentary by-elections, the county council contests and the European Parliament elections, some Tory MPs were revealing their concern over what they saw as a new phase of anti-Market rhetoric from Downing Street.

Labour's campaign strategists-- Mr Kinnock, the party's communications chief Mr Peter Mandelson and Mr Bryan Gould, the campaign co-ordinator-- set out after the Vale of Glamorgan by-election victory on May 4 to use the European elections to convince the public they were back in business as a potential party of government. They determined to present Labour as a party ready to play a constructive and co-operative role in Europe, believing that Mrs Thatcher had made a crucial mistake in taking a "destructive and chauvinist" line on Europe.

At the Scottish Conservative Party conference in Perth on May 12, Mrs Thatcher raised her standard for the European elections battle by saying that Labour would fight on a platform of more controls, more bureaucracy, more regulations and more controls on businessmen. The Tories would fight on a platform of more jobs through the coming Single European Market, more opportunity for financial institutions as exchange controls were removed and for a free-trading Europe open to the world.

She insisted: "We are good Europeans. We joined the Community in good faith. And we shall work through the Community -- let there be no mistake about that-- for our kind of Europe, not a socialist super-state in Brussels which submerges our identity and snuffs out our sovereignty, but a free Europe, whose many different states have room to breathe".

Mr Michael Heseltine that weekend published a book on the Common Market which warned that Britain could not hope to lead Europe from the touchlines and which urged that there were gains in the pooling of sovereignty. Leadership of the second eleven, he said, was there for the taking.

Mr Heseltine urged that Britain should join the EMS and said that our national interests would only be served by "the determined building up of a stronger, closer Community". Attacking no-one by name, he criticised the "sock it to 'em defence of to-day's interests with yesterday's phrases" and warned "every negative speech by a senior politician on European affairs delivered in ringing nationalist tones to a domestic audience is heard abroad and can have damaging consequences".

Mr Heseltine also warned that little would be achieved on environmental problems without working closely with the European community.

Mr Heath's accusations

On May 14 came much starker evidence of the Conservative divisions on Europe. Mr Heath, speaking on television, accused Mrs Thatcher of trying to mislead the British people about the nature of Europe. Her policy, he said, could leave Britain as a second-rate power in a two-tier Community. He accused Mrs Thatcher of being abusive, laying down the law and talking "absolute rubbish". When it was put to him that these were serious charges, he replied: "The time has come when these things have got to be said".

He was immediately rebuked by Mr Norman Fowler, the Employment Secretary, who accused him of talking "total nonsense". He added: "I think many people will deeply resent and oppose the way Mr Heath put his case".

But that, it turned out, was only the start.

Two days later Lord Plumb, the British President of the European Parliament, delivered a speech taking issue with the Prime Minister on virtually every aspect of the European Community, accusing her of failing to understand the nature of the EC and attacking it for being something which nobody sought to make it. Reflecting the fears then already apparent of Conservative European candidates that their party was drifting into an anti-European stance, he argued that sovereignty was being pooled and exercised jointly, not surrendered.

Mr Heath went further. He accused Mrs Thatcher of "dictatorship" and "authoritarianism", declaring: "It is quite clear that this Government and Mrs Thatcher are going to oppose every positive thing put forward by the Commission".

The Government meanwhile had been living up to Mrs Thatcher's exhortations to ministers to challenge attempts by Brussels to increase its competence by opposing plans for a standardised EC health ruling to be printed on cigarette packets. Health Secretary Kenneth Clarke had lost on a majority vote in the European Council and

Mr Heath declared:"If Mrs Thatcher and Kenneth Clarke take this to the European Court they will make absolute idiots of this country".

On May 18, the day Labour published its policy review document *"Meet the Challenge, Make the Change, a new Agenda for Britain"*, Mrs Thatcher told MPs at question time in the House of Commons that the Social Charter planned in Brussels was a "Socialist Charter", full of unnecessary controls and regulations which would tie up industry and make it uncompetitive. In a newspaper interview, she had labelled it "Marxist" to the mystification of many of Britain's European partners.

All this was by way of prelude to the campaign itself, but it set the tone. And at the weekend that tone was confirmed when we saw the first Conservative campaign advert. Beside a photograph of the famous entry to Number Ten Downing Street it proclaimed *"Don't let Labour in through the back door"*.

Tory strategists revealed that the aim was to maximise Conservative turnout by warning the Tory faithful of the risks of letting Labour win by default. The plan was to attribute Labour's warmer attitude to Europe to the party's hopes of getting its policies imposed on Britain via Brussels. The aim was to give Conservative supporters a compelling reason to vote, rather than seeking to convert doubters to the Tory cause, and the campaign was drawn up by Mr Brendan Bruce, the new Director of Communications at Conservative Central office, with Mr Tim Bell, the Prime Minister's long-standing publicity adviser.

The Conservative Election manifesto *"Leading Europe into the 1990s"*, published on May 22, attempted to square the circle between the Prime Minister's determination to counter attempts to force countries into a European identikit personality and the willingness to work practically with other independent sovereign states for common ends. The detailed 62-page document (covered in detail elsewhere in this book) reaffirmed the Government's rejection of economic and monetary union and the Social Charter and focussed heavily on the Single European market to be created from 1992. It claimed: "We are leading Europe into the 1990s on a Conservative agenda" and said that only the Conservatives could be trusted to safeguard the achievements of the past decade.

At a press conference to introduce the document, Mrs Thatcher said that she did not know of anyone at that moment seriously suggesting Britain should join the ERM. Before it could be contemplated, Britain's inflation would have to come down and the other nations in Europe would have to get rid of exchange controls and restrictions on capital movements as Britain had already done.

She brushed aside Mr Heath's criticisms, saying that it was her Government, not his, which had brought "sanity" to Common Market practices.

Labour's tactics became apparent the next day when Mr Kinnock launched his party's manifesto *"Meeting the Challenge in Europe"*, a much slimmer document of just seven pages. Mr Kinnock and his colleagues urged the electorate to turn the European contest into a referendum on ten years of Thatcherism.

The Labour Leader said: "Mrs Thatcher makes enemies in Europe more easily than she makes friends. The Tories are virtually isolated in the European Parliament. Her style is to talk tough and maximise resentment against Britain, but she has too often given way on the issues that really matter".

Much in common

What the two manifestoes clearly showed was that Labour and Conservative policies actually had much in common on Europe. Both were against joining the EMS for the present, both opposed any creation of a further tier of government in Brussels and any further tax harmonisation.

Mr Kinnock's own list of conditions for Britain joining the exchange rate mechanism included proper arrangements for financial support of the transitional period, an agreed EC growth strategy, an expanding role for the Social and Regional funds and joining at a "competitive rate". There would need to be "regular swap arrangements" to counter speculative currency flows.

Though Mr Peter Brooke, the Conservative Party chairman, issued a list of quotes that day detailing Labour splits on European issues, the Conservatives never succeeded in making much of those during the campaign which followed, while the Tory divisions remained high profile.

Mr Kinnock, who had in 1983 been proclaiming "We want out of the Common Market" now began preaching "closer and closer co-operation with Europe" with the electorate seemingly little aware of the irony.

One reason for that was the relative exposure of the leading figures. The Labour Party held daily press conferences in London with their front benchers: the Conservatives restricted theirs to three days a week. Mr Kinnock toured the country throughout, Mrs Thatcher only really entered the campaign in the final week, speaking to audiences where there were no converts to be made.

The Conservative campaign was dogged by reports of differences on economic policy between Mrs Thatcher and her Chancellor of the Exchequer after he had been forced to make ten increases in interest rates within the year as he sought to counter inflationary pressures.

Early in the campaign, in a BBC World Service television interview, Mrs Thatcher appeared to blame the Chancellor for higher inflation. News that Number Ten had subsequently telephoned with an apology significantly came from the Treasury, not from Downing Street. It did not help that Professor Sir Alan Walters, who had the previous year been publicly critical of the Chancellor's strategy, had rejoined Mrs Thatcher as her economic adviser. And it was well known that Mr Lawson and Sir Geoffrey Howe favoured ERM entry sooner than the Prime Minister would permit it.

One theme on which Labour made little progress, however, was that chosen by Mr Kinnock for his opening press conference.

He attacked the Government's preparation of British industry for 1992, saying that 1992 would prove to be a "desperate struggle for survival" rather than a great opportunity for British industry. British companies, he said, would be too busy "repelling boarders" to take advantage of the new opportunities. Labour favoured tax incentives to encourage firms to gear up.

Three day wonder

But Mr Kinnock hit his own troubles when he appeared on a BBC *World at One* interview on May 25. Transcripts of the original version of his interview, in which he refused to answer questions on what Labour would do, leaked out and the Labour leader was accused of "temperamental failings" by Tory MPs.

Despite that setback for Labour, which proved a three day wonder, Mr Kinnock's party was soon confirmed by the opinion polls as in the lead. And the Conservative disarray was made still further evident by a speech from Mr Edward Heath, pointedly delivered in Brussels, in which he attacked the Prime Minister in astonishing terms.

Ignoring the convention that you do not set about British political opponents, let alone those in the same party, when you are abroad , Mr Heath told the Belgian Royal Society of International Affairs that he had come to Brussels to "wipe away the stain" of the Prime Minister's Bruges speech.

He accused Mrs Thatcher of breaking treaties which he had signed on Britain's behalf and of "patronizing, self-seeking hypocrisy". Her attitude, he said, was "preposterous and insulting".

Explaining what he saw as the British way in approaching Europe, Mr Heath went on: "That way is not to Euro-bash. It is not to smear the Community as being Socialist, let alone Marxist, nor should our leaders treat the Community in such a derisory fashion".

That the Tory leadership had been ready for such a vituperative attack was evidenced by the fact that the first denunciations of Mr Heath's speech came from Mr Douglas Hurd, the Home Secretary and once Mr Heath's political secretary as Prime Minister, and from Mr Kenneth Baker, then the Education Secretary and once Mr Heath's PPS.

The former Tory leader reacted by calling them "scared stiff" of Mrs Thatcher. Mr Heath went on to accuse the Tory Party of running a "dirty tricks campaign" against him, saying that he had been prevented from speaking in some constituencies. When this was denied by Mr Peter Brooke, the Conservative Party chairman, Mr Heath called him a liar.

That brought even Lord Whitelaw into the act, to say that the popular and respected Mr Brooke could never have been any such thing.

Mr Heath and Mr Brooke eventually linked up and agreed in Mr Brooke's words that "organisational analysis by megaphone was not the best way of conducting our affairs". He added that Mr Heath had agreed that he was an honourable man which was "a perfectly satisfactory way of going to sleep at night". But by then the damage was well and truly done.

Conservative candidates were by this point in some despair at the muddled message from their party, and Labour naturally exploited the Tory divisions to the fullest extent.

Dr Barry Seal, then the leader of the Labour group in the European Parliament, wrote to all Tory candidates asking them to make clear which of the two Tory parties available they were standing for. Mr Bryan Gould said that there was a state of civil war in the Conservative Party over Europe.

Meanwhile the voice of the third party Democrats was almost lost. Their leader, Mr Paddy Ashdown, insisted that his was the only party dealing in the realities of Europe. Mr Kinncok and Mrs Thatcher, he declared, were bashing each other round the head while the world passed them by. "Good entertainment for the children but disastrous for the country".

But Democrat campaigners, with few resources left after the county council campaigns to devote to the European contest, were already alarmed at the tide of votes moving the way of the Green Party, campaigning on a shoestring from cramped premises in Balham High Street and virtually ignored by the press until the final days of the campaign.

Mr Kinnock, on one of his forays outside London, promised that Labour would reverse the rule whereby aid won from European Community funds was deducted from British Government aid to particular regions . The process of "additionality" by which the deductions were made was "grand larceny" by the Government, he said. He called for the development of a better road and rail infrastructure to see that the benefits of the Channel Tunnel reached all parts of the country.

Meanwhile, Mr Heseltine denounced Labour as "a cynical bunch of Johnny-come-Latelies" masquerading as Europeans. Nothing could be more damaging to Britain's national interests, he said, than to allow Labour to undermine the competitive thrust of the European marketplace.

As the campaign unwound and as the opinion polls confirmed a growing Labour lead, the Opposition began to turn it more into a personal attack on the Prime Minister and her style of Government. The celebrations of Mrs Thatcher's ten years as Prime Minister, shortly before the campaign began, and which she had deliberately kept to a minimum, enabled Labour to play on the "time for a change" theme.

Howe hits back

Another interview by Mrs Thatcher provided scope for the Opposition when she was asked about the danger to the pound of speculation that Mr Lawson and Sir Geoffrey Howe might be moved in the forthcoming reshuffle.

The Prime Minister said: "Nigel is a very good neighbour of mine and a very good Chancellor. Geoffrey is a very good Foreign Secretary" and added: "I'm not going any further".

This enabled the Opposition to claim that she was undermining senior ministers, although it was explained she was merely trying to be non-committal about her reshuffle, as Prime Ministers must always be.

Sir Geoffrey hit at Labour, saying that Mr Kinnock's team had a hidden manifesto. Their seven page policy document was "short on specifics and long on linguistics, just as one would expect from Neil Kinnock".

Labour, he said, would impose capital controls and import controls—"a fortress Britain in a fortress Europe, cut off from the world". The Labour manifesto, he said, had made little mention of employment because the Conservatives were the party of jobs.

Sir Geoffrey accused Labour of employing smear tactics against the Prime Minister to hide their own policies. Meanwhile for Labour, transport spokesman John Prescott blamed Government under-spending for the series of transport disasters. He confirmed that his party's radical review of transport issues included the possibility of scrapping the road fund licence.

Mr Peter Brooke, not only Conservative chairman but a Treasury Minister, said that if Labour reverted to the policy of raising the equivalent revenue by increasing the petrol tax that would mean an extra 38p per gallon.

Mr Kinnock, at one of his increasingly frequent press conferences, pledged that Labour would bring the privatised water industry back under public control.

The constant spate of stories about pressure from Brussels for Britain to fall into line with European standards on drinking water and sewage discharges enabled Labour to play up its willingness to co-operate with European initiatives on the environment while the Government appeared to be dragging its feet. Water privatisation, which opinion polls confirmed to be highly unpopular with the public, became one of the sub-issues of the campaign.

Ministers argued that privatisation would result in higher environmental standards because there would be more funds available in the private sector, where water treatment works would not be competing with education, defence and social security for spending priority.

Flow of votes to Greens

Mr Michael Howard, the water minister, said that every other country besides Britain had been threatened with court action over not meeting the EC standards on drinking water. He pointed out that investment in sewage treatment and the like had been cut by 50 per cent under the previous Labour Government. But it seemed to have done little to stop the flow of votes to the Green party.

Attack tends to be easier than defence, especially when a Government is still in mid-term after pushing through its most unpopular legislation in the first two years of a Parliament.

Another theme pursued by Labour was that the Government's drive for privatisation had resulted in costs to British industry being increased as a result of electricity, gas and water price increases designed to help make the industries appeal to investors. This had been a factor in the increased rate of inflation and the higher interest rates, said economic spokesman Gordon Brown. The economic miracle, said Shadow Chancellor John Smith, was a mirage.

Attacking Britain's growing trade deficit, he said "We have lost the role as the workshop of the world to become a nation of shopkeepers selling goods made in the rest of the world".

Ministers could do little to counter such attacks but warn that things would be worse if the Opposition were to take over, a theme which becomes somewhat harder to sell to the electorate after you have been in office for ten years.

Conservative prospects were not helped when the Chancellor had to admit that inflation was likely to go up above eight per cent before it came down.

On June 8, a week before polling, Mrs Thatcher ventured out for the first time onto the campaign trail. But a somewhat sanitised visit to an agricultural college in Shropshire and to a Bilston factory producing enamel boxes and trinkets, surrounded all the while by a swarm of television cameras, was not exactly a meet-the-people occasion. By the end of the penultimate week there was considerable alarm among Conservative party workers and candidates at the way the campaign was going.

Labour's private polling had shown there were four themes on the mind of the electorate --the poll tax, water privatisation, the health service (for which Mr Kinnock pledged an extra £3 billion) and interest rates. On all four the Government had been forced onto the defensive. Labour was clearly succeeding in its attempt to turn the election not into a contest about how the country should be represented in a Strasbourg Parliament with new powers over European legislation (powers denied to the Westminster Parliament) but into a referendum on ten years of Thatcherite economics.

The elections were becoming a sort of large-scale parliamentary by-election. Labour campaigners were delighted by the "Downing Street" advertisement, with its "Don't let Labour in by the Back Door" theme. They reckoned it a tactical blunder: the Conservatives had never previously admitted there was the possibility of Labour getting into Downing Street, and thus into Government, by any kind of door. It boosted the Opposition's credibility.

The Conservative divisions on Europe were widely apparent, so was the latest reported round of tension between Mrs Thatcher and her Chancellor of the Exchequer. Candidates and party workers, having for years believed that theirs was the party of Europe, now found the Prime Minister seemingly leading an assault on Brussels and all its works.They were confused about the Tory message and it showed.

Those who worried and made their protests known were told that European elections were won or lost in the last week and that it would all come good then as the Prime Minister adopted a higher profile. But the Conservatives, used to their opponents undermining themselves, had been too complacent.

As Mr Norman Fowler, the Employment Secretary, prepared to go to Brussels on the Monday of the final week to make it clear that Britain wanted nothing to do with any compulsory Social Charter, Labour trumpeted its support for the charter, emphasising that it would bring more generous benefits for pensioners, mothers, workers and other groups. Mr Michael Meacher, their employment spokesman, gave details over the final weekend of a "leaked" EC report showing that Britain lagged behind other Community countries in the provision of hoidays, minimum wages and controlled working hours. Labour pressed the theme that a vote for them in Europe would be a vote for raised social standards.

At this late stage, the Conservative party began efforts to pull things together. Lord Whitelaw sought to bridge the gap between Mr Heath and Mrs Thatcher by saying that he had been proud to serve under Mr Heath's leadership, when the former Prime Minister's skills had gained Britain entry to the EC, and that he was equally proud to have served under Mrs Thatcher, whose firm leadership and successful policies had won Britain a place in the vanguard of that Community.

Mr Brooke visited Mr Heath at his London flat and persuaded him to make a "helpful" speech urging the electorate to support Conservative candidates and Mrs Thatcher even managed a tribute to her predecessor during Question Time in the Commons.

But the other Tory tensions were showing again. In a TV interview Chancellor Lawson described the view of Mrs Thatcher's adviser Sir Alan Walters that the EMS was "half-baked" as "very difficult to reconcile with the facts".

Thatcher warning

Mrs Thatcher addressed a rally in Nottingham on the final Monday, insisting that Conservatives were "good Europeans". She said that it was the Government led by Mr Heath which had had the "vision" to take Britain into the Common market and that it was her Government which had made a success of it.

But her language was still reminiscent of the Bruges speech as she insisted that Britain did not want to be swallowed up in some huge European conglomerate and warned: "We haven't rolled back the frontiers of socialism in this country to see them reimposed from Brussels". She would continue to fight any attempt from Brussels to interfere in Britain's taxation, social security, health service, education or industrial relations.

Addressing the fears that Britain could become isolated, she went on: "Sometimes you have to stand alone and give a lead... I didn't get where I am to-day by not fighting Britain's corner". To which Labour's response was that it was Mrs Thatcher's actions which had got us put in the corner.

As the Conservative big guns pitched into the campaign, Mr Lawson declared that Labour's policies were past their sell-by date. The lines had not changed at all. There was renationalisation, subsidies, regulations and controls, with higher public spend-ing and heavier taxation.The only new thing compared with the 1987 election was that government interference and bureaucracy would increase with four new minis-tries, four new regulatory commissions, ten regional women's units, twelve new assemblies and dozens of new quangoes.

But with renewed speculation about the state of relations between Mrs Thatcher and her Chancellor and the deal agreed between them on the EMS (it appeared to be that he would stop pressing for it in the immediate future if she would stop appearing to rule it out for ever) Mrs Thatcher was forced once again to declare her confidence in Mr Lawson in terms which made it virtually impossible for her then to move him in any subsequent reshuffle.

With sterling under pressure at its lowest level for two years and the markets in some turmoil, Mrs Thatcher went to the third time of asking at the Tuesday Question Time before she announced: "I give full and unequivocal and generous backing to my Chancellor of the Exchequer, of whom I am very proud".

That same day Mr Brooke, the party chairman, conceded that the Tories own private polls showed Labour 5 per cent ahead, figures which he knew would give Labour greater representation in Strasbourg than the Conservatives .But he claimed that the Tory voting intention had risen fifty per cent over the previous week. At that point Mr Heath duly made his speech urging Conservatives to turn out and vote, despite his earlier criticisms of the Government.

Last minute news was not too helpful to the Conservative cause, with senior Conservative MPs and the CBI combining in pressing the Chancellor not to raise interest rates a further two points as some in the markets feared he might.

Mr John Banham, the Director General of the CBI, urged the Chancellor not to react to "City panics based on dubious statistics". Labour leaders predicted, predictably, that the Government would be forced into increases of that level the day after the European polls, though in the event they were proved wrong.

Mrs Thatcher, at the final Tory press conference, continued lauding her Chancellor, saying that she supported him "fully, gladly, joyfully, unequivocally, generously".But equally she made it clear that she was not willing to dispense with the services of Sir Alan Walters.

The Prime Minister said that polls now showed that the Conservatives and Labour were running neck and neck, though it transpired there had actually been no further private Tory poll since the one less favourably interpreted by Mr Brooke. And it was perhaps not the best of signs, given the tenor of the Conservative campaign, that a Gallup survey commissioned by the European Commission and published that day, showed public support for British membership of the European Community on an all-time high at 55 per cent. A further 23 per cent were ambivalent, thinking membership neither a good nor a bad thing, and only 18 per cent were opposed.

When the results came, most of them on Sunday night and the rest on Monday, June 19, the political world was ready for them, prepared by a BBC exit poll on the Thursday night which had indicated the scale of the Conservative disaster and the scope of the Green advance.

Tories blamed their first election defeat under Mrs Thatcher's leadership and the first to Labour since 1974 on the muddled message of their campaign, the obvious divisions within the party and a willingness by voters with little at stake to indulge in a protest vote.

There were immediate calls, responded to by Mrs Thatcher in the subsequent reshuffle, for a strong party chairman to be appointed with a position in the Cabinet. But there was little disposition to blame Mr Brooke. She had set the tone of the campaign, it was conceded.

Noting that the Conservative performance was worse in the European elections than it had been in the county council elections and Parliamentary by-elections which also offered the opportunity of protest voting, many MPs concluded that there was an error in the approach on the question of Europe.

Euro MPs in particular felt that the campaigning had been too little and too late and that they had been offered no opportunity to make their own input.

There were few admirers of the Prime Ministers neo-Gaullist style among the Conservative MEPs, who found that her denunciation of most things European had left them short of working partners in Strasbourg. Their former Spanish Popular party allies in the European Democrat Group swiftly departed after the European contest to join the Christian Democrats, content no longer to be bracketed with Thatcherite rhetoric on Europe.

There was also bitter criticism of the campaigning basics on the Tory side, notably of the poster advertising , especially the one which told voters: "Stay at home on June 15 and you'll live on a diet of Brussels".

Mr Norman Tebbit, the former party chairman, having suffered in the 1987 General Election aftermath as rival advertising teams squabbled over who deserved the glory for victory, ridiculed the advertising campaign as "the worst in living memory". Sir Leon Brittan, the former Cabinet Minister now a European Commissioner, said it was "quite extraordinarily negative, damaging and confusing". But the poster campaign was personally approved by the Prime Minister.

Mrs Thatcher herself appeared to blame the party organisation at first for the failing to get out the vote, telling reporters outside Downing Street "not enough of our supporters came out".

She said that it had been an organisational election and added: "The message that we had was that a bigger proportion of our people were intending to come out. But it did not turn out to be true on a hot and very nice day".

At the subsequent Madrid EC Summit, however, she did maintain a significantly softer line on European integration.

Tories believed that they had been damaged by the criticisms of Mr Edward Heath, but perhaps more by the appearance of disunity between Mrs Thatcher and her Chancellor.

The Labour campaign team ,which had set out believing it might make four or six gains overall, was understandably jubilant. Their campaign once again was well-co-ordinated , eye-catching and energetic. Labour did well where it needed to recover lost ground, in the Midlands and in London.But there were warning signs for Mr

Kinnock too. The Labour vote actually fell half a per cent in Scotland, where turnout was up to nearly 42 per cent and where the Scottish National Party vote nearly doubled to 25 per cent.

If the Euro-poll voting were repeated at a General Election it would only have been enough to give Mr Kinnock a small working majority and this was a contest in which fewer than half the number of voters who turn out in a General Election had bothered to vote.

Politicians were left puzzling over how much the voting had been on European issues and how much on the economy, interest rates, water and electricity privatisation and the general style of Mrs Thatcher's Government, criticised on other issues for "going too far".

Labour better placed

Opinion poll studies showed that Labour supporters had become noticeably warmer about Europe during the campaign and that the Tory showing was adversely affected by the perceived differences on exchange rates between Mrs Thatcher and Mr Lawson and by the cigarette packets row.

For the Democrats, whose campaigning was ill-funded and desultory, the results were a disaster. Their 6.2 per cent of the vote was less than the Liberals alone had polled in a British election at their weakest 35 years before.

Had the results been divided on proportional representation lines,incidentally, the result would have been Labour 32, Conservatives 28, Green Party 12, SLD 4, Nationalists 2.

The biggest question mark for the future was over the astonishing rise by the Green Party. Those in other parties immediately set to studying whether their showing was likely to be a flash in the pan or whether a significant new force had arrived in British politics.

Certainly the Greens more than doubled their best hope of amassing a million votes and forced all the other parties to re-examine their environment policies.

What politicians in all parties were left puzzling was how much the contest had been about Europe and how much about domestic politics in general and Mrs Thatdcher's governmental style in particular. It left Labour in a much better position on the starting grid for the General Election campaign and the Tory Government struggling to regain momentum.

It also left many more Conservative MPs, at least in private, willing to criticise Mrs Thatcher's style. Some felt that her new wave of anti-European rhetoric had been set off by a belated realisation of what she had signed away in agreeing to the Single European Act and that she had become out of touch with a new and more co-operative public mood on Europe.The British readiness to fight agggrandisement by Brussels Commissioners and civil servants, it was felt, became focussed on the wrong issues, like cigarette packet warnings and pensioners' bus passes . And the rich populist vein which the Tory campaigners thought they would tap with their "diet of Brussels" advertising proved to have disappeared, or to be offering a temporary transfusion to the Greens.

Review of the Campaign in Eire

European results mirrored general election crisis

By Edward Gorman
Irish Affairs Correspondent of *The Times*

In the Irish Republic in 1989 the European election was swamped by an unexpected domestic general election called for the same day, just three weeks in advance of polling for Strasbourg.

Hopes that Community issues, most notably the debate on how structural funds due to Ireland should be spent over the next five years, would be discussed and widely publicized, proved sadly premature. In the event, despite considerably increased spending by all parties on European electoral budgets, it was domestic political issues that dominated voting patterns.

The main question was the desirability or otherwise of allowing Mr Charles Haughey, the Fianna Fail leader and Taoiseach, his first majority government, after a string of four minority administrations.

As the campaign developed, the unpopular effects of two years of difficult financial retrenchment on the part of Mr Haughey's outgoing government, threw up three key issues; the need for increased spending on the health service, and the problems of unemployment and the continuing high levels of emigration. Two subsidiary special cases also played a part, though their impact was somewhat uneven; a dispute over an unpopular fishing rod licence in the West of the country, and a campaign for improved Army pay.

The European question intervened in two ways. Mr Haughey pitched his campaign on the need to complete the task of economic reform, and to implement his nine billion plan for economic recovery, much of which is based on Community structural funds.

He also attempted to justify calling what was a generally unpopular election, by arguing that during Ireland's presidency of the EC (January-July 1990), he did not want to be distracted from concentration on European issues during a particularly important time for the Community, by unstable and vulnerable minority government in Dublin.

The domestic election led to a prolonged political crisis. It produced a decisive swing to the left and an erosion of support for Fianna Fail, which was eventually forced, through agreement with the small Progressive Democrats, into its first ever coalition after almost a month of political deadlock.

The European results mirrored those trends with a break-up of the two-party dominance of Fianna Fail and Fine Gael at Strasbourg which each lost two seats, and a return of the left. The Irish Labour Party has one seat in the shape of Mr Barry Desmond and the Workers Party are represented at Strasbourg for the first time by Mr Proinsias De Rossa, the party leader, who was at one time interned as a member of the IRA. Making up Ireland's 15 seats in Europe, is a first seat for the Progressive Democrats which helped to offset its poor performance in the domestic election, and the return of two independents.

The net effect, is a much more evenly spread representation for the Republic in Europe with MEPs forming part of six political groups in the new European Parliament.

The turnout, at 68 per cent, was high and a considerable improvement on the 47 per cent participation in 1984, reflecting to a large extent the coincidence of the Dail poll on the same day for which turnout was around 75 per cent. Community officials in Dublin believe publicity about 1992 had got through to some extent despite the primacy of domestic issues, and helps to explain the heightened interest.

In the new Parliament, Fianna Fail and Fine Gael continue to sit with the European Democratic Alliance and the European People's Party respectively, while both Mr Pat Cox for the Progressive Democrats and Mr T J Maher, the independent, are attached to the Liberal group. Mr Neil Blaney, also an independent, sits with the Rainbow group.

A cause of potentially serious friction between the two parties of the left, was the destination of Mr De Rossa who wanted to join the European Socialist group where Mr Desmond sits. But objections from the Irish Labour Party amongst others, prevented his affiliation with the Socialist International and Mr De Rossa settled for the new European United Left Group.

One notable unsuccessful candidate for Europe was Father Patrick Ryan who is wanted by Scotland Yard detectives for alleged involvement in IRA terrorist offences. Father Ryan ran as a single-issue anti-extradition candidate in the five-seat Munster constituency where he did better than expected, polling just under 30,000 votes. He was eliminated on the sixth count.

Advancing towards democratic control

By George Clark

former European Political Correspondent of *The Times* and Chairman of the U.K. Association of European Journalists, 1986-89

In its marathon struggle to secure greater democratic control over the law-makers of Europe - alias, the Council of Ministers and the European Commission - the European Parliament achieved a major break-through in its second five year stint as an elected assembly. The turning point came with the passing of the Single European Act, ratified by all Parliaments of the member States, which came into force on July 1, 1987. After that, MEPs could no longer be brushed aside or ignored by the Council when they put forward amendments to proposed legislation.

The first directly-elected Parliament (1979-84) suffered frustration and humiliation. At the end of the five years, the Council of Ministers had failed to take final decisions on at least 750 reports and recommendations sent to them by the Parliament. The Single European Act, giving Parliament an explicit role in deciding certain Community policies and introducing a "cooperation procedure" for settling new laws, came as a result of continuous pressure from MEPs for more power in Community decision-making. They wanted to shed the somewhat unkind gravy train image bestowed on them by public and press. To a considerable extent they have succeeded.

The pressure culminated in the passing, by a large majority, of Parliament's own draft Treaty on European Union in February 1984. Those voting against included some British Conservative and Labour MEPs who were opposed to the idea of a United States of Europe, as it was then envisaged. To give greater weight to its plan and demonstrate its legitimacy as a representative body, Parliament submitted the draft Treaty direct to member state Governments and Parliaments.

Consultations on that draft Treaty led the member Governments to accept important innovations which are now enshrined in the Single European Act. In the House of Commons, the Conservative Government used the Whips to get through the Bill that endorsed the provisions of the Act. And, in spite of Mrs Thatcher's protestations, it specifically re-affirms that the aim is "to transform relations as a whole. . . into a European Union". In the preamble, the Act refers to "the need for new developments (to) correspond to the wishes of the democratic peoples of Europe, for whom the European Parliament. . . is an indispensable means of expression".

To speed up the legislation needed to make the Single Market a reality by the end of 1992, the Act specified that the Council of Ministers could take decisions by majority vote. The unanimity vote procedure had caused many delays. At the same time, it allowed some matters to remain subjected to a single veto. These include fiscal harmonisation - for instance a Europe-wide basis for Value Added Tax - the free movement of persons (where immigration rules are important), the rights and interests of salaried workers, and legislation dealing with professional qualifications.

MEPs faced a lot of extra work, but the legislative log-jam was broken. In July 1988, M. Jacques Delors, President of the European Commission, reported to the Parliament: "In the first six months of 1988 the Community took more decisions than in the ten years from 1974 to 1984. . . This progress could never have been achieved without the determination, the drive and the spirit of cooperation consistently shown by the European Parliament".

In fact, the whole legislative process had changed. Previously, the Council of Ministers' decision on any parliamentary proposal was final (apart from budgetary matters, where there was joint responsibility). There was no way of bringing the Council to account. Often recommendations were sent to the Council and nothing more was heard of them, or there were long delays, sometimes for two years or more. The Council was under no obligation or requirement to give reasons for rejecting a proposition from Parliament. If it did, it was on a grace and favour basis.

What kind of democracy was that? Under the Single Act, Parliament can put forward amendments to proposed legislation on first reading. These go to the Council of Ministers who then consider them and report back, setting out their "common position" on the proposed changes. Often this amounts to an acceptance of Parliament's view, perhaps slightly modified. Sometimes Parliament gets the "thumbs down", but the Council must set out their reasons for rejection.

The matter does not rest there. Parliament is able to reject the Council's "common position" and insist on its amendments if an absolute majority of MEPs (at least 260 of them) is in favour of so doing, at second reading. After the second reading, provided that Parliament's position is supported by the Commission in Brussels, the Council can reverse Parliament's view only by acting unanimously. That is for a rejection. The acceptance of a re-drafted law can be settled by qualified majority vote. It has three months, from the date of second reading, to decide. If no decision is reached, the proposal falls.

In the first 16 months' operation of the new procedure, the Commission adopted in part or fully 60 per cent of Parliament's first reading amendments; Council adopted 44 per cent. At second reading, the Commission accepted 58 per cent of Parliament's amendments, and the Council 23 per cent. On the face of it, Parliament would seem to have achieved a high rate of acceptance, but the proposals rejected at the last stage usually involve the tricky, most sensitive issues.

However, Parliament has made a good start. Mr Martyn Bond, Head of the Parliament's London Office, commented: "Roughly one in four of second reading amendments are confirmed by Council and become law: not a bad record if you liken them either to Lords amendments or even to Opposition amendments at Westminster".

Foreign policy cooperation

For many years, foreign policy cooperation in the Community had been achieved by Foreign Ministers meeting regularly to work out a common "European" approach on international relations - often involving a quick reaction to a sudden emergency, as when the US air force bombed Libyan targets in 1987 - although this was not provided for in the Treaty of Rome.

MEPs have not been backward in expressing their views on foreign events, passing resolutions on all manner of subjects. Indeed, some critics have alleged that the MEPs spend far too much time debating the situation in far-away places, and not enough on European problems! Their views were taken into account by the Foreign Ministers, but the authority for such proceedings was vague.

In the Single European Act, however, member Governments committed themselves to endeavour jointly "to formulate and implement a European foreign policy". They also agreed that they should coordinate policies on "the political and economic aspects of security". Thus foreign policy and security were brought into a binding legal text of the Community for the first time. Parliamentary foreign affairs resolutions gained in authority from this.

Under the heading of foreign policy, Parliament was given additional power over trade and aid agreements with non-Community countries. Previously, MEPs had the right to be informed about negotiations with other countries, but their influence was severely limited. The Single European Act gave them the right of veto on the accession to the Community of any new member State, and on the terms of trade and economic association agreements with other States or organisations. A vote of at least 260 of Parliament's 518 members is required for the approval of any such agreement.

Experience since September 1987 has shown that Parliament intends to use this power as an instrument of direct political influence - not only on the Council, but also on the third countries concerned. Thus, in March 1988, three protocols amending the agreement with Israel failed to receive an absolute majority. MEPs were worried about the conditions in the occupied territories where there was severe unrest. Parliament wanted guarantees that the Israeli Government would afford Palestinian fruit growers adequate opportunities for exporting their products to the Community. When these assurances were given, in October 1988, the protocols were approved.

Earlier, in December 1987, Parliament refused to approve an association agreement with Turkey until it had received additional information and guarantees from the Turkish Government. Political developments in Turkey, including the suppression of human rights, were the subject of several resolutions. In April 1987, Turkey applied for membership of the Community but the Commission has put off a decision until after 1992 and, in any case, Parliament's approval will be needed. There are many MEPs who believe that true democracy must be established in Turkey before that happens.

During the last two years, Parliament has used its delaying powers on more than thirty occasions. It has also sought assurances about civil rights and other political issues from developing states having aid and trade agreements with the Community under the Lomé Conventions.

Right of Address

Lord Plumb, the British Conservative MEP who was elected President of the Parliament in January 1987, had an important role to play after the Single European Act came into force. He won the right to address the opening session of each bi-ennial summit meeting of Heads of Government. In his down-to-earth, forthright manner, he outlined the views and demands of the MEPs as they confronted the big issues holding up progress towards closer unity. Often he upset the top brass. His protests at a summit in 1988 about the failure of the member Governments to agree on a permanent seat for the Parliament had particular force at a time when MEPs were being asked to do so much extra work in connection with the Single Market Programme.

Another concession obtained by Lord Plumb and the Bureau of Parliament (consisting of leading members of all party groups) concerned the legislative programme. Under the old system, proposals flowed from the Commission and passed on through various stages without any clear time-table. Now, at Lord Plumb's request, the Commission provides an annual legislative programme, rather like the Queen's Speech at Westminster each autumn that sets out the British Government's plans.

Before the February session at Strasbourg, the Commission's programme is submitted and in March, associated with a vote of confidence in the Commission, Parliament gives its verdict. Progress is evaluated at quarterly meetings. The first adopted programme covered the period April 1988 to end of March, 1989.

Slaving away at their increased work-load, MEPs have become more and more dissatisfied with their working arrangements. They have their plenary week-long sessions once a month in Strasbourg (August excepted); the 18 committees meet at least one week every month in Brussels; and Parliament's staff and records are housed in Luxembourg. Political groups also meet two or three days a month to prepare tactics for the monthly plenaries. To keep interest alive in the different EC countries, they also switch from Brussels to other European capitals for political group meetings, with full facilities for documentation and interpreters/translators provided from the parliamentary budget.

Travel facilities are often disrupted in winter by snow, ice or fog. In summer, air traffic control failings often intervene. This circus-like existence is irksome, time-wasting, inefficient and expensive. The additional costs, compared with work in one centre, are put at more than £49 million a year. Outsiders can only marvel at the idiocy of the whole set-up. "Why do they put up with it?" is the question everybody asks. "They must be crazy!" But - and it is a big but - it is not entirely the MEPs' fault. Parliament has to work in three centres because the member Governments, for 32 years, have failed to reach agreement on a single seat for Parliament.

The Rome Treaty specifically states: "The seat of the Community institutions shall be fixed by common accord between the governments of the member States" (Article 216). In January 1989, by 223 votes to 173, Parliament passed a resolution declaring its intention to concentrate more of its activities in Brussels and to transfer many of the staff from Luxembourg to the Belgian capital. Already, in October 1985, Parliament had decided, by resolution, to have a building constructed with a hall providing seating for not less than 600 people, a visitors' gallery and ancilliary facilities, in Brussels. The French Government, noting that 121 MEPs had not voted in 1989, indicated again that they would resist any down-grading of Strasbourg. They also make sure the Mayor is an MEP! The city was chosen as the seat for the Council of

Europe and European Parliament as a symbol of the reconciliation between France and Germany, in a territory (Alsace) fought over in two world wars.

Luxembourg had already been snubbed because, on its own initiative, it built a new parliamentary precinct eight years ago at great expense, yet Parliament used it only once (July 1985). It again felt affronted. It moved in the Court of Justice to try to prevent the removal of Parliamentary staff to Brussels, but the court has already said that MEPs can make their own working arrangements to help efficiency. France has objected to every open or covert attempt to shift Parliament's seat from France to Belgium.

Parliament's resolution of 1989, put forward on behalf of the Political Affairs Committee by Mr Derek Prag, Conservative MEP for Hertfordshire, emphasised that on grounds of efficiency and economy a single permanent seat was essential. It drew "the clear conclusion, from all the information available, that there was no prospect of action by the member Governments in the foreseeable future" and resolved in consequence "to make more satisfactory arrangements for carrying out Parliament's tasks in accordance with its obligations under Community law and the self-evident right of a Parliament elected by universal suffrage".

While Governments bicker and the French protest, a Belgian consortium is building a 600-seat chamber (call it what you will) alongside Parliament's existing committee rooms and offices in the Rue Belliard, Brussels. This may be a gamble, but most MEPs have no doubt that one day, perhaps coinciding with the advent of the Single Market in 1993, the aim will be achieved - one working place in Brussels.

Community Budget clashes

Conflict between the Parliament and Council of Ministers over the size and shape of the EC Budget came to a head during the last Parliament. The breakthrough came, after sustained pressure from Parliament, at the Brussels summit in 1988 when legally-binding limits were placed on Community spending, and the basis of member States contributions was changed to take account each year of the relative prosperity (Gross Domestic Product) of each country.

To curb spending on agriculture, which was producing surpluses - food mountains and wine lakes - that embarrassed farmers and politicians alike, the member States accepted the UK proposition, not unlike the plan put forward by Lord Plumb and the Parliament's agriculture committee in 1982, that a ceiling should be set each year for agricultural support and that a system of "stabilisers" (automatic price reductions) should be imposed when production of certain crops exceeded the level of the fixed annual target.

In fact, Parliament could only show the way. Its ability to change the Common Agricultural Policy (CAP) is limited by the Rome Treaty. That part of the annual European budget dealing with farm subsidies and related price levels is classified as "obligatory", where the Commission and Council have the final say. MEPs can give their opinions, suggest price changes and the like; Ministers take note, but they do the fixing. Farming debates and the long voting sessions on price levels at the Parliament followed a predictable pattern. MEPs with a strong farming lobby in their areas were anxious to defend farmers' incomes, and MEPs from the industrial wastelands, suffering from high unemployment, voted to cut down CAP payments and make more money available to support new industries, research and development, and projects to promote economic growth supported from the Social and Regional Funds.

In the 1985 draft Budget, the Council of Ministers made provision for agricultural funding for only 10 months instead of 12 and failed to include agreed rebates to Germany and the UK. Parliament rejected it, and a new Budget was produced. Amazingly, the next year's Budget overlooked the new members, Spain and Portugal, concerning social and regional expenditure, and also commitments entered into in earlier budgets that now had to be met in payments. Parliament included a high increase in the draft. In response, the Council of Ministers claimed that Parliament had exceeded its powers and referred the matter to the Court of Justice. In its judgment, the Court found in favour of Parliament and required Parliament and Council to negotiate a solution within their two responsibilities: a) the obligatary spending, and b) the non-compulsory section of the Budget. That is now a ratio of about 6 to 4; in 1985 it was 7 to 3.

Another clash came at the end of 1987 when proceedings on the 1988 Budget did not begin at the usual time. The reason: the Council could not agree on the draft. So the Commission and Parliament took the Council of Ministers to the Court of Justice for the offence of not keeping to the time-table. Eventually the dispute went to the Summit meeting, where directions were given for a settlement and the President of Parliament signed the agreed Budget in February 1988.

In May 1988, Parliament got into a ridiculous tangle. It had earlier approved the draft overall Budget. Then the farmers' friends got to work on the prices, and came up with a total for farm support which exceeded the figure MEPs had originally approved. A certain amount of juggling with figures and crops was necessary to get back to the original overall figure.

The 10-year-long "battle of the Budgets" ended with the Brussels summit agreement of 1988. December came, and for the first time since the joint settlement procedure was introduced in 1983, Parliament and Council agreed the Budget for 1989 before the end of the preceding year. It was a time for rejoicing!

Mrs Thatcher, as president of the Council in Office, had warned Parliament in December 1986: "Too much money is still being swallowed by the CAP....Half the Community's total Budget goes not for support which directly helps the farmer but on storage and disposal of agricultural surpluses". The CAP had to be changed to meet the needs of a Community in which only 10 per cent of the population were engaged in agriculture. "You in Parliament have suggested setting aside funds for disposing of the surpluses," she said. "We all want to do that, but you cannot drain the tank when the tap is still turned full on.... You cannot spend more on research and development if you have already spent it on subsidising sales of surplus butter to the Soviet Union, unless you put a bigger hand into taxpayers' pockets."

There was more in the same vein, pungent and true. No doubt her continuous challenge to the accepted norms and the stupidities of the CAP led to the sensible changes made at the Brussels summit. Apart from introducing a new source of finance based on GDP, it put agricultural spending under sharp control, doubled the funds for social and regional funds for the next few years, and established the five-year frame of reference for Community spending.

Detection of fraud

Parliament continued to demand more drastic action from national Governments to combat fraud. Estimates in 1989 put the amount obtained illegally from the agricultural budget at £2.5 billion or up to 10 per cent of the total allotted. Investigators claimed that some of this illegal haul found its way into the hands of the Mafia and the IRA. At the prompting of the Parliament, the European Court of Auditors was set up in 1977 and every year since then its reports have disclosed an amazing picture of false accounting and fraud. In 1984 Parliament called for a fraud squad to be set up; in 1985 it sanctioned funds for a "flying squad" to be employed.

The Committee on Budgetary Control held its first open hearing on fraud cases in 1986 highlighting some of the methods used to obtain payments illegally. In the same year, it refused to discharge the 1984 Budget because it disclosed growing fraudulent practices. Herr Heinrich Eigner, chairman of the committee, toured the EC capitals in 1987 to try to persuade Governments to step up their action against fraudsters, and to give more powers to the Commission to track down offences. However, in 1986 and again in 1989 the Council of Ministers rejected Parliament's demand for greater powers to be given to the Commission to organise the detection of fraud on a Europe-wide basis.

In April 1989, while member Governments still procrastinated, Parliament presented its own five-point plan to tackle the scandal. Produced by Mr Piet Dankert, the Dutch MEP and former President, it proposed:

(1) A central computer network for the exchange of information between all countries and the Commission's small fraud unit;

(2) EC funds to be used to pay for this quickly if member Governments were reluctant to pay for it themselves;

(3) Better cooperation between Member States to speed up extradition, cross-border prosecutions, and sentencing;

(4) Power for the Commission itself to impose fines and penalties;

(5) Better training of national officials in Community rules and regulations.

When this plan was adopted by Parliament, to be sent to the Council for action, one Sicilian MEP complained that there had been no response to Parliament's earlier demand for action against the Mafia and its involvement in Community finances.

The European Parliament was strongly supported in the same month by the House of Lords European Communities Committee. It referred to "a grave situation which has existed for many years, involving weak administration, corrupt practices, and heavy losses of Community funds".

The Greening of Europe

Undoubtedly, the most significant development in the 1984-89 period was the "Greening of Europe" and Parliament's concern for the environment was demonstrated at every session. Partly this was due to the influx of young MEPs from the Green parties in the Rainbow Group. But as scientific evidence became more alarming, all the political groups - reacting to their constituents' fears - demanded tougher joint action to stop the dangerous pollution of the air, sea, soil and water. Pollution knows no national boundaries. Here was a subject that needed international collaboration, with commonly-accepted laws to limit or stop man's harmful activities in industry, farming and in the home.

MEPs came up with a whole series of proposals for legislation and many of them were adopted by the Commission and national Governments. Joint action on exhaust gases was an example where Parliament insisted on faster application of new restrictions than the Council of Ministers first accepted. Most concern centred on the build-up of the "greenhouse effect". Mr Stanley Clinton Davis then UK Commissioner in charge of environment policy, told Parliament in 1988: "The greenhouse effect will become increasingly apparent during our own lifetimes, building to a major crisis within a generation....We owe it to this planet and to future generations to act with speed and determination."

A report from the Commission stated that scientists had advised that significant changes in the earth's atmosphere would lead to changes in the thermal balance on earth. Gases such as carbon dioxide, methane, nitrous oxide and chloroflurocarbons (CFCs) allowed solar radiation to penetrate to the Earth but retained some of the infra-red radiation which the Earth would normally emit back into space. Concentrations of these gases would therefore result in more heat being trapped in the Earth's atmosphere, followed by warming and associated climatic changes.

Parliament was first in the field, asking for restrictions on emissions from power stations. Local MEPs produced dramatic pictures showing how European forests were being damaged by acid rain which was traced back to these emissions. In the Single European Act, provisions were included, based on Parliament's draft treaty, giving a legal basis for Europe-wide legislation on environmental protection. This was a big step forward, and Parliament took the initiative on several fronts. The Year of the Environment (1987-88) brought to the public a greater awareness of the threats to life on Earth.

Parliament's fourth action programme, sent to the Commission in June 1987, called for action on previous Parliamentary resolutions, proposed an overall waste-disposal strategy, and listed a general set of rules for the use and disposal of chemical substances. Member States responded to Parliament's requests without enthusiasm - in part because huge costs were involved in reducing emissions. In 1986, for example, Parliament was told that of the 198 EC approved directives relating to the environment and consumer protection, 55 had encountered problems of incorporation into national law.

In March 1988, Parliament urged the more stringent monitoring of member States' application of EC laws, possibly by having a separate environmental inspectorate, and asked that non-compliance cases should be taken to the Court of Justice. Mr Ken Collins, Labour MEP for Strathclyde, produced a report in 1988 for the Committee on Public Health and the Environment about the implementation of EC laws on water pollution. Again, MEPs protested about the way member Governments were refusing to implement directives.

Taking on board the main points of a Parliamentary resolution passed in 1987 on pollution of the North Sea, the Council of Ministers decided to put a ban on the incineration of pollutants at sea, to end the dumping of toxic industrial waste into the North Sea by the end of 1989; a 50 per cent reduction in the nitrates, phosphates and dangerous substances discharged into that sea by 1995; a ban on the dumping of solid waste from ships; and a strict limit, under close control, on the dumping of radioactive waste into the sea. Emissions of CFCs are to be virtually eliminated by the year 2000 through the revision of a Montreal Convention protocol. The

Commission is engaged in international talks to get agreement on other international measures to protect the atmosphere.

In May 1989, the new procedure of the Single Act was used by Parliament to change the Council of Ministers' minds on car exhaust pollution. MEPs voted for the stronger, US-style controls, but a majority of Ministers favoured weaker standards and a longer period of transition. Parliament stood firm and, at second reading, by threatening to reject in toto the Council's scheme, won the Commission's support. As a result, the tougher scheme was adopted; this has the added advantage of putting European car producers in a position to fight off competition from the US and Japan where the higher controls have already led to changes in car and HGV design.

Another advantage of the Single Act was that Parliament was able to lay down guidelines for the future development of the CAP to take account of environmental protection - limiting the use of pollutant chemicals.

Several times, delegations of MEPs visited the nuclear waste reprocessing plant at Sellafield following complaints, mostly from Irish MEPs, about the discharge of radioactive waste into the Irish Sea. They learnt that changes in the process, then (1987) being put in hand, would reduce the effluents to a level far below that permitted by the International Commission on Radiological Protection. MEPs reported that they were impressed, if not fully satisfied, by the precautions taken to prevent contamination.

Commission President Jacques Delors told Parliament in January 1989, that a new European Environmental Agency was being set up, independent of the Commission, to gather data from EC countries on problems such as air, water and soil pollution.

Recalling Henry Ford's dictum that "all history is bunk", a majority of MEPs rallied to defeat a resolution calling for a standard European history book to counter the national bias in the books used in member States' schools. One Labour MEP thought the chances of getting agreement on what the book should contain were nil when he thought of all the other topics on which the 12 countries disagreed!

Nonetheless, Parliament did press for several Europe-wide schemes to promote greater awareness among young people of the history and culture of other EC countries, and to establish closer partnership between colleges and industry.

In 1984 and again when the programme for achieving a Single Market in 1992 appeared, Parliament asked governments to agree on the recognition of diplomas and degrees, and the harmonisation of training. (EC directives for professional qualifications for architects took 17 years to agree, for pharmacists 16 years!).

There were massive complications. The Council eventually decided on a new approach and agreed that, henceforth, a system of mutual recognition of each country's diplomas and degrees would be adopted. "Phony" degrees will be strictly eliminated. The object is to allow individuals free movement in their chosen calling within the whole Community.

Slow-moving transport policies

A coherent transport policy for the Community has been demanded by Parliament in repeated resolutions for 30 years, with little result. Frustrated and angry, the MEPs decided to arraign the Council of Ministers before the Court of Justice for failing to act on Treaty requirements. Giving judgment in May 1985, the Court declared the Council to be in breach of its duty. This evoked some action, but the Council kept to the terms of the judgment that it had "failed to ensure freedom to provide transport services".

Much more was needed, Parliament insisted, if there was to be a "level playing field" for all competitors in the Single Market of 1993. Council came back with new proposals, covering free movement of goods and access to cabotage. A most welcome change was the substitution of a single customs document for lorry drivers to produce at frontier checks - in place of the 17 they formerly had to carry. Harmonised transport legislation still has to be hammered out that will remove distortions caused by quotas, national rules, driving hour limits, road tests, safety requirements, and fuel and road taxes. Slowly, the way for the free passage of goods is being opened. At many frontier posts between member States traffic already flows without hindrance.

In the air, things are different. Air travellers find that fares remain high, national monopolies are stubbornly defended, and the crowded air lanes are subject to an inefficient system of traffic control. Only in July, 1989, did the Council agree on a unified air control system and this is not due to come into operation until 1993. A £40 million computer control will be established in Brussels to coordinate flights within

51

the 23 countries which are members of the European civil aviation conference.

Nationalism reared its unwelcome head when Parliament debated measures to liberalise air passenger and freight services in September 1985. Parliament voted 198 to 67 to ask the Commission to modify its proposals. The majority did not want to jeopardise their own national airlines. No-one could deny the critics' claim, however, that these lines operated as a cartel to keep prices high. The Commission sought to limit the right of national governments to veto lower air fares or to restrict the "independents". Where innovator airlines had been given the go-ahead, they said, customers had a wider choice of fares and routes.

Lord Bethell, Conservative MEP for London North West, continued to campaign tirelessly in this cause. In 1988 further progress was made. Parliament approved a scheme from the Commission authorising scheduled inter-regional services. In practice, the independent operators often found that national airport controllers restricted their landings and take-offs to inconvenient times of the day and night.

Following a series of accidents, Parliament led in demanding that more attention should be given to safety, in construction of aircraft and in their operation. They had complaints from the thousands of holidaymakers who spent substantial periods of their holidays in airport waiting lounges, and urged the Commission to work for the establishment of a central traffic control centre for the whole of Europe. That is coming, as indicated above, but there is a long wait.

High Technology

As part of the strategy to boost economic development and provide more jobs, Parliament advocated several schemes to bring high technology industries up to the competitive ability of the Japanese and the Americans. At a special session in October 1985, it approved a resolution giving guidelines for future improvement. It wanted budget provision to be increased from 3 to 6 per cent for research - even then a modest figure - and backed a Commission plan for 1987-91 only to see the Council prune it down. On three occasions in 1987, MEPs complained about the Council's dilatory stance.

All the prodding and urging brought little response. The Euronet Diane project was not supported so generously as they thought necessary, with the result, the MEPs say, that the Community is falling far behind the US in key sectors of the information technology sector. Europe is opening up only half as many on-line databases as the Americans.

On a practical level, Parliament asked for the more rapid adoption of a European strategic plan for telecommunications, embracing European common standards, mutually-compatible mobile telephone systems, and the liberalisation of monopoly-dominated markets. Praise came where it was due. MEPs welcomed the Eureka project which is fostering research and coordination in the new technologies, both as a non-military response to the US strategic defence initiative and to the Japanese human frontier science programme. One side-effect should be the prevention of wasteful duplication of projects in member countries.

Ahead of the Commission, MEPs called on Governments to agree on a common market for broadcasting services (*TV without Frontiers*) and the removal of national restrictions on the film industries. The aim: to allow access by every Community citizen to the greatest number of television programmes, the production of more programmes with a European content, and a coherent policy among member States in respect of broadcasting de-regulation. Responding favourably, the Commission issued a draft directive (1986) setting out requirements on programme content. These concerned community broadcasting, advertising standards, the protection of youth, and copyright.

For their part, MEPs pressed for new copyright provisions to deal with audiovisual piracy, home copying equipment, and software protection. They also pointed out that a common technical standard for satellite broadcasting is essential if a variety of differing transmission systems is to be avoided. Such a mix-up would repeat the confusion existing in the 1960s when countries had differing TV systems.

Problems concerning the fragmentation of production and distribution of European programmes were highlighted in Parliament's comments (December 1986) on the proposed subsidy scheme for non-documentary cinema and TV productions in Europe. Here the objective was to counter the flood of North American programmes. Even more to the point, Parliament asked that all member States should support a multilingual TV service which would form a link between diverse European cultures.

Catching the drug pedlars

Closer cooperation to catch "the pedlars of death and destruction" - the drug barons - operating in Europe was the theme of a Parliamentary debate in 1986 after a special inquiry, mounted by the Committee on Social Affairs and Employment. Its rapporteur, Sir Jack Stewart-Clark, Conservative MEP for Sussex East, said the "the world's filthiest trade" was believed to be worth about £208,333 million a year, or ten times the entire annual budget of the European Community.

He quoted estimates that there were about 1.9 million heroin addicts in the Community, with about 200,000 each in the major states (the UK, France, Germany, Italy and Spain). Parliament called for specific measures, asking the Commission to act swiftly. These were: (1) A combined onslaught against every link in the drugs chain. (2) More money to be provided to drug-producing countries to persuade them to grow alternative crops. (3) Stricter controls over the import and export of chemicals used in illegal drug-making. (4) Common rules for sentencing drug traffickers - for extraditing them and for confiscating their assets.

Ms Eileen Lemass, an Irish MEP, argued that an EC task force should be set up to track down the drugs dealers. "These faceless barons and profiteers are blind to pain, immune to suffering; they are without conscience and they are continuously devising new drugs to boost their empire of fear and profit," she said. Prompted by Parliament, the Council of Ministers adopted a plan for concerted action, and several member States passed legislation to allow the courts to order the confiscation of the assets of drug dealers when convicted.

New measures on a Europe-wide scale to combat the spread of AIDS were sent from Parliament to the Commission in May 1987, and eventually the Council of Ministers acted on many of the suggestions, including the pooling of information and the coordination of research.

Tobacco is also a drug, and a cause of cancer. Parliament approved stronger warnings on cigarette packets, later adopted by the Council of Ministers. The UK was the sole dissenting voice in voting against the directive, coming into force in January 1993, requiring manufacturers to print "Tobacco seriously damages health" on packet fronts and a choice of 16 warnings on the back. These back-of-pack messages are to be changed regularly, ranging from "Smoking kills" to "Pregnant women: smoking harms your baby".

Mrs Thatcher explained to the Commons that the UK Government objected to the dictat of the bureaucrats in Brussels on matters that could be decided in national Parliaments. It appeared that the heart of the British objections was the interpretation of the powers of the Commission and Council in implementing measures under the Single Act. Cigarettes and health warnings seemed subject to majority decision, therefore the UK would have to accept the decision from Brussels.

A small matter, maybe, but it put the spotlight on the growing power of the Commission, and the use of the majority vote to over-rule the wishes of an objecting member State. It is a point of historical importance that, in the European Parliament, there was a democratic majority in favour of the stronger warnings.

Parliament also expressed firm views on radiation dangers, harmful food additives, health and safety at work, research in biotechnology, and innovations in surgery, including organ transplants and surrogate motherhood, subjects certain to be explored again in the new Parliament.

Crocodile and Kangaroo

Away from the formal business, MEPs have set up all-party groups (called inter-groups in Euro-jargon) to deal with a variety of subjects. At the last count, there were nearly 60 groups, dealing directly with outside bodies and individuals who want to get their complaints and interests on to the parliamentary agenda. The most influential of the groups, in the long term, will be seen to be the Crocodile Club, set up in 1981 and named after the restaurant in Strasbourg in which MEPs from all parties and EC countries met to debate the institutional changes that were needed to bring about European union - or, if that was pie in the sky, much closer unity among the member States.

Crocodile reports impressed the larger body of MEPs so much that Parliament decided to set up a special committee, under the guidance of the late Altiero Spinelli, an Italian Communist MEP, chairman of the EP Committee on Institutional Affairs, to produce a blue-print for the future. This draft Treaty on European Union got the backing of Parliament and went to the Council of Ministers. It pressed the claims of MEPs to a stronger position in the law-making process, and the result came - much watered down - in the Single European Act.

So Crocodile was a fringe group of historic importance. Another, formed early in 1983, was the Kangaroo Group, so called because it was devoted to leaping across fences without hindrance. Its leading members were the late Mr Basil de Ferranti, Conservative MEP for West Hampshire, and Herr Karl von Wogau, a German Christian Democrat. Their aim was to break down border restrictions on the free movement of people and goods, and the removal of nationalistic protective rules, usually carried out through silly technical requirements. They gained wide support from all parties, and from Mrs Thatcher and other leaders. They were supplied with hundreds of examples of irksome restrictions, sometimes involving the bribing of customs men or officials.

Mr de Ferranti in the first issue of *Kangaroo News* in 1983 told that the first constituent who came to see him after being elected was a trader unable to export fork-lift trucks to France because ridiculous technical conditions were imposed, one or two of them ignoring safety needs. The Kangaroos brought immense pressure to bear on the Commission and the national Governments who could not rebut their accusations. Without their hard work, it is doubtful whether the 1992 Single Market would have come on to the agenda. Too many vested interests had to be exposed.

Another effective inter-group, operative since 1979, deals with animal welfare. They were the motivating force, backed by crowds of lobbyists who surrounded the entrance to Parliament whenever animal protection was debated, in getting the ban on seal skin imports. It was Europe's condemnation of the trappers' cruel method of clubbing seal pups to death in the icy wastes.

Other inter-groups cover such issues as the welfare of the elderly, the disabled, handicapped children, federal union, the promotion of regional dialects and culture, tourism, science in industry and European broadcasting.

The Right to Petition

No right of citizens to petition the European Parliament is to be found in the Treaties; it has been granted and established by Parliament through its own rules of procedure. Collective and individual petitions are now reaching Parliament at the rate of 600 a year. Since January 1987, Parliament has had a committee charged with looking into the petitions, rather like the Ombudsmen/women who deal with complaints against maladministration in central and local government in member States. A condition of acceptance is that the petition must either involve some European regulation or directive, Treaty provisions, basic human rights, or has a general European dimension.

Many concern alleged discrimination based on sex or nationality, pensions and social security rights of people who have worked in more than one member State, transport or trade restrictions, freedom of movement, the right to provide services, rights of residence and so on. Some petitions are sent for action by the Commission; others are channelled to the appropriate authority, or legal action is recommended, and others are passed on to Ombudsman offices in member States.

Petitions can be passed to the President of Parliament, if it seems likely that he can help people whose national Governments have failed. A touching example of Lord Plumb's success in this delicate area of international relations was when he got several mothers re-united with children who had been taken to Algeria by run-away husbands. Parliament's work was recognised by the wider community in June 1988, when Mr Raphaël Chanterie, of Belgium, chairman of the Committee on Petitions, was invited to take part in the round-table discussion held by European Ombudsmen and their officials.

Countering the extremist

Disturbed by the rise of right-wing, extremist political parties in Community countries, the Socialist Group in Parliament led a demand for a special committee of inquiry into the growth of fascism and racism in Europe. Support for a full-scale inquiry was luke-warm among the Conservatives and Christian Democrats, but there was a majority in favour. The committee began its work early in 1985 under the chairmanship of Mr Glyn Ford, Labour MEP for Greater Manchester East. The French National Front members, after seeking to prevent the inquiry, decided to boycott its proceedings. For their part, the Socialists, with Mrs Barbara Castle to the fore, decided to ostracise the FN members and attack everything they did.

After many sessions, taking evidence from all sections of society at public hearings, the committee reported back with details of the extremist groups active in member States and stated that there was an increase in xemophobia and intolerance towards immigrant communities in all countries. Calling for stricter application of the laws on discrimination, the committee also advocated greater emphasis in schools and universities on civic education and on instilling more tolerant attitudes.

A resolution endorsing the committee's conclusions was passed by 317 votes to 22, and was followed by a joint declaration by Parliament, Council and Commission in June, 1986. This vigorously condemned all forms of intolerance, hostility and use of force against persons or groups on grounds of racial, religious, cultural, social or national differences. All three institutions re-affirmed their resolve to protect the freedom and dignity of every member of society, and to reject any form of segregation of foreigners.

Later, a report from the Socialist Group stated that one of the disturbing features of the Far Right incursions into working class youth culture was the spillover of politically-motivated violence into sport, notably soccer. After the Heysel Stadium disaster in 1985, they said, investigators uncovered the fact that agitators from the British National Party had been distributing their literature both on the terraces and on the ferries en route to the match.

After the Heysel tragedy and a series of other incidents involving hooliganism by "lager louts" at other football matches, the Committee on Youth, Culture, Education and Sport organised a public hearing (December 1985). Some of the recommendations put forward by well known sporting figures were later adopted, such as: special security at "high-risk games", separation of rival groups of supporters, controls on the sale of alcohol and tickets, and supervision of travelling fans. Mr Alex Falconer, Labour MEP for Mid Scotland and Fife, blamed the behaviour of some young fans on high youth unemployment in the inner cities. Others saw a strong connexion between violence on the field and fighting on the terraces.

The committee's ideas were taken up by the Council of Sports Ministers. The British Government proceeded with legislation requiring the issue of identity cards for supporters. Various bans on the sale of alcohol were enforced.

Committee on Women's Rights

Women in the Community have probably gained more in the way of equal pay and equal treatment through European Parliament and Commission initiatives than through national Parliaments. There are 165 million women in the EC; in mid-1989 21 million were in paid employment, 7 million were unemployed. Believing that the Rome Treaty obligation on member States to work for equal pay for women when doing the same jobs as men, was not being seriously accepted, Parliament stepped into the gap.

In the first elected Parliament, with a woman, Mme Simone Veil of France, as its first President, the MEPs set up an ad hoc committee to tackle women's problems (1977). In 1984, it replaced this with a permanent Committee on Women's Rights which has monitored Governments' actions in response to the scandal of women's low pay, especially for part-time jobs.

When Governments have fallen short, the Committee and the European Court of Justice have acted in test cases to show the way towards equal treatment. Prompted by Parliament, the Commission produced a second action programme covering the period 1986 to 1990 commending legislation to eliminate pay and social security anomalies. Parliament wanted the burden of proof rules reversed in discrimination cases, and the Commission has adopted its recommendation. The Council has yet to agree (July 1989).

Repeatedly during the 1984-89 Parliament, MEPs protested at the slow rate of legislation to protect women's rights. In 1986 they sent the Council a report stating that wage differentials were still widespread, as high as 30 per cent in some occupations (for equal work). Some MEPs backed the idea of husbands paying housewives salaries.

For the Commission, M. Manual Marin told them there was little chance of a directive on taxation of women being accepted, or of getting agreement on

Parliament's proposals regarding part-time work and parental leave. If the Council could not agree, it should say so and the public could see who was holding up progress, he said.

In October, 1987, Parliament went on the offensive again, passing four major reports showing discrimination still existed in employment and training, social security, taxation, the media, business opportunities, education, sport, and the treatment of immigrant women.

Poor Relationships

Relations between the British party groups at Strasbourg and their colleagues in the Westminster Parliament continued to be minimal. "When we go to the Commons, we are treated like pirates trying to board a treasure ship" one Labour MEP told me. Other phrases used to describe their reception - "interlopers", "visitors from outer space", "pariahs" "unwanted immigrants". . . There is a lot of bitterness.

After ten years of a directly-elected Parliament, the British MEPs have only this year (1989) been granted, by vote of the Commons, admission passes - and these are by no means the equal of an MP's pass. The MEPs have the same right of entry and movement as MPs' research assistants. Time and again, British MEPs - notably Mr Bill Newton Dunn, Conservative MEP for Lincolnshire - have called for closer collaboration with party colleagues in the Commons to improve democratic control over the Commission and Council of Ministers. In no sense can the Commons scrutiny of draft legislation from Brussels be called effective. What remains is a glaring democratic deficit.

Take the period July 1987 to the end of June 1988. During that time 931 Commission documents - regulations, directives, proposals - were considered by the Commons Standing Committee on European Legislation. It is charged with the task of checking the documents, and recommending those which raise matters of important public interest and deserve full debate on the floor of the Commons. Of the 931, 94 were selected as being of such importance.

There were, in fact, 19 debates in the House and these covered 66 documents, grouped for the sake of convenience. In Standing Committee there were 11 debates on 23 documents. Thus only 10 per cent of the Commission's output came under discussion in debate. Usually the Commons debates on Euro legislation take place late in the evening or middle of the night. There is little media coverage, and a low turn-out of MPs - the same regulars. What is more, debates rarely result in more than "taking note". Ministers get a general impression of the views of the House, and take them into account when decisions are made in the Council of Ministers.

Most MPs have accepted the reality of the new situation created by the Single European Act. The Commons and the Lords could theoretically order the British Minister to vote in a particular way on a piece of legislation, or part of it, and the Minister could do so. However, under the new process, on nearly all legislation connected with the creation of a Single Market, the Council can act by majority vote. Thus the veto in that situation is a thing of the past.

This is where the democratic deficit becomes so obvious, where national sovereignty vanishes and European sovereignty takes over. And the cooperation procedure used by the European Parliament now puts MEPs in a much stronger position to influence the details of legislation than national Parliaments. As Lord Plumb, the retiring President, has pointed out - the European Parliament must take over the task of democratic control from the national MPs. An increasing number of the MEPs' amendments are being accepted, and an increasing number of new laws are being passed over by national parliaments.

Pro-European MPs and peers at Westminster became alarmed about this unsatisfactory state of affairs in 1988 and formed an all-party pressure group, chaired by Mr Hugh Dykes, Conservative MP for Harrow East, to try to bridge the democratic gap. As a result the House of Commons Procedure Committee was persuaded to investigate improved methods for examining the Brussels output. Mr Christopher Prout, Leader of the British Conservative MEPs, told the committee that it was common practice for MEPs of other countries to work closely with national Parliaments and pass on advance information about pending legislation.

When asked whether Euro-MPs would be willing to attend joint committees in Westminster to help check on Euro legislation, he said, "Yes, willingly". Labour MEPs would also be willing, according to veteran members of their group. Sir Peter Emery, chairman of the Commons Procedure Committee, said during one hearing:

"It is time for an end to the rivalry between the two Parliaments, especially from the Westminster end. It is time we all got into the same boat and started rowing in the same direction". In the back of people's minds is the memory of M. Jacques Delors forecast: "In ten years, 80 per cent of the economic legislation - and perhaps tax and social legislation - will be directed from the Community". Like it or not, the Westminster MPs have to recognise that if they do nothing the reins of power will gradually slip from their hands.

Over the last ten years the Conservative MEPs - partly, I suspect, because of their isolation from Conservative MPs at Westminster - have become more Europe-oriented than the rest of their party, and often take a policy line which infuriates Mrs Thatcher. Their compromise on proportional representation was an instance.

They are welcome at Tory back-benchers' group meetings dealing with specialised subjects whenever they have time to get there, but not the weekly 1922 Committee meetings although even this situation was changed after the June 1989 Euro reverses and a group of Tory MEP attended a 1922 Committee meeting. Tory MEPs have no vote in the annual election of the leader. They have an annual get-together with the Prime Minister, whose message is usually admonitionary, on the lines of: "I expect you to stand up for British interests, just as the Germans and French stand up for theirs!"

However, Conservative and Labour MEPs are regularly invited to give evidence at the investigatory sessions of the House of Lords European Communities Committee. Usually specialists on the subject being discussed, they bring valuable enlightenment about the political under-currents influencing affairs in Brussels and Strasbourg. This Lords Committee continues to issue the most comprehensive and hard-hitting reports on proposed European directives and regulations. The high standard of their reports and their recommendations cannot be matched by any other Parliament or committee in the Community. And Commissioners are most ardent readers.

Labour now loves Europe

Within the Labour group of MEPs the tensions which existed after the first direct election were carried over to the 32-strong contingent in 1984. Relations with party headquarters were not good; the party conference was still critical of Britain's membership of the EC, but the leadership had come round to accepting that withdrawal was not feasible and that the best efforts must be made to advance Socialism through combining with comrades in Europe.

Mrs Barbara Castle was again elected leader of the far from cohesive group. Its members were roughly divided into three factions:- the centre-right, pro-Europeans; those who were allied with the Tribune Group at Westminster; and a third who were Campaign Group members, on the hard left of the party. Mrs Castle had become pro-European and wanted to get the best deal possible for the UK, championing the cause of industrial revival, the needs of the unemployed in the hard-hit regions, and attacking the scandalous treatment of consumers in contrast to the mollycoddling of farmers.

But in June 1985 she was defeated by 18 votes to 14 in the annual leadership election, the result reflecting the critical attitude still being adopted by a majority of Labour MEPs about Europe. Mr Alf Lomas, Labour MEP for London North East, a former signalman, who was elected in her place, declared that he would continue to campaign for Britain's withdrawal from the Community on the grounds that Labour's policy for a planned economy could not be achieved inside the Community. He wrote a book on the subject.

On the other hand, even he said: "We must face reality. So long as Britain remains a member - which is certain for the foreseeable future - I will lead the British Labour members in campaigning for the policies which we believe are in the best interests of working people throughout Europe". He added that the group would not hesitate to pursue the policies of the Labour Party where these were in conflict with the majority of the Europe-wide Socialist Group. "Our policies are decided by our national conference, not by socialist manifestos drawn up in Brussels," he declared.

After two years, in 1987, Mr Lomas was voted out, to be replaced by Mr David Martin, former accounts clerk, MEP for the Lothians, who had the support of the centre-right and some of the Tribune group. He appeared with Mr Neil Kinnock, the party leader, at a press conference in 1988 to launch the first of the pre-election statements on the party's European aims. But, a year later, Dr Barry Seal, MEP for West Yorkshire, former polytechnic college lecturer, was elected leader. By this time most of the group had fallen in behind Mr Kinnock and accepted that the new-look Labour Party was going places.

Trade unions were also looking to the Labour MEPs for help in ensuring that the 1992 revolution did not become just a bonanza for the bosses, with workers' pay and conditions taking a very low priority. After M. Delors had addressed the TUC in 1988 on what he saw as the essential elements in the Charter of Workers' Rights (then being drawn up) and had been tumultuously received, the unions and the left-wingers saw a new dawn breaking - a way of escape from the restrictions imposed on the unions through Mrs Thatcher's "oppressive legislation".

In spite of all this, the group's links with the party were tenuous. There was little consultation. The Chair of the group had the right to attend meetings of the National Executive, and speak on European topics, but not to vote. There were no joint meetings of the PLP and the Euro group, only occasional contacts at the Tribune and Campaign group meetings. However, the group, reinforced by 13 new members with no particular allegiance to the old groupings, elected Mr Glyn Ford, MEP for Greater Manchester East, as the new leader within a few days of the 1989 election triumph. Labour's new look had paid off handsomely! They are now demanding closer links with the party leadership, and would like a constitutional change giving them the right to take part in the election of the party leader and other officers, equal to the PLP. And, they say, they will use Europe to enable Labour to win the next UK general election.

Harmonization of VAT

For two years, controversy raged over the Commission plan, proposed and defended by Lord Cockfield, Commissioner and former Conservative Treasury Minister, to harmonize VAT rates throughout the Community. Seven states have one or more reduced rates, in addition to the normal rate. This "normal" level is variable. It can differ by anything up to 10 per cent on crossing a frontier. The Commission proposed at the end of 1988 a "normal" band rate of between 14 per cent and 20 per cent, and a single, reduced rate band, between 4 and 9 per cent. There was outrage. No zero rate!

Mrs Thatcher had already hoisted the storm cones in 1987. She declared: "The Government is fully prepared to use its veto to preserve our zero rates if necessary". British zero rates apply to food, electricity, gas, fuel, transport, children's clothes, and books and newspapers. Labour's Treasury spokesman, Mr Gordon Brown, estimated that the Commission proposals could add between £3 and £7 a week to the bills of an ordinary family. Relations between Mrs Thatcher and Lord Cockfield became extremely sour at this stage, although he had been her appointment to the Commission.

In the European Parliament, also, the controversy raged. Eventually, MEPs came up with a compromise: the normal VAT rate should be fixed between 16 and 22 per cent, and the second, reduced, band, should range from zero to 9 per cent. This was carried. On this occasion, British MEPs of all parties were united in favour!

A serious blow was yet to come, however. The European Court of Justice, dealing with an submission by the Commission, that VAT must be charged on new building, except housing, in the UK as elsewhere in the Community, came down in favour of the bureaucrats. It raised fears that it would place a new burden on industry, and add to the cost of building hospitals and schools - and to the costs of charities providing homes for the poor and the sick.

This Court decision was historic. It has deep - some would say sinister - significance, as one tries to predict the future, in the Single Market. The principle of the Single European Act is that only those tasks that can be more effectively carried out in common, rather than nationally, should be taken over by the Commission and Community.

Here was an example where a country's policy could be seriously affected by a European Court decision. Charities could be put in jeopardy. In spite of Mrs Thatcher's repeated declarations that Britain will not be ruled by the bureaucrats in Brussels, here was proof of her impotence. However, a new EC Commissioner, Mrs Scrivener, came round to the view, in contrast to Lord Cockfield, that zero rating on domestic housing, children's clothing and food could remain.

Unemployment still high

Looking back on the 1984-89 activities in Strasbourg, the greatest frustration for

MEPs was the block placed on their efforts to tackle unemployment. In spite of the rosy predictions when the United Kingdom joined the Community, unemployment rose from 5 million in 1975 to 16 million in 1986 and at the beginning of 1989 was just over 15 million. Some increase in the money allocated to the Social and Regional Funds was brought about in the European Parliament by exploiting the power over the non-compulsory sector of the Budget. Unfortunately, the money was far short of what was needed.

Optimistically, the Community's economic advisers say that expansion of the European economy, due to the advantages of the 1992 Single Market, will bring a huge increase in jobs. That is a hope for the future, but in the period under review, as was reported to MEPs in a 1988 debate, employment in most member States had remained stagnant in the last 10 years while the US had created 21 million new jobs, and Japan six million. In the free market, Europe had "imported" unemployment.

In 1986, Parliament held a major debate on unemployment. It criticised the puny level of grants available from the Social Fund and the Regional Fund (in total representing only 6 per cent of the Budget in 1985 while 70 per cent went to the guarantee section of the agricultural fund). The Social Fund, the main instrument for supporting job training and re-training, has been doubled in the last five years, but Parliament claimed that disbursements had failed to target the most deprived sectors of the population. At Parliament's request, the Council adopted a revised code for the fund, and more attention is now given to helping the long-term unemployed and concentrating more on the new technologies.

On the wider front, the Regional Fund is used to promote development in regions where unemployment is high, usually due to the run-down of traditional industries, like steel and shipbuilding. Between 1975 and 1987, the UK share of the Regional Fund came to £3.1 billion or 20 per cent of the total. Hundreds of schemes were supported. In March 1986, the town of Corby, one of the beneficiaries, sent a delegation to Strasbourg to say "Thank you" for the £100 million revival programme. That followed the closure of the steel works, in which 13,000 workers had been employed. Grants from the EC Regional Fund had created 8,000 new jobs; more than 300 new companies had started up.

The Social Charter

Attention now turns to the Charter on Workers' Rights which the new Parliament will be asked to approve. The Commission says it is intended to protect jobs and living standards that could be jeopardised by the industrial adjustments which will be made to strengthen competition in the Single Market. Rights specified include the right to form trade unions, to strike, and to enter into collective bargaining; and the right to information for, and consultation with, the workforce when company plans are formed or changed.

This will revive the controversy which dominated the 1979-84 Parliament over the so-called Vredeling Directive on company law. There was an acrimonious debate in Parliament, the centre-right siding with employers and refusing to make it a general rule that workers should have a guaranteed place on the management board of companies, and the Socialists demanding more than the Commission was prepared to give. Lobbying was intense.

Battered from both sides, the Commission - always keen on worker participation - eventually gave up the struggle. This time, however, workers' participation will be more loosely defined, to allow nationally-accepted practices to be continued. All the signs are that the TUC, modifying its 1982 position, will be active in the defence of more flexibility. On the other side, Mrs Thatcher regards the proposed Charter as "back-door socialism", a burden which will add to costs and handicap European companies when competing on the world market.

So the scene is set for another classic battle in which the European Parliament, with its political balance evenly poised, will play an important role. The crucial question remains: when it comes to final decisions on the controversial parts of the Charter, who will have the final say? Will it be the European Parliament or the Council of Ministers? Will they at last succeed in getting their act together? The next five years will be the test. Certainly the European intrusion into domestic politics will cause all parties to pay more attention to the potentialities of their MEPs at Strasbourg: to the role they can play in shaping laws that MPs at Westminster have neither the time, nor - on present evidence - the inclination, to examine in detail.

The First Session in Strasbourg

Serious work ahead on important and controversial issues

By Alan Wood

Former Head of Parliamentary Staff, *The Times*

Unlike five years previously when the United Kingdom rebate and the EC budget dominated events, the first week in Strasbourg of the third directly-elected European Parliament confined its political activities to sorting itself into shape in terms of the political groups and the composition of its committees and a few easily forecast postures on future business.

Although there are now more political groups and committees with larger member-ships, everything emerged in fairly workmanlike fashion. And what debate there was looked ahead to the implications of economic and monetary union, the social charter, the fall of internal trade barriers at the end of 1992 and the environment - all important and needless to say controversial issues. The Spanish and French Foreign Ministers were particularly strong in their determination to see the social charter implemented. So was the President of the Commission, M. Jacques Delors, and the new Labour group leader, Mr Glyn Ford. It was all predictable material.

For the first time, the directly-elected Parliament succeeded in electing a new President on the first ballot - Señor Enrique Barón Crespo, the Spanish Socialist MEP, former Vice-President of the Parliament and President of the European Movement since 1987. He gained the full backing of the Christian Democrats who did not put up a candidate in the hope that mid-term, January 1992, the Socialists will similarly support a candidate from the European People's Party. The new President obtained 301 votes, exactly equal to the combined strength of the Socialists (180) and the EPP Christian Democrats (121).

Votes obtained by the other presidential candidates were: Herr Rüdiger von Wechmar (LDR) 93; Sra María Santos (co-chair of Les Verts) 31; Mrs Winifred Ewing, of the Scottish National Party (Arc-en-Ciel) 23; M. Jean-Marie Le Pen (Droites Européenes) 18 and Sgr Marco Pannella (Non-attached) 12. Señor Crespo was warmly welcomed to office by all the groups and he, in acknowledging the honour being bestowed upon him, paid a warm, sincere tribute to the work of his predecessor, Lord Plumb. The new President pointed out that they shared the same birthday and Christian name; it was a case of the Red Baron succeeding the Blue cavalier.

Sadly, the process of electing the new President was marred by a huge walk-out of MEPs and demonstrations by the Greens. This was because the oldest MEP, who by custom presides and speaks before the election, was a member of the extreme right group led by M. Le Pen. It was widely felt that he put former film director M. Autant Laurent (date of birth - August 5 1901) on the National Front list merely because of his age and so that he could preside over this important parliamentary occasion.

M. Autant-Lara duly spoke at great length to an almost empty chamber, the Socialist Group and others leaving behind red roses at their desks. Many of the Conservative group did not at first join in the walkout but most decided to do so when M. Autant-Lara, who admitted he had only recently joined M. Le Pen's National Front, launched a savage attack on the United States followed by a similar tirade against the English language.

Mrs Caroline Jackson, Tory MEP for Wiltshire, who stayed the course, said she did so out of respect for the Parliament, its rules and the right of free speech. The lesson to be learned was that their rules should be changed. This is certain to happen. It would be rather pleasantly formal if the last act of the outgoing President could be the handing over of, say, a badge of office to the incoming President.

There were 14 candidates for the 14 Vice-Presidencies and a considerable time was expended balloting them into office. The reason was the need to determine the pecking order and, again, the block votes of the two big political groups determined that nine of the first ten Vice-Presidencies settled in the first ballot were held by members of those groups - five by Socialists and four by the EPP.

Those elected on the first ballot were: Mme Nicole Pery (France, Soc) 286 votes; Herr Siegbert Alber (Germany, EPP) 279; Mr Georgios Anastassopoulos (Greece, EPP) 275; Herr Hans Peters (Germany, Soc) 259; Mme Nicole Fontaine (France, EPP) 254; Mr David Martin (United Kingdom, Soc) 246; Mr Georgios Romeos (Greece, Soc) 242; Sgr Roberto Formigoni (Italy, EPP) 240; Sir Fred Catherwood (United Kingdom, European Democrat - Conservative) 238; Senhor Joâo Cravinho (Portugal, Soc) 237. Those elected on the second ballot were: M. Yves Galland (France, LDR - Liberal and Democrat) 310 votes; Senhor Antonio Capucho (Portugal, LDR) 295; Señor Fernando Pérez Royo (Spain, European United Left) 292, and Herr Wilfried Telkämper (Germany, Verts) 272.

In the only other ballot for elected offices, the Parliament chose its five quaestors, who look after backbench interests. Those elected were: Sgr Gerardo Gaibisso (Italy, EPP) 302; Mr Ernest Glinne (Belgium, Soc) 301; Mr Paddy Lalor (Ireland, RDE - European Democratic Alliance); Sgr Andrea Raggio (Italy, EUL) 225, and Mr Anthony Simpson (United Kingdom, ED) 224.

The two big groups also neatly carved up most of the 18 committee chairmanships, the Socialists taking eight and the EPP five, leaving two for the Liberals and Democrats, and one each for the European Democrats, the Greens and the European United Left, one of the two Communist groups.

The walk-out during M. Autant-Lara's speech and the leaving of red roses in the chamber led to the first faux-pas of the week by the Conservatives. A press release emerged from them castigating the Socialists for heavy expenditure on flowers for this and other occasions. Sadly, the amount expended was calculated over high on an incorrect rate of exchange for the European current unit (the Ecu) so the manoeuvre fell rather flat and caused a few wry smiles.

This was matched by a later press release from the British Labour group of MEPs protesting about expenditure on certain gifts for MEPs by the French Government and authorities of Strasbourg. There was a filofax for every MP and the promise of a telefax and TV set in every member's office and other items of equipment like an electronic pager and message receiver. The Labour group burst forth with a shock-horror-bribery-corruption complaint just as if none of them had not been around for the last 10 years. All well and good, but the French Socialist MEPs were definitely not amused, particularly Mme Trautmann, who just happens to be the Socialist Mayor of Strasbourg faithfully carrying on hospitality activities for which a Christian Democrat predecessor, M. Pflimlin, ex-President of the EP, was rather well known.

Bearing in mind the principle of subsidiarity which particularly the United Kingdom Government wants applied to more European activities, if the French taxpayers in general and the Strasbourg taxpayers in particular wish to expend money in this way then so be it. In PR terms, both Labour and Conservatives from the UK, must aim for a higher plain.

MEPs have already indicated a desire to move to Brussels but the final say is not theirs yet. The French have certainly been seeking to influence MEPs to stay in Strasbourg since 1973 when the late Sir Peter Kirk and his nominated colleagues from the UK first took their seats in the European Parliament and the then hostile anti-EEC Labour Party stayed away.

The actions of the French are undoubtedly linked to plans for the construction of another extension to the European Parliament building at the Palais de l'Europe. This is due to begin in January 1990 and be completed by April 1991. The new facilities will include a press centre, a visitors' area including a restaurant, and offices for the administrative services of the Parliament permanently based in Strasbourg.

While debates in the chamber concentrated on economic and monetary union, the social charter, 1992, the environment and events in Poland, several interesting items during the first week of the new Parliament were outside the Chamber, like the final press conference by Lord Plumb; the press conference held by Mr Neil Kinnock, the Labour leader, and that jointly held by Herr Klepsch, EPP Group leader, and Mr Christopher Prout, European Democratic (Conservative) Group leader, over Tory moves for closer collaboration between the two or even a link-up.

61

The Greens held a celebratory reception; the Tories a postmortem on the disastrous outcome of their campaign in which they lost 13 Euro seats; Labour were understandably jubilant and heartened through a visit by the party leader. They also picked up the chairs of two important committees - Mr Ken Collins becoming environment committee chairman yet again and Mrs Christine Crawley heading the women's rights committee. The top priority of Mr Collins is to bring Governments to book if they are not observing existing directives and regulations.

The Tories were certainly not downhearted in European Parliament terms, picking up the chairmanship of the Committee on Budgetary Control through Mr Peter Price, and an all-important vice-chairmanship of the environment committee, held by Sir Jim Scott-Hopkins, the former Tory group leader.

The Tories spent much time considering the campaign in the UK and used the first week to draw together various recommendations which could be put to Conservative Central Office. This was duly done in September, three months after the Euro voting. Various propositions were aired. One idea was that a vice-chairmanship of the Conservative Party should be held by an MEP. Another was that MEPs, like MPs, should have a vote in choosing a future leader. Other propositions embraced more say in future Euro manifestos and closer collaborations with backbench committees in the House of Commons and with Conservative Central Office.

Mr Kinnock, in the course of his visit to Strasbourg, had useful talks with the new President of the Parliament and with M. Delors, President of the EC Commission. And he also, quite properly, attended a reception given by the Mayor of Strasbourg. At his press conference, Mr Kinnock was at his most verbose. There was a considerable amount of edging and fudging over the lengths to which the UK should agree to economic and monetary union and joining the European monetary system. But this only reflected the cautious words in the Labour Euro manifesto. However, so much was his care that one wag at the press conference could not make up his mind whether it was being held by Margaret Kinnock or Neil Thatcher!

While accusing Mrs Thatcher of confusing sovereignty with vanity, Mr Kinnock did make clear that he would not participate in any development that would be in conflict with the interests of Britain. 'No one would expect us to' he commented. Mr Kinnock indicated his talks with the enlarged Labour Euro group would cover ways of working together to secure the progressive policies which they wanted to see implemented across the Community as well as in the UK. Improved liaison between MEPs and MPs would be introduced and they would also be considering what part the Labour group could play in a restructured Labour Party conference and national executive committee.

At his farewell press conference, Lord Plumb said the emerging European political debate needed European politicians to shape it and conduct it. He believed that the future would see the emergence of the politician who is concerned more about Europe than the immediate national political concerns of his country of birth. The next five years would certainly see the emergence of such a politician.

And 1992 was only the beginning of a much larger quest for political and economic unity in the European Community as a whole. He declared: 'I look forward in this parliamentary mandate to the recognition of the European Parliament's objective of real and permanent responsibilities over the whole of Community legislation and not just a part of it.'

Asked what role he intended to play in future, Lord Plumb, an acknowledged non-linguist, at least revealed he had learned one word of French. He indicated he intended to take things easier but would be an active MEP and if his opinion was ever sought as an 'ancien' President, he would be only too pleased to offer it.

The Klepsch-Prout press conference proved highly useful in bringing out into the open the search for closer collaboration between the EDG and the EPP, the latter having already decided that now was not the right time for a more direct and apparent link up between the two. That will be pronounced upon in two years' time in the light of how things worked out in practice in the Parliament and whether Christian Democrats and Conservatives could sink their differences on key items of policy.

The application to the EPP by the members of the ED Group was for allied membership, not full membership, and Mr Prout made quite clear that no member of the group he led had approached the EPP to apply for individual membership. During the week one or two names were bandied about but for the moment everyone stays where they are. Both group leaders pointed out how the political game in the Parliament had changed as a result of the Single European Act because 260 votes are now required at second reading and neither the centre-left nor centre-right can achieve those votes on their own.

Mr Prout, making one of his rare appearances before the press, tactfully but correctly emphasized that as a group of 34 in a Parliament of 518 members, putting up their hands on their own in relation to every issue was rather useless politically. The influential decisions of the Parliament would be shaped by decisions taken by other like-minded parties.

In the chamber itself, the new President said that national Parliaments must see MEPs as partners in the democratic monitoring of institutions. He called on the political groups and committees to improve collaboration with national parliaments. Their prime concern must be the immediate problems which directly affected European citizens although they must not forget other problems further away. He was convinced the new European Parliament must of necessity have more powers.

He particularly wanted mechanisms established whereby European Commissioners were appointed subject to Parliament's approval and Parliament was also consulted on the appointment of the President of the Commission. He described the social charter as a necessity; and as for the next Euro elections in 1994 the President urged the Parliament and national governments to work towards a uniform electoral system for all the countries.

This raised the issue of proportional representation and the list system which varies from country to country. In the new European Parliament, the Institutional Affairs Committee has been given the task of framing a common electoral system, a rather difficult assignment bearing in mind the immense differences in the systems used. Events in the Italian Euro election bring out some aspects of the list system which cause difficulties and which certainly do not add to the prestige of the Parliament. Not until the day before the Parliament met was a list available identifying accurately all the Italian MEPs. Three resignations came because the MEPs became Prime Minister and Ministers but where candidates were elected in more than one region or area, their replacements were difficult to ascertain.

On top of that, one of the Italian Greens, Sgr Ronchi, of the Verdi Arcobaleno per l'Europa, was MEP for one day - July 25 1989 - during which he voted in the election of President and Vice-Presidents and then resigned. He was immediately replaced by Sgr Franco Corleone until the end of October 1989 when he was due to be succeeded by Sgr Virginio Bettini until the end of 1991; from 1992 to 1994, according to a press release from Les Verts, a certain Francesca Scopelliti will step into the role of MEP. The same party has another seat and in that instance, the present woman MEP will be replaced at the end of 1991. Similarly, eight French Green MEPs look like being replaced mid-term by eight others duly named. Corporate leadership which the Greens like in order to avoid the cult of the individual leader, could in the end prove to be a grave disadvantage

The Institutional Affairs Committee would be well advised to look into this system of chopping and changing. It would hardly go down well in the UK although it could be discouraged if non-list system by-elections had to be held if a party decided that A should be succeeded by B. The habit of party leaders standing for Europe at the head of their list, being elected but not taking their seats also ought to cease. The Euro election list should only include the names of those who intend to take their seats.

Both the French Foreign Minister, M. Dumas, and the President of the Commission, M. Delors, emphasized that the proposed social charter, accepted by eleven of the twelve member states, was still on the agenda. M. Dumas said social Europe could not be dissociated from economic Europe; it was not its by-product. France would seek to obtain the adoption of the Community charter of fundamental social rights. As for events at the Madrid summit after the Euro elections when the go-ahead for the first of the three stages in the Delors report went through, he considered the way ahead to economic and monetary union had been marked out and had proposed that the European Council set up a group of ministers' personal representatives to start work on preparatory texts for the drafting of a new treaty.

On that it is a case of wait and see. These and other challenges he set out will form the main political debates in the European Parliament over the next five years. The Parliament is slowly but surely gaining in influence and the MEPs, despite their political differences, appear united in their desire to see that continue. That is something which is really up to them. And it is a reasonably safe bet that the next general election campaign in the United Kingdom will have more in it about Europe than the 1987 Euro elections. Only the British could do that!

Results of voting in the third direct elections to the European Parliament

BELGIUM

Polling day: June 18
Electorate: 7,096,273   (1984 electorate: 6,975,677)
Votes cast: 5,899,285   Turnout: 90.7%   (1984 votes cast 5,725,837 Turnout: 92.2%.)
Seats: 24

Party	1989 Votes 1st pref	1989 % of poll	1989 Seats	1984 votes 1st pref	1984 % of poll	1984 Seats
Socialist (SP- Flanders)	733,247		3	980,668	17.1	4
Socialist (PS-Wallonia)	854,148	26.9	5	762,377	13.3	5
Christian People's (CVP-Flanders)	1,247,090		5	1,134,012	19.8	5
Social Christian (PSC-Wallonia)	476,802	29.2	2	436,126	7.6	2
Reform and Freedom (PRL-Flanders)	625,566		2	540,597	9.4	3
Freedom and Progress (PVV-Wallonia)	423,511	17.8	2	494,585	8.6	2
People's Union, Flanders (VU-Eva)	318,146	5.4	1	484,925	8.5	2
Ecologists (Agalev-Flanders)	446,524		1	246,879	4.3	1
Ecologists (Ecolo-V- Wallonia)	371,053	13.9	2	220,704	3.9	1
Walloon Rally (PWE)	85,870	1.5	–	142,871	2.5	–
Vlaams Blok (Flemish National Pty)	241,117	4.1	1	73,222	1.3	–
Others	76,211	1.2	–	209,271	3.7	–
Totals	5,899,285	100.0	24	5,725,837	100.0	24

Voting system: Regional list, PR. One Flemish constituency of 13 seats and one Walloon constituency of 11 seats.

Those elected were:

FLANDERS
Christian Democrats (CVP, 5 seats)
Leo Tindemans
An Hermans
Karel Pinxten
*Raf Chanterie
*Pol Marck

Socialists (SP, 3 seats)
Mark Galle
Lode Van Outrive
*Marijke Van Hemeldonck

Freedom and Progress (PVV, 2 seats)
Willy de Ciercq
*Karel de Gucht

People's Union (VU-Eva, 1 seat)
*Jaak Vandemeulebroucke

Green (Agalev, 1 seat)
*Paul Staes

Vlaams Blok (VB, 1 seat)
Karel Dillen

WALLONIA
Socialists (PS, 5 seats)
*Raymonde Dury
*José Happart
*Ernest Glinne
*Claude Desama
Elio Di Rupo

Liberals (PRL, 2 seats)
Francois-Xavier de Donnea
Jean Defraigne

Social Christian (PSC, 2 seats)
*Gérard Deprez
*Fernand Herman

Green (Ecolo, 2 seats)
Paul Lannoye
Brigitte Ernst de la Graete

DENMARK

Polling day: June 15

Electorate: 3,923,549 (1984: 3,804,660)

Votes cast: 1,789,395   Turnout: 46.2%   (1984: 2,002,726 Turnout: 52.2%)

Seats: 16

Party	Votes	1989 % of poll	seats	Votes	1984 % of poll	Seats
Social Democratic Party (S)	417,076	23.3	4	387,098	19.5	3
Popular Movement against EC	338,953	18.9	4	413,808	20.8	4
Liberal (V)	297,565	16.6	3	248,397	12.5	2
Conservative People's (KF)	238,760	13.3	2	417,177	20.8	4
Centre Democracy (CD)	142,190	8.0	2	131,984	6.6	1
Socialist People's (SF)	162,902	9.1	1	183,580	9.2	1*
Progress	93,985	5.3	—	68,747	3.5	—
Others	97,964	5.5	—	142,489	7.1	—
Totals	1,789,395	100.0	16	1,990,280	100.0	15

*Socialist People's Party had second seat when Greenland left EC on Jan 1 1985.

Voting system: National list with all Denmark a 16 seat constituency. PR.

Those elected were:

Social Democratic Party (S, 4 seats)

Kirsten Jensen
Joanna Ronn
Freddy Blak
*Ejner Hovgaard Christiansen

Liberal Party (V, 3 seats)
Niels Anker Kofoed
Klaus Riskaer Pedersen
*Tove Nielsen

Centre Democracy (CD, 3 seats)
*Erhard Jacobsen
Frode Nor Christensen

Popular Movement against EC
(F mod EF, 4 seats)
*Jens-Peter Bonde
*Ib Christensen
*Birgit Bjornvig
Ulla M Sandbaek

Conservative People's Pty (KF, 2 seats)
*Marie Jepsen
Christian Rovsing

Socialist People's Party (SF, 1 seat)
*John Iversen

FRANCE

Polling day: June 18
Electorate: 38,348,191   (1984 electorate: 36,880,688)
Votes cast: 18,145,588   Turnout: 48.7%   (1984: 20,180,934 Turnout: 56.7%)
Seats: 81

Party	Votes	1989 % of poll	seats	Votes	1984 % of poll	Seats
Union UDF/RPR (Giscard d'Estaing list)	5,241,354	28.88	26	8,683,596	43.02	41
Centre Party (Simone Veil list)	1,528,931	8.42	7	–	–	–
Socialist Party (PS)	4,284,734	23.61	22	4,188,875	20.75	20
National Front (FN)	2,128,589	11.73	10	2,210,344	10.95	10
Green Party (Verts)	1,922,353	10.59	9	680,080	3.37	–
Communist Party (PCF)	1,399,939	7.71	7	2,261,312	11.20	10
Others	1,639,688	9.06	–	2,156,737	10.65	–
Totals	18,145,588	100	81	20,180,944	100	81

Voting system: PR national list. Minimum of 5 per cent needed to obtain seat. The Centre Party, led by Simone Veil, stood in 1984 as part of the single UDF/RPR right/centre list.

Those elected were:

UDF/RPR (26 seats)
Valéry Giscard d'Estaing
Alain Juppé
Simone Martin
Michèle Barzach
Yves Galland
Michele Alliot-Marie
Jeannou Lacaze
*Christian de la Malène
Alain Madelin
Dick Ukeiwé
*Charles Baur
François Guillaume
Claude Malhuret
Yvon Briant
Marc Reymann
*Jean-Claude Pasty
Alain Lamassoure
Henry Chabert
*Robert Hersant
Alain Pompidou
*Jean-Thomas Nordmann
*Alain Marleix
Yves Verwaerde
*Jacques Vernier
Jean-Pierre Raffarin
*Pierre Lataillade

National Front (FN, 10 seats)
*Jean-Marie Le Pen
*Martine Lehideux
Bruno Megret
*Jean-Marie le Chevallier
Yvan Blot
*Bernard Antony
Bruno Gollnisch
Pierre Ceyrac
Claude Autant-Lara
Jacques Tauran

Centre Party (7 seats)
*Simone Veil
Jean-Louis Borloo
Adrien Zeller
*Nicole Fontaine
Pierre Bernard-Reymond
Philippe Douste-Blazy
Jean-Louis Bourlanges

Socialist Party (PS, 22 seats)
Laurent Fabius
Catherine Trautmann
Claude Cheysson
*Alain Bombard
Léon Schwartzenberg
*Jean-Pierre Cot
*Jean-Marie Alexandre
*Henry Saby
*Nicole Pery
Jean-François Hory
Claude Allègre
*Martine Buron
Gérard Fuchs
*Bernard Thareaux
André Sainjon
*Max Gallo
Frédéric Rosmini
*Marie-Claude Vayssade
Marie-Jo Denys
Nora Zaidi
Jean-Paul Benoit
Gérard Caudron

Green (Verts, 9 seats)
Antoine Waechter
Solange Fernex
Max Siméoni
Claire Joanny-Schlecht
Yves Cochet
Marie-Christine Aulas
Gérard Monnier-Besombes
Djida Tazdait
Didier Anger

Communist Party (PCF, 7 seats)
Philippe Herzog
Sylviane Ainardi
*René Piquet
Sylvie Mayer
*Francis Wurtz
Maximé Gremetz
Mireille Elmalan

GERMANY

Polling day: June 18

Electorate: 45,723,901   (1984 electorate: 44,451,981)

Valid votes: 28,203,266 Turnout: 62.4%   (1984: 24,851,371 Turnout: 56.8%)

Seats: 81

Party	1989 Votes	% of poll	seats	1984 Votes	% of poll	Seats
Christian Democratic Union (CDU)	8,334,433	29.6	25	9,308,411	37.5	34
Christian Social Union (CSU)	2,324,655	8.2	7	2,109,130	8.5	7
Social Democrat Party (SDP)	10,524,859	37.3	31	9,296,417	37.4	33
Greens (GRÜNE)	2,381,278	8.4	8	2,025,972	8.2	7
Republicans	2,005,555	7.1	6	-	-	-
Free Democrat Party (Liberals)	1,576,280	5.6	4	1,192,624	4.8	-
Others	1,056,206	3.7	-	918,817	3.6	-
Totals	28,203,266	99.9	81	24,851,371	100	81

Voting system: PR on the national or Land list system.

Those elected were:

CDU/CSU (32 seats)

CDU (25 seats)
Reimer Böge
Hartmut Perschau
*Hans-Gert Pöttering
*Werner Münch
Godelieve Quisthouot-Rowohl
Karsten Hoppenstedt
Hedwig Keppelhoff-Wiechert
*Günter Rinsche
*Marlene Lenz
*Elmar Brok
*Kurt Malangre
*Gerd Lemmer
Friedrich Lerz
Karl Heinz Florenz
*Bernhard Sälzer
*Axel Zarges
*Egon Klepsch
*Horst Langes
*Siegbert Alber
*Diemut Theato
*Karl von Wogau
Winfried Menra
Honor Funk
Doris Pack
*Rudolf Luster

CSU (7 seats)
*Friedrich Pirkl
*Ursula Schleicher
*Otto Habsburg
*Ingo Friedrich
*Reinhold Backlet
Gerd Müller
*Franz Graf von Stauffenberg

Green (GRÜNE, 8 seats)
Dorothea-Gertrud Piermont
Friedrich-Wilhelm Graefe zu Baringdorf
Claudia Roth
Karl Partsch
Eva-Maria Quistorp
*Wilfried Telkämper
Hiltrud Breyer
Brigit Cramon-Daiber

Social Democrat Party (SDP, 31 seats)
*Gerd Walter
*Magdalene Hoff
*Klaus Hänsch
*Gerhard Schmid
*Klaus Wettig
Mechtild Rothe
*Heinke Salisch
*Karl-Heinrich Mihr
*Kurt Vittinghoff
*Johannes-Wilhelm Peters
Heinz Köhler
Guenter Lüttge
Christa Ranozio-Plath
Helwin Peter
*Thomas von der Vring
*Dieter Schinzel
Karin Junker
*Rolf Linkohr
Willi Görlach
Gepa Maibaum
*Jannis Sakellariou
*Barbara Simons
*Beate Weber
*Willi Rothley
*Guenter Topmann
*Dieter Rogalla
Barbara Onur
*Barbara Schmidbauer
Detlev Samland
Lieselotte Gröner
Dagmar Roth-Behrendt

Liberals (FDP, 4 seats)
Rüdiger Freiherr von Wechmar
Mechtild von Alemann
Martin Holzfuss
Manfred Vohrer

Republicans (6 seats)
Franz Schönhuber
Klaus-Peter Köhler
Harald Neubauer
Johanna-Christina Grund
Hans-Günter Schodruch
Emil Schlee

GREECE

Polling day: June 18   General election also held
Electorate: 8,347,387   (1984 electorate: 7,790,309)
Valid votes: 6,544,669 Turnout: 79.9%   (1984: 5,956,060 Turnout: 77.2%)
Seats: 24

Party	Votes	1989 % of poll	Seats	Votes	1984 % of poll	Seats
New Democracy (ND)	2,647,215	40.45	10	2,266,568	38.05	9
Socialist (PASOK)	2,352,271	35.94	9	2,476,491	41.58	10
Communist Alliance (SAP)	936,175	14.30	4	693,304	11.64	3
Communist, Interior (KKE-es)	–	–	–	203,813	3.42	1
Centre/Right Alliance (DI-ANA)	89,469	1.37	1	–	–	–
Extreme Right Wing (EPEN)	75,877	1.16	–	136,642	2.29	1
Others	443,662	6.78	–	179,242	3.02	-
Totals	6,544,669	100	24	5,956,060	100	24

Voting system: National list. PR.

Those elected were:
New Democracy (ND, 10 seats)
Ioannis Pesmazoglou
*Marietta Giannakou-Koutsikou
Pavlos Sarlis
*Panayotis Lambrias
*Georgios Anastasopoulos
*Konstantinos Stavrou
*Georgios Saridakis
*Efthymios Christodoulou
Efstathios Lagakos
Filippos Pierros

Socialist Party (PASOK, 9 seats)
*Georgios Romeos
*Christos Papoutsis
*Paraskevas Avgerinos
Panayotis Roumeliotis
Dionysis Livanos
Dimitrios Pagoropoulos
Konstantinos Tsimas
Ioannis Stamoulis
Sotiris Kostopoulos

Communist Alliance (SAP, 4 seats)
*Vassilis Ephremidis
Mihail Papayiannakis
*Alexandros Alavanos
*Dimitrios Desyllas

Centre/Right (DI-ANA, 1 seat)
Dimitrios Nianios

IRELAND

Polling day: June 15   General election held at same time
Electorate: 2,453,451   (1984 electorate: 2,413,404)
1989 - **Valid votes:** 1,632,728   **Spoiled votes:** 42,391   **Turnout:** 68.3%
1984 - **Valid votes:** 1,120,416   **Spoiled votes:** 27,329   **Turnout:** 47.6%
Seats: 15

Party	Votes 1st pref	1989 % of poll	seats	votes 1st pref	1984 % of poll	seats
Fianna Fail (FF)	514,537	31.5	6	438,946	39.2	8
Fine Gael (FG)	353,094	21.6	4	361,034	32.2	6
Progressive Democrats (PD)	194,059	11.9	1	–	–	–
Independents (Ind)	193,823	11.9	2	113,067	10.1	1
Labour Party (Lab)	155,782	9.5	1	93,656	8.4	–
Workers' Party (WP)	123,265	7.5	1	48,449	4.3	–
Green Alliance (Grn)	61,041	3.8	–	5,242	0.5	–
Sinn Fein (PSF)	37,127	2.3	–	54,672	4.9	–
Democratic Socialist	–	–	–	5,350	0.5	–
Totals	1,632,728	100	15	1,120,416	100	15

Voting system: Regional list. Country divided into four constituences and seats allotted on PR.
Those elected were:

Fianna Fail (FF, 6 seats)
*Niall Andrews
*Gene Fitzgerald
*Jim Fitzsimons
*Mark Killilea
*Paddy Lalor
Paddy Lane

Independents
Neil T Blaney
*Thomas Maher

Workers' Party (WP, 1 seat]
Proinsias de Rossa

Fine Gael (FG, 4 seats)
*Mary Banotti
Pat Cooney
John Cushnahan
*Joe McCartin

Labour Party (Lab, 1 seat)
Barry Desmond

Progressive Democrats (PD, 1 seat)
Pat Cox

Voting details in Ireland's four constituencies

DUBLIN 4 seats

	1989			**1984**		
Electorate	711,416			704,873		
Total poll	455,939	64.1%		288,831	41.0%	
Spoiled votes	7,137			6,153	0.9%	
Total valid poll	448,802			282,678	40.1%	
Quota	89,681			56,536		
Candidates	11			12		

First preferences	Number	% of poll	Seats	Number	% of poll	Seats
Fianna Fail	130,402	29.1	1	94,350	33.4	2
Fine Gael	77,240	17.2	1	89,674	31.7	2
Labour	57,225	12.8	1	28,384	10.0	—
Workers' Party	71,041	15.8	1	19,590	6.9	—
Progressive Democrats	36,402	8.2	—	—	—	—
Sinn Fein	11,582	2.6	—	14,604	5.2	—
Green Party	37,317	8.3	—	5,242	1.9	—
Others	27,193	6.1	—	30,834	10.9	—

Elected: De Rossa (WP) and Banotti (FG); Desmond (Lab) and Andrews (FF) each elected without reaching quota after six counts.

LEINSTER 3 seats

	1989			**1984**		
Electorate	571,694			545,878		
Total poll	391,697	68.5%		268.491	49.2%	
Spoiled votes	14,106			9,197	1.7%	
Total valid poll	377,591			259,292	47.5%	
Quota	94,398			64,824		
Candidates	14			9		

First preferences	Number	% of poll	Seats	Number	% of poll	Seats
Fianna Fail	139,424	36.9	2	113,512	43.8	2
Fine Gael	101,567	26.9	1	94,877	36.6	1
Labour	49,766	13.2	—	30,773	11.9	—
Workers' Party	16,540	4.4	—	8,943	3.4	—
Progressive Democrats	31,623	8.4	—	—	—	—
Sinn Fein	9,959	2.6	—	11,189	4.3	—
Green Party	23,724	6.3	—	—	—	—
Others	4,988	1.3	—	—	—	—

Elected: Cooney (FG) elected on tenth count. Fitzsimons (FF) and Lalor (FF) elected without reaching quota after eleven counts. A recount took place and it was announced that the result stood.

MUNSTER 5 seats

	1989			1984		
Electorate	703,913			691,076		
Total poll	505,219	71.7%		349,179	50.5%	
Spoiled votes	10,786			6,216	0.9%	
Total valid poll	494,433			342,963	49.6%	
Quota	82,406			57,161		
Candidates	15			9		
First preferences	Number	% of poll	Seats	Number	% of poll	Seats
Fianna Fail	142,581	28.8	2	133,521	38.9	2
Fine Gael	86,854	17.6	1	98,068	28.6	2
Labour	43,822	8.9	–	26,162	7.6	–
Progressive Democrats	85,558	17.3	1	–	–	–
Workers' Party	26,828	5.4	–	17,304	5.6	–
Sinn Fein	–	–	–	12,829	3.7	–
Independent	55,499	11.2	1	55,079	16.0	1
Others	53,291	10.8	–	–	–	–

Elected: Cox(PD) and Fitzgerald (FF) who reached quota; Cushnahan (FG), Lane (FF) and Maher (Ind), each without reaching quota after ten counts.

CONNACHT-ULSTER 3 seats

	1989			1984		
Electorate	464,661			471,577		
Total poll	322,664	69.4%		241,244	51.2%	
Spoiled votes	10,362			5,763	1.2%	
Total valid poll	312,302			235,481	50.0%	
Quota	78,076			58,871		
Candidates	13			11		
First preferences	Number	% of poll	Seats	Number	% of poll	Seats
Fianna Fail	102,130	32.7	1	97,563	41.4	2
Fine Gael	87,433	28.0	1	78,415	33.3	1
Labour	4,969	1.6	–	8,337	3.5	–
Progressive Democrats	40,476	13.0	–	–	–	–
Workers' Party	8,856	2.8	–	2,612	1.1	–
Sinn Fein	15,586	5.0	–	16,050	6.8	–
Other	52,852	16.9	1	32,504	13.8	–

Elected: McCartin (FG), Blaney (IFF) and Killilea (FF) each elected without reaching quota after nine counts.

71

Details of the six counts in Dublin

Quota: 89681	1st count	2nd count		3rd count		4th count		5th count		6th count	
		Transfer of Cahill & Speed		Transfer of O'Malley's		Transfer of Crotty's		Transfer of Harney's		Transfer of Sargent's	
Name/party	Votes	Votes	Result	Votes	Result	Votes	Result	Votes	Result	Votes	Result
Andrews, Niall (FF)	72057	+975=73032		+975=74007		+2859=76866		+3144=80010		+5551=85561	
Banotti, M (FG)	50666	+286=50952		+15224=66176		+2797=68973		+14516=83489		+9931=93420	
Cahill, T (Ind)	1668	-1668= –		–		–		–		–	
Crotty, R (Ind)	25525	+2329=27854		+559=28413		-28413= –		–		–	
De Rossa, P (WP)	71041	+2815=73856		+1065=74921		+5554=80475		+4868=85343		+11658=97001	
Desmond, B (Lab)	57225	+960=58185		+2365=60550		+3772=64322		+7774=72096		+10168=82264	
Harney, M (PD)	36402	+371=36773		+3456=40229		+2142=42371		-42371= –		–	
Lemass, E (FF)	58345	+836=59181		+711=59892		+2204=62096		+3664=65760		+5175=70917	
O'Malley, C (FG)	26574	+321=26845		-26845= –		–		–		–	
Sargent, T (GP)	37317	+2285=39602		+1165=40767		+6145=46912		+4287=51199		-51199= –	
Speed, A (SF)	11582	-11582= –		–		–		–		–	
non-transferable:		2072		1375		2904		4118		8734	

Details of the eleven counts in Leinster

Quota: 94398

Name/party	1st count Votes	2nd count Transfer of De Groot's Votes / Result	3rd count Transfer of Moore's Votes / Result	4th count Transfer of Boland's Votes / Result	5th count Transfer of McGeough's Votes / Result	6th count Transfer of Dunphy's Votes / Result	7th count Transfer of Enright's & Murphy's Votes / Result	8th count Transfer of English's Votes / Result
Bell, M (Lab)	49766	+104=49870	+84=49954	+344=50298	+239=50537	+5677=51104	+4650=55754	+5852=61606
Boland, K (Ind)	3362	+100= 3462	+34= 3496	-3496= –	–	–	–	–
Cooney, P (FG)	65775	+151=65926	+36=65962	+468=66430	+79=66504	+229=66733	+1230=67963	+3326=71298
Dardis, J (PD)	31623	+107=31730	+59=34789	+370=32159	+35=32194	+199=32393	+1310=33703	+3787=37490
De Groot, C (Ind)	1626	-1626= –	–	–	–	–	–	–
Dunphy, K (SF)	4534	+86=4620	+416=5036	+293=5329	+2064=7393	-7393= –	–	–
English, S (GP)	23724	+198=23922	+70=23992	+317=24309	+92=24401	+761=25162	+2037=27199	-27199= –
Enright, M (WP)	9451	+280=9731	+66=9707	+185=9982	+111=10093	+610=10703	-10703= –	–
Fitzsimons, J (FF)	63797	+109=63906	+88=63994	+350=64344	+184=64528	+686=65214	+1260=66474	+3165=69639
Lalor, P (FF)	75627	+88=75715	+141=75856	+342=76198	+172=76370	+544=76914	+1839=78753	+2802=81555
McDonald, C (FG)	35792	+71=35863	+81=35944	+119=36063	+105=36168	+199=36367	+1543=37910	+2052=39962
McGeough, P (SF)	3001	+8=3009	+854=3863	+67=3930	-3930= –	–	–	–
Moore, T (SF)	2424	+14=2438	-2438= –	–	–	–	–	–
Murphy, C (WP)	7089	+36=7125	+196=7321	+92=7413	+271=7684	+171=8155	-8155= –	–
non-transferable:			313	549	583			

73

Details of the eleven counts in Leinster-continued

Quota: 94398	9th count		10th count		11th count	
	Transfer of Dardis's Votes	Result	Transfer of McDonald's Votes	Result	Transfer of Cooney's surplus Votes	Result
Name/party						
Bell, M (Lab)	+4062=65668		+2347=68015		+7224=75239	
Boland, K (Ind)	–	–	–	–	–	–
Cooney, P (FG)	+11412=82701		+29359=112060		–	–
Dardis, J (PD)	–	–	–	–	–	–
De Groot, C (Ind)	–	–	–	–	–	–
Dunphy, K (SF)	–	–	–	–	–	–
English, S (GP)	–	–	–	–	–	–
Enright, M (WP)	–	–	–	–	–	–
Fitzsimons, J (FF)	+3100=72739		+1265=74000		+1245=75249	
Lalor, P (FF)	+3535=85090		+3778=88868		+1605=90473	
McDonald, C (FG)	+6969=46931		-46931=		–	–
McGeough, P (SF)	–	–	–	–	–	–
Moore, T (SF)	–	–	–	–	–	–
Murphy, C (WP)	–	–	–	–	–	–

non-transferable:
A recount took place and it was announced that the result stood.

Details of the ten counts in Munster

Quota: 82406

Name/party	1st count Votes	2nd count Transfer of Cox's Surplus Votes	Result	3rd count Transfer of Fitzsimmon's & O'Shea's & Slater Townsend's Votes	Result	4th count Transfer of Ferris's Votes	Result	5th count Transfer of Noonan's Votes	Result	6th count Transfer of Sherlock's Votes	Result	7th count Transfer of Ryan's Votes	Result	8th count Transfer of Fahey's Votes	Result	9th count Transfer of Fitzgerald's surplus Votes	Result	10th count Transfer of Raftery's Votes	Result
Cox, P (PD)	85558	-3152	—	—	—	—	—	—	—	—	—	—	—	—	—	—	—	—	—
Cushnahan, John (FG)	43326	+882=44208		+896=45104		+932=46036		+1155=47191		+1547=48738		+1659=50397		+1047=51444		+164=51608		+27450=79058	
Desmond, Eileen (Lab)	29979	+376=30355		+475=30830		+4879=35709		+2342=38051		+7633=45684		+3791=49435		+1677=51112		+222=51334		+4073=55407	
Fahey, Jackie (FF)	37290	+140=37430		+489=37919		+1073=38992		+425=39417		+953=40370		+2241=42611		-42611=	—	—	—	—	—
Ferris, M (Lab)	13243	+84=13927		+223=14150		-14150=	—	—	—	—	—	—	—	—	—	—	—	—	—
Fitzgerald, Gene (FF)	64139	+211=64350		+381=64371		+546=65277		+1314=66591		+2397=68988		+3401=72389		+20102=92491		-10085=	—	—	—
Fitzsimmons, Abbey of the Holy Cross (Ind)	1794	-1794=	—	—	—	—	—	—	—	—	—	—	—	—	—	—	—	—	—
Lane, Paddy (FF)	41152	+199=41351		+207=41558		+466=42024		+492=42516		+1026=43542		+2761=46303		+8921=55224		+9063=64287		+1384=65671	
Maher, T J (Ind)	55499	+473=55972		+681=56653		+1671=58324		+2527=60851		+2664=63515		+5380=68895		+2328=71223		+515=71738		+7369=79107	
Noonan, Joe (People first)	15975	+101=16076		+390=16466		+196=16662		-16662=	—	—	—	—	—	—	—	—	—	—	—
O'Shea, W (Ind)	2011	+10=2021		-2021=	—	—	—	—	—	—	—	—	—	—	—	—	—	—	—
Raftery, Thomas (FG)	43528	+397=43925		+572=44497		+426=44923		+1758=46681		+1970=48651		+1320=49971		+545=50516		+1211=50637		-50637=	—
Ryan, Patrick (Ind)	30934	+71=31005		+351=31356		+665=32021		+1008=33029		+2590=35619		-35619=	—	—	—	—	—	—	—
Salter Townsend, G (Ind)	2577	+18=2595		-2595=	—	—	—	—	—	—	—	—	—	—	—	—	—	—	—
Sherlock, Joe (WP)	26828	+172=27000		+382=27382		+839=28221		+2489=30710		-30710=	—	—	—	—	—	—	—	—	—
non-transferable:				3081		2457		3152		9930		15906		7991		10085		10361	

75

Details of the nine counts in Connacht-Ulster

Quota: 78076

Name/party	1st count Votes	2nd count Transfer of Dermot's Votes / Result	3rd count Transfer of Roger's Votes / Result	4th count Transfer of McPhillip's Votes / Result	5th count Transfer of O'Caolin's Votes / Result	6th count Transfer of Brick's Votes / Result	7th count Transfer of Lupton's & P Doherty's Votes / Result	8th count Transfer of Harte's Votes / Result	9th count Transfer of Molloy's Votes / Result
Blaney, N (IFF)	52852	+223=53075	+847=53922	+503=54425	+1556=55981	+959=56940	+1340=59954	+3239=63193	+6664=69857
Brick, J (WP)	4759	+81=4840	+493=5333	+1377=6710	+131=6841	-6841= —	—	—	—
Dermot, G (SF)	1697	-1697= —	—	—	—	—	—	—	—
Doherty, P (SF)	7716	+403=8119	+118=8237	+78=8315	+2353=10668	+426=11094	-11094= —	—	—
Doherty, S (FF)	48388	+79=48467	+202=48569	+156=48725	+461=49186	+288=49474	+1220=50694	+868=51562	+2079=53641
Harte, P (FG)	30745	+53=30798	+427=31225	+334=31559	+156=31715	+422=32137	+2526=34663	-34663= —	—
Killilea, M (FF)	53842	+108=53950	+172=54122	+237=54395	+273=54668	+427=55095	+2591=57686	+1109=58795	+8451=67246
Lupton, A (FG)	10165	+47=10212	+42=10254	+299=10553	+62=10615	+539=11154	-11154= —	—	—
McCartin, J J (FG)	46523	+56=46579	+115=46694	+351=47045	+283=47328	+261=47589	+5148=52737	+18354=71091	+13606=84697
McPhillips, I (Lab)	4969	+43=5012	+294=5306	-5306= —	—	—	—	—	—
Molloy, B (PD)	40476	+88=40564	+190=40754	+859=41613	+191=41804	+1450=43254	+2367=45621	+2606=48227	-48227= —
O'Caolain, C (SF)	6173	+268=6441	+112=6553	+103=6656	-6656= —	—	—	—	—
Rogers, S (WP)	4097	+15=4112	-4112= —	—	—	—	—	—	—
non-transferable:		233	1100	973	11090	269	5382	8487	17427

ITALY

Polling day: June 18

Electorate: 46,805,457   1984 electorate: 44,438,303

Votes cast: 34,829,128   Turnout: 81.0%   (1979 valid votes 35,098,046 Turnout 83.4%)

Seats: 81

Party	Votes	1989 % of poll	Seats	Votes	1984 % of poll	Seats
Christian Democracy (DC)	11,460,702	32.9	26	11,574,318	33.0	26
Communist (PCI)	9,602,618	27.6	22	11,693,415	33.3	27
Socialist (PSI)	5,154,515	14.8	12	3,935,966	11.2	9
Green Alliance (Verdi/Arco)	2,148,723	6.2	5	–	–	–
Centre Parties (PRI/PLI)	1,533,053	4.4	4	2,137,768	6.1	5
Radical (PR)	–	–	–	1,197,858	3.4	3
Social Movement (MSI)	1,922,761	5.5	4	2,274,489	6.5	5
Social Democrat (PSDI)	946,856	2.7	2	1,224,003	3.5	3
Lombardy Regional (Lega-L)	636,546	1.8	2	–	–	–
Proletarian Democracy (DP)	450,058	1.3	1	505,037	1.4	1
De-criminalise drug offences movement (Antiproibizionisti)	429,554	1.2	1	–	–	–
Sardinian Action (UV-PSDA)	208,775	0.6	1	193,055	0.5	1
South Tyrol People's (SVP)	172,488	0.5	1	198,850	0.6	1
Others	162,479	0.5	–	163,287	0.5	–
Totals	34,829,128	100	81	35,098,046	100	81

Voting system: Regional list with five regional constituencies

Those elected after resignations of MEPs holding Ministerial office and replacements for those elected in more than one seat were:

Christian Democracy (DC, 26 seats)
Giovanni Goria
*Roberto Formigoni
Mario Ruffini
*Nino Pisoni
*Maria Luisa Cassanmagnago
Andrea Bonetti
Rosy Bindi
*Franco Borgo
Gabriele Sboarina
Francesco Guidolin
Arnaldo Forlani
*Gerardo Gaibisso
Giulio Gallenzi
*Carlo Casini
*Alberto Michelini
Emilio Colombo
*Antonio Iodice
Mario Forte
Giuseppe Mottola
Lorenzo de Vitto
Antonio Fantini
Calogera Lo Giudice
Felicetto Contu
*Salvo Lima
*Chiabrando Mauro
*Pisoni Ferruccio

Communist Party (PCI, 22 seats)
Achille Occhetto
Maurice Duverger (French politician)
Anna Catasta
Tullio Regge
Renzo Imbeni
Dacia Valent
Cesare de Piccoli
Giulio Fantuzzi
Pasqualina Napoletano
*Luciana Castellina
Giacomo Porrazini
Giorgio Napolitano
Biagio de Giovanni
Luigi Colajanni
*Andrea Raggio
*Roberto Barzanti
Rinaldo Bontempi
Adriana Ceci
*Georgio Rossetti
Roberto Speciale
*Renzo Trivelli
Luciano Vecchi

Italian Social Movement (MSI-DN, 4 seats)
Gianfranco Fini
Giuseppe Rauti
Antonio Mazzone
Cristiana Muscardini

Socialist Party (PSI, 12 seats)
Bettino Craxi
*Enzo Bettiza
Maria Magnani Noya
Pierre Carniti
Nereo Laroni
Giuliano Ferrara
*Enzo Mattina
Franco Iacono
Antonio la Pergola
*Gianni Baget Bozzo
Lelio Lagorio
Luigi Vertemati
Social Democrat Party (PSDI, 2 seats)
Enrico Ferri
Antonio Cariglia
Lombardy Regional Party (Lega L, 2 seats)
Luigi Moretti
Francesco Speroni
South Tyrol People's Party (SVP, 1 seat)
*Joachim Dalsass

Centre Parties (PRI/PLI, 4 seats)
*Jas Gawronsky
Giorgio La Malfa
Bruno Visentini
*Marco Pannella

Green Alliance (Verdi Arcob, 5 seats)
Gianfranco Amendola
Enrico Falqui
Alexander Langer
†Franco Corleone
Maria Adelaide Aglietta

Proletarian Democracy (DP, 1 seat)
Eugenio Melandri

De-crime drug offences (1 seat)
Marco Taradash

Sardinia Action (UV-PSDA, 1 seat)
Mario Melis

†to be replaced at end of October 1989 by Virginio Bettini

Voting details in Italy's five regional constituencies

Italy, North-West (Italia Nord Occidentale)
Piemonte, Valle d'Aosta, Liguria and Lombardia

Party	Votes	1989 % of poll	seats	Votes	1984 % of poll	seats
DC	2,910,135	30.2	7	3,213,010	32.5	7
PCI	2,425,789	25.2	5	3,138,246	31.7	7
PSI	1,467,160	15.2	4	1,217,232	12.3	3
MSI	430,328	4.5	1	450,255	4.5	1
PRI-PLI-FED	497,899	5.2	1	—	—	—
PLI-PRI	—	—	—	897,300	9.1	2
PR	—	—	—	397,498	4.0	1
Lista Verde	387,812	4.0	1	—	—	—
Verdi Arcob	282,998	2.9	1	—	—	—
PSDI	228,590	2.4	1	324,481	3.3	1
Lega-L	542,526	5.6	2	30,226	0.3	—
DP	152,218	1.6	1	189,482	1.9	1
Antiproibiz	111,096	1.1	1	—	—	—
UV-PSDA	43,613	0.4	—	35,324	0.4	—
Mov. Pension	162,479	1.7	—	—	—	—
Totals	9,641,663	100	25	9,893,054	100	23

The following were elected, with preferences in brackets:

DC (7 seats): Goria (640,403), Formigoni (468,248), Martinazzoli (465,871), Ruffini (174,730), Pisoni (149,905), Cassanmagnago (140,556), Bonetti (137,226).
PCI (5 seats): Occhetto (532,611), Cervetti (126,554), Duverger (101,586), Catasta (80,421), Regge (69,388).
PSI (4 seats): Craxi (472,910), Magnani Noya (84,548), Romita (76,537), Bettiza (59,300).

MSI (1 seat): Fini (117,880).
PLI-PRI-FED (1 seat): Gawronski (84,207).
Lista Verde (1 seat): Amendola (35,906).
Verdi Arcob (1 seat): Ronchi (11,980).
PSDI (1 seat): Ferri (34,046).
Lega-L (2 seats): Bossi (68,501), Moretti (52,697).
DP (1 seat): Melandri (22,975).
Antiproibiz (1 seat): Taradash (7,425).

Italy, North-East (Italia Nord Orientale)
Veneto, Trentino-Alto-Adige, Friuli Venezia Giulia, Emilia-Romagna

Party	Votes	1989 % of poll	seats	Votes	1984 % of poll	Seats
DC	2,377,949	33.2	5	2,426,067	33.9	5
PCI	2,024,755	28.3	5	2,352,153	32.9	6
PSI	1,011,934	14.2	2	729,821	10.2	1
MSI	302,001	4.2	1	288,015	4.0	–
PRI-PLI-FED	295,715	4.1	1	–	–	–
PLI-PRI	–	–	–	469,022	6.6	1
PR	–	–	–	202,544	2.8	–
Lista Verde	350,778	4.9	1	–	–	–
Verdi Arcob	194,494	2.7	1	–	–	–
PSDI	143,139	2.0	–	252,922	3.5	1
Lega-L	70,972	1.0	–	113,807	1.6	–
DP	77,436	1.1	–	104,388	1.5	–
Antiproibiz	88,944	1.3	–	–	–	–
UV-PSDA	45,134	0.6	–	15,026	0.2	–
SVP	172,488	2.4	1	198,850	2.8	1
Totals	7,155,739	100	17	7,152,615	100	17

The following were elected, with preferences in brackets:
DC (5 seats): Andreotti (530,858), Bindi (211,102), Borgo (173,517), Sboarina (169,007), Guidolin (117,834).
PCI (5 seats): Occhetto (268,168), Imbeni (135,477), Valent (70,526), De Piccoli (46,841), Fantuzzi (34,142)

PSI (2 seats): Carniti (151,068), Laroni (55,426).
MSI (1 seat): Fini (83,961).
PLI-PRI-FED (1 seat): La Malfa (59,830).
Lista Verde (1 seat): Langer (35,387).
Verdi Arcob (1 seat): Aglietta (9,072).
SVP (1 seat): Dalsass (106,324.

Italy, Central (Italia Centrale)
Toscana, Umbria, Marche and Lazio

Party	Votes	1989 % of poll	seats	Votes	1984 % of poll	Seats
DC	2,091,079	29.5	5	2,088,194	29.1	5
PCI	2,479,876	35.2	6	2,973,778	41.5	7
PSI	982,640	13.8	2	763,745	10.6	2
MSI	443,208	6.2	1	471,001	6.6	1
PRI-PLI-FED	262,671	3.7	1	–	–	–
PLI-PRI	–	–	–	363,946	5.1	1
PR	–	–	–	214,016	3.0	1
Lista Verde	273,612	3.9	1	–	–	–
Verdi Arcob	173,505	2.4	–	–	–	–
PSDI	176,022	2.5	–	192,099	2.7	–
Lega-L	11,158	0.2	–	7,272	0.1	–
DP	84,709	1.2	–	85,077	1.2	–
Antiproibiz	89,428	1.3	–	–	–	–
UV-PSDA	7,349	0.1	–	9,963	0.1	–
Totals	7,093,257	100	16	7,169,091	100	17

The following were elected, with preferences in brackets:
DC (5 seats): Forlani (425,824), Gaibisso (158,164), Gallenzi (156,257), Casini (143,616), Michelini (128,804).
PCI (6 seats): Occhetto (650,137), Duverger (83,453), Napoletano (80,603), Valent (76,138), Castellina (75,338), Porrazzini (72,636).

PSI (2 seats): Craxi (344,585), Ferrara (160,999).
MSI (1 seat): Rauti (96,139).
PLI-PRI-FED (1 seat): Visentini (61,998).
Lista Verde (1 seat): Amendola (42,036).

Italy, South (Italia Meridionale)
Abruzzi, Molise, Campania, Puglian Basilicata and Calabria

	1989			1984		
DC	2,798,062	37.8	6	2,677,596	36.6	6
PCI	1,805,192	24.4	4	2,215,663	30.3	5
PSI	1,210,300	16.3	3	833,139	11.4	2
MSI	503,012	6.8	1	756,906	10.3	2
PRI-PLI-FED	304,900	4.1	1	-	-	-
PLI-PRI	-	-	-	222,098	3.0	1
PR	-	-	-	211,176	2.9	1
Lista Verde	204,171	2.8	-	-	-	-
Verdi Arcob	123,274	1.7	-	-	-	-
PSDI	262,869	3.6	1	309,368	4.2	1
Lega-L	7,738	0.1	-	7,003	0.1	-
DP	92,395	1.2	-	81,664	1.1	-
Antiproibiz	84,562	1.1	-	-	-	-
UV-PSDA	9,373	0.1	-	10,480	0.1	-
Totals	7,405,848	100	16	7,325,093	100	18

The following were elected, with preferences in brackets:

DC (6 seats): Colombo (363,209), Iodice (335,147), Forte (333,048), Mottola (269,064), De Vitto (247,654), Fantini (223,837).
PCI (4 seats): Napolitano (356,912), Rodota (205,480), Castellina (175,227), De Giovanni (143,943).

PSI (3 seats): Craxi (650,461), Mattina (215,911), Iacono (195,312).
MSI (1 seat): Tatarella (142,030).
PLI-PRI-FED (1 seat): Pannella (59,152).
PSDI (1 seat): Cariglia (98,620).

Italy, Islands (Italia Insulae)
Sicilia and Sardegna

Party	Votes	1989 % of poll	seats	Votes	1984 % of poll	Seats
DC	1,283,477	36.3	3	1,169,451	32.9	3
PCI	849,006	24.0	2	1,013,575	28.5	2
PSI	482,481	13.7	1	392,029	11.0	1
MSI	244,212	6.9	–	308,312	8.7	1
PRI-PLI-FED	171,868	4.9	–	–	–	–
PLI-PRI	–	–	–	185,407	5.2	–
PR	–	–	–	172,624	4.9	–
Lista Verde	100,350	2.8	–	–	–	–
Verdi Arcob	58,729	1.7	–	–	–	–
PSDI	136,236	3.9	–	145,133	4.1	–
Lega-L	4,152	0.1	–	4,979	0.1	–
DP	43,300	1.2	–	44,426	1.2	–
Antiproibiz	55,524	1.6	–	–	–	–
UV-PSDA	103,306	2.9	1	122,262	3.4	1
Totals	3,532,641	100	7	3,558,193	100	8

The following were elected, with references in brackets:

DC (3 seats): Lo Giudice (299,442), Contu (256,061), Lima (246,257).
PCI (2 seats): Colajanni (150,376), Raggio (145,333).

PSI (1 seat): La Pergola (184,554).
UV-PSDA (1 seat): Melis (69,604).

Italy valid votes cast in the other member states of the European Community

Party	Votes	1989 % of poll	1984 % of poll
DC	48,716	24.2	22.9
PCI	49,954	24.8	36.1
PSI	38,057	18.9	13.9
MSI	7,165	3.6	4.5
PRI-PLI-FED	4,758	2.4	–
PLI-PRI	–	–	3.5
PR	–	–	2.5
Lista Verde	10,311	5.1	–
Verdi Arcob	10,064	5.0	–
PSDI	13,813	6.9	8.2
Lega-L	1,662	0.8	1.2
DP	9,582	4.8	5.2
Antiproibiz	2,595	1.4	–
UV-PSDA	2,475	1.2	1.5
SVP	1,561	0.7	0.9
Pension	295	0.2	.2
Totals	201,008	100	100

LUXEMBOURG

Polling day: June 18 (Voting compulsory and coinciding with general election)

Electorate: 218,019 (1984: 215,792)

Each elector has up to six votes. Votes cast: 191,442 (turnout 87.4%) 1984 - votes cast: 162,898 (turnout 88.8%)

Seats: 6

Party	Votes	1989 % of poll	seats	Votes	1984 % of poll	Seats
Christian Social People's (PCS)	346,621	34.87	3	345,586	34.9	3
Socialist Workers (POSL)	252,920	25.45	2	296,382	29.9	2
Democratic (PD)	198,254	19.95	1	218,481	22.1	1
Others	196,951	19.73	–	129,693	13.1	–
Totals	993,951	100	6	990,142	100	6

Voting system: National list, PR.

Those elected after Ministers who headed lists stood down, were:
Christian Socialist People's Party (PCS, 3 seats)
*Nicolas Estgen
Astrid Lulling
Viviane Reding
Socialist Workers' Party (POSL, 2 seats)
Robert Krieps
Ben Fayot
Democratic Party (PD, 1 seat)
Colette Flesch

THE NETHERLANDS

Polling day: June 15
Electorate: 11,121,477 (1984 electorate: 10,476,161)
Valid votes: 5,243,911 Turnout: 47.2% (1984: 5,297,621 Turnout: 50.57%)
Seats 25

Party	Votes	1989 % of poll	seats	Votes	1984 % of poll	Seats
Christian Democrats (CDA)	1,813,935	34.6	10	1,590,601	30.02	8
Labour (PvdA)	1,609,408	30.7	8	1,785,399	33.72	9
Freedom and Democracy (VVD)	715,721	13.6	3	1,002,825	18.93	5
Green Progressive Alliance	365,527	7.0	2	296,516	5.60	2
Coalition of Protestants	309,059	5.9	1	275,824	5.21	1
Democrats '66	311,973	5.9	1	120,848	2.28	—
Others	117,260	2.3	—	225,608	4.26	—
Totals	5,241,883	100	25	5,297,621	100	25

Voting system: National lists, PR.
Those elected were:
Christian Democrats (CDA, 10 seats)
*J J M Penders
*J R H Maij-Weggen
*B Beumer
J Sonneveld
*P A M Cornelissen
M G H C Oomen-Ruitjten
K M H Peijs
*J L Janssen van Raay
A M Oostlander
M J M Verhagen
Freedom and Democracy (Liberals) (VVD, 3 seats)
*G M de Vries
*J E S Larive
*L van der Waal
Green Progressive Alliance (CPN 2 seats)
H A Verbeek
*P B M van Dijk
Coalition of Protestants (SGP 1 seat)
*L van der Waal
Democrats '66 (1 seat)
J-W Bertens

Socialist (PvdA, 8 seats)
*P Dankert
*H d'Ancona
*E P Woltjer
*H J Muntingh
M J A van Putten
W J van Velzen
*B Visser
*A Metten

PORTUGAL

Polling day: June 18
Electorate: 8,052,025   Turnout: 51.27%   1987 turnout: 72.62%
Seats 24

Party	Votes	1989 % of poll	seats	Votes	1984 % of poll	Seats
Social Democrat (PSD)	1,349,996	32.7	9		37.4	10
Socialist (PS)	1,175,671	28.5	8		22.5	6
Social Democratic Centre (CDS)	584,602	14.2	3		15.4	4
United Democratic Alliance (Communist/Green)	594,771	14.4	4		11.5	3
Democratic Renewal	—	—	—		4.4	1
Others (incl. invalid votes)	423,644	10.3	—		8.7	—
Totals	4,128,684	100.0	24		100.0	24

Those elected were:

Socialist Democratic Party (PSD, 9 seats)
Antonio Capucho
*Rui Amarel
*Carlos Pimenta
Manuel Lopes Porto
*Antonio Marques Mendes
Maria Margarida Salema
José Mendes Bota
*Virgilio Pereira
*Vasco Garcia

Communist (PCP, 4 seats)
Carlos Carvalhas
*Joaquim Miranda da Silva
*José Barros Moura
Maria Santos

Socialist Party (PS, 8 seats)
João Cravinho
J Torres Couto
*Fernando Santos Gomes
Pedro Canavarro
*Antonio Coimbra Martins
Artur Cunha Oliviera
*Luis Marinho
*Maria Belo

Centre Party (CDS, 3 seats)
*Francisco Lucas Pires
Luis Beiroco
*José Carvalho Cardoso

SPAIN

Polling day: June 18
Electorate: 29,160,830
Votes cast: 15,980,882   Turnout: 54.8%   (1987 Turnout: 68.9%)
Seats: 60

Party	Votes	1989 % of poll	Seats	Votes	1987 % of poll	Seats
Socialists (PSOE)	6,258,749	39.56	27	7,522,706	39.10	28
Popular Party (PP)	3,389,341	21.42	15	4,918,149	25.54	17
Centre Party (CDS)	1,129,599	7.14	5	1,976,093	10.26	7
Communist and Allies (IU)	959,270	6.06	4	1,011,830	5.24	3
Catalan Party (CiU)	662,757	4.19	2	842,331	4.41	3
José María Ruiz–Mateos (JMRM)	609,171	3.85	2	116,761	0.61	–
Andalucia Regional Party (PA)	297,218	1.88	1	185,550	1.82	–
Nationalist Coalition (CN)	295,741	1.87	1	336,090	0.98	–
Izquierda de los Pueblos (IP)	289,915	1.83	1	261,328	1.88	1
Basque Party (HB)	269,743	1.71	1	360,950	1.34	–
European People's Coalition (EP)	238,528	1.51	1	326,911	1.70	1
PTE–UCE	196,174	1.24	–	222,680	1.15	–
LV	163,703	1.03	–	–	–	–
VE	161,486	1.02	–	107,625	0.55	–
FPR	152,129	0.96	–	216,050	1.10	–
PCPE	80,303	0.51	–	–	–	–
FN	59,964	0.38	–	122,799	0.63	–
PV	58,626	0.37	–	–	–	–
CSD	55,868	0.35	–	25,058	0.15	–
AV–MEC	47,548	0.30	–	65,574	0.34	–
BNG	45,941	0.29	–	53,116	0.28	–
PST–PORE	39,592	0.25	–	107,289	0.54	–
EV	29,434	0.19	–	–	–	–
FE–JONS	24,185	0.15	–	23,411	0.12	–
CLL	19,586	0.12	–	–	–	–
PH	19,139	0.12	–	22,333	0.12	–
AR	17,079	0.11	–	–	–	–
UNA	13,132	0.08	–	–	–	–
UC–PED	10,716	0.07	–	9,146	0.04	–
LA	9,384	0.06	–	9,881	0.04	–
IDE	8,647	0.05	–	–	–	–
PC	8,419	0.05	–	–	–	–
PAR	–	–	–	105,765	0.55	–
ANEMYA	–	–	–	30,143	0.16	–
POSI	–	–	–	25,270	0.14	–
UCE	–	–	–	21,482	0.12	–
UM	–	–	–	19,066	0.10	–
CV	–	–	–	14,749	0.08	–
Totals	15,621,087	100	60	19,060,138	100	60

The following are the Spanish political parties:

PSOE: Partido Socialista Obrero Español. **PP:** Partido Popular. **CDS:** Centro Democrático y Social. **IU:** Izquierda Unida. **CiU:** Convergència i Unió. **JMRM:** José María Ruiz–Mateos. **CN:** Coalición Nacionalista (Partido Nacionalista Vasco, Coalición Galega, Agrupación Independiente Canaria, Partido Nacionalista de Castilla y León). **PA:** Partido Andalucista. **HB:** Herri Batasuna. **IP:** Izquierda de los Pueblos (Euskadiko Ezquerra, Entesa del Nacionalistes d'Esquerra, Partit Socialista de Mallorca, Unió del Poble Valencià, Asamblea Canaria, Unión Aragonesista–Chunta Aragonesista, Partido Socialista Galego–Esquerda Galega). **EP:** Por la Europa de los Pueblos (Eusko Alkartasuna, Esquerra Republicana de Catalunya, Partido Nacionalista Galego). **PTE–UC:** Partido de los Trabajadores de España–Unidad Comunista. **FPR:** Federación de Partidos Regionalistas (Unión Valenciana, Extremadura Unida, Partido Riojano Progresista, Partido Regionalista de Madrid, Unión del Pueblo Melillense, Partido Regionalista de Cantabria). **FN:** Frente Nacional. **VE:** Los Verdes Ecologistas. **PST–PORE:** Partido Socialista de los Trabajadores–Partido de los Obreros Revolucionarios de España.

AV–MEC: Alternativa Verda–Moviment Ecologista de Catalunya. BNG: Bloque Nacionalista Galego. CSD: Coalición Socialdemócrata. FE–JONS: Falange Española de las JONS. PH: Partido Humanista. LA: Liberación Andaluza. UC–PED: Unidad Centrista–Partido Español Demócrata. PCPE: Partido Comunista de los Pueblos de España. EV: Europa por la vida. CLL: Catalunya LLiure. AR: Alianza por la República. IDE: Iniciativa para una Democracia Europea. PC: Partido Carlista. LV: Lista Verde. UNA: Unidad Nacionalista Asturiana. PV: Partido Verde. PAR: Partido Aragonés Regionalista. ANEMYA: Asamblea Nacional de Estudiantes de Medicina y Asociados. POSI: Partido Obrero Socialista Internacionalista. UCE: Unificación Comunista de España. UM: Unió Mallorquina. CV: Coalición Valenciana.

Those elected were:

Socialists (PSOE, 27 seats)
*Fernando Morán López
*Enrique Carlos Barón Crespo
*Manuel Medina Ortega
*Josep Verde i Aldea
*Luis Planas Puchades
*Juan Luis Colino Salamanca
*Ana Clara Miranda de Lage
*José Enrique Pons Grau
*Francisco Oliva García
*Joan Colom i Naval
*Ludivina García Arias
María Izquierdo Rojo
*José Alvarez de Paz
*José Vazquez Fouz
*Carmen Diez de Rivera
Juan José de la Cámara Martínez
*Barbara Dührkop Dührkop
*Enrique Sapena Granell
*Mateo Sierra Bardaji
*Xavier Rubert de Ventos
*Pedro Bofill Abeilhe
*Carlos María Bru Puron
*Jesús Cabazón Alonso
*Eusebio Cano Pinto
*Juan de Dios Ramírez Heredia
*Victor Manuel Arbeloa Muru
*Javier Sanz Fernández

Catalan Party (CiU, 2 seats)
*Carles-Alfred Gasòliba i Böhm
*Concepcio Ferrer i Casals

European People's Coalition (EA, 1 seat)
*Carlos Garaikoetxea Urriza

Nationalist Coalition (CN, 1 seat)
Juan Antonio Gangoiti Llaguno

**Supporters of election
of Ruiz–Mateos** (2, seats)
José María Ruiz–Mateos
Carlos Perreau de Pinninck Domenech

Popular Party (PP, 15 seats)
Marcelino Oreja Aguirre
*Fernando Suarez González
Gerardo Fernández Albor
*Carlos Robles Piquer
*Pio Cabanilla Gallas
José María Gil-Robles Gil Delgado
*Miguel Arias Canete
*Antonio Navarro Velasco
*Carmen Llorca Vilaplana
Leopoldo Ortiz Climent
*Manuel García Amigo
Joaquim Siso Cruellas
*Domènec Romera i Alcázar
*Arturo Juan Escuder Croft
*José Luis Valverde

Centre Party (CDS, 5 seats)
José Ramón Caso García
*Eduardo Punset i Casals
*Raúl Morodo Leoncio
*Rafael Calvo Ortega
Guadalupe Ruiz-Giménez Aguilar

Communist and Allies (IU, 4 seats)
*Fernando Pérez Royo
*Antoni Gutiérrez Díaz
*Alonso José Puerta Gutiérrez
Teresa Domingo Segarra

Basque Party (HB, 1 seat)
*José María Montero Zabala

Izquierda de los Pueblos (IP, 1 seat)
Juan María Bandres Molet

Andalucia Regional Party (PA, 1 seat)
Pedro Pacheco Herrera

The Popular Party has joined the European People's Party Group (EPP) in the European Parliament. It was previously in the European Democratic (Conservative) Group.

UNITED KINGDOM

England, Scotland and Wales   78 seats

Polling day: June 15
Electorate: 42,590,060   (1984 electorate: 41,917,313)
Votes cast: 15,353,154   Turnout: 35.9%   (1984: 13,312,963 Turnout: 31.8%)

Party	Votes	1989 % of poll	seats	Votes	1984 % of poll	Seats
Labour	6,153,640	40.1	45	4,865,261	36.5	32
Conservative	5,331,077	34.7	32	5,426,821	40.8	45
Alliance*	–	–	–	2,591,635	19.5	–
Green	2,292,705	14.9	–			
SLD	986,292	6.2	–	–	–	–
Scot Nat	406,686	2.7	1	230,594	1.7	1
Pl Cymru	115,062	0.8	–	103,031	0.8	–
SDP	75,886	0.5	–	–	–	–
Others	41,295	0.3	–	95,531	0.7	–
Totals	15,353,154	–	78	13,312,963	–	78

*Liberal and Social Democratic candidates formed Alliance

Voting system: Simple majority - first-past-the-post

Those elected were:

Labour (45 seats)
*Gordon Adam
*Richard Balfe
Roger Barton
*John Bird
David Bowe
*Janey Buchan
Ken Coates
*Ken Collins
Peter Crampton
*Christine Crawley
Alan Donelly
*Michael Elliot
*Alex Falconer
*Glyn Ford
Pauline Green
Lyndon Harrison
*Michael Hindley
*Geoffrey Hoon
*Stephen Hughes
*Alfred Lomas
*Michael McGowan
Henry McGubban
*Hugh McMahon
*David Martin
*Tom Megahy
*David Morris
*Stanley Newens
*Edward Newman
Christine Oddy
Anita Pollack
Mel Read
*Barry Seal
Brian Simpson
Alex Smith
*Llewellyn Smith
*George Stevenson
*Ken Stewart
Garry Titley
*John Tomlinson
*Carole Tongue
David Wayne
*Norman West
Ian White
Anthony Wilson
Terence Wynn

Conservative (32 seats)
*Christopher Beazley
*Peter Beazley
*Lord Bethell
*Bryan Cassidy
*Sir Frederick Catherwood
*Margaret Daly
*James Elles
*Paul Howell
*Caroline Jackson
*Christopher Jackson
*Edward Kellett-Bowman
Anne McIntosh
*Edward McMillan-Scott
*James Moorhouse
*William Newton Dunn
*Lord O'Hagan
*Ben Patterson
*Lord Plumb of Coleshill
*Derek Prag
*Peter Price
*Christopher Prout
Patricia Rawlings
*Sir James Scott-Hopkins
*Madron Seligman
*Richard Simmonds
*Anthony Simpson
Tom Spencer
John Stevens
*Sir Jack Stewart-Clark
*Amedee Turner
Richard Vane
*Michael Welsh

Scottish National Party
*Winifred Ewing

Northern Ireland (3 seats)
(See separate table on page 87)

Democratic Unionist Party
*Ian Paisley
Social Democratic and Labour Party
*John Hume

Official Unionist Party
James Nicholson

United Kingdom
England, Scotland and Wales

There are 78 European constituencies in England, Scotland and Wales contested under the first-past-the-post-system. The 1989 Euro elections are on almost the same boundaries as in 1984, all changes being so small that comparisons with 1984 can be made in each constituency. In 1984 31.8% of an electorate of 41,917,313 voted. *In 1979, only Liberals stood. In 1984 Liberals and SDP stood as Alliance candidates. Figures in brackets in the % of poll and MEP lines are those for 1984.

	Lab	C	Green	SLD	SDP	SNP/PlC	Others	Totals
ENGLAND								
1989	5,052,647	4,790,269	2,078,131	847,932	72,733	–	39,938	12,873,680
1984	3,963,213	4,879,964	67,357	–	–	–	21,348	11,174,788
% of poll	29.2(35.5)	37.2(43.7)	16.1(0.6)	6.6(–)	0.5(–)	–	0.3(0.2)	–
MEPs	34(24)	32(42)	–(–)	–(–)	–(–)	–	–	66
SCOTLAND								
1989	664,263	331,495	115,028	68,056	–	406,686	1,357	1,586,885
1984	526,066	332,771	2,560	–	–	230,594	–	1,293,773
% of poll	41.9(40.7)	20.9(25.7)	7.2(0.2)	4.2(–)	–(–)	25.6(17.8)	0.9(–)	–
MEPs	7(5)	– (2)	–(–)	–(–)	–(–)	1(1)	–	8
WALES								
1989	436,730	209,313	99,546	28,785	3,153	115,062	–	892,589
1984	375,982	214,086	4,266	–	–	103,031	4,266	844,312
% of poll	48.9(44.5)	23.4(25.4)	11.2(0.5)	3.2(–)	0.4(–)	12.9(12.2)	–(0.5)	–
MEPs	4(3)	–(1)	–(–)	–(–)	–(–)	–	–	4
Totals								
1989	5,331,077	6,153,640	2,292,705	986,292	75,886	521,748	41,295	15,353,154
1984	5,426,821	4,865,261	74,183	–	–	333,625	28,174	13,312,963
% of poll	34.7(40.8)	40.1(36.5)	14.9(0.6)	6.2(–)	0.5(–)	3.4(2.5)	0.3(0.2)	35.9(31.8)
MEPs	32 (45)	45 (32)	– (–)	– (–)	– (–)	1 (1)	– (–)	78

Northern Ireland

Electorate: 1,120,508   (1984: 1,064,035) Total poll: 540,254 (696,971)   Turnout: 48.8% (65.4%)
Spoiled votes: 5,443 (11,654) Valid poll: 534,811 (685,317) Quota: 133,703 (171,330)   Number of seats: 3

Name and party	1st pref	1989 % of poll	Seats	1st pref	1984 % of poll	Seats
*Paisley, Rev I (Dem U)	160,110	29.6	1	230,251	33.6	1
*Hume, J (SDLP)	136,335	25.2	1	151,399	22.1	1
Nicholson, J (OUP)	118,785	22.0	1	147,169	21.5	1
Morrison, D (PSF)	48,914	9.1	–	91,476	13.3	–
Alderdice, J T (All)	27,905	5.2	–	34,046	5.0	–
Kennedy, A (C)	25,789	4.8	–	–	–	–
Samuel, MH (Ecol)	6,569	1.2	–	2,172	0.3	–
Lynch, S (WP)	5,590	1.0	–	8,712	1.3	–
Langhammer (Lab Rg)	3,540	0.7	–	–	–	–
Caul, B (Lab 87)	1,274	0.2	–	–	–	–

Candidates elected (*seeking re–election): Paisley, Hume and Nicholson

Voting system: All 17 Ulster parliamentary constituencies make up the single multi–member European constituency with single transferable voting system.

Details of two counts in Northern Ireland:	1st count	2nd count Transfer of Paisley's	
Name and party	Votes	surplus	Result
*Paisley, Rev I (Dem U)	160,110	–26,407	133,703
*Hume, J (SDLP)	136,335	–	136,335
Nicholson, J (OUP)	118,785	+22,798	141,583
Morrison, D (PSF)	48,914	+73	48,987
Alderdice, J T (All)	27,905	+728	28,633
Kennedy, A (C)	25,789	+1,082	26,871
Samuel, MH (Ecol)	6,569	+306	6,875
Lynch, S (WP)	5,590	+78	5,668
Langhammer (Lab Rg)	3,540	+120	3,660
Caul, B (Lab 87)	1,274	+30	1,304
Non-transferable	1,189		1,189

UK constituency results in England, Scotland and Wales

Results in the 78 constituencies of England, Scotland and Wales contested under the first-past-the-post electoral system were as follows with * denoting MEPs of the outgoing Parliament who were seeking re-election. The boundaries of the Euro constituencies were virtually the same as those contested in 1984, all changes being so small as to enable comparisons with 1984 voting to be made in each seat. The 1987 figures are the last general election voting totals in the Westminster seats making up the Euro constituency. Key to parties: C - Conservative; Lab - Labour; SLD - Social and Liberal Democrat; SDP - Social Democrat; Grn - Green; Comm - Communist; PC - Plaid Cymru; SNP - Scottish National; OUP - Official Unionist; DUP - Democratic Unionist; SDLP - Social Democratic Labour; SF - Sinn Fein; All - Alliance.

Additional Abbreviations: Ind - Independent; SPGB - Socialist Party of Great Britain; Hum - Humanist; Meb Ker: Mebyon Kernow (Cornwall in Europe); ICO - International Communist Party; WP - Workers Party; NF-GBO - National Front-Get Britain Out; Lab RG - Labour for Representative Government; PRP - Protestant Reformation Party; Corr - Corrective; Wes Rg - Wessex Regionalist; Loony - Raving Loony; Comm L - Communist League; UPUP - Ulster Popular Unionist Party.

BEDFORDSHIRE SOUTH

Electorate: 569,512 (524,963)

Bedfordshire South West; Hertfordshire North; Hertfordshire West; Luton North; Luton South; Milton Keynes; Stevenage.

*P G Beazley (C)	73,406	38.6%
T McWalter (Lab)	70,429	37.0%
D Everett (Grn)	34,508	18.1%
W M Johnston (SLD)	8,748	4.6%
R Muller (SDP)	3,067	1.6%
C majority	2,977	1.6%

Total vote 190,158 (33.4%). **No change.**

1984: Total vote 165,638 (31.6%). C 72,088 (43.5%); Lab 57,106 (34.5%); L/All 36,444 (22.0%). C majority 14,982 (9.1%).

1987 Total vote: 431,027 (78.5%). C 214,346 (49.7%); Lab 103,862 (24.1%); SDP/All 81,733 (18.9%); L/All 29,454 (6.8%); Others 1,632 (0.4%). C maj 110,484 (25.6%).

BIRMINGHAM EAST

Electorate: 535,951 (548,899)

The Birmingham seats of Edgbaston, Erdington, Hall Green, Hodge Hill, Northfield, Selly Oak, Small Heath, Sparkbrook and Yardley.

*Mrs C M Crawley (Lab)	96,588	54.1%
M I C Harbour (C)	49,640	27.8%
P Simpson (Grn)	22,589	12.7%
J C Binns (SDP)	5,424	3.0%
J M E C Roodhouse (SLD)	4,010	2.3%
M Wingfield (NF-GBO)	1,471	.8%
Lab majority	46,948	26.3%

Total vote 178,251 (33.3%). **No change.**

1984: Total vote 154,738 (28.2%). Lab 76,377 (49.4%); C 54,994 (35.5%); SDP/All 21,927 (14.2%); Other 1,440 (0.9%). Lab majority 21,383 (13.9%).

1987 Total vote: 377,098 (69.7%). Lab 160,099 (42.5%); C 149,906 (39.8%); SDP/All 37,818 (10.0%); L/All 26,330 (7.0%); Others 2,945 (0.8%). Lab maj 10,193 (2.7%).

BIRMINGHAM WEST

Electorate: 521,662 (518,707)

Aldridge Brownhills; Birmingham Ladywood; Birmingham Perry Barr; Sutton Coldfield; Walsall North; Walsall South; West Bromwich East; West Bromwich West.

*J E Tomlinson (Lab)	86,545	50.6%
C F Robinson (C)	55,685	32.6%
J D Bentley (Grn)	21,384	12.5%
S Reynolds (SLD)	7,673	4.5%
Lab majority	30,860	18.0%

Total vote 171,287 (32.8%). **No change.**

1984: Total vote 137,070 (26.4%). Lab 61,946 (45.2%); C 55,702 (40.6%); SDP/All 19,422 (14.2%). Lab majority 6,244 (4.6%).

1987 Total vote: 375,769 (72.4%). C 164,845 (43.9%); Lab 150,181 (40.0%); L/All 42,600 (11.3%); SDP/All 17,493 (4.7%); Others 650 (0.2%). C maj 14,664 (4.0%).

BRISTOL

Electorate 567,225 (569,765)

Bath; the Bristol seats of East, North West, South, and West; Kingswood; Northavon; Wansdyke.

I White (Lab)	87,753	39.5%
*R J Cottrell (C)	77,771	34.5%
D N Wall (Grn)	39,436	17.8%
C Boney (SLD)	16,309	7.3%
G McEwen (Wes Rg)	1,017	.5%
Lab majority	9,982	4.5%

Total vote 222,286 (39.2%). **Lab gain from C.**

1984: Total vote 205,358 (36.0%). C 94,652 (46.1%); Lab 77,008 (37.5%); SDP/All 33,698 (16.4%). C majority 17,644 (8.6%).

1987 Total vote: 447,710 (78.6%). C 204,401 (45.6%); Lab 102,543 (22.9%); L/All 62,586 (14.0%); SDP/All 533,22 (11.9%); Others 2,952 (0.7%). C maj 101,858 (22.7%).

CAMBRIDGE AND BEDFORDSHIRE NORTH

Electorate: 568,664 (523,899)

Bedfordshire Mid; Bedfordshire North; Cambridge; Cambridgeshire North East; Cambridgeshire South West; Huntingdon; Peterborough;

*Sir F Catherwood (C)	84,044	44.6%
M Strube (Lab)	51,723	27.3%
Ms M E Wright (Grn)	37,956	20.1%
A N Duff (SLD)	15,052	8.0%
C majority	32,321	17.1%

Total vote 188,775 (33.2%). No change.
1984: Total vote 161,359 (30.8%). C 86,117 (53,4%); (Lab) 38,901 (24.1%); L/All 36,341 (22.5%). C majority 47,216 (29.3%).
1987 Total vote: 420,881 (76.5%). C 223,639 (53.1%); Lab 82,970 (19.7%); L/All 67,250 (16.0%) SDP/All 44,610 (10.6%); Others 2,412 (0.6%). C maj 140,669 (33.4%).

CHESHIRE EAST

Electorate: 524,202 (498,568)

Congleton; Crewe and Nantwich; Macclesfield; Staffordshire Moorlands; Tatton; Warrington North; Warrington South.

B Simpson (Lab)	74,721	41.2%
*Sir T Normanton (C)	72,857	40.2%
C C White (Grn)	21,456	11.8%
Mrs B Fraenkel (SLD)	12,344	6.8%
Lab majority	1,864	1.0%

Total vote 181,378 (34.6%). Lab gain from C.
1984: Total vote 155,362 (31.2%). C 71,182 (45.8%); Lab 52,806 (34.0%); SDP/All 31,374 (20.2%). C majority 18,376 (11.8%).
1987 Total vote: 402,530 (78.3%). C 190,045 (47.2%); Lab 124,398 (31.0%); L/All 45,772 (11.4%); SDP/All 42,052 (10.4%); Others 263 (0.1%). C maj 65,647 (16.3%).

CHESHIRE WEST

Electorate: 549,338 (539,761)

Birkenhead; City of Chester; Eddisbury; Ellesmere Port and Neston; Halton; Wallasey; Wirral South; Wirral West.

L Harrison (Lab)	102,962	47.2%
*A Pearce (C)	79,761	36.6%
G L Nicholls (Grn)	25,933	11.9%
J Rankin (SLD)	9,333	4.3%
Lab majority	23,201	10.6%

Total vote 217,989 (39.7%). Lab gain from C.
1984: Total vote 169,936 (31.5%). C 74,579 (43.9%); Lab 64,887 (38.2%); SDP/All 30,470 (17.9%). C majority 9,692 (5.7%).
1987 Total vote: 426,044 (78.3%). C 182,066 (42.7%); Lab 165,443 (38.8%); L/All 51,790 (12.2%); SDP/All 24,778 (9.3%); Others 1,967 (0.5%). C maj 16,623 (4.0%).

CLEVELAND AND YORKSHIRE NORTH

Electorate: 577,379 (566,083)

Hartlepool; Langbaurgh; Middlesbrough; Redcar; Richmond (Yorks); Skipton and Ripon; Stockton North; Stockton South.

D Bowe (Lab)	94,953	47.6%
*Sir P Vanneck (C)	70,861	35.5%
O Dumpleton (Grn)	17,225	8.7%
T M Mawston (SLD)	8,470	4.2%
R I Andrew (SDP)	7,970	4.0%
Lab majority	24,092	12.0%

Total vote 199,479 (34.5%). Lab gain from C.
1984: Total vote 179,725 (31.8%). C 73,217 (40.7%); Lab 70,592 (39.3%); SDP/All 35,916 (20.0%). C majority 2,625 (1.4%).
1987 Total vote: 429,699 (75.5%). C 175,130 (40.8%); Lab 154,470 (36.0%); L/All 57,419 (13.4%); SDP/All 40,069 (9.3%); Others 2,611 (0.6%). C maj 20,660 (4.8%).

CORNWALL AND PLYMOUTH

Electorate: 548,246 (506,004)

Cornwall North; Cornwall South East; Falmouth and Camborne; Plymouth Devonport; Plymouth Drake; Plymouth Sutton; St Ives; Truro.

*C J P Beazley (C)	88,376	38.9%
P A Tyler (SLD)	68,559	30.1%
Ms D Kirk (Lab)	41,466	18.2%
H Hoptrough (Grn)	24,581	10.8%
C Lawry (Meb Ker)	4,224	1.9%
C majority	19,817	8.7%

Total vote 227,206 (41.8%). No change.
1984: Total vote 191,973 (41.4%). C 81,627 (42.5%); SDP/All 63,876 (33.3%); Lab 35,952 (18.7%); Others 10,518 (5.5%). C majority 17,751 (9.2%).
1987 Total vote: 417,279 (78.6%). C 185,145 (44.4%); L/All 93,933 (22.5%); SDP/All 70,414 (16.9%); Lab 66,921 (16.0%); Others 866 (0.2%). C maj 91,212 (21.9%).

COTSWOLDS

Electorate: 564,582 (527,081)

Banbury; Cheltenham; Cirencester and Tewkesbury; Gloucester; Stratford-on-Avon; Stroud; Witney.

*Lord Plumb of Coleshill (C)	94,852	45.0%
Mrs S Limb (Grn)	49,174	23.4%
T Levitt (Lab)	48,180	22.9%
L A Rowe (SLD)	18,196	8.6%
C majority	45,678	21.7%

Total vote 210,402 (37.3%). No change.
1984: Total vote 177,276 (33.6%). C 94,740 (53.5%); L/All 45,798 (25.8%); Lab 36,738 (20.7%). C Maj 48,942 (27.7%).
1987 Total vote: 426,836 (78.0%). C 232,009 (54.4%); L/All 115,322 (27.0%); Lab 66,836 (15.7%); SDP/All 12,386 (3.0%); Others 283 (0.1%). C maj 116,687 (27.3%).

CUMBRIA & LANCASHIRE NORTH

Electorate: 567,412 (547,433)

Barrow and Furness; Carlisle; Copeland; Lancaster; Morecambe and Lunesdale; Penrith and the Border; Westmorland and Lunesdale; Workington; Wyre.

†W R F Vane (C)	84,035	41.2%
J M P Hutton (Lab)	81,644	40.0%
Mrs C E Smith (Grn)	21,262	10.4%
E E Hill (SLD)	12,590	6.2%
J Bates (SDP)	4,206	2.0%
C majority	2,391	1.2%

Total vote 203,737 (35.9%). **No change.**
1984: Total vote 188,081 (34.4%). C 86,127 (45.8%); Lab 62,332 (33.1%); L/All 39,622 (21.1%). C majority 23,795 (12.7%).
1987 Total vote: 434,262 (78.0%). C 212,607 (49.0%); Lab 132,825 (30.6%); L/All 44,977 (10.4%); SDP/All 42,187 (9.7%); Others 1,666 (0.4%). C maj 79,782 (18.4%).
†following the death of his father shortly after the election, inherited title of Lord Inglewood

DERBYSHIRE

Electorate: 570,752 (553,020)

Amber Valley; Ashfield; Bolsover; Derby North; Derby South; Derbyshire West; Erewash; High Peak.

*G W Hoon (Lab)	106,018	51.0%
P Jenkinson (C)	72,630	34.9%
E Wall (Grn)	20,781	10.0%
S Molloy (SLD)	4,613	2.2%
Mrs A M Ayres (SDP)	3,858	1.9%
Lab majority	33,388	13.4%

Total vote 207,900 (36.4%). **No change.**
1984: Total vote 182,903 (33.1%). Lab 79,466 (43.5%); C 72,613 (39.7%); SDP/All 30,824 (16.8%). Lab majority 6,853 (3.8%).
1987 Total vote: 437,969 (77.8%). C 193,065 (44.1%); Lab 153,702 (35.1%); L/All 49,411 (11.3%); SDP/All 41,275 (9.4%); Others 291 (0.1%). C maj 39,363 (9.0%).

DEVON

Electorate: 601,931 (560,807)

Devon North; Devon West and Torridge; Exeter; Honiton; South Hams; Teignbridge; Tiverton; Torbay.

*Lord O'Hagan (C)	110,518	46.4%
P S Christie (Grn)	53,220	22.3%
W J Cairns (Lab)	40,675	17.0%
M Edmunds (SLD)	23,306	9.8%
R Edwards (SDP)	7,806	3.3%
S B F Hughes (Loony)	2,241	0.9%
Lady Rous (Wes Rg)	385	0.2%
C majority	57,298	24.1%

Total vote 238,151 (39.6%). **No change.**
1984: Total vote 210,243 (35.9%). C 110,121 (54.7%); L/All 53,519 (26.6%); Lab 30,017 (14.9%); Others 7,578 (3.8%). C majority 56,610 (28,1%).
1987 Total vote: 461,109 (79.0%). C 243,223 (52/7%); L/All 128,830 (27.9%); Lab 46,499 (10.1%); SDP/All 37,635 (8.2%); Others 4,922 (1.1%). C maj 114,393 (24.8%).

DORSET EAST AND HAMPSHIRE WEST

Electorate: 615,135 (565,709)

Bournemouth East; Bournemouth West; Christchurch; Dorset North; Dorset South; New Forest; Poole; Romsey and Waterside.

*B M D Cassidy (C)	111,469	50.4%
Ms K I Bradbury (Grn)	49,695	22.4%
H R White (Lab)	38,011	17.2%
H R Legg (SLD)	21,809	9.9%
C majority	61,774	27.9%

Total vote 220,984 (35.9%). **No change.**
1984: Total vote 189,476 (33.5%). C 109,072 (57.6%); L/All 49,181 (26.0%); Lab 31,223 (16.4%). C majority 59,891 (31.6%).
1987 Total vote: 453,882 (76.0%). C 266,386 (58.7%); SDP/All 70,130 (15.5%); L/All 67,762 (14.9%); Lab 49,360 (10.9%); Others 244 (0.1%). C maj 196,256 (43.2%).

DURHAM

Electorate: 535,728 (530,104)

Bishop Auckland; Blaydon; Darlington; Durham, City of; Durham North; Durham North West; Easington; Sedgefield.

*S S Hughes (Lab)	124,448	65.8%
R Hull (C)	37,600	19.9%
Ms H I Lennox (Grn)	18,770	9.9%
P Freitag (SLD)	8,369	4.4%
Lab majority	86,848	45.9%

Total vote 189,187 (35.3%). **No change.**
1984: Total vote 183,226 (34.6%). Lab 106,073 (57.9%); C 44,846 (24.5%); L/All 32,307 (17.6%). Lab majority 61,227 (33.4%).
1987 Total vote: 402,801 (76.0%). Lab 208,583 (51.8%); C 112,050 (27.8%); SDP/All 49,888 (12.4%); L/All 32,280 (8.0%). Lab maj 96,533 (24.0%).

ESSEX NORTH EAST

Electorate: 604,807 (574,022)

Braintree; Colchester North; Colchester South and Malden; Harwich; Rochford; Saffron Walden; Southend East; Southend West.

Miss A C B McIntosh (C)	92,758	44.5%
Ms H J Bryan (Lab)	53,360	25.6%
C R Keene (Grn)	45,163	21.7%
Miss D P Wallis (SLD)	16,939	8.1%
C majority	39,398	18.9%

Total vote 208,220 (34.4%). **No change.**
1984: Total vote 174,743 (30.4%). C 97,138 (55.6%); Lab 42,836 (24.5%); SDP/All 34,769 (19.9%). C majority 54,302 (31.1%).
1987 Total vote: 453,354 (75.8%). C 250,945 (55.3%); L/All 69,795 (15.4%); Lab 66,858 (14.7%); SDP/All 64,562 (14.2%); Others 1,194 (0.3%). C maj 181,150 (40.0%).

ESSEX SOUTH WEST

Electorate: 575,882 (557,704)

Basildon; Billericay; Brentwood and Ongar; Castle Point; Chelmsford; Epping Forest; Harlow; Thurrock.

Miss P E Rawlings (C)	77,408	41.1%
J W Orpe (Lab)	68,005	36.1%
Mrs M E Willis (Grn)	32,242	17.1%
T P Allen (SLD)	10,618	5.6%
C majority	9,403	

Total vote 188,273 (32.7%). **No change.**
1984: Total vote 157,744 (28.3%). C 72,190 (45.8%); Lab 56,169 (35.6%); L/All 29,385 (18.6%). C maj 16,021 (10.2%).
1987 Total vote: 437,491 (76.8%). C 230,849 (52.8%); Lab 101,733 (23.3%); SDP/All 53,066 (12.1%); L/All 49,946 (11.4%); Others 1,867 (0.4%). C maj 129,116 (29.5%).

GREATER MANCHESTER CENTRAL

Electorate: 484,767 (507,941)

Altrincham and Sale; Davyhulme; the Manchester seats of Blackley, Central, Gorton, Withington, and Wythenshawe; Stretford.

*E Newman (Lab)	86,914	51.7%
Miss C E Gillan (C)	48,047	28.6%
B Candeland (Grn)	19,742	11.8%
J H Mulholland (SLD)	9,437	5.6%
S M Millson (SDP)	2,769	1.6%
S Knight (Hum)	1,045	0.6%
Lab majority	38,867	23.1%

Total vote 167,954 (34.6%). **No change.**
1984: Total vote 151,205 (29.8%). Lab 76,830 (50.8%); C 48,753 (32.2%); L/All 24,192 (16.0%); Other 1,430 (1.0%). Lab maj 28,077 (18.6%).
1987 Total vote: 364,783 (73.0%). Lab 168,932 (46.3%); C 125,558 (34.4%); L/All 44,963 (12.3%); SDP/All 24,337 (6.7%); Others 993 (0.3%). Lab maj 43,374 (11.9%).

GREATER MANCHESTER EAST

Electorate: 511,510 (510,586)

Ashton under Lyne; Cheadle; Denton and Reddish; Hazel Grove; Oldham Central and Royton; Oldham West; Stalybridge and Hyde; Stockport.

*J G Ford (Lab)	93,294	49.7%
R N Greenwood (C)	58,793	31.3%
M J Shipley (Grn)	19,090	10.2%
A B Leah (SLD)	16,645	8.9%
Lab majority	34,501	18.4%

Total vote 187,822 (36.7%). **No change.**
1984: Total vote 152,475 (29.9%). Lab 65,101 (42.7%); C 56,415 (37.0%); SDP/All 27,801 (18.2%); Ecol 3,158 (2.1%). Lab maj 8,651 (5.7%).
1987 Total vote: 388,414 (75.8%). C 153,708 (39.6%); Lab 142,811 (36.8%); L/All 56,647 (14.6%); SDP/All 34,329 (8.8%); Others 919 (0.2%). C maj 10,897 (2.8%).

GREATER MANCHESTER WEST

Electorate: 527,443 (528,896)

Bolton North East; Bolton South East; Bolton West; Bury North; Bury South; Eccles; Salford East; Worsley.

G Titley (Lab)	109,228	53.9%
P H Twyman (C)	59,093	29.2%
D W Milne (Grn)	22,778	11.2%
A H Cruden (SLD)	6,940	3.4%
Mrs B Archer (SDP)	4,526	2.2%
Lab majority	50,135	24.8%

Total vote 202,565 (38.4%). **No change.**
1984: Total vote 167,676 (31.7%). Lab 93,740 (55.9%); C 56,042 (33.4%); SDP/All 17,894 (10.7%). Lab maj 37,698 (22.5%).
1987 Total vote: 404,673 (76.9%). Lab 184,331 (45.6%); C 158,872 (39.3%); SDP/All 37,797 (9.3%); L/All 23,472 (5.8%); Others 201 (0.1%). Lab maj 25,459 (6.3%).

HAMPSHIRE CENTRAL

Electorate: 552,976 (524,649)

Aldershot; Basingstoke; Eastleigh; Hampshire North West; Southampton Itchen; Southampton Test; Winchester.

*E T Kellett-Bowman (C)	78,651	43.5%
Ms A Mawle (Lab)	50,977	28.2%
Mrs S J Penton (Grn)	33,186	18.3%
D W G Chidgey (SLD)	18,418	10.2%
C majority	27,674	15.3%

Total vote 180,962 (32.7%). **No change.**
1984: Total vote 162,579 (31.0%). C 84,086 (51.8%); SDP/All 39,265 (24.2%); Lab 39,228 (24.0%). C maj 44,821 (27.6%).
1988 by-election: Total vote 77,582 (14.4%). Kellett-Bowman (C) 38,039 (49.0%); John Arnold (Lab) 16,597 (21.4%); David Chidgey (SLD) 13,392 (17.3%); Earl Attlee (SDP) 5,952 (7.7%); Mrs Sally Penton (Grn) 3,603 (4.6%). C maj 21,442 (27.6%).
1987 Total vote: 416,841 (77.3%). C 218,319 (52.4%); Lab 74,771 (17.9%); L/All 69,700 (16.7%); SDP/All 53,486 (12.8%); Others 565 (0.1%). C maj 143,548 (34.4%).

HEREFORD AND WORCESTER

Electorate: 602,355 (560,654)

Bromsgrove; Gloucestershire West; Hereford; Leominster; Worcester; Worcestershire Mid; Worcestershire South; Wyre Forest

*Sir J Scott-Hopkins (C)	87,898	41.3%
C A Short (Lab)	62,233	29.2%
Ms F M Norman (Grn)	49,296	23.1%
Mrs J D Davies (SLD)	13,569	6.4%
C majority 25,665		12.0%

Total vote 212,996 (35.4%). **No change.**
1984: Total vote 174,253 (31.1%). C 84,077 (48.3%); Lab 44,143 (25.3%); L/All 37,854 (21.7%); Ecol 8,179 (4.7%). C maj 39,934 (23.0%).
1987 Total vote: 450,925 (77.5%). C 230,081 (51.0%); Lab 87,152 (19.3%); L/All 78,058 (17.3%); SDP/All 53,443 (11.9%); Others 2,191 (0.5%). C maj 142,929 (31.7%).

HERTFORDSHIRE

Electorate: 522,292 (505,206)

Broxbourne; Hertford and Stortford; Hertfordshire South West; Hertsmere; St Albans; Watford; Welwyn Hatfield.

*D N Prag (C)	86,898	46.6%
V S Anand (Lab)	43,556	23.4%
M F Ames (Grn)	37,277	20.0%
M D Phelan (SLD)	13,456	7.2%
Mrs C Treves Brown (SDP)	5,048	2.7%
C majority	43,342	23.3%

Total vote 186,235 (35.7%). **No change.**

1984: Total vote: 170,151 (33.7%). C 87,603 (51.5%); Lab 41,671 (24.5%); SDP/All 40,877 (24.0%). C majority 45,932 (27.0%).

1987 Total vote: 403,072 (77.9%). C 218,201 (54.1%); Lab 75,076 (18.6%); L/All 61,596 (15.3%); SDP/All 46,086 (11.4%); Others 2,113 (0.5%). C maj 143,125 (35.5%).

HUMBERSIDE

Electorate: 512,062 (503,080)

Beverley; Bridlington; Brigg and Cleethorpes; Great Grimsby; Hull East; Hull North; Hull West.

P D Crampton (Lab)	74,163	45.4%
*R C Battersby (C)	57,835	35.4%
Mrs J C Clark (Grn)	23,835	14.6%
F L Parker (SLD)	3,989	2.4%
S W Unwin (SDP)	3,419	2.1%
Lab majority	16,328	10.0%

Total vote 163,241 (31.9%). **Lab gain from C.**

1984: Total vote 143,207 (28.5%). C 61,952 (43.3%); Lab 53,937 (37.7%); SDP/All 27,318 (19.0%). C majority 8,015 (5.6%).

1987 Total vote: 369,003 (73.0%). C 146,163 (39.6%); Lab 130,830 (35.4%); SDP/All 46,118 (12.5%); L/All 44,911 (12.2%); Others 983 (0.3%). C maj 15,333 (4.2%).

KENT EAST

Electorate: 575,975 (554,808)

Ashford; Canterbury; Dover; Faversham; Folkestone and Hythe; Maidstone, Thanet North; Thanet South.

*C M Jackson (C)	85,667	43.9%
G N J Perry (Lab)	56,706	29.1%
Ms P A Kemp (Grn)	36,931	18.9%
A F C Morris (SLD)	15,470	7.9%
C majority	28,961.	14.9%

Total vote 194,774 (33.8%). **No change.**

1984: Total vote 175,819 (31.7%). C 92,340 (52.5%); Lab 43,473 (24.7%); SDP/All 34,601 (19.7%); Ecol 5,405 (3.1%). C majority 48,867 (27.8%).

1987 Total vote: 427,680 (75.8%). C 228,043 (53.3%); Lab 77,410 (18.1%); L/All 64,359 (15.1%); SDP/All 54,273 (12.7%); Others 3,595 (0.8%). C maj 150,633 (35.2%).

KENT WEST

Electorate: 575,667 (565,693)

Dartford; Gillingham; Gravesham; Kent Mid; Medway; Sevenoaks; Tonbridge and Malling; Tunbridge Wells.

*G B Patterson (C)	82,519	43.4%
P L Sloman (Lab)	58,469	30.7%
J Tidy (Grn)	33,202	17.4%
J B Doherty (SLD)	16,087	8.4%
C majority	24,050	12.6%

Total vote 190,277 (33.1%). **No change.**

1984: Total vote 174,495 (30.9%). C 85,414 (49.0%); Lab 50,784 (29.1%); L/All 33,306 (19.1%); Ecol 4,991 (2.9%). C majority 34,630 (19.9%).

1987 Total vote: 440,383 (75.9%). C 240,941 (54.7%); Lab 90,202 (20.5%); L/All 71,426 (16.2%); SDP/All 36,450 (8.3%); Others 1,364 (0.3%). C maj 150,739 (34.2%).

LANCASHIRE CENTRAL

Electorate: 543,245 (524,132)

Blackpool North; Blackpool South; Chorley; Fylde; Lancashire West; Preston; Ribble Valley; South Ribble.

*M J Welsh (C)	81,125	42.0%
G W T Smith (Lab)	75,437	39.1%
Ms H Ingham (Grn)	28,777	14.9%
Ms J Ross-Mills (SLD)	7,378	3.8%
C majority	5,688	2.9%

Total vote 192,717 (35.5%). **No change.**

1984: Total vote 163,481 (31.2%). C 82,370 (50.4%); Lab 56,175 (34.4%); SDP/All 24,936 (15.2%). C majority 26,195 (16.0%).

1987 Total vote: 408,670 (76.6%). C 197,031 (48.2%); Lab 131,812 (32.3%); L/All 50,723 (12.4%); SDP/All 27,985 (6.8%); Others 1,119 (0.3%). C maj 65,219 (16.0%).

LANCASHIRE EAST

Electorate: 535,179 (534,542)

Blackburn; Burnley; Heywood and Middleton; Hyndburn; Littleborough and Saddleworth; Pendle; Rochdale; Rossendale and Darwin.

*M J Hindley (Lab)	96,926	51.5%
R W Sturdy (C)	57,778	30.7%
S Barker (Grn)	20,728	11.0%
M Hambley (SLD)	12,661	6.7%
Lab majority	39,148	20.8%

Total vote 188,093 (35.1%). **No change.**

1984: Total vote 169,837 (31.8%). Lab 75,711 (44.6%); C 67,806 (39.9%); L/All 26,320 (15.5%). Lab majority 7,905 (4.7%).

1987 Total vote: 415,307 (77.7%). Lab 168,600 (40.6%); C 157,362 (37.9%); L/All 59,829 (14.4%); SDP/All 24,179 (5.8%); Others 297 (0.1%). Lab maj 11,238 (2.7%).

LEEDS

Electorate: 508,109 (526,133)

Elmet; the Leeds sets of Central, East, North East, North West, South and Morley, and West; Pudsey.

*M McGowan (Lab)	97,385	52.2%
J W Tweddle (C)	54,867	29.4%
C R Lord (Grn)	22,558	12.1%
Mrs J Ewens (SLD)	11,720	6.3%
Lab majority	42,518	22.8%

Total vote 186,530 (36.7%). **No change.**
1984: Total vote 166,810 (31.7%). Lab 70,535 (42.3%); C 60,178 (36.1%); L/All 36,097 (21.6%). Lab majority 10,357 (6.2%).
1987 Total vote: 384,316 (73.8%). C 143,078 (37.2%); Lab 140,050 (36.4%); L/All 63,270 (16.5%); SDP/All 36,484 (9.5%); Others 1,434 (0.4%). C maj 3,028 (0.8%).

LEICESTER

Electorate: 585,877 (564,350)

Bosworth; Leicester East; Leicester South; Leicester West; Loughborough; Nuneaton; Rutland and Melton; Warwickshire North.

Ms I M Read (Lab)	90,798	42.6%
*F A Tuckman (C)	75,476	35.4%
C J Davis (Grn)	33,081	15.5%
A G Barrett (Ind C)	6,996	3.3%
G W Childs (SLD)	6,791	3.2%
Lab majority	15,322	7.2%

Total vote 213,142 (36.4%). **Lab gain from C.**
1984: Total vote 175,029 (31.0%). C 72,508 (41.3%); Lab 69,616 (39.8%); SDP/All 29,656 (17.0%); Ind C 3,249 (1.9%). C majority 2,892 (1.7%).
1987 Total vote: 450,581 (78.3%). C 219,361 (48.7%); Lab 146,480 (32.5%); SDP/All 43,074 (9.6%); L/All 38,953 (8.6%); Others 2,713 (0.6%). C maj 72,881 (16.2%).

LINCOLNSHIRE

Electorate: 592,709 (551,904)

Bassetlaw; Gainsborough and Horncastle; Grantham; Holland with Boston; Lincoln; Lindsey East; Newark; Stamford and Spalding.

*W F Newton Dunn (C)	92,043	45.4%
S Taggart (Lab)	71,393	35.2%
Ms J Steranka (Grn)	24,908	12.3%
J P Heppell (SLD)	14,341	7.1%
C majority	20,650	10.2%

Total vote 202,685 (34.2%). **No change.**
1984: Total vote 177,011 (32.1%). C 92,606 (52.3%); Lab 47,161 (26.6%); L/All 37,244 (21.1%). C majority 45,445 (25.7%).
1987 Total vote: 434,671 (76.0%). C 225,024 (51.8%); Lab 100,701 (23.2%); L/All 78,841 (18.2%); SDP/All 28,768 (6.6%); Others 1,337 (0.3%). C maj 124,323 (28.6%).

LONDON CENTRAL

Electorate: 493,067 (543,825)

Chelsea; City of London and Westminster South; Fulham; Hampstead and Highgate; Holborn and St Pancras; Islington North; Islington South and Finsbury; Kensington; Westminster North.

*A S Newens (Lab Co-op)	78,561	42.2%
Ms H S Crawley (C)	67,019	36.0%
Ms N Kortvelyessy (Grn)	28,087	15.1%
Miss S A Ludford (SLD)	7,864	4.2%
W D E Mallinson (SDP)	2,957	1.6%
Lord D E Sutch (Loony)	841	.5%
Ms L St-Claire (Corr)	707	.4%
J S Swinden (Hum)	304	.2%
Lab Co-op majority	11,542	6.2%

Total vote 186,036 (37.7%). **No change.**
1984: Total vote 180,170 (33.1%). Lab and Co-op 77,842 (43.2%); C 64,545 (35.8%); SDP/All 30,269 (16.8%); Ecol 5,945 and other 1,569 (4.2%). Lab and Co-op majority 13,297 (7.4%).
1987 Total vote: 348,391 (67.0%). C 146,038 (41.9%); Lab 129,728 (37.2%); SDP/All 55,169 (15.8%); L/All 13,118 (3.8%); Others 4,346 (1.3%). C maj 16,310 (4.7%).

LONDON EAST

Electorate 535,582 (537,831)

Barking; Dagenham; Hornchurch; Ilford North; Ilford South; Newham North East; Romford; Upminster; Wanstead and Woodford.

*Miss C Tongue (Lab)	92,803	49.5%
A R Tyrrell (C)	65,418	34.9%
Ms E L Crosbie (Grn)	21,388	11.4%
J K Gibb (SLD)	7,341	3.9%
D A O'Sullivan (ICP)	717	.4%
Lab majority	27,385	14.6%

Total vote 187,667 (35.0%). **No change.**
1984: Total vote 161,960 (30.1%). Lab 73,870 (45.6%); C 61,711 (38.1%); SDP/All 26,379 (16.3%). Lab majority 12,159 (7.5%).
1987 Total vote: 380,633 (71.0%). C 184,759 (48.5%); Lab 122,426 (32.2%); L/All 47,129 (12.4%); SDP/All 25,934 (6.8%); Others 385 (0.1%). C maj 62,333 (16/4%).

LONDON NORTH

Electorate: 577,420 (564,359)

Chipping Barnet; Edmonton; Enfield North; Enfield Southgate; Finchley; Hendon North; Hendon South; Hornsey and Wood Green; Tottenham.

Ms P Green (Lab Co-op)	85,536	41.2%
R M Lacey (C)	79,699	38.3%
S Clark (Grn)	30,807	14.8%
Ms H F Leighter (SLD)	8,917	4.3%
P Burns (Ind)	2,016	.8%
Ms L Reith (Comm)	850	.4%
Lab Co-op majority	5,837	2.8%

Total vote 207,825 (36.0%). **Lab gain from C.**
1984: Total vote 180,865 (32.1%). C 74,846 (41.4%); Lab 69,993 (38.7%); L/All 31,344 (17.3%); Ecol 4,682 (2.6%). C majority 4,853 (2.7%).
1987 Total vote: 411,177 (70.0%). C 210,721 (51.3%); Lab 123,955 (30.1%); L/All 42,695 (10.4%); SDP/All 29,535 (7.2%); Others 4,271 (1.0%). C maj 86,766 (21.1%).

LONDON NORTH EAST

Electorate: 513,302 (513,781)

Bethnal Green and Stepney; Bow and Poplar; Chingford; Hackney North and Stoke Newington; Hackney South and Shoreditch; Leyton; Newham North West; Newham South; Walthamstow.

*A Lomas (Lab)	76,085	53.9%
M Trend (C)	28,318	20.1%
Mrs J D Lambert (Grn)	25,949	18.4%
S Banks (SLD)	9,575	6.8%
Ms N C Temple (Comm)	1,129	.8%
Lab majority	47,767	33.9%

Total vote 141,056 (27.5%). **No change.**
1984: Total vote 129,290 (25.2%). Lab 79,907 (61.8%); C 27,242 (21.1%); L/All 17,344 (13.4%); Ecol 4,797 (3.7%). Lab majority 52,665 (40.7%).
1987 Total vote: 321,049 (62.5%). Lab 132,981 (41.4%); C 105,397 (32.8%); L/All 51,183 (15.9%); SDP/All 27,825 (8.7%); Others 3,663 (1.2%). Lab maj 27,584 (8.6%).

LONDON NORTH WEST

Electorate: 510,858 (518,365)

Brent East; Brent North; Brent South; Harrow East; Harrow West; Hayes and Harlington; Ruislip-Northwood; Uxbridge.

*Lord Bethell (C)	74,900	41.3%
A K Toms (Lab)	67,500	37.2%
I E Flindall (Grn)	28,275	15.6%
C D Noyce (SLD)	10,553	5.8%
C majority	7,400	4.1%

Total vote 181,228 (35.5%). **No change.**
1984: Total vote 161,793 (31.2%). C 69,803 (43.1%); Lab 62,381 (38.6%); L/All 29,609 (18.3%). C majority 7,422 (4.6%).
1987 Total vote: 375,076 (72.2%). C 193,974 (51.7%); Lab 105,335 (28.1%); SDP/All 56,646 (15.1%); L/All 16,882 (4.5%); Others 2,300 (0.6%). C maj 88,639 (23.6%).

LONDON SOUTH AND SURREY EAST

Electorate: 499,933 (505,393)

Carshalton and Wallington; Croydon Central; Croydon North East; Croydon North West; Croydon South; Reigate; Surrey East; Sutton and Cheam.

*C J O Moorhouse (C)	78,256	45.4%
R J E Evans (Lab)	47,440	27.5%
G F Brand (Grn)	31,854	18.5%
P H Billenness (SLD)	14,967	8.7%
C majority	30,816	17.9%

Total vote 172,517 (34.5%). **No change.**
1984: Total vote 154,109 (30.5%). C 82,122 (53.3%); Lab 37,465 (24.3%); l/All 34,522 (22.4%). C majority 44,657 (29.0%).
1987 Total vote: 369,612 (73.1%). C 189,275 (51.2%); Lab 67,422 (18.2%); L/All 43,024 (11.6%); SDP/All 41,890 (11.3%); Others 28,001 (7.6%). C maj 121,853 (33.0%).

LONDON SOUTH EAST

Electorate: 564,156 (561,984)

Beckenham; Bexleyheath; Chislehurst; Eltham; Erith and Crayford; Greenwich; Old Bexley and Sidcup; Orpington; Ravensbourne; Woolwich.

*P N Price (C)	80,619	38.2%
D J Earnshaw (Lab)	73,029	34.6%
Dr E C McPhee (Grn)	37,576	17.8%
A A Kinch (SDP)	10,196	4.8%
Mrs M C Williams (SLD)	9,052	4.3%
W E Turner (Ind)	456	.2%
C majority	7,590	3.6%

Total vote 210,928 (37.4%). **No change.**
1984: Total vote 182,604 (32.5%). C 81,508 (44.6%); Lab 61,493 (33.7%); L/All 38,614 (21.2%); other 989 (0.5%). C majority 20,015 (10.9%).
1987 Total vote: 428,044 (75.5%). C 211,213 (49.3%); Lab 95,799 (22.4%); L/All 65,423 (15.3%); SDP/All 54,962 (12.8%); Others 647 (0.2%). C maj 115,414 (27.0%).

LONDON SOUTH INNER

Electorate: 530,615 (530,672)

Dulwich; Lewisham Deptford; Lewisham East; Lewisham West; Norwood; Peckham; Southwark and Bermondsey; Streatham; Vauxhall.

*R Balfe (Lab Co-op)	90,378	51.9%
R J Wheatley (C)	45,360	26.1%
Ms P A Shepherd (Grn)	26,230	15.0%
M J Pindar (SLD)	10,277	5.9%
P N Power (Comm)	1,277	.7%
Ms D Weppler (Comm L)	323	.2%
Lab Co-op majority	45,018	25.9%

Total vote 173,845 (32.8%). **No change.**
1984 Total vote 152,513 (28.7%). Lab & Co-op 77,661 (50.9%); (C) 46,180 (30.3%); SDP/All 25,391 (16.7%); Ecol 3,281 (2.2%). Lab & Co-op majority 31,481 (20.6%).
1987 Total vote: 357,824 (66.8%). Lab 155,879 (43.6%); C 127,279 (35.6%); L/All 36,860 (10.3%); SDP/All 34,638 (9.7%); Others 3,168 (0.9%). Lab maj 28,600 (8.0%).

LONDON SOUTH WEST

Electorate: 490,242 (499,273)

Battersea; Epsom and Ewell; Kingston upon Thames; Mitcham and Morden; Putney; Surbiton; Tooting; Wimbledon

Ms A J Pollack (Lab)	74,298	38.3%
*Dame S M Roberts (C)	73,780	38.0%
Ms M A Elson (Grn)	35,476	18.3%
J C Field (SLD)	10,400	5.4%
Lab majority	518	.3%

Total vote 193,954 (39.6%). **Lab gain from C.**
1984: Total vote: 169,447 (33.9%). C 70,490 (41.6%); Lab 63,623 (37.6%); L/All 32,268 (19.0%); Ecol 3,066 (1.8%). C Maj 6,867 (4.0%).
1987 Total vote: 371,640 (75.0%). C 189,902 (51.1%); Lab 104,620 (28.1%); L/All 44,567 (12.0%); SDP/All 30,107 (8.1%); Others 2,444 (0.7%). C maj 83,282 (22.4%).

LONDON WEST

Electorate: 519,646 (516,661)

Brentford and Isleworth; Ealing Acton; Ealing North; Ealing Southall; Feltham and Heston; Hammersmith; Richmond and Barnes; Twickenham.

*M N Elliott (Lab)	92,959	43.0%
B Donnelly (C)	78,151	36.2%
J R Hywell-Davies (Grn)	32,686	15.1%
J G Parry (SLD)	9,309	4.3%
J Rogers-Davies (SDP)	2,877	1.3%
Lab majority	14,808	6.9%

Total vote 215,982 (41.6%). No change.
1984: Total vote 194,927 (37.7%). Lab 79,554 (40.8%); C 74,325 (38.1%); SDP/All 36,687 (18.8%); Ecol 4,361 (2.2%). Lab majority 5,229 (2.7%).
1987 Total vote: 401,778 (75.2%). C 190,590 (47.4%); Lab 118,748 (29.6%); L/All 60,504 (15.1%); SDP/All 28,222 (7.0%); Others 3,714 (0.9%). C maj 71,842 (17.9%).

MERSEYSIDE EAST

Electorate: 523,254 (537,285)

Knowsley North; Knowsley South; Leigh; Liverpool Garston; Makerfield; St Helens North; St Helens South; Wigan.

T Wynn (Lab)	107,288	63.7%
E N Farthing (C)	30,421	18.6%
R L Georgeson (Grn)	20,018	12.2%
R M Clayton (SLD)	5,658	3.5%
Lab majority	76,867	47.0%

Total vote 163,385 (31.2%). No change.
1984: Total vote 142,392 (26.5%). Lab 87,086 (61.2%); C 38,047 (26.7%); SDP/All 17,259 (12.1%). Lab majority 49,039 (34.5%).
1987 Total vote: 397,957 (74.7%). Lab 233,905 (58.8%); C 96,063 (24.1%); SDP/All 34,127 (8.6%); L/All 33,226 (8.3%); Others 636 (0.2%). Lab maj 137,842 (34.6%).

MERSEYSIDE WEST

Electorate: 506,337 (551,532)

Bootle; Crosby; the Liverpool seats of Broadgreen, Mossley Hill, Riverside, Walton, and West Derby; Southport.

*K A Stewart (Lab)	93,717	52.4%
M D Byrne (C)	43,900	25.6%
L Brown (Grn)	23,052	12.9%
Mrs H F Clucas (SLD)	16,327	9.1%
D J E Carson (PRP)	1,747	.8%
Lab majority	49,817	27.9%

Total vote 178,743 (35.3%). No change.
1984: Total vote 155,936 (28.3%). Lab 65,915 (42.3%); C 52,718 (33.8%); L/All 37,303 (29.9%). Lab majority 13,197 (8.5%).
1987 Total vote: 400,400 (74.4%). Lab 180,685 (45.1%); C 102,098 (25.5%); L/All 74,745 (18.7%); SDP/All 41,618 (10.4%); Others 1,254 (0.3%). Lab maj 78,587 (19.6%).

MIDLANDS CENTRAL

Electorate: 544,904 (533,798)

The Coventry seats of North East, North West, South East, and South West; Meriden; Rugby and Kenilworth; Solihull; Warwick and Leamington.

Ms C M Oddy (Lab)	76,736	38.5%
*J de Courcy Ling (C)	71,643	35.9%
Ms J A Alty (Grn)	42,622	21.4%
I Cundy (SLD)	8,450	4.2%
Lab majority	5,093	2.6%

Total vote 199,451 (36.6%). Lab gain from C.
1984: Total vote 152,445 (28.6%). C 67,884 (44.5%); 55,155 (36.2%); SDP/All 27,912 (18.3%); Other 1,494 (1.0%). C majority 12,720 (8.3%).
1987 Total vote: 409,751 (75.3%). C 188,180 (45.9%); Lab 134,505 (32.8%); L/All 46,069 (11.3%); SDP/All 38,994 (9.5%); Others 2,003 (0.5%). C maj 53,675 (13.1%).

MIDLANDS WEST

Electorate: 535,395 (533,796)

Dudley East; Dudley West; Halesowen and Stourbridge; Warley East; Warley West; Wolverhampton North East; Wolverhampton South East; Wolverhampton South West.

*J A W Bird (Lab Co-op)	105,529	53.4%
M J Whitby (C)	63,165	31.9%
J Raven (Grn)	21,787	11.0%
Mrs F M Oborski (SLD)	6,974	3.5%
Lab Co-op majority	42,364	21.4%

Total vote 197,455 (36.9%). No change.
1984: Total vote 146,206 (27.4%). Lab 74,091 (50.7%); C 54,406 (37.2%); L/All 17,709 (12.1%). Lab majority 19,685 (13.5%).
1987 Total vote: 399,213 (74.5%). C 172,459 (43.2%); Lab 158,734 (39.8%); SDP/All 36,635 (9.2%); L/All 31,385 (7.9%). C maj 13,725 (3.4%).
1987 Euro by-election: Total vote 152,603 (27.4%). Lab 59,761 (39.1%); C 55,736 (36.5%); L/All 37,106 (24.4%). Lab majority 4,025 (2.6%).

NORFOLK

Electorate: 584,054 (543,214)

Great Yarmouth; the Norfolk seats of Mid, North, North West, South, and South West; Norwich North; Norwich South.

*P F Howell (C)	92,385	42.3%
Ms M Page (Lab)	71,478	32.7%
M Macartney-Filgate (Grn)	40,575	18.6%
R A Lawes (SLD)	8,902	4.1%
S D Maxwell (SDP)	4,934	2.3%
C majority	20,907	9.6%

Total vote 218,274 (37.4%). No change.
1984: Total vote 191,764 (35.3%). C 95,459 (49.8%); Lab 58,602 (30.6%); SDP/All 37,703 (14.7%). C majority 36,857 (19.2%).
1987 Total vote: 440,441 (78.2%). C 224,842 (51.1%); Lab 101,027 (22.9%); SDP/All 68,113 (15.5%); L/All 45,499 (10.3%); Others 960 (0.2%). C maj 123,815 (28.1%).

95

RESULTS OF VOTING

NORTHAMPTONSHIRE

Electorate: 594,492 (547,188)

Blaby; Corby; Daventry; Harborough; Kettering; Northampton North; Northampton South; Wellingborough.

*A M H Simpson (C)	86,695	41.8%
M Coyne (Lab)	66,248	31.9%
Ms A Bryant (Grn)	43,071	20.7%
R Church (SLD)	11,619	5.6%
C majority	20,447	9.8%

Total vote 207,633 (34.9%). **No change.**

1984: Total vote 178,228 (32.6%). C 88,668 (49.8%); Lab 48,809 (27.4%); SDP/All 37,421 (21.0%); Other 3,330 (1.8%). C majority 39,859 (22.4%).

1987 Total vote: 444,284 (78.1%). C 239,874 (54.0%); Lab 104,125 (23.4%); L/All 73,167 (16.5%); SDP/All 25,844 (5.8%); Others 1,274 (0.3%). C maj 135,749 (30.6%).

NORTHUMBRIA

Electorate: 521,980 (512,979)

Berwick-upon-Tweed; Blyth Valley; Hexham; Newcastle upon Tyne Central; upon Tyne North; Tynemouth; Wallsend; Wansbeck.

*G J Adam (Lab)	110,688	53.1%
P Yeoman (C)	50,648	25.7%
Ms A Lipman (Grn)	24,882	12.6%
Viscount Morpeth (SLD)	10,983	5.6%
Lab majority	60,040	30.4%

Total vote 197,201 (37.8%). **No change.**

1984: Total vote 184,080 (35.9%). Lab 78,417 (42.6%); C 62,717 (34.1%); L/All 42,946 (23.3%). Lab majority 15,700 (8.5%).

1987 Total vote: 396,527 (76.8%). Lab 161,226 (40.7%); C 121,369 (30.6%); L/All 75,125 (18.9%); SDP/All 37,563 (9.5%); Others 1,244 (0.3%). Lab maj 39,857 (10.0%).

NOTTINGHAM

Electorate: 570,908 (554,473)

Broxtowe; Gedling; Mansfield; Nottingham East; Nottingham North; Nottingham South; Rushcliffe; Sherwood.

K Coates (Lab)	92,261	43.8%
*M L Kilby (C)	77,748	36.8%
Mrs S E Blount (Grn)	34,097	16.2%
A Swift (SLD)	6,693	3.2%
Lab majority	14,513	6.9%

Total vote 210,799 (36.9%). **Lab gain from C.**

1984: Total vote 182,043 (32.8%). C 82,500 (45.3%); Lab 66,374 (36.5%); L/All 33,169 (18.2%). C majority 16,126 (8.8%).

1987 Total vote: 431,043 (76.7%). C 205,669 (47.7%); Lab 142,432 (33.1%); SDP/All 59,835 (13.9%); L/All 19,445 (4.5%); Others 3,662 (0.9%). C maj 63,237 (14.7%).

OXFORD AND BUCKINGHAMSHIRE

Electorate: 567,292 (542,343)

Aylesbury; Beaconsfield; Buckingham; Chesham and Amersham; Henley; Oxford East; Oxford West and Abingdon; Wycombe.

*J E M Elles (C)	92,483	46.8%
R Gifford (Lab)	44,965	22.8%
T H Andrewes (Grn)	42,058	21.3%
R Johnston (SLD)	14,405	7.3%
R C Turner (Ind)	3,696	1.9%
C majority	47,518	24.0%

Total vote 197,607 (34.8%). **No change.**

1984: Total vote 178,355 (32.9%). C 94,136 (52.8%); SDP/All 45,055 (25.3%); Lab 39,164 (22.0%). C majority 49,081 (27.5%).

1987 Total vote: 422,932 (76.2%). C 236,133 (55.8%); Lab 72,519 (17.1%); L/All 61,229 (14.5%); SDP/All 51,095 (12.1%); Others 1,956 (0.5%). C maj 163,614 (38.7%).

SHEFFIELD

Electorate: 563,375 (558,984)

Chesterfield; Derbyshire North East; the Sheffield seats of Attercliffe, Brightside, Central, Hallam, Heeley, and Hillsborough.

R Barton (Lab)	109,677	58.2%
T S R Mort (C)	40,401	21.4%
P L Scott (Grn)	26,844	14.2%
A H Rogers (SLD)	10,910	5.8%
D E Hyland (ICP)	657	0.3%
Lab majority	69,276	36.8%

Total vote 188,489 (33.5%). **No change.**

1984: Total vote 164,712 (29.5%). Lab 93,530 (56.8%); C 47,247 (28.7%); L/All 23,935 (14.5%). Lab majority 46,283 (28.1%).

1987 Total vote: 409,621 (73.4%). Lab 200,548 (49.0%); C 109,151 (26.6%); L/All 63,323 (15.5%); SDP/All 35,659 (8.7%); Others 940 (0.2%). Lab maj 91,397 (22.3%).

SHROPSHIRE AND STAFFORD

Electorate: 605,021 (562,823)

Cannock and Burntwood; Ludlow; Newcastle-under-Lyme; Shrewsbury and Atcham; Shropshire North; Stafford; Staffordshire South; The Wrekin.

*C J Prout (C)	85,896	41.0%
D J A Hallam (Lab)	83,352	39.8%
R T C Saunders (Grn)	29,637	14.2%
C Hards (SLD)	10,568	5.0%
C majority	2,544	1.2%

Total vote 209,453 (34.6%). **No change.**

1984: Total vote 176,859 (31.4%). C 82,291 (46.5%); Lab 57,359 (32.4%); L/All 37,209 (21.1%). C majority 24,932 (14.1%).

1987 Total vote: 455,584 (78.2%). C 216,434 (47.5%); Lab 125,165 (27.5%); L/All 86,357 (19.0%); SDP/All 26,571 (5.8%); Others 1,057 (0.2%). C maj 91,269 (20.0%).

SOMERSET & DORSET WEST

Electorate: 588,614 (540,393)

Bridgwater; Dorset West; Somerton and Frome; Taunton; Wells; Weston-super-Mare; Woodspring; Yeovil.

*Mrs M E Daly (C)	106,716	45.0%
Dr R H Lawson (Grn)	54,496	22.9%
Ms D M Organ (Lab)	46,210	19.5%
M Mactaggart (SLD)	28,662	12.0%
A P B Mockler (Wes Rg)	930	0.4%
C majority	52,220	22.0%

Total vote 237,014 (40.3%). No change.
1984: Total vote 194,468 (36%). C 98,928 (50.9%); L/All 58,677 (30.2%); Lab 36,863 (18.9%). C majority 40,251 (20.7%).
1987 Total vote: 444,255 (78.6%). C 229,527 (51.7%); L/All 100,960 (22.7%); SDP/All 56,399 (12.7%); Lab 53,960 (12.2%); Others 3,409 (0.8%). C maj 128,567 (28.9%).

STAFFORDSHIRE EAST

Electorate: 587,571 (563,376)

Burton; Derbyshire South; Staffordshire South East; Leicestershire North West; Staf-fordshire Mid; Stoke-on-Trent Central; Stoke-on-Trent North; Stoke-on-Trent South.

*G W Stevenson (Lab)	94,873	50.3%
M F Spungin (C)	63,104	33.4%
S Parker (Grn)	23,415	12.4%
R C Dodson (SLD)	7,046	3.7%
Lab majority	31,769	16.9%

Total vote 188,438 (32.1%). No change.
1984: Total vote 171,732 (30.5%). Lab 76,753 (44.7%); C 68,886 (40.1%); SDP/All 26,093 (15.2%). Lab majority 7,867 (4.6%).
1987 Total vote: 442,561 (77.3%). C 193,477 (43.7%); Lab 162,949 (36.8%); SDP/All 44,866 (10.1%); L/All 39,863 (9.0%); Others 1,406 (0.3%). C maj 30,528 (6.9%).

SUFFOLK

Electorate: 556,169 (516,050)

Bury St Edmunds; Cambridgeshire South East; Ipswich; Suffolk Central; Suffolk Coastal; Suffolk South; Waveney.

*A E Turner (C)	82,481	43.6%
M D Cornish (Lab)	56,788	30.0%
A C Slade (Grn)	37,305	19.7%
P R Odell (SLD)	12,660	6.7%
C majority	25,693	13.6%

Total vote 189,234 (34.0%). No change.
1984: Total vote 163,472 (31.7%). C 88,243 (54.0%); Lab 41,145 (25.2%); L/All 34,084 (20.9%). C majority 47,098 (28.8%).
1987 Total vote: 412,445 (76.8%). C 220,196 (53.4%); Lab 146,500 (21.9%); SDP/All 65,608 (15.9%); L/All 33,861 (8.2%); Others 2,280 (0.5%). C maj 129,696 (31.5%).

SURREY WEST

Electorate: 520,571 (504,923)

Chertsey and Walton; Esher; Guildford; Mole Valley; Surrey North West; Surrey South West; Woking.

T N B Spencer (C)	89,674	49.8%
E Haywood (Grn)	40,332	22.4%
H G Trace (Lab)	28,313	15.7%
A Davis (SLD)	18,042	10.0%
B M Collignon (SDP)	3,676	2.0%
C majority	49,342	27.4%

Total vote 180,037 (34.6%). No change.
1984: Total vote 163,293 (32.3%). C 96,675 (59.2%); SDP/All 44,087 (27.0%); Lab 22,531 (13.8%). C majority 52,588 (32.2%).
1987 Total vote: 391,963 (75.7%). C 236,195 (60.3%); L/All 81,966 (20.9%); Lab 38,956 (9.9%); SDP/All 34,547 (8.8%); Others 299 (0.1%). C maj 154,229 (39.3%).

SUSSEX EAST

Electorate: 558,325 (537,397)

Bexhill and Battle; Brighton Kemptown; Brighton Pavilion; Eastbourne; Hastings and Rye; Hove; Lewes; Wealden.

*Sir J Stewart-Clark (C)	96,388	48.2%
Ms G Roles (Lab)	43,094	21.6%
Ms R Addison (Grn)	42,316	21.3%
Mrs D Venables (SLD)	16,810	8.4%
D Howells (Loony)	1,181	0.6%
C majority	53,294	26.7%

Total vote 199,789 (35.8%).No change.
1984: Total vote 176,567 (32.9%). C 102,287 (57.9%); SDP/All 36,666 (20.8%); Lab 32,213 (18.2%); Ecol 5,401 (3.1%). C majority 65,621 (37.1%).
1987 Total vote: 407,455 (74.0%). C 235,529 (57.8%); Lab 61,887 (15.2%); L/All 59,956 (14.7%); SDP/All 47,288 (11.6%); Others 2,795 (0.7%). C maj 173,642 (42.6%).

SUSSEX WEST

Electorate: 560,124 (531,934)

Arundel; Chichester; Crawley; Horsham; Shoreham; Sussex Mid; Worthing.

*R M Seligman (C)	95,821	47.4%
I F N Bagnall (Grn)	49,588	24.5%
M Shrimpton (Lab)	32,006	15.8%
Dr J M M Walsh (SLD)	24,855	12.3%
C majority	46,233	22.9%

Total vote 202,270 (36.1%). No change.
1984: Total vote 177,711 (33.4%). C 104,257 (58.7%); L/All 46,755 (26.3%); Lab 22,857 (12.9%); Ecol 3,842 (2.2%). C majority 57,502 (32.4%).
1987 Total vote: 411,020 (75.2%). C 246,678 (60.0%); L/All 84,724 (20.6%); Lab 48,497 (11.8%); SDP/All 28,542 (7.0%); Others 2,579 (0.6%). C maj 161,954 (39.4%).

RESULTS OF VOTING

THAMES VALLEY

Electorate: 548,243 (519,564)

Berkshire East; Reading East; Reading West; Slough; Spelthorne; Windsor and Maidenhead; Wokingham.

J C C Stevens (C)	73,070	42.7%
Ms H B de Lyon (Lab)	46,579	27.2%
P Gordon (Grn)	36,865	21.5%
D B Griffiths (SLD)	14,603	8.5%
C majority	26,491	15.5%

Total vote 171,117 (31.2%). **No change.**
1984: Total vote 143,755 (27.7%). C 74,928 (52.1%); Lab 36,123 (25.1%); L/All 32,704 (22.8%). C majority 38,805 (27.0%).
1987 Total vote: 403,096 (74.4%). C 228,125 (56.6%); Lab 75,080 (18.6%); SDP/All 48,646 (12.1%); L/All 46,934 (11.6%); Others 4,311 (1.1%). C maj 153,045 (38.0%).

TYNE AND WEAR

Electorate: 536,205 (543,955)

Gateshead East; Houghton and Washington; Jarrow; Newcastle upon Tyne East; South Shields; Sunderland North; Sunderland South; Tyne Bridge.

A J Donnelly (Lab)	126,682	69.3%
N C Gibbon (C)	30,902	16.9%
R Stather (Grn)	18,107	9.9%
P J Arnold (SLD)	6,101	3.3%
T P Kilgallon (SPGB)	919	0.5%
Lab majority	95,780	52.4%

Total vote 182,711 (34.1%).**No change.**
1984: Total vote 147,715 (27.2%). Lab 89,024 (60.3%); C 39,610 (26.8%); SDP/All 19,081 (12.9%). Lab majority 49,414 (33.5%).
1987 Total vote: 379,347 (70.6%). Lab 221,631 (58.4%); C 96,206 (25.4%); SDP/All 38,748 (10.2%); L/All 21,476 (5.7%); Others 1,286 (0.3%). Lab maj 125,425 (33.1%).

WIGHT & HAMPSHIRE EAST

Electorate: 580,357 (544,189)

Fareham; Gosport; Hampshire East; Havant; Isle of Wight; Portsmouth North; Portsmouth South.

*R J Simmonds (C)	90,658	44.9%
Dr A D Burnett (Lab)	51,228	25.3%
S L Rackett (Green)	40,664	20.1%
Ms V A Rayner (SLD)	19,569	9.7%
C majority	39,430	19.5%

Total vote 202,119 (34.8%). **No change.**
1984: Total vote 186,849 (34.3%). C 96,666 (51.7%); L/All 53,738 (28.8%); Lab 36,445 (19.5%). C majority 42,928 (22.9%).
1987 Total vote: 428,054 (75.9%). C 239,211 (55.9%); L/All 87,107 (20.3%); SDP/All 54,242 (12.7%); Lab 46,666 (10.9%); Others 828 (0.2%). C maj 152,104 (35.5%).

WILTSHIRE

Electorate: 575,333 (531,501)

Devizes; Newbury; Salisbury; Swindon; Wantage; Westbury; Wiltshire North.

*Mrs C F Jackson (C)	93,200	44.4%
G A Harris (Lab)	46,887	22.3%
J V Hughes (Grn)	46,735	22.3%
P N Crossley (SLD)	18,302	8.7%
J A Cade (Ind)	4,809	2.3%
C majority	46,313	22.1%

Total vote 209,933 (36.5%). **No change.**
1984: Total vote 182,734 (34.4%). C 86,873 (47.5%); L/All 60,404 (33.1%); Lab 35,457 (19.4%). C majority 26,469 (14.4%).
1987 Total vote: 431,895 (77.7%). C 230,151 (53.3%); L/All 85,679 (19.8%); Lab 66,615 (15.4%); SDP/All 49,078 (11.4%); Others 372 (0.1%). C maj 144,472 (33.5%).

YORK

Electorate: 549,050 (517,592)

Boothferry; Glanford and Scunthorpe; Harrogate; Ryedale; Scarborough; Selby; York.

*E H C McMillan-Scott (C)	81,453	43.4%
J T Grogan (Lab)	66,351	35.3%
R Bell (Grn)	27,525	14.7%
A Collinge (SLD)	12,542	6.7%
C majority	15,102	8.0%

Total vote 187,871 (34.2%). **No change.**
1984: Total vote 158,226 (30.6%). C 80,636 (51.0%); Lab 44,234 (28.0%); SDP/All 33,356 (21.0%). C majority 36,402 (23.0%).
1987 Total vote: 408,013 (76.7%). C 204,416 (50.1%); Lab 101,720 (24.9%); SDP/All 50,971 (12.5%); L/All 50,165 (12.3%); Others 741 (0.2%). C maj 102,696 (25.2%).

YORKSHIRE SOUTH

Electorate: 526,040 (516,431)

Barnsley Central; Barnsley East; Doncaster Central; Doncaster North; Don Valley; Rotherham; Rother Valley; Wentworth.

*N West (Lab)	121,060	69.4%
W J Clappison (C)	29,276	16.8%
A Grace (Grn)	19,063	10.9%
B Boulton (SLD)	5,039	2.9%
Lab majority	91,784	52.6%

Total vote 174,438 (33.2%). **No change.**
1984: Total vote 147,597 (28.6%). Lab 98,020 (66.4%); C 30,271 (20.5%); SDP/All 19,306 (13.1%). Lab majority 67,749 (45.9%).
1987 Total vote: 376,810 (72.7%). Lab 227,425 (60.4%); C 93,368 (24.8%); SDP/All 29,669 (7.9%); L/All 26,203 (7.0%); Other 145 (0.04%). Lab maj 134,057 (35.6%).

YORKSHIRE SOUTH WEST

Electorate: 529,788 (518,423)

Barnsley West and Penistone; Colne Valley; Dewsbury; Hemsworth; Huddersfield; Normanton; Pontefract and Castleford; Wakefield.

*T Megahy (Lab)	108,444	57.9%
G T Horton (C)	42,543	22.8%
Mrs S Leyland (Grn)	25,677	13.7%
J A D Ridgway (SLD)	10,352	5.5%
Lab majority	65,901	35.2%

Total vote 187,016 (35.3%). No change.

1984: Total vote 159,719 (30.8%). Lab 88,464 (55.4%); C 44,291 (27.7%); L/All 26,964 (16.9%). Lab majority 44,173 (27.7%).

1987 Total vote: 396,903 (76.3%). Lab 196,865 (49.6%); C 126,653 (31.9%); L/All 41,455 (10.4%); SDP/All 30,383 (7.7%); Others 1,547 (0.4%). Lab maj 70,212 (17.7%).

YORKSHIRE WEST

Electorate 570,228 (560,190)

Batley and Spen; Bradford North; Bradford South; Bradford West; Calder Valley; Halifax; Keighley; Shipley.

*B H Seal (Lab)	108,644	49.9%
G T Hall (C)	70,717	32.5%
N Parrott (Grn)	28,308	13.0%
P Wrigley (SLD)	9,765	4.5%
Lab majority	37,927	17.4%

Total vote 217,434 (38.1%). No change.

1984: Total vote 180,373 (32.2%). Lab 86,259 (47.8%); C 65,405 (36.2%); SDP/All 28,709 (15.9%). Lab majority 20,854 (11.6%).

1987 Total vote: 431,877 (76.6%). C 184,298 (42.7%); Lab 167,718 (38.8%); SDP/All 40,552 (9.4%); L/All 38,113 (8.8%); Others 1,196 (0.3%). C maj 16,580 (3.8%).

SCOTLAND

GLASGOW

Electorate: 491,905 (518,178)

The Glasgow seats of Cathcart, Central, Garscadden, Govan, Hillhead, Maryhill, Pollok, Provan, Shettleston, and Springburn.

*Mrs J O Buchan (Lab)	107,818	55.4%
A Brophy (SNP)	48,586	24.9%
Mrs A K Bates (C)	20,761	10.7%
D L Spaven (Grn)	12,229	6.3%
J Morrison (SLD)	3,887	1.9%
D Chalmers (Comm)	1,164	0.6%
J Simons (ICP)	193	0.1%
Lab majority	59,232	30.4%

Total vote 194,638 (39.6%). No change.

1984: Total vote 153,620 (29.6%). Lab 91,015 (59.3%); C 25,282 (16.5%); L/All 20,867 (13.6%); SNP 16,456 (10.7%). Lab majority 65,733 (42.8%).

1987 Total vote: 359,357 (70.5%). Lab 224,810 (62.6%); C 45,684 (12.7%); SNP 37,431 (10.4%); SDP/All 30,391 (8.5%); L/All 18,779 (5.2%); Others 2,262 (0.6%). Lab maj 179,126 (49.8%).

HIGHLANDS AND ISLANDS

Electorate: 317,129 (307,265)

Argyll and Bute; Caithness and Sutherland; Inverness, Nairn and Lochaber; Moray; Ross, Cromarty and Skye; Orkney and Shetland; Western Isles.

*Mrs W M Ewing (SNP)	66,297	51.6%
Sir Albert McQuarrie (C)	21,602	16.8%
N MacAskill (Lab)	17,848	13.9%
M Gregson (Grn)	12,199	9.5%
N Michison (SLD)	10,644	8.3%
SNP majority	44,695	34.8%

Total vote 128,590 (40.5%). No change.

1984: Total vote 118,034 (38.4%). SNP 49,410 (41.9%); L/All 33,133 (28.1%); C 18,847 (16.0%); Lab 16,644 (14.1%). SNP majority 16,277 (13.8%).

1987 Total vote: 228,187 (72.3%). C 56,687 (24.9%); L/All 44,753 (19.6%); SNP 44,372 (19.4%) Lab 43,306 (19.0%); SDP/All 34,566 (15.2%); Others 4,503 (2.0%). C maj 11,934 (5.2%).

LOTHIANS

Electorate: 527,785 (526,068)

The Edinburgh seats of Central, East, Leith, Pentlands, South and West; Linlithgow; Livingston; Midlothian.

*D W Martin (Lab)	90,840	41.3%
Mrs C M Blight (C)	52,014	23.6%
J Smith (SNP)	44,935	20.4%
R C M Harper (Green)	22,983	10.4%
K Leadbetter (SLD)	9,222	4.2%
Lab majority	38,826	17.6%

Total vote 219,994 (41.7%). No change.

1984: Total vote 185,581 (35.3%). Lab 74,989 (40.4%); C 49,065 (26.4%); SDP/All 36,636 (19.7%); SNP 22,331 (12.0%); Ecol 2,560 (1.4%). Lab majority 25,924 (14.0%).

1987 Total vote: 397,858 (75.1%). Lab 162,096 (40.7%); C 108,274 (27.2%); SDP/All 45,955 (11.6%); SNP 41,943 (10.6%); L/All 38,146 (9.6%); Others 1,444 (0.4%). Lab maj 53,822 (13.5%).

SCOTLAND MID AND FIFE

Electorate: 539,276 (528,529)

Clackmannan; Dunfermline East; Dunfermline West; Falkirk East; Falkirk West; Fife Central; Fife North East; Kirkcaldy; Perth and Kinross; Stirling.

*A Falconer (Lab)	102,246	46.1%
K W MacAskill (SNP)	50,089	22.6%
A Christie (C)	46,505	20.9%
G Moreton (Grn)	14,165	6.4%
M Black (SLD)	8,857	3.9%
Lab majority	52,157	23.5%

Total vote 221,862 (41.1%). No change.

1984: Total vote 187,641 (35.5%). Lab 80,038 (42.7%); C 52,872 (28.2%); SNP 30,511 (16.3%); SDP/All 24,220 (12.9%). Lab majority 27,166 (14.5%).

1987 Total vote: 410,063 (76.3%). Lab 176,014 (43.0%); C 102,720 (25.0%); SNP 59,247 (14.5%); L/All 48,091 (11.7%); SDP/All 23,991 (5.9%). Lab maj 73,294 (17.9%).

99

SCOTLAND NORTH EAST

Electorate: 559,275 (548,711)

Aberdeen North; Aberdeen South; Angus East; Banff and Buchan; Dundee East; Dundee West; Gordon; Kincardine and Deeside; Tayside North.

H McGubbin (Lab)	65,348	30.7%
Dr A Macartney (SNP)	62,735	29.4%
*J L C Provan (C)	56,835	26.7%
M Hill (Grn)	15,584	7.3%
S Horner (SLD)	12,704	5.9%
Lab majority	2,613	1.2%

Total vote 213,206 (38.1%). **Lab gain from C.**

1984: Total vote 157,395 (28.7%). C 53,809 (34.2%); Lab 44,648 (28.4%); SNP 33,448 (21.3%); SDP/All 25,490 (16.2%). C majority 9,161 (5.8%).

1987 Total vote: 411,627 (73.1%). C 125,386 (30.5%); Lab 110,171 (26.8%); SNP 93,538 (22.7%); L/All 51,489 (12.5%); SDP/All 30,436 (7.4%); Others 607 (0.1%). C maj 15,215 (3.7%).

SCOTLAND SOUTH

Electorate: 497,108 (484,760)

Ayr; Carrick, Cumnock and Doon Valley; Clydesdale; Cunninghame South; Dumfries; Galloway and Upper Nithsdale; East Lothian; Roxburgh and Berwickshire; Tweeddale, Ettrick and Lauderdale.

A Smith (Lab)	81,366	39.8%
*A H Hutton (C)	65,673	32.2%
M Brown (SNP)	35,155	17.2%
J Button (Grn)	11,658	5.7%
J E McKercher (SLD)	10,368	5.0%
Lab majority	15,693	7.7%

Total vote 204,220 (41.1%). **Lab gain from C.**

1984: Total vote 164,389 (33.9%). C 60,843 (37.0%); Lab 57,706 (35.1%); L/All 23,598 (14.4%); SNP 22,242 (13.5%). C majority 3137 (1.9%).

1987 Total vote: 381,016 (77.3%). Lab 138,420 (36.3%); C 118,120 (31.0%); L/All 57,202 (15.0%); SNP 46,165 (12.1%); SDP/All 20,079 (5.3%); Others 1,030 (0.3%). Lab maj 20,300 (5.3%).

WALES

WALES MID AND WEST

Electorate: 553,711 (533,644)

Brecon and Radnor; Carmarthen; Ceredigion and Pembroke North; Gower; Llanelli; Neath; Pembroke; Swansea East; Swansea West.

*Rev D R Morris (Lab)	105,670	46.9%
O J Williams (C)	53,758	23.9%
Ms B I McPake (Grn)	29,852	13.2%
Dr P J S Williams (PC)	26,063	11.6%
G A Sinclair (SLD)	10,031	4.6%
Lab majority	51,912	23.0%

Total vote 225,374 (40.7%). **No change.**

1984: Total vote 214,586 (40.2%). Lab 89,362 (41.6%); C 52,910 (24.7%); L/All 35,168 (16.4%); PlC 32,880 (15.3%); Ecol 4,266 (2.0%). Lab majority 36,452 (16.9%).

1987 Total vote: 430,532 (79.3%). Lab 186,710 (43.4%); C 120,707 (28.0%); L/All 67,137 (15.6%); PlC 33,227 (7.7%); SDP/All 20,980 (4.9%); Others 1,771 (0.4%). Lab maj 66,003 (15.3%).

STRATHCLYDE EAST

Electorate: 500,935 (498,458)

Cumbernauld and Kilsyth; East Kilbride; Glasgow Rutherglen; Hamilton; Kilmarnock and Loudoun; Monklands East; Monklands West; Motherwell North; Motherwell South.

*K D Collins (Lab)	109,170	56.2%
G A Leslie (SNP)	48,853	25.1%
M Dutt (C)	22,233	11.4%
A Whitelaw (Grn)	9,749	5.0%
G Lait (SLD)	4,276	2.2%
Lab majority	60,317	31.0%

Total vote 194,281 (38.8%). **No change.**

1984: Total vote 154,862 (31.1%). Lab 90,792 (58.6%); SNP 27,330 (17.7%); C 24,857 (16.1%); L/All 11,883 (7.7%). Lab majority 63,462 (40.9%).

1987 Total vote: 387,024 (77.3%). Lab 222,872 (57.6%); C 55,215 (14.3%); SNP 53,122 (13.7%); SDP/All 31,495 (8.1%); L/All 24,097 (6.2%); Others 223 (0.1%). Lab maj 167,657 (43.3%).

STRATHCLYDE WEST

Electorate: 499,616 (499,162)

Clydebank and Milngavie; Cunninghame North; Dumbarton; Eastwood; Greenock and Port Glasgow; Paisley North; Paisley South; Renfrew West and Inverclyde; Strathkelvin and Bearsden.

*H R McMahon (Lab)	89,627	42.6%
C M Campbell (SNP)	50,036	23.8%
S J Robin (C)	45,872	21.8%
G Campbell (Grn)	16,461	7.8%
D J Herbison (SLD)	8,098	3.9%
Lab majority	39,591	18.8%

Total vote 210,094 (42.1%). **No change.**

1984: Total vote 172,251 (34.5%). Lab 70,234 (40.8%); C 47,196 (27.4%); SNP 28,866 (16.8%); SDP/All 25,955 (15.0%). Lab majority 23,038 (13.4%).

1987 Total vote: 392,676 (78.1%). Lab 180,443 (45.0%); C 101,005 (25.7%); SDP/All 45,920 (11.7%); SNP 40,655 (10.4%); L/All 24,653 (6.3%). Lab maj 79,438 (20.2%).

WALES NORTH

Electorate: 546,071 (516,153)

Alyn and Deeside; Caernarfon; Clwyd North West; Clwyd South West; Conwy; Delyn; Meirionnydd Nant Conwy; Montgomery; Wrexham; Ynys Mon.

J Wilson (Lab)	83,638	33.1%
*Miss B A Brookes (C)	79,178	31.3%
Dr D E Thomas (PC)	64,120	25.4%
P H W Adams (Grn)	15,832	6.3%
R K Marshall (SLD)	10,056	3.9%
Lab majority	4,460	1.8%

Total vote 252,824 (46.3%). **Lab gain from C.**

1984: Total vote 218,885 (42.4%). C 69,139 (31.6%); SDP/All 56,861 (26.0%); Lab 54,768 (25.0%); Plc 38,117 (17.4%). C majority 12,278 (5.6%).

1987 Total vote: 423,815 (79.7%). C 153,084 (36.1%); Lab 124,257 (29.3%); PlC 62,208 (14.7%); L/All 59,538 (14.1%); SDP/All 24,728 (5.8%). C maj 28,827 (6.8%).

100

WALES SOUTH

Electorate: 526,058 (509,434)

Bridgend; the Cardiff seats of Central, North, South and Penarth, and West; Ogmore; Pontypridd; Vale of Glamorgan.

W David (Lab)	108,550	54.7%
A R Taylor (C)	45,993	23.2%
G P Jones (Grn)	25,993	13.1%
P J Keelan (PC)	10,727	5.4%
P K Verma (SLD)	4,037	2.0%
D A T Thomas (SDP)	3,153	1.6%
Lab majority	62,557	31.6%

Total vote 198,453 (37.7%). **No change.**

1984: Total vote 195,403 (38.4%). Lab 99,936 (57.1%); C 55,678 (28.5%); L/All 26,588 (13.6%); Plc 13,201 (6.8%). Lab majority 44,258 (22.7%).

1987 Total vote: 360,680 (78.6%). Lab 161,122 (44.7%); C 125,015 (34.7%); SDP/All 46,067 (12.8%); L/All 18,962 (5.3%); PIC 8,862 (2.5%); Others 652 (0.2%). Lab maj 36,107 (10.0%).

WALES SOUTH EAST

Electorate: 568,811 (565,739)

Blaenau Gwent; Caerphilly; Cynon Valley; Islwyn; Merthyr Tydfil and Rhymney; Monmouth; Newport East; Newport West; Rhondda; Torfaen.

*L T Smith (Lab)	138,872	64.3%
R J Young (C)	30,384	14.1%
M J Witherden (Grn)	27,869	12.9%
Ms J Evans Plaid Cymru	14,152	6.6%
P Nicholls-Jones (SLD)	4,661	2.2%
Lab majority	108,488	50.2%

Total vote 215,938 (38.0%). **No change.**

1984: Total vote 215,438 (38.1%). Lab 131,916 (61.2%); C 36,359 (16.9%); SDP/All 28,330 (13.1%); PIC 18,833 (8.7%). Lab majority 95,557 (44.3%).

1987 Total vote: 442,408 (78.3%). Lab 265,994 (60.1%); C 96,616 (21.8%); SDP/All 31,028 (7.0%); L/All 29,273 (6.6%); PIC 18,178 (4.1%); Others 1,319 (0.3%). Lab maj 169,378 (38.3%).

Abbreviations

Most frequently used abbreviations in the biographies of MEPs are as follows:

AHA	Area Health Authority	Lab	Labour
B	Born	Ldr	Leader
BC	Borough Council	LSE	London School of Economics
Bd	Board	MBC	Metropolitan Borough Council
CC	County Council	Mbr	Member
Chmn	Chairman	MDC	Metropolitan District Council
Cl	Council	MEP	Member of European Parliament
Cllr	Councillor	N	North
CLP	Constituency Labour Party	Nat	National
Cmte	Committee	NE	North East
CND	Campaign for Nuclear Disarmament	NI	Northern Ireland
		NW	North West
Coll	College	Parly	Parliamentary
Cons	Conservative	PPS	Parliamentary Private Secretary
DC	District Council	Pres	President
Dept	Department	Pty	Party
E	East	Reg	Regional
EC	European Community	S	South
Ed	Education	Sch	School
EP	European Parliament	SE	South East
Exec	Executive	Sec	Secretary
FCO	Foreign and Commonwealth Office	SW	South West
Fed	Federation	TC	Town Council
Govt	Government	Tech	Technical or Technology
Gp	Group	Treas	Treasurer
GS	Grammar School	Univ	University
HS	High School	Vice Pres	Vice President
Inst	Institute	W	West
Jt	Joint	WEU	Western European Union

101

The European Parliament

The biographical information on members of the European Parliament has been compiled from information supplied to *The Times* by the Directorate-General of Information and Public Relations and its offices in the EC member states, the Secretariats and Press Officers of the Political Groups of the Parliament, and by the successful candidates and their party headquarters in the United Kingdom. Occupations and political group memberships are those at the time of election to the Parliament. Addresses and telephone numbers were those published at the July 1989 plenary session in Strasbourg, and for some MEPs, especially among the new ones, are subject to change.

All MEPs can also be contacted at the EP political group offices, 97-113 rue Belliard, 1040 Brussels, at the Palais de l'Europe in Strasbourg during plenary sessions, the various offices of the European Parliament in the member states (see page 288 for addresses and telephone numbers), and through their political party headquarters in their member states.

ADAM, GORDON
UK, Northumbria, Soc (Lab)

Mr Gordon Adam, a mining engineer with NCB, 1959-79, was first elected to EP in 1979; since then been a vice-chmn of Cmte on Energy, Research and Technology; mbr, Cmte on Petitions, 1989- . Contested Tynemouth, 1966 election, and Berwick-upon-Tweed in Nov 1973 by-election and Feb 1974. Mbr, Whitley Bay BC, 1971-74; North Tyneside MBC, 1973-80 (chmn, 1973-74; mayor, 1974-75; dep ldr, 1975-80); Northern Economic Planning Cl, 1974-79; Northern Arts General Cl, 1975- . B Mar 28 1934. Vice-pres, Tynemouth branch, UNA; Pres, Northumberland area cmte of Physically Handicapped Able Bodied. Hon Pres, Felling male voice choir. BACM.

Addresses: 10 Coach Road, Wallsend, Tyne and Wear NE28 6JA. Tel: (091) 263 5838. 2 Queen's Road, Whitley Bay, Tyne and Wear NE26 3BJ. Tel: (091) 252 8616.

AGLIETTA, SIGNORA MARIA ADELAIDE
Italy, Verts (Verdi Arcob)

Signora Maria Adelaide Aglietta sits in the Italian Chamber of Deputies as mbr of Radical Party and Federal Europe Gp. Elected to EP in 1989 on list of Verdi Arcobaleno per l'Europa. (Green Rainbow for Europe). Became mbr, Cmte on Institutional Affairs and Cmte on External Economic Relations. B Jun 4 1940.

Address: Gruppo Federalista Europeo, Camera dei Deputati, Via Uffici del Vicario 21, 00186 Roma. Tel: (06) 678 08 04.

AINARDI, MME SYLVIANE
France, CG (PCF)

Mme Sylviane Ainardi, teacher, was elected to EP in 1989 and joined Cmte on Regional Policy and Regional Planning. Mbr, Midi-Pyrenees Regional Council; municipal councillor at Toulouse; federal first secretary of PCF at Haute-Garonne. B 1948.

Address: Comité Central du Parti Communiste Français, 2 place du Colonel Fabien, 75940 Paris Cedex 19.

ALAVANOS, ALEXANDROS
Greece, CG (SAP/Comm)

Mr Alexandros Alavanos was first elected to EP in 1984. After 1989 elections joined Cmte on Environment, Public Health and Consumer Protection. Former mbr, Cmte on Regional Policy and Regional Planning; former vice-chmn, Cmte on Social Affairs and Employment. B May 22 1950.

Addresses: Kentriki Epitropi tou KKE, Leoforos Irakleiou 145, 142 31 Nea Ionia. Tel: (1) 25 22 591. Eleftheriou Venizelou 49 a, 152 36 Palaia Pendeli. Tel: (1) 80 44 480.

ALBER, SIEGBERT
Germany, EPP (CDU)

Herr Siegbert Alber was elected a Vice-President of the EP in 1984 and was re-elected as such in 1987 and 1989; mbr, Cmte on Environment, Public Health and Consumer Protection and Cmte on Institutional Affairs. MEP since 1977; first elected 1979; a former vice-chmn of EPP Gp; has served on gp bureau. Chaired EP cmte of inquiry into treatment of toxic and dangerous substances by EC and its mbr states. Mbr, Bundestag, 1969-80; assemblies of Cl of Europe and WEU, 1970-77. Chmn, Stuttgart CDU, 1971-79. B Jul 27 1936. Read law and became junior legal official and public prosecutor.

Address: Gammertinger Strasse 35, 7000 Stuttgart 80. Tel: (0711) 72 54 45.

103

ALEMANN, FRAU MECHTILD VON
Germany, LDR (FDP)

Frau Mechtild von Alemann returned to EP in 1989 having been an elected MEP, 1979-84, when she served on Cmte on Transport and was a vice-chair of the EP cmte of inquiry into situation of women in Europe. Librarian. After 1989 elections became a vice-chair of LDR Gp and mbr, Cmte on Transport and Tourism. Secretary-General Federation of European Liberal and Democratic Parties and previously on its executive cmte. Former mbr, North Rhine-Westphalian regional assembly, which she joined in 1975. Was responsible for European affairs in North Rhine-Westphalian FDP. B Jan 29 1937.

Address: Kaiserswerther Markt 10, 4000 Dusseldorf.

ALEXANDRE, JEAN-MARIE
France, Soc (PS)

M. Jean-Marie Alexandre became an MEP during the outgoing Parliament; re-elected 1989 and appointed a vice-chmn, EP Cmte on Regional Policy and Regional Planning; former mbr, EP Cmte on Youth, Culture, Education, Information and Sport. Mbr, Nord-Pas-de-Calais Regional Cl; has also been municipal councillor at Souchez, Pas-de-Calais. Teacher. B Nov 25 1946.

Addresses:4 rue Beffara, 62000 Arras. Tel: 21 23 47 35.
35 rue Carnot, 62153 Souchez. Tel: 21 45 19 95.

ALLEGRE, CLAUDE
France, Soc (PS)

M.Claude Allegre, university professor and scientist, was elected to EP in 1989 joining Cmte on Energy, Research and Technology. Special adviser to M Lionel Jospin, Minister of State for Education. Mbr, municipal council at Lodeve (Herault). B 1937.

Address: 88 boulevard Saint Germain, 75007 Paris.

ALLIOT-MARIE, MME MICHÈLE
France, RDE (RPR)

Mme Michèle Alliot-Marie, mbr of French National Assembly and Secretary of State for Education, 1986-88, was elected to EP in 1989 on UDF/RPR list; became mbr, Political Affairs Cmte. Deputy for Pyrenées-Atlantiques; town councillor for Biarritz. University professor. B 1946.

Address: RPR, 123 rue de Lille, 75007 Paris.

ALVAREZ DE PAZ, JOSÉ
Spain, Soc (PSOE)

Señor José Alvarez De Paz has been an MEP since 1986; elected in 1987 and re-elected 1989 when he rejoined EP Cmte on Social Affairs, Employment and Working Environment. Former mbr of regional government of Castilla-Leon; mbr, Spanish national Parliament. B Nov 19 1935.

Addresses: Genral Cives, 16, entreplanta, Ponferrada. c/los Claveles, 1, 9°, Ponferrada. Tel: (87) 41 29 25/41 20 02/40 35 17.

AMARAL, RUI
Portugal, LDR (PSD)

Senhor Rui Amaral was a Vice-President of EP, 1987-89; first elected to EP in 1987 and was a vice-chmn, LDR Gp. After 1989 elections became chmn, Cmte on Transport and Tourism; former mbr, Cmte on Budgets. B Sep 25 1943.

Addresses: Rua Augusto Lessa 153, 4°-D, 4200 Porto. Tel: (2) 40 26 05. Palacio di S Bento, Largo das Cortes, 1296 Lisboa Codex. Tel: (1) 66 01 41.

AMENDOLA, GIANFRANCO
Italy, Verts (Verde)

Sgr Gianfranco Amendola, university professor, magistrate and journalist, was elected to EP in 1989 and joined Cmte on Environment, Public Health and Consumers. National delegate to World Wildlife Fund and mbr, executive, League for the Environment. B Apr 8 1942.

Address: Via Raffaele Cappelli 67, 00191 Roma. Tel: (06) 327 67 13.

ANASTASSOPOULOS, GEORGIOS
Greece, EPP (ND)

Mr Georgios Anastassopoulos was elected a Vice-President of EP in July 1989. Elected MEP in 1984; chmn, Cmte on Transport, 1984-89; mbr, Cmte on Legal Affairs and Citizen's Rights, 1989- . Journalist. In 1978 was first Greek appointed to Cl of International Federation of Journalists; former President, Athens Union of Journalists. Worked for many newspapers and been general manager, Athens News Agency. Acting Secretary of State attached to President's Office in 1977 and 1981 caretaker governments. B Sep 25 1935; ed Athens Coll and Faculty of Law; graduate in law and European law.

Address: Levidou 13, Nea Erythrea, 14671 Athina. Tel: (1) 801 25 09.

d'ANCONA, MEVR HEDY
Netherlands, Soc (PvdA)

Mevr Hedy d'Ancona became chair of EP Cmte on Social Affairs, Employment and Working Environment after 1989 elections; mbr of cmte since first elected MEP in 1984; chaired Cmte on Women's Rights in outgoing Parliament and is still a mbr of cmte. Former mbr of First Chamber; was Secretary of State for Social Affairs and Employment. Former lecturer in planning. B Oct 1 1937.

Address: Amstel 274, 1017 AM   Amsterdam. Tel: (020) 25 65 80.

ANDREWS, NIALL
Ireland, RDE (FF)

Mr Niall Andrews was first elected to the EP in 1984, serving on the Cmte on Development and Cooperation in outgoing Parliament and rejoining it after 1989 elections. Mbr, Dail (Irish Parliament) since 1977. Former television programmes officer with RTE. Minister of State, Dept of Environment, Oct to Dec 1982. Delegate, Cl of Europe, 1981- . B Aug 19 1937.

Address: 48 Westbrook Road, Dundrum, Dublin 14. Tel: (01) 98 47 69.

ANGER, DIDIER
France, Verts (Verts)

M.Didier Anger, teacher, was elected to EP in 1989; became mbr, Cmte on Energy, Research and Technology. Mbr, Basse-Normandie regional council. Named by regional press as "best representative of the region", he headed list of Les Verts for European elections in 1984. For a long time has opposed nuclear developments in Lower Normandie and elsewhere. B 1939.

Address: Route d'etang Val, 50340 Les Pieux. Tel: 33 52 45 59.

ANTONY, BERNARD
France, DR (FN)

M. Bernard Antony, known as Romain Marie, was first elected to EP in 1984; became mbr, Cmte on Regional Policy and Regional Planning after 1989 elections; former mbr, Cmte on External Economic Relations. Regional councillor for Midi-Pyrenees; chmn, Christianity-Solidarity cmtes; founder of *Present.* Company director; former teacher. B Nov 28 1944.

Addresses: 40 rue de Tivoli, 67000 Strasbourg. 61 avenue Lucien Coudert, 81100 Castres.

ARBELOA MURU, VICTOR MANUEL
Spain, Soc (PSOE)

Señor Victor Manuel Arbeloa Muru became an MEP in 1986; elected in 1987 and re-elected 1989. Has served on Committees on Regional Policy and Regional Planning and on Petitions. Former Spanish senator and former president of the regional parliament of Navarra. Theologian and historian; writer. B Sep 1 1936.

Addresses: Apartado de Correos 384, 31080 Pamplona. Vuelta del Castillo, 5 11°-A, 31007 Pamplona. Tel: (48) 26 59 18.

ARIAS CAÑETE, MIGUEL
Spain, EPP (PP)

Señor Miguel Arias Cañete has been an MEP since Jan 1986; first elected 1987; a vice-chmn, EP Cmte on Budgetary Control, 1989- ; mbr, Cmte on Budgets. State lawyer in Exchequer delegations for Jerez de la Frontera and Cadiz. Former mbr, Andalusian regional assembly. Senator for Cadiz, 1982-86; chmn, Senate Budget Cmte, 1982-86. Head of Studies and Programmes Department, Alianza Popular. Civil law lecturer, Law Department, Jerez de la Frontera, 1979-82. President, Alianza Popular, Cadiz. B Feb 24 1950.

Addresses: Sevilla 41-43, Jerez de la Frontera, Cadiz. Tel: 32 18 55. Santo Domingo 11 10°N, Jerez de la Frontera, Cadiz. Tel: 34 36 85.

AULAS, MME MARIE-CHRISTINE
France, Verts (Verts)

Mme Marie-Christine Aulas, journalist, specialising in Near and Middle East affairs having spent much of her life in the Third World. Elected an MEP in 1989, joining Cmte on Development and Cooperation and becoming one its vice-chairs. B 1945 in Oran, Algeria, she moved to France in 1962 and lives in Paris.

Address: 16 rue Vandrezanne, 75013 Paris. Tel: 45 88 86 17.

AUTANT-LARA, CLAUDE
France, DR (FN)

M.Claude Autant-Lara, as the oldest elected MEP, presided at the opening of the new Parliament. His speech was marked by a walk-out and other demonstrations. Film director and film dubber. Former president of theatre and cinema organizations including film technician trade unions. Became mbr, Cmte on Youth, Culture, Education, the Media and Sport. B Aug 5 1901.

Address: 7 Calade St Roch, 06410 Biot.

AVGERINOS, PARASKEVAS
Greece, Soc (PASOK)

Mr Paraskevas Avgerinos, first elected to EP in 1984, served on Cmte on Regional Policy and Regional Planning, 1984-89, being a cmte vice-chmn, 1987-89; became mbr, Institutional Affairs Cmte and Cmte on Environment,Public Health and Consumer Protection, in 1989; former mbr, Cmte on Rules of Procedure, Verification of Credentials and Immunities. Founder mbr of PASOK (Pan-Hellenic Socialist Movement) and mbr of its central cmte. A former Minister of Health. Doctor. B Aug 19 1927.

Address: Knossou 10, 175 64 P. Faliro. Tel: (1) 942 64 20.

BAGET BOZZO, GIANNI
Italy, Soc (PSI)

Sgr Gianni Baget Bozzo, priest, theologian and journalist, was first elected to EP in 1984; re-elected 1989 when he joined Political Affairs Cmte; mbr, Cmte on Development and Cooperation in outgoing Parliament. Founder and director of theological magazine *Renovatio.* B Mar 8 1925.

Address: Via Corsica 9, 16128 Genova. Tel: (010) 56 44 83.

109

BALFE, RICHARD
UK, London South Inner, Soc (Lab)

Mr Richard Balfe joined EP Cmtes on Political Affairs and on Institutional Affairs after 1989 elections; mbr, Cmte on Development and Cooperation, 1984-89; former secretary, British Labour MEPs. Elected to EP 1979. Contested Paddington South, 1970 election. Chmn, SE Branch, Co-op Wholesale Soc, 1987- ; director, Royal Arsenal Co-op Soc and associated companies, 1978-85, being political sec, 1973-79. Mbr, GLC, 1973-77. B May 14 1944. Mbr, exec, London Lab Pty, 1973- .

Addresses: 132 Powis Street, London SE18 6JN. Tel: (01) 855 2128. 53 Chatsworth Way, London SE27 9NH. Tel: (01) 761 2510.

BANDRES MOLET, JUAN MARIA
Spain, Verts (IP)

Señor Juan María Bandres Molet was elected to EP in 1989; previously MEP 1986-87 when he was on Cmte on Legal Affairs and Citizens' Rights. In 1989 joined Cmte on Institutional Affairs; also became treasurer of Green Gp. Former senator and mbr, Spanish national Parliament. President of the party *Eusdkadiko Ezquerra*. B Feb 12 1932.

Address: Okendo 10-5°, 20004 San Sebastion.

BANOTTI, MRS MARY
Ireland, EPP (FG)

Mrs Mary Banotti was elected to the EP in 1984 and is mbr, Cmte on Environment, Public Health and Consumer Protection; after 1989 elections also became a vice-chair, Cmte on Youth, Culture, Education, the Media and Sport; was mbr, cmte of inquiry into drugs. Social worker and broadcaster; contributor to newspapers and magazines on social welfare issues. Worked as nurse in Kenya; chairs treatment centre for alcoholism in Dublin; co-founder of hostel for battered wives. Assistant Secretary, Dublin Central Fine Gael constituency. B May 29 1939.

Address: 8 Cambridge Avenue, Ringsend, Dublin 4. Tel: (1) 68 0341

BARÓN CRESPO, ENRIQUE
Spain, Soc (PSOÉ)

Señor Enrique Barón Crespo was elected President of EP in Jul 1989; a Vice-President of EP, 1987-89. MEP since 1986 and first elected in 1987; mbr, Cmte on Budgets, in outgoing Parliament; led Spanish delegation in Socialist Gp being on its bureau and a former vice-chmn. Spanish Minister for Transport, Tourism and Communications, 1982-85; mbr, Cortes (Spanish Parliament), 1977-87. President, International European Movement, since 1987. B Mar 27 1944; qualified in law and economics at Madrid Univ. Between 1966 and 1970 taught land economy at National Institute of Agriculture, Vallodolid, and economics at Madrid Univ.

Address: Oficina de informacion del Parlamento Europeo, c/Fernanflor n° 4, 28014 Madrid. Tel: (1) 429 02 38.

BARROS MOURA, JOSÉ
Portugal, CG (PCP)

Senhor José Barros Moura became an MEP in 1986; first elected in 1987 and re-elected 1989. Was mbr, EP Cmte on Social Affairs, Employment and Working Environment, in outgoing Parliament and rejoined it after 1989 elections. Lawyer; university lecturer. B Oct 8 1944.

Addresses: Partido Comunista Portugues, Rua Soeire Pereira Gomes, 1699 Lisboa Codex. Tel: (1) 77 91 42. Telefax: (01) 76 91 26. Rua dos Soeiros 327 5°, 1500 Lisboa. Tel: (1) 726 28 84.

BARTON, ROGER
UK, Sheffield, Soc (Lab)

Mr Roger Barton, secretary of Sheffield District Lab Pty and Sheffield TUC since 1981, was elected to EP in 1989 and joined Cmte on Economic and Monetary Affairs and Industrial Policy. Worked as an engineering fitter with Davy United, now Davy McKee, until 1981. Mbr, Sheffield City Cl, 1972- . Founding activist within local authorities' nuclear free zones movement, until recently chairing UK and international steering cmtes. B Jan 1 1945; ed in Sheffield primary sch; sec modern sch; night sch and day release. AEU, becoming branch sec and district cmte mbr.

Address: 50 Hartley Brok Avenue, Sheffield S5 0HN.

BARZACH, MME MICHÈLE
France, RDE (RPR)

Mme Michèle Barzach, doctor, deputy for Paris and Deputy Mayor of Paris, was elected to EP in 1989; became mbr, Cmte on Youth, Culture, Education, the Media and Sport. Former minister with responsibilities for health and family affairs. B 1943.

Address: RPR, 123 rue de Lille, 75007 Paris.

BARZANTI, ROBERTO
Italy, EUL (PCI)

Sgr Roberto Barzanti was first elected to EP in 1984; re-elected 1989 and became chmn of Cmte on Youth, Culture, Education, the Media and Sport; in outgoing Parliament was on Cmte on Legal Affairs and Citizens, and was a vice-chmn, Cmte on Rules of Procedure, the Verification of Credentials and Immunities. Has served as Mayor (1969-74) and deputy mayor of Siena; from 1974-79 was regional assessor for Tuscany. Student of literature and history. B Jan 24 1939.

Address: Via di Citta 85, 53100 Siena. Tel: (0577) 40444

BAUR, CHARLES
France, LDR (UDF/RPR)

M. Charles Baur became an MEP during the 1984-89 Parliament; re-elected 1989. Former mbr, Cmte on Transport. Managing director. President, Regional Cl of Picardy. B Dec 20 1929.

Addresses: Comet SA, BP 100, 27 av. Etienne Audibert, 60304 Senlis Cedex. Tel: 44 53 62 22. Telex: 14 00 29. 9 rue Catulle Mendès, 75017 Paris.

BEAZLEY, CHRISTOPHER
UK, Cornwall and Plymouth, ED (C)

Mr Christopher Beazley was first elected to EP for this seat in 1984. A vice-chmn, EP Cmte on Transport and Tourism, 1989- ; Cmte on Regional Policy and Regional Planning Cmte, 1984-89; former mbr, Institutional Affairs Cmte; mbr, bureau, ED gp, 1988- ; deputy whip, ED gp, 1986-87, and in 1986 was mbr, EDG rural policy working pty. Was Nuffield Research Fellow, School of European Studies, Sussex Univ. Vice-chmn, Lewes and Eastbourne branch, European Movement, 1980-83. Mbr, Wealden DC, 1979-83. B Sep 5 1952. Son of Mr Peter Beazley, MEP for Bedfordshire South.

Address: "The Grange", Devoran, nr Truro, Cornwall TR3 6PF. Tel: (0872) 862132 and (0736) 63664.

BEAZLEY, PETER
UK, Bedfordshire South, ED (C)

Mr Peter Beazley, MEP for Bedfordshire, 1979-84, first won this seat in 1984. A vice-chmn, EP Economic and Monetary Affairs and Industrial Policy Cmte, 1984-89; still mbr of cmte; mbr, bureau, ED gp, 1982-83. With ICI from 1947 to 1978, 17 years being spent abroad in Frankfurt, Brussels, Portugal, S America and S Africa; was manager, general manager, divisional bd director, vice-chmn and managing director of associated companies. Research Fellow, Royal Inst of International Affairs. B Jun 9 1922; ed Highgate Sch; St John's Coll, Oxford. His son, Christopher, is Cons MEP for Cornwall and Plymouth.

Address: "Rest Harrow", 14 The Combe, Ratton, Eastbourne, Sussex BN20 9DB. Tel: (0323) 504460.

BEIRÔCO, LUIS
Portugal, EPP (CDS)

Senhor Luis Beirôco was Chef de Cabinet at Ministry of Commerce and Tourism, 1978. Secretary-General of CDS. Former deputy and former mbr, North Atlantic Assembly. Elected to EP in 1989 and joined Cmte on Institutional Affairs; was elected mbr, 1986-87, serving on Cmte on Economic and Monetary Affairs and Industrial Policy. Lawyer; business manager. B Jul 4 1939.

Addresses: Av. da Igreja, 63-7°E, 1700 Lisboa. Tel: (1) 77 93 87.

113

BELO, SRA MARIA
Portugal, Soc (PS)

Sra Maria Belo became an elected MEP in 1988 and served on EP Cmte on Development and Cooperation; after 1989 elections she became a vice-chair of that cmte and also mbr, Cmte on Women's Rights; former mbr, Cmte on Regional Policy and Regional Planning. Psychoanalyst. B Apr 27 1938.

Address: R.Guilherme Braga, 1-2° Dt., 1100 Lisboa. Tel: (1) 87 25 88.

BENOIT, JEAN-PAUL
France, Soc (PS)

M. Jean-Paul Benoit, director-general of forecasting organization, became an elected MEP in 1989 and joined EP Cmte on External Economic Relations. Delegate to Association of Democrats. B 1936.

Address: Association des Democrates, 5 rue Chaillot, 75016 Paris. Tel: 45 61 07 01.

BERNARD-REYMOND, PIERRE
France, EPP (Centre)

M. Pierre Bernard-Reymond became elected MEP in 1989 joining EP Cmte on Economic and Monetary Affairs and Industrial Policy; first elected to EP in 1984 and before leaving served on Political Affairs Cmte and was a vice-chmn, EP-Canada interparliamentary delegation. Foreign Secretary with responsibility for European Affairs, 1978-81; Hautes Alps deputy (UDF), 1971-81; vice-chmn, Hautes-Alpes Regional Cl; Mayor of Gap (Hautes Alps); previously Deputy Mayor. Vice-chmn of CDS. B Jan 16 1944.

Address: 11 Bd Bellevue, 05000 Gap. Tel: 92 51 12 40.

BERTENS, JAN-WILLEM
Netherlands, LDR (D'66)

Mr Jan-Willem Bertens was elected to EP in 1989, regaining a seat for his party that was previously held in 1979. Became mbr, Cmte on Youth, Culture, Education, the Media and Sport, and Cmte on Environment, Public Health and Consumer Protection. Formerly in diplomatic service. B Jan 23 1936.

Address: St. Bernardusstraat 11, 6211 HK Maastricht.

BETHELL, LORD
UK, London North West, ED (C)

Lord Bethell is a prominent campaigner for lower air fares in Europe being chmn of 'Freedom of the Skies'; also chmn, Gibraltar in Europe Representation Gp; Friends of Cyprus, 1981- ; vice-chmn, EP human rights sub-cmte, 1984- . Elected to EP in 1979; served in nominated Parliament, 1975-79; mbr, EP Political Affairs Cmte. B Jul 19 1938; ed Harrow; Pembroke Coll, Cambridge. On editorial staff of *The Times Literary Supplement*, 1962-64; a script editor in BBC Drama Dept, 1964-67. A Lord-in-Waiting (Govt whip and a junior Govt spokesman), House of Lords, 1970-71. Freelance writer and a translator from Russian and Polish.

Address: 73 Sussex Square, London W2 2SS.

BETTIZA, VINCENZO
Italy, Soc (PSI)

Sgr Vincenzo Bettiza, a mbr of the nominated Parliament, was first elected to the EP on PLI list in 1979 and was a vice-chmn of the Liberal and Democratic Gp until 1984 and remained with gp until 1989 election when he was on the PSI list. Mbr, Cmte on External Economic Relations, 1989- ; former mbr, Political Affairs Cmte. Journalist; on editorial board of *Il Nuovo Giornale*. Senator, 1976-79. Was correspondent of *La Stampa* and *Corriere della Sera* in various capitals of the world, including Moscow. B Jun 7 1927.

Address: Via Anelli 5, 20100 Milano. Tel: (02) 58 30 03 32.

BEUMER, BOUKE
Netherlands, EPP (CDA)

Mr Bouke Beumer was first elected to EP in 1979. Chmn, EP Cmte on Economic and Monetary Affairs and Industrial Policy, since 1987, and mbr of cmte since 1984; chmn, EP Cmte on Youth, Culture, Education, Information and Sport, 1982-84. On bureau of EPP Gp. Mbr, Dutch Second Chamber, 1975-79. Director of NW Overijssel Regional Cl, 1962-66; Burgomaster of Midwolda, 1966-75. B Nov 21 1934; studied economics at Rotterdam, 1952-58.

Address: Oude Middelhorst 9, 9751 TK Haren. Tel: (050) 34 31 81.

BINDI, SIGNORA ROSARIA
Italy, EPP (DC)

Signora Rosaria (Rosy) Bindi, teacher and director, Vittorio Bachelet Institute, is vice-chair, *l'Action Catholique Italienne*, the Catholic action gp. Former town councillor. Elected to EP in 1989 and became a vice-chair of Cmte on Development and Cooperation; also mbr, Cmte on Institutional Affairs and Cmte on Women's Rights. B Feb 12 1951; doctor of political science.

Address: Via Umberto I 44, 53048 Sinalunga (Siena). Tel: (0577) 60 34 70.

BIRD, JOHN
UK, Midlands West, Soc (Lab)

Mr John Bird was elected chairman of Labour group of MEP immediately after 1989 Euro elections. First elected to EP in 1987 by-election. Mbr, EP Cmte on External Economic Relations; former mbr, Budgets Cmte. Mbr, Wolverhampton Cl, 1962-88; West Midlands CC, 1973-81; AMA ed cmte, 1974-80; AMA Cl, 1974-87; W Midlands Economic Dev Cl, 1973-81; W Midlands Regional Economic Forum, 1986-87. Was chmn, Wolverhampton Dist Lab Pty and Midlands West Euro-constituency. B Feb 4 1926. Former occupations: policeman for two years; centre lathe turner, industrial welfare officer. AEU. Lifelong supporter of Wolverhampton Wanderers FC and led campaign to save club in 1986.
Addresses: Campaign Office, Old Bank Chambers, Lich Gates, Wolverhampton WV1 1TY. Tel: (0902) 712366. 5 Giffard Road, Bushbury, Wolverhampton WV10 8EG. Tel: (0902) 782830.

BJORNVIG, FRU BIRGIT
Denmark, ARC (Folkebevaegelsen mod EF)

Fru Birgit Bjornvig became an MEP during 1984-89 Parliament; re-elected 1989 and became a co-chair of Arc-en-Ciel (Rainbow) Gp; joined EP Cmte on Environment, Public Health and Consumer Protection and Cmte on Women's Rights; former mbr, EP Cmte on Youth, Culture, Education, Information and Sport. Teacher of the handicapped. B Jan 4 1936.

Address: Issehoved 41 p, 8795 Nordby. Tel: (06) 59 62 59. Folkebevaegelsen mod EF, Norrebrogade 188, 2200 Kobenhavn N.

BLAK, FREDDY
Denmark, Soc (S)

Mr Freddy Blak was elected to EP in 1989 and joined Cmte on Budgetary Control being appointed one of its vice-chmn. Fitter; trade unionist. B Mar 8 1945.

Address: Marie Bregendahlsvej 18, 4700 Naestved. Tel: (53) 73 47 81.

BLANEY, NEIL
Ireland, ARC (Ind)

Mr Neil Blaney was returned to the EP by the Connacht-Ulster constituency in 1989 having been one of its elected MEPs, 1979-84; rejoined Cmte on Agriculture, Fisheries and Rural Development; has also served on Budgetary Control Cmte. Minister for Agriculture and Fisheries, 1966-70; Minister for Local Govt, 1957-66; Minister for Posts and Telegraphs, 1957. Has farming and business interests. First elected to Dail for Donegal, 1948, and returned as FF deputy up to and including 1969 election. Expelled from party, 1971. Since 1973 has contested elections as Ind FF Republican Party. Mbr, Donegal CC, 1948-57 (chmn, 1955-57). President, Football Assocn of Ireland, 1968-73 and a patron since 1973. B Oct 29 1922.

Address: Rossnakill, Letterkenny, Co. Donegal. Tel: (074) 59014.

BLOT, YVAN
France, DR (FN)

M.Yvan Blot, former mbr of French National Assembly as deputy for Calais, was elected to EP in 1989 joining Cmtes on Budgets and on Institutional Affairs. Lecturer at Institute for Political Studies in Paris; county councillor for Pas-de-Calais; town councillor at Calais. Secretary-General of cmte for l'Europe des patries, for which the party campaigned. B 1948.

Address: 12 rue des Dardanelles, 75017 Paris.

BOCKLET, REINHOLD
Germany, EPP (CSU)

Herr Reinhold Bocklet, first elected to EP in 1979, rejoined the Cmte on Agriculture, Fisheries and Rural Develop after the 1989 elections. Former official of Bavarian Landtag. Mbr, CSU Regional Association for Upper Bavaria, since 1975. B Apr 5 1943. Lectured in political science at Geschwister-Scholl Institute (Munich Univ).

Address: Grasslfingerstrasse 22a, 8038 Gröbenzell. Tel: (08142) 5523.

BÖGE, REIMER
Germany, EPP (CDU)

Herr Reimer Böge, agricultural engineer and farmer, was elected to EP in 1989; joined Cmte on Budgets. Former municipal councillor; former chmn, European Cl of Young Farmers. B Dec 18 1951.

Address: Dorfstrasse 50, 2359 Hasenmoor. Tel: (04195) 412.

BOFILL ABEILHE, PEDRO
Spain, Soc (PSOE)

Señor Pedro Bofill Abeilhe, an MEP since 1986, was elected to the EP in 1987 and re-elected in 1989 when he joined Cmte on Economic and Monetary Affairs and Industrial Policy. Member, Spanish national Parliament. University professor. B Feb 14 1946.

*photograph
unavailable*

Address: Ferraz 84, 28008 Madrid.

BOMBARD, ALAIN
France, Soc (PS)

M. Alain Bombard became an MEP in 1981 and re-elected since then. Mbr, EP Cmte on Environment, Public Health and Consumer Protection; former mbr, Cmte on Rules of Procedure. A biologist, he was mbr of EP cmte of inquiry into treatment of toxic and dangerous substances by EC and member states. Former State Secretary for Environment; former Var county councillor. Biologist. Director, laboratory ships 'Coryphene', 1958-60, and 'Captain Cap', 1960-62. Chaired aquaculture cmte, Provence-Alpes-Cote d'Azur regional council. Author of works about the sea. B Oct 27 1924.

Address: La Baou de la Garduère, 83150 Bandol.

BONDE, JENS-PETER
Denmark, ARC (Folkebevaegelsen mod EF)

Mr Jens-Peter Bonde, first elected to the EP in 1979, has joined EP Cmte on Transport and Tourism; former mbr, Cmte on Budgets. Largely responsible for starting up Danish anti-EC popular movement journal *Det ny Notat* (The New Report). Mbr, central cmte, Danish Communist Party. B Mar 27 1948.

Address: Folkebevaegelsen mod EF, Norrebrogade 18B, 2200 Kobenhavn N. Tel: (01) 37 20 66. Telefax (01) 37 52 14. Skovbrynet 39, 2880 Bagsvaerd. Tel: (02) 49 02 51. Telefax: (02) 49 02 51.

119

BONETTI, ANDREA
Italy, EPP (DC)

Sgr Andrea Bonetti is Deputy President of Brescia provincial workers' union; mbr, Italian Chamber of Deputies; director of Italian craft workers' confederation. Elected to EP 1989; joined Cmte on Transport and Tourism. B 1946; doctor of economic science.

Address: Via Achille Papa 14, 25100 Brescia. Tel: (030) 38 31 68.

BONTEMPI, RINALDO
Italy, EUL (PCI)

Sgr Rinaldo Bontempi was elected to EP in 1989 and joined Cmte on Social Affairs, Employment and Working Environment. Regional councillor. Mbr, regional secretariat of PCI in Piemonte. B Jan 2 1944; degree in jurisprudence.

Address:

BORGO, FRANCO
Italy, EPP (DC)

Sgr Franco Borgo, livestock farmer and former farmers' union official, was first elected to EP in 1984. After 1989 elections became a vice-chmn of Cmte on Agriculture, Fisheries and Rural Development, having served on it in the outgoing Parliament, and rejoined Cmte on Development and Cooperation. Has served as chmn of Vicenza Farmers' Association and Veneto Farmers' Regional Federation, been Chamber of Commerce assessor on agriculture, and on party's regional cmte in Veneto. Joined Veneto regional cl in 1970; provincial adviser of Cooperative Union. B Oct 10 1932.

Addresses: Via Campogallo 10, 36060 Schiavon (Vicenza). Tel: (0444) 46 20 72 - 46 20 36. Via Fontanella Borghese, 00186 Roma.

BORLOO, JEAN-LOUIS
France, NI (Centre)

M.Jean-Louis Borloo was elected to EP in 1989 on French Centre Party list headed by Mme Simone Veil. Became mbr, Cmte on Regional Policy and Regional Planning. Mayor of Valenciennes (Nord). Director of business consultancy; mbr, small firms section of French employers' organization; lawyer. B 1951.

photograph unavailable

Address: 3 rue Saint Gery, 59300 Valenciennes.

BOURLANGES, JEAN-LOUIS
France, EPP (Centre; ex-RPR)

M.Jean-Louis Bourlanges was elected to EP in 1989 on French Centre Party list led by Mme Simone Veil; appointed to Cmte on Agriculture, Fisheries and Rural Protection. Regional councillor for Haute-Normandie. B 1946; diploma on political science.

Address: 8 rue du Commendant Riviere, 75000 Paris.

BOWE, DAVID
UK, Cleveland and Yorkshire North, Soc (Lab)

Mr David Bowe, science teacher, won this Euro seat in 1989 and became mbr, EP Cmte on Environment, Public Health and Consumer Protection. He was elected to Middlesbrough Borough Cl in 1983 (chmn, Monitoring and Review Cmte). Northern regional sec and Cleveland branch sec, Socialist Educational Assocn; former mbr, Northern regional exec, Lab Pty. B Jul 19 1953; ed Sunderland Poly; Bath Univ. Nupe.

Address: 14 Thornfield Grove, Middlesborough TS5 5LG. Tel: (0642) 82 60 78.

BREYER, FRAU HILTRUD
Germany, Verts (Grüne)

Frau Hiltrud Breyer was elected to EP in 1989; became mbr, Cmte on Energy, Reseach and Technology. Began political career towards end of 1970s with her fight against pollution at Saarland, near French border. Campaigning against nuclear contamination. B 1957.

Address: Ormersheimer Strasse 3, 6676 Mandelbachtal 5.

BRIANT, YVON
France, RDE (CNI)

M. Yvon Briant, company managing director, was elected to EP in 1989; became a vice-chmn, RDE Gp, and mbr, Cmte on Legal Affairs and Citizens' Rights. General secretary of CNI (National Centre of Independents). B 1954.

Address: 106 rue de l'Universite, 75007 Paris.

BROK, ELMAR
Germany, EPP (CDU)

Herr Elmar Brok is honorary chairman of the International Young Democratic Union. MEP since 1980; after 1989 elections rejoined Cmte on Social Affairs, Employment and Working Environment, on which he was EPP Gp spokesman in outgoing Parliament. Journalist. Chmn of several party organizations; has served as deputy Federal chmn of Junge Union; mbr, federal cmte for foreign policy and management cmte, East Westphalia-Lippe CDU. B May 14 1946.

Address: Thomas-Mann-Strasse 15, 4800 Bielefeld 17. Tel: (0521) 33 14 56.

BRU PURON, CARLOS
Spain, Soc (PSOE)

Señor Carlos Bru Puron, President of Spanish Council of European Movement, became an MEP in 1986; elected in 1987 and re-elected 1989 when he became a vice-chmn of Cmte on Institutional Affairs, on which he had previously served. Was a vice-chairman, Committee on Rules of Procedure, Verification of Credentials and Immunities, and stayed a cmte mbr after 1989 elections. Solicitor. Born Feb 28 1927.

Address: c/Huesca 25-27, Alcobendas, 28100 Madrid.

BUCHAN, MRS JANEY
UK, Glasgow, Soc (Lab)

Mrs Janey Buchan was first elected to EP in 1979; chaired British Labour gp of MEPs 1988-89; gp secretary, 1984-88. In 1989 rejoined Cmte on Youth, Culture, Education, the Media and Sport; former mbr, EP Cmte on Development and Cooperation. Former chair of Lab Pty in Scotland and of Scottish Gas Consumers Cl. Served from 1974 on Strathclyde Regional Cl, being former vice-chair of its education cmte. B Apr 30 1926; ed sec sch; commercial coll. Married to Mr Norman Buchan, Lab MP for Paisley South. MSFU.

Address: 72 Peel Street, Glasgow G11 5LR. Tel: (41) 339 2583.

BURON, MME MARTINE
France, Soc (PS)

Mme Martine Buron became an MEP in 1988; re-elected 1989; mbr, Cmte on Social Affairs, Employment and Working Environment. Architect. Municipal councillor at Chateaubriant (Loire-Atlantique); regional councillor, Pays-de-Loire. B Jan 12 1944.

Address: 15 rue des Déportes-Résistants, 44110 Chateaubriant. Tel: 40 81 21 44.

CABANILLAS GALLAS, PIO
Spain, EPP (PP)

Señor Pio Cabanillas Gallas became a nominated MEP in 1986; first elected 1987; re-elected 1989. Mbr, EP Cmte on Legal Affairs and Citizens Rights; bureau of EPP gp and leader of Spanish delegation. Under Secretary for Tourism and Information, 1962-68; Minister of Tourism and Information, 1974; Mbr of Parliament, 1977-79; Minister of Culture, 1977-79; Minister of State, 1980, Minister of Presidency, 1981; Minister of Justice, 1982; Mbr of Parliament, 1982-86. Mbr, Royal Academy of Law and Jurisprudence. B Nov 13 1923.

Addresses: c/Alberto Alocer n° 13, 28036 Madrid. Tel (1) 250 31 03. Pazo de Pompean, Vilanovina-Paradela, Villagarcia, Pontevedra. Tel: 71 20 77. Paseo Castellana 134, Madrid. Tel: (1) 262 54 06.

CABAZÓN ALONSO, JESÚS
Spain, Soc (PSOE)

Señor Jesús Cabazón Alonso, former Spanish senator, became an MEP in 1986; elected 1987 and re-elected 1989; mbr, Cmte on Social Affairs, Employment and Working Environment, on which he served in outgoing Parliament. Former senator; former civil servant with special responsibility for social security.

Addresses: Apartado de Correos 2211, 39080 Santander. c/Ruiz Zorrilla, n° 15-7° D, 39009 Santander.

CALVO ORTEGA, RAFAEL
Spain, LDR (CDS)

Señor Rafael Calvo Ortega was first elected to EP in 1987 serving on Cmte on Budgets; after 1989 elections joined Cmte on Regional Policy and Regional Planning. Lawyer; university professor. Secretary-General, Centre Democratic Union (UCD). Former Minister of Labour; former senator and mbr, Spanish national Parliament. B Aug 26 1933.

Address: c/Quintana 28, 28008 Madrid. Tel: (1) 247 64 69.

CÁMARA MARTÍNEZ, JUAN JOSÉ DE LA
Spain, Soc (PSOE)

Señor Juan José de la Cámara Martínez was elected to EP in 1989. Former civil servant. Member, regional government of Castilla-La-Mancha. B Jul 1 1945.

Address: Avda. Castilla, 8 5°D, 19003 Guadalajara.

CANAVARRO, PEDRO
Portugal, Soc (PS)

Senhor Pedro Canavarro, university professor, was elected to EP in 1989 and joined Cmte on Environment, Public Health and Consumer Protection. Head of several cultural organizations. Secretary-General of Democratic Renewal Party (PRD). B May 9 1937.

Address: R. dos Navegantes 58-1° Dto, 1200 Lisboa.

CANO PINTO, EUSEBIO
Spain, Soc (PSOE)

Señor Eusebio Cano Pinto, an MEP since 1986, was appointed a vice-chmn of EP Cmte on External Economic Relations in 1989; previously mbr, Cmte on Environment, Public Health and Consumer Protection. Former member, Spanish national Parliament and regional government of Extremadura. B Aug 17 1940.

Address: c/Asura 131, 28043 Madrid. Tel: (1) 200 07 98.

CAPUCHO, ANTÓNIO
Portugal, LDR (PSD)

Senhor António Capucho who became an elected MEP in 1989, was elected a Vice-President of EP in July 1989; mbr, Political Affairs Cmte and Cmte on Energy, Research and Technology. Business manager. Former mbr, Portuguese National Parliament, to which he was elected in 1980 being leader, PSD parliamentary gp. Secretary-General, PSD, 1978-84. Became Minister for Parliamentary Affairs; has held other ministerial offices. B Jan 3 1945.

Address: Av. Marques Leal 5A R/C, S. João do Estoril, 2765 Estoril.

CARIGLIA, ANTONIO
Italy, Soc (PSDI)

Sgr Antonio Cariglia, Italian senator and MEP 1979-84, returned as elected MEP in 1989 and joined Political Affairs Cmte on which he previously served. National secretary of Italian Social Democrat Party (PSDI). Italian MP, 1963-76. Was freelance journalist; also official of Court of Auditors. Former national secretary, Italian Union of Labour (UIL). B Mar 28 1924; degree in political science.

Address: Partito Socialdemocratico Italiano, Via Santa Maria in Via 12, 00187 Roma. Tel: (06) 672 71.

CARNITI, PIERRE
Italy, Soc (PSI)

Sgr Pierre Carniti, journalist and trade unionist, was elected to EP in 1989. Became mbr, Cmte on Social Affairs, Employment and Working Environment. Former Secretary-General, Italian Confederation of Trade Unions; former President, European Confederation of Trade Unions. B Sep 25 1936.

Address: Via Oppido Mamertina 4, Zona Statuario, 00178 Roma. Tel: (06) 779 10 91.

CARVALHAS, CARLOS
Portugal, CG (PCP)

Senhor Carlos Carvalhas was elected to EP in 1989 on list of *Coligacao Democratica Unitaria* (CDU) and joined Cmte on Economic and Monetary Affairs and Industrial Policy. Was elected vice-chairman of CG Gp. Economist. Former Secretary of State; mbr of Portuguese national Parliament from 1976; on political commission of PCP Central Cmte; vice-chmn, National Cl for Central Plan. B Nov 9 1941.

Address: Rua Professor, Reinaldo dos Santos, N° 1-8°Dt°, 1500 Lisboa.

CARVALHO CARDOSO, JOSÉ
Portugal, EPP (CDS)

Senhor José Carvalho Cardoso, elected MEP since 1987, is a former Secretary of State and former Deputy. Agriculturalist; director of agricultural research, Portugal. After 1989 elections joined EP Cmte on Energy, Research and Technology; former mbr, Cmte on Agriculture, Fisheries and Food. Vice-chmn, National Federation of Agricultural Savings Banks. B Sep 19 1923.

Addresses: Rua do Salitre 62, 2°, Lisboa. Tel: (1) 56 13 68. Av Padre Manuel da Nobrega 3, 4°, 1000 Lisboa. Tel: (1) 88 36 53.

CASINI, CARLO
Italy, EPP (DC)

Sgr Carlo Casini, first elected to EP in 1984, is on the Cmte on Legal Affairs and Citizens' Rights. A graduate in jurisprudence, became magistrate in Empoli, then assistant public prosecutor in Florence; in 1973 elected mbr of Law Cl of Tuscany; former magistrate in Cassazionne. Former judge in Court of Appeal to which he was appointed in 1977. Former mbr, Chamber of Deputies. B Mar 4 1935.

Addresses: Via Cavour 92, 50129 Firenze. Tel: (05) 55 71 754. Via del Corso 176, 00186 Roma. Tel: (06) 67 17 93 78.

CASO GARCÍA, JOSÉ RAMÓN
Spain, LDR (CDS)

Señor José Ramón Caso García was elected to EP in 1989 and joined Cmte on Agriculture, Fisheries and Rural Development. Secretary-General, CDS Party, since 1982 and became deputy in Spanish national Parliament in 1986. B Sep 17 1946.

photograph unavailable

Address: Marques del Duero 7, 28001 Madrid.

CASSANMAGNAGO CERRETTI, SIGNORA MARIA LUISA
Italy, EPP (DC)

Signora Maria Luisa Cassanmagnago Cerretti was Senior Vice-President of EP, 1984-87; also Vice-President, 1982-84. Mbr of EP since 1976; elected since 1979. A vice-chmn, EPP Gp, 1979-82; mbr of EPP Gp bureau as leader of Italian delegation. Former chair, EPP Gp working party on social affairs. Joined Political Affairs Cmte in 1989; a vice-chmn, EP Cmte on Development and Cooperation, 1987-89; former mbr, Cmtes on Social Affairs and Employment and on Women's Rights. In Italian Chamber of Deputies, 1972-79, and has served on DC national cl and executive of DC women's movement. Adviser on social services to Milan provincial administration, 1963-72. B Apr 7 1929.

Addresses: Segretario, Via Nirone 15, Milano. Tel: (02) 801120. Via della Mendola 57, 00135 Roma. Tel: (06) 32 82 154.

CASSIDY, BRYAN
UK, Dorset East and Hampshire West, ED (C)

Mr Bryan Cassidy was first elected to EP 1984. EDG spokesman on External Economic Relations Cmte, 1987-89; mbr, Cmte on Economic and Monetary Affairs and Industrial Policy, 1984-87 and 1989- ; Cmte on Petitions, 1987- . Director-General, Cosmetic, Toiletry and Perfumery Assocn, 1981-84; previously with Ever Ready, Beecham's, Reed International (director, European associates). Contested Wandsworth Central for Cons in 1966 general election. Mbr, Cl of CBI, 1981-84; GLC (for Hendon N), 1977-86 (Opposition spokesman on industry and employment, 1983-84). B Feb 17 1934; ed Ratcliffe Coll; Sidney Sussex Coll, Cambridge.

Addresses: 11 Esmond Court, Thackeray Street, London W8 5HB. Tel: (01) 973 3558. The Stables, White Cliff Gardens, Blandford Forum, Dorset DT11 7BU.

CASTELLINA, SIGNORA LUCIANA
Italy, EUL (PCI)

Signora Luciana Castellina was elected to EP in 1979 on PDUP list and became a vice-chmn of CDI gp for defence of independent gps. Elected in 1984 and 1989 on Communist list. Mbr, EP Political Affairs Cmte, 1989- ; bureau of EUL Group; former mbr, Cmte on Development and Cooperation. In Chamber of Deputies from 1976. Journalist; served on Cmte on Justice and the Interparliamentary Cmte on general guidance and supervision of broadcasting services. Mbr, PCI central cmte. B Aug 9 1929; degree in jurisprudence. President, Union of Italian Women.

Addresses: c.o. Lega Internazionale dei Popoli, Via della Dogana Vecchia 5, 00186 Roma. Tel: (06) 687 77 74 or 654 14 68. c.o. C. R. S., Via della Vite 13, 00187 Roma. Via San Valentino 32, 00197 Roma. Tel: (06) 804808.

CATASTA, SIGNORA ANNA
Italy, EUL (PCI)

Signora Anna Catasta was elected to EP in 1989; became mbr, Cmte on Social Affairs, Employment and Working Environment. Trade unionist, being mbr, Milan General Workers' Union, and provincial CGIL (trade union) organization in Milan. B May 6 1952.

Address: Via Ramazzini 8, 20129 Milano. Tel: (02) 29 40 29 13.

CATHERWOOD, SIR FREDERICK
UK, Cambridgeshire and Bedfordshire North, ED (C)

Sir Frederick Catherwood was elected a Vice-President of EP in July 1989; also became mbr, Cmte on Social Affairs Employment and Working Environment. Deputy chmn of ED (Cons) Gp, 1983-87. Elected for this seat 1984; MEP for Cambridgeshire, 1979-84. Mbr, EP Cmte on Institutional Affairs, 1987-89; Budgets Cmte, 1984-87; chmn, EP External Economic Relations Cmte, 1979-84;. Director-General, Nat Economic Development Cl, 1966-71; chief industrial adviser, Dept of Economic Affairs, 1964-66. Managing director and chief executive, John Laing and Son Ltd, 1972-74; director, Goodyear Tyre and Rubber Co (GB) Ltd. Chartered accountant. Chmn, British Overseas Trade Bd, 1975-79; Vice-pres, British Inst of Management, 1976- ; chmn, 1974-76. B Jan 30 1925; ed Shrewsbury; Clare Coll, Cambridge.
Address: Shire Hall, Castle Hill, Cambridge CB3 0AW. Tel: (0223) 317672.

CAUDRON, GÉRARD
France, Soc (PS)

M.Gérard Caudron, lecturer in business management, was elected to EP in 1989 and joined Cmte on Economic and Monetary Affairs and Industrial Policy. Mayor of Villeneuve-d'Ascq; vice-chmn, Northern General Council. B 1945.

photograph unavailable

Address: Hotel de Ville, Place S. Allende, 59650 Villeneuve d'Ascq. Tel:20 72 36 88.

CECI, SIGNORA ADRIANA
Italy, EUL (PCI)

Signora Adriana Ceci was elected to EP in 1989 and joined Cmte on Legal Affairs and Citizens' Rights. Former Italian deputy. B Dec 9 1942.

Address:

CEYRAC, PIERRE
France, DR (FN)

M.Pierre Ceyrac, journalist and businessman, became mbr, EP Cmte on External Economic Relations, upon being elected MEP in 1989. Former deputy for Nord. B Sep 18 1946.

Address: 37 rue de Cambrai, 59800 Roubaix.

CHABERT, HENRY
France, RDE (RPR)

M.Henry Chabert was elected to EP in 1989 and joined Cmte on External Economic Relations. Deputy Mayor of Lyon and Mayor of 9th District. Former company chief executive. B 1945.

Address: 76 Cours de la Liberte, 69003.

CHANTERIE, RAPHAËL
Belgium, EPP (CVP)

Mr Raphaël Chanterie has been an MEP since 1981 and became a vice-chmn, EPP Gp, in 1989; on gp bureau of EPP in outgoing Parliament; mbr, Cmte on Environment, Public Health and Consumer Protection, 1989- ; chmn, EP Cmte on Petitions, 1987-89, and previously a vice-chmn; former mbr, EP Cmte on Economic and Monetary Affairs and Industrial Policy. Modern languages teacher, 1963-70. Former Secretary-General of European Union of Christian Democratic Workers (EUCDW). B Nov 22 1942.

Address: Eikenlaan 26, 8790 Waregem. Tel: (056) 60 35 87.

CHEYSSON, CLAUDE
France, Soc (PS)

M.Claude Cheysson was EC Commissioner with responsibility for development policy and relations with Third World, 1973-81; from 1973-77 also responsible for budgets and financial control. Minister for Foreign Affairs, 1981-84. Elected to EP 1989; on bureau of Socialist Gp; mbr, Political Affairs Cmte. Ambassador to Indonesia, 1966-70, when he became chmn of board of *Enterprise minière et chimique*, leading French state-owned chemical company. Secretary-General, Commission for Technical Cooperation in Africa, 1957-62; Director-General, Technical Organisation for Exploitation of Sahara Minerals, 1962-65. In 1971, joined board of *Le Monde*. B Apr 13 1920.

Address: 52 rue de Vaugirard, 750006 Paris.

131

CHIABRANDO, MAURO
Italy, EPP (DC)

Sgr Mauro Chiabrando was first elected to EP in 1984; re-elected in 1989 when he rejoined Cmte on Energy, Research and Technology and also joined Cmte on External Economic Relations. Became mbr of Piedmont regional council in 1970; state assessor; has also worked in Turin's municipal administration. Former provincial secretary of DC in Turin. Agricultural consultant; holds diplomas in land surveying and agronomy. B Mar 29 1932.

Addresses: Piazza Roma 12, 10064 Pinerolo (Torino). Tel: (0121) 793600. Strada Baudenasca 8, 10064 Oinerolo (Torino). Tel: (0121) 70333.

CHRISTENSEN, FRODE NOR
Denmark, EPP (CD)

Mr Frode Nor Christensen was Danish Minister of Traffic, 1987-88; formerly led the CD gp in the Folketing, the Danish Parliament, to which he was elected in 1981. Became elected MEP in 1989; mbr, bureau, EPP Gp, as leader of Danish delegation, and was appointed a vice-chmn, EP Cmte on Transport and Tourism. Former policeman. B Oct 9 1948.

Addresses: Folketinget, Christiansborg, 1240 Kobenhavn K. Tel: (01) 11 66 00 - 4214. Telefax: (01) 14 54 20. Kirkestrade 16, Hodsager, 7490 Aulum. Tel: (07) 47 63 51.

CHRISTENSEN, IB
Denmark, ARC (Folkebevaegelsen mod EF)

Mr Ib Christensen was first elected to EP in 1984; mbr, Political Affairs Cmte, 1989- ; former mbr, Cmte on Agriculture, Fisheries and Food. Chmn, Single-Tax Party (*Retsforbundet*) which he represented in Danish Parliament, 1973-75 and 1978-79 when his party lost all seats. Mbr, nominated EP, 1978-79. Hs bn mbr, Cl of Europe and leading figure in One World organization, the UN Association and various Nordic organizations. B Mar 15 1930.

Address: Gortlervej 26, 8900 Randers. Tel: (86) 42 68 53.

CHRISTIANSEN, EJNER HOVGAARD
Denmark, Soc (S)

Mr Ejner Hovgaard Christiansen became elected MEP in 1984; a former vice-chmn of Socialist Gp; mbr, EP Cmte on Economic and Monetary Affairs and Industrial Policy. Secretary-General, Social Democratic Party, since 1971; in 1979 was candidate for post of Secretary-General of Socialist International. Electrician. B May 28 1932.

Address: Jacobys Alle 12 3. tv., 1806 Frederiksberg C. Tel: (01) 31 69 75.

CHRISTODOULOU, EFTHIMIOS
Greece, EPP (ND)

Mr Efthimios Christodoulou is former head of EPP Gp Greek delegation and is mbr of Cmte on Budgets and Cmte on Budgetary Control. Became elected MEP in 1984. President and Governor of National Bank of Greece, 1979-81. Participated on many international conference on economics and in the work of international banking organizations such as the IMF and OECD. Economist. Worked as consultant director, director-general and chmn of a number of major banks and enterprises including ETVA (Commercial Bank for Industrial Development and Olympic Airways. B Dec 2 1932; ed Athens Coll; Hamilton Coll and Columbia Univ.

Addresses: Lamachou 3, 105 57 Athina. Tel: (1) 32 29 658. Louki Akrita 1B, 152 37 Filothei. Tel: (1) 68 17 923.

CLERCQ, WILLY DE
Belgium, LDR (PVV)

Mr Willy de Clercq was Belgian Deputy Prime Minister and Minister for Finance and Foreign Trade from Dec 1981 to 1985; an EC Commissioner from 1985 to Jan 1989. Elected MEP, 1979-81, leaving to take ministerial office; re-elected 1989 and became chmn, Cmte on External Economic Relations. First chmn of PVV in 1971; re-elected PVV chmn in 1977. Representative for Ghent-Eeklo. Under-Secretary of State for the Budget, 1960-61; Deputy Prime Minister and Minister for the Budget, 1966-68; Deputy Prime Minister and Minister for Finance, 1973-74; President of EC Cl of Ministers of Finance, first half of 1973; Minister for Finance, 1974-77. Has twice been chmn, Interim Cmte of IMF. B Jul 8 1927.

Address: Cyriel Buyssestraat 12, 9000 Gent. Tel: (091) 21 18 13/22 59 47. Telefax: (091) 20 07 77.

COATES, KENNETH
UK, Nottingham, Soc (Lab)

Mr Kenneth Coates won this seat in 1989 having contested it in 1984 and Nottingham South in 1983 general election. Joined EP Political Affairs Cmte in 1989. University lecturer and author; former miner; active in helping launch the Movement for European Nuclear Disarmament and now sec of its liaison cmte; mbr, Bertrand Russell Peace Foundation. B Sep 16 1930; Nottingham Univ, being former tutor in univ's Adult Ed Dept, now Reader in Adult Ed. Founder mbr, Inst of Workers' Control. AUT. Sec, Rushcliffe CLP, 1970-82.

Address: 112 Church Street, Matlock DE4 3BZ. Tel: (0629) 57159. Telefax: (0629) 58 06 72.

COCHET, YVES
France, Verts (Verts)

M. Yves Cochet was elected to EP in 1989 and joined Cmte on Budgets and Cmte on Budgetary Control. Became co-vice-chmn of Green Gp. Information technologist. Town councillor at Rennes (Ille-et-Vilaine). Former militant campaigner for Friends of the Earth, he was co-founder of Les Verts in 1984; mbr of executive college of Les Verts, responsible for publications. He built his own solar-powered house; prominent mbr of ecological movement in Brittany for many years, where the Greens were successful in the last municipal elections. B 1946.

Address: 16 rue de la Plesse, 35510 Cesson Sevigne. Tel: 99 83 14 64.

COIMBRA MARTINS, ANTÓNIO
Portugal, Soc (PS)

Senhor António Coimbra Martins became an MEP in 1986; elected 1987 and re-elected 1989. Mbr, Cmte on Youth, Culture, Education, the Media and Sport, and Cmte on Petitions. Minister of Culture and deputy in Portuguese national assembly, 1983-85. Senior executive with Calouste Gulbenkian Foundation. B Jan 30 1927.

Addresses: 93 Rue Archimède 1 C, B. P. 46, 1040 Bruxelles. Tel: (02) 734 24 93. Av. Elias Garcia, 174 - R/C Esq., 1000 Lisboa. Tel: (1) 77 78 21.

COLAJANNI, LUIGI
Italy, EUL (PCI)

Sgr Luigi Colajanni was elected to EP in 1989 and was elected leader of the new European United Left (EUL) Gp - *Grupo por la Izquierda Unitaria Europea.* Mbr, EP Cmte on Budgets, 1989- . Architect. Mbr, central cmte and management caucus of Italian Communist Party (PCI) and Sicilian regional cmte. Mbr, Sicilian Regional Assembly and local councillor at Palermo. B Oct 2 1943.

Address: c.o. Comitato Regionale PCI, Corso Calatafimi 633, 90129 Palermo. Tel: (091) 42 10 42.

COLINO SALAMANCA, JUAN LUIS
Spain, Soc (PSOE)

Señor Juan Luis Colino Salamanca was reappointed in July 1989 as chairman of the Committee on Agriculture, Fisheries and Rural Development, a position he held in the outgoing Parliament. MEP since 1986. Former member, Spanish national Parliament. Lawyer. Lawyer and civil servant. B May 5 1947.

Address: Plaza de Santa Cruz 1 7° C, 47002 Valladolid. Tel: 30 38 31.

COLLINS, KENNETH
UK, Strathclyde East, Soc (Lab)

Mr Kenneth Collins again became chmn of EP Cmte on Environment, Public Health and Consumer Protection in 1989; previously chmn, 1979-84; a vice-chmn, 1984-87; cmte mbr since 1979, the year he was first elected MEP. Dep ldr, Labour gp of MEPs, 1979-84. European adviser to ACTT and Nalgo. Hon vice-pres, Royal Environmental Health Inst of Scotland; International Fed on Environmental Health; European Food Law Assocn; Inst of Trading Standards Administration. Teacher, Glasgow Coll of Building, 1967-69; lecturer in urban studies, Paisley Coll of Tech, 1969-79. Planning officer, Glasgow and W Yorkshire, 1965-67; organiser tutor, WEA, 1966-67. Mbr, East Kilbride T and DC, 1973-79; Lanark CC, 1973-75; East Kilbride Development Corporation, 1976-79. B Aug 12 1939.
Address: 11 Stuarton Park, East Kilbride G74 4lA. Tel: (03552) 37282. Telefax;: (03552) 49670.

COLOMBO, EMILIO
Italy, EPP (DC)

Sgr Emilio Colombo was President of the European Parliament, 1977-79, when he became an elected MEP resigning to return to political duties in Italy. Elected MEP again in 1989 and became mbr, Cmte on External Economic Relations. Prime Minister of Italy, 1970-72. Between 1955 and 1988 he was Minister of agriculture, of external trade, of industry, of the Treasury, for the budget and of finance. Joined Chamber of Deputies, 1948. Became nominated MEP in 1976; chmn, Political Affairs Cmte, 1976-77. B Apr 11 1920.

Address: Ministero delle Finanze, Viale Boston, 00144 Roma. Tel: (06) 599 71.

COLOM I NAVAL, JOAN
Spain, Soc (PSOE)

Señor Joan Colom i Naval, MEP since 1986; elected 1987 and re-elected 1989, rejoined the EP Committee on Budgets; also mbr, Cmte on Budgetary Control. Economist and university professor. Former member, Portuguese national Parliament. B Jul 5 1945.

Address: c/Nàpols 352 6°, 08025 Barcelona. Tel: (?) 207 00 76.

CONTU, FELICETTO
Italy, EPP (DC)

Sgr Felicetto Contu was elected to EP in 1989; mbr, Cmte on Regional Policy and Regional Planning. Mbr, Italian Chamber of Deputies; has served as Under Secretary of State. Former Sardaigne regional chmn of Italian farmers' union. Solicitor. B Sep 10 1927.

Address: Piazza Dettori 5, 09100 Cagliari. Tel: (070) 65 27 68.

COONEY, PATRICK
Ireland, EPP (FG)

Mr Patrick Cooney was elected to EP in 1989 and joined Cmte on Institutional Affairs and Cmte on Legal Affairs and Citizens' Rights. First elected to Dail, 1970; deputy for Longford Westmeath since then with exception of 1977-81 when Leader, Fine Gael Party, in Senate. Minister for Defence, 1982-86; Minister for Education, 1986-87; Minister for Transport and Minister for Posts and Telegraphs, 1981-82; Minister for Justice, 1973-77. Vice-chmn, Joint Oireachtas Cmte on State Sponsored Bodies, 1977-81; mbr, Oireachtas Jt Cmte on EC secondary legislation, 1987. B Mar 2 1931; ed St Vincent's Coll, Castlenock; Univ Coll, Dublin. Solicitor. Mbr, Westmeath CC, 1967-73.

Address: Garnafailigh, Athlone, Co. Westmeath. Tel: (0902) 75531.

CORLEONE, FRANCO
Italy, Verts (Verdi Arcob)

Sgr Franco Corleone became an MEP in July 1989 replacing Sgr Edoardo Ronchi who was an MEP for one day - July 24 1989 - when he voted in the elections of the President and Vice-Presidents and then resigned. Sgr Corleone became mbr, Cmte on Energy, Research and Technology. According to the Green Group, he was due to be replaced at the end of October 1989 by Virginio Bettini who will be MEP until the end of 1991 followed by replacement by somone else for the latter half of the Parliament.

Address:

CORNELISSEN, PETRUS
Netherlands, EPP (CDA)

Mr Petrus Cornelissen, first elected to EP in 1984, joined the Budgets Cmte and in 1987 became one of its vice-chairmen; remained on cmte after 1989 elections. Mbr, Dutch Second Chamber, 1967-81 during which time he was chmn of the chamber's cmte on housing and town and country planning; also chmn of the parliamentary party's transport cmte. B Jan 13 1934; civil engineer. Former mbr, assemblies of Cl of Europe and WEU, being a vice-president of WEU, 1970-81.

Address: Willem-II-straat 47, 5682 AG Best. Tel: (04998) 72279.

COT, JEAN-PIERRE
France, Soc (PS)

M. Jean-Pierre Cot was elected chmn of the Socialist GP of the EP in July 1989; first elected to EP in 1984; chmn, EP budgets cmte, 1984-89, and still mbr of cmte. Mbr, central cmte, French Socialist Party. From 1983 he chaired French Unesco delegation. Minister of Cooperation and Development, 1981-82; Savoie deputy, 1973-81; Mayor of Coise-St-Jean-Pied-Gauthier since 1971. Lecturer at Faculty of Law first of Amiens, then of Paris.

Address: Coise-St-Jean-Pied-Gauthier, 73800 Montmelian. Tel: 79 28 81 97.

COX, PAT
Ireland, LDR (PD)

Mr Pat Cox, elected to the EP in 1989, joined Cmte on Economic and Monetary Affairs and Regional Policy. General Secretary of Progressive Democrats since March 1986, just after its formation. Previously presenter/reporter for RTE current affairs on *Today Tonight* programme; lecturer in economics at NIHE Limerick, now Limerick Univ, being at present a mbr of its governing body. He was the party's national director of elections for 1987 general election. B Nov 28 1952; ed in Limerick.

Address: 7 Maretimo Gardens East, Blackrock, Co. Dublin. Tel: 880372.

CRAMON-DAIBER, FRAU BIRGIT
Germany, Verts (Grüne)

Frau Birgit Cramon-Daiber was elected to EP in 1989 and joined Cmte on Social Affairs, Employment and Working Environment. Educationalist; has degree in pedagogy and engaged in research into women's problems in Berlin; representative of Berlin women's group. B 1944.

Address: Essholtzstrasse 7, 1000 Berlin 30. Tel (030) 216 57 83.

CRAMPTON, PETER
UK, Humberside, Soc (Lab)

Mr Peter Crampton, former lecturer, statistician, teacher and education officer in Uganda, won this Euro seat for Lab in 1989; contested it, 1984. Became a vice-chmn, EP Political Affairs Cmte. Mbr, nat exec, CND, chairing CND International Cmte; nat chair, European Nuclear Disarmament, 1984-86; mbr, International END liaison cmte and nat coordinating cmte of END, 1982- ; chair, Hull CND, 1981- ; regional coordinator for One World. B Jun 1932; ed Nottingham, Birmingham and Hull Univs. Chmn, Humberside Ed Appeals Panel. TGWU; Co-op Pty.

Address: 135 Westbourne Avenue, Hull HU5 3HU. Tel: (0482) 494 796.

CRAVINHO, JOÃO
Portugal, Soc (PS)

Senhor João Cravinho, former Minister for Industry and Technology, was elected to EP in 1989. Was elected a Vice-President of EP in July 1989 and became mbr, Cmte on Economic and Monetary Affairs and Industrial Policy. Civil engineer. Also became a vice-chmn of Socialist Gp and leader of Portuguese delegation on the gp. Mbr, Portuguese national Parliament, 1979-83 and 1985-89. A national secretary of PS. B Sep 19 1936.

Address: Rue Particular à Rue António Ferro, S. Pedro do Estoril, 2765 Estoril.

CRAWLEY, MRS CHRISTINE
UK, Birmingham East, Soc (Lab)

Mrs Christine Crawley was first elected to the EP for this seat in 1984. After 1989 elections was appointed chair of EP Women's Rights Cmte; a vice-chair, 1984-89; and mbr, Cmte on Environment, Public Health and Consumer Protection; former mbr, Agriculture, Fisheries and Food Cmte. Former teacher; then held part-time position with Manpower Services Commission. B Jan 1 1950; ed Notre Dame Catholic Sec Girls Sch, Plymouth; Digby Stuart Training Coll, Roehampton. Mbr, Didcot TC and S Oxfordshire DC, 1979-83; parly candidate, Staffordshire SE, 1983. NUT and MSFU; represents interests of Nupe in Europe.

Addresses: Euro Office, Birmingham District Labour Party, 16 Bristol Street, Birmingham B5 7AF. Tel: (021) 622 2270. 70 Melton Road, West Bridgford, Nottingham NG2 7NF. Tel: (0602) 813262.

CRAXI, BETTINO
Italy, Soc (PSI)

Sgr Bettino Craxi, former Prime Minister and President of the Council of Ministers, was first elected Secretary-General of the Italian Socialist Party in 1976. First elected to EP in 1979 but resigned during that Parliament; re-elected 1989; mbr, Cmte on Budgetary Control. Mbr, Italian Chamber of Deputies since 1968 and has been chmn of PSI parliamentary gp. Was freelance journalist and author. Former president, Institute for the Science of Public Administration. Party representative on Socialist International. B Feb 1934.

Address: Direzione PSI, Via del Corso 262, 00186 Roma. Tel: (06) 677 81.

CUNHA OLIVEIRA, ARTUR
Portugal, Soc (PS)

Senhor Artur Cunha Oliveira, theologian, university professor and journalist, was elected to EP in 1989. Became mbr, Cmte on Agriculture, Fisheries and Rural Development. Undertaken various functions in regional administration of the Azores. B Sep 30 1924.

Address: Cidade da Horta 8, 9500 Ponta Delgada, Açores. Tel: 270 38.

CUSHNAHAN, JOHN
Ireland, EPP (FG)

Mr John Cushnahan was elected to EP in 1989 and joined Cmte on Regional Policy and Regional Planning. Since 1987 has run a public relations and public affairs consultancy. Leader, Alliance Party in N Ireland, 1984-87; chief whip of Alliance Party, 1982-84; general secretary of party, 1974-82. Mbr, N Ireland Assembly being education cmte chmn, 1982-86; Belfast City Council, 1977-85. N Ireland Housing Executive, 1978-82. B Jul 23 1948; ed St Mary's CBS, Belfast; St Joseph's Coll of Ed, Belfast; Queen's Univ.

Address: The Rock Lodge , Castleconnell, Co. Limerick. Tel: (061) 377376.

DALSASS, JOACHIM
Italy, EPP (SVP)

Sgr Joachim Dalsass was first elected to EP in 1979 and is serving on Cmte on Agriculture, Fisheries and Rural Development, being EPP Gp spokesman in outgoing Parliament. Former chmn, Bolzano Provincial Cl; vice-chmn of South Tyrol People's Party (SVP) since 1969; chmn, South Tyrol Regional Cl from 1978, mbr from 1956. Deputy councillor for social welfare for South Tyrol, 1956-60; mbr, regional executive, in charge of public works, 1960-72; in charge of agriculture, forestry, hunting and fishing, 1972-78. B Dec 3 1926.

Address: 39040 Petersberg (Bozen) (Südtirol). Tel: (0471) 61 51 91.

DALY, MRS MARGARET
UK, Somerset and Dorset West, ED (C)

Mrs Margaret Daly, first elected to EP in 1984, joined Cmte on Development and Cooperation, being a vice-chmn, 1987-89, and EDG spokesman on it since 1989 elections; delegate to joint EEC/ACP Assembly; mbr, Cmte on Women's Rights, since 1984. Nat director of Cons Trade Unionists, 1979-84; consultant to trade union dept, Cons Central Office, 1976-79; trade union official, Guild of Insurance Officials, then Union of Insurance Staffs which merged with ASTMS, 1960-71; departmental head with Phoenix Assurance Co, 1956-60. Was a CTU representative on all-pty trade union gp for Europe and a mbr of EDG/CTU jt cmte. B Jan 1938.

Address: The Old School House, Aisholt, Spaxton, nr Bridgwater, Somerset TA5 1AR. Tel: (027867) 688.

DANKERT, PIETER
Netherlands, Soc (PvdA)

Mr Pieter Dankert was President of the EP, 1982-84; unsuccessfully contested Presidency in July 1984, and was a Vice-President, 1987-89. From 1984-89, he was a vice-chmn of the Socialist Gp and then mbr of its bureau. Mbr, Cmte on Budgetary Control, 1989- ; Budgets Cmte, 1984-89. Became MEP in 1977, being first elected in 1979. Former mbr, Dutch Second Chamber. Has also served in Cl of Europe, WEU and North Atlantic assemblies, PvdA international secretary, 1975-81. B Jan 8 1934. Former teacher.

Address: Hoogstraat 1, 1135 BZ Edam. Tel: (02993) 71668.

DAVID, WAYNE
UK, South Wales, Soc (Lab)

Mr Wayne David was elected to EP in 1989 and became mbr, Cmte on Regional Policy and Regional Planning, Cmte on Rules of Procedure, Verification of Credentials and Immunities, and treasurer of enlarged group of Labour MEPs. Mid-Glamorgan tutor-organiser for WEA; previously history teacher. Part-time researcher and writer for Mr Neil Kinnock, Lab leader, since 1985. Mbr, Welsh Lab Pty exec, 1981-82 and 1986-89; Wales South Euro-constituency gen management cmte, 1984- ; chmn, Welsh Lab Pty local govt cmte, 1986- , and mbr, Lab Pty NEC's local govt advisory cmte, 1986- ; chmn, Welsh Lab Pty political ed team, 1986- ; chmn, Bridgend CLP, 1987-88, and its junior and senior vice-chmn, 1985-87. B Jul 1 1957. Has chaired War on Want Cymru since 1985.
Address: Claren House, Cefn Road, Cefn Cribwr, Bridgend CD32 0ae, Mid-Glamorgan. Tel: (0656) 741142.

DEFRAIGNE, JEAN
Belgium, LDR (PRL)

Mr Jean Defraigne was elected to EP in 1989 becoming a vice-chmn of its Political Affairs Cmte; also mbr, Cmte on Rules of Procedure, Verification of Credentials and Immunities. Former president, Belgian Chamber of Deputies; former Minister of Public Works; deputy for Liege; Minister of State, lawyer. B Apr 19 1929.

Address: 55 quai Bonaparte, 4020 Liege. Tel: (041) 41 25 55 or 43 67 78.

DENYS, MME MARIE-JO
France, Soc (PS)

Mme Marie-Jo Denys, administrative director of the French National School of Music and Dance at Rochelle, was elected to EP in 1989; became mbr, Cmte on Transport and Tourism. Mbr, Poitou-Charentes Regional Council. First Secretary, Socialist Federation of Charente-Maritime. B 1950.

*photograph
unavailable*

Address: Résidence Dupleix Appt 17, 12 rue de l'Ouvrage à Cornes, 17000 La Rochelle. Tel: 46 41 46 28.

DEPREZ, GÉRARD
Belgium, EPP (PSC)

Mr Gérard Deprez was first elected to the EP in 1984. After 1989 elections, joined Cmte on Social Affairs, Employment and Work Environment. Chmn of PSC since Dec 1981; former party political adviser. Sociologist. Served on staffs of ministers, 1979-81. Local councillor at Ottignies-Louvain-la-Neuve. B Aug 13 1943.

Addresses: Avenue des Combattants 26, 1340 Ottignies. Tel: (010) 41 85 44. PSC, 45 rue des Deux Eglises, 1040 Bruxelles. Tel: (02) 238 01 11.

DESAMA, CLAUDE
Belgium, Soc (PS)

Mr Claude Desama became an MEP in 1988 and was re-elected in 1989. Mbr, EP Cmte on Energy, Research and Technology. University professor. B Oct 9 1942; Doctor of Philosphy.

Addresses: Floréal, 7 Crapaurue, 4800 Verviers. Tel: (087) 33 95 95. 161E rue du Paradis, 4821 Dison. Tel: (087) 31 01 25.

DESMOND, BARRY
Ireland, Soc (Lab)

Mr Barry Desmond, elected to EP in 1989, joined Cmte on Economic and Monetary Affairs and Industrial Policy and became a vice-chmn; also a vice-chmn, Socialist Gp. Minister for Social Welfare, 1982-86; Minister of State, Dept of Finance, with responsibility for Economic Planning, 1981-82. Asst Govt Chief Whip and Chief Whip, Lab Party, 1973-77. First elected to Dail in 1969; mbr, Cl of State, 1973- ; Dail Cmte of Public Accounts, 1987. On Dublin CC, 1974-82 (chmn, 1980-81); trustee, Dalkey School Project, 1976- . Lab spokesman on finance and public service, 1987; deputy ldr, Lab Party, since 1982; vice-president, Irish Cl of European Movement, 1972- ; Irish delegate, Cl of Europe, 1973-81. Education and industrial officer, Irish Congress of Trade Unions, 1964-69. B May 1935.

Address: 2 Taney Avenue, Dublin 14. Tel: (01) 985719.

143

DESYLLAS, DIMITRIOS
Greece, CG (SAP/Comm)

Mr Dimitrios Desyllas became an MEP during the 1984-89 Parliament and was re-elected in 1989. Mbr, EP Cmte on Agriculture, Fisheries and Rural Development. Agronomist. Mbr of Greek Young Communist Party and several agricultural organizations. B Nov 12 1947.

Addresses: Leof. Irakliou 145, Nea Ionia, 142 31 Nea Ionia. Tel: (1) 252 25 91. Pithagora 11 be Mytsinis, 142 31 Nea Ionia. Tel: (1) 252 25 91.

DIEZ DE RIVERA ICAZA, SRA CARMEN
Spain, Soc (POSE)

Sra Carmen Diez de Rivera Icaza rejoined the EP Committee on Environment, Public Health and Consumer Protection after the 1989 elections; first elected MEP in 1987. Was head of Prime Minister's office in 1976. B Aug 29 1942.

Address: Henares 10-A, 28002 Madrid. Tel: (1) 411 51 51.

DIJK, MEVR P (NEL) VAN
Netherlands, Verts (CPN)

Mevr P (Nel) B van Dijk, an MEP since 1987 and re-elected 1989, is serving on the EP Cmte on Social Affairs and Employment and the EP Cmte on Women's Rights; was on these cmtes in outgoing Parliament. Archivist. Former mbr of Communist Party. Worked for trade union movement; action on union side in management of steel industry, 1982-84. B Oct 22 1952.

Address: Heistraat 14, 6136 Bd Sittard. Tel: (04498) 117 68.

DILLEN, KAREL
Belgium, DR (VB)

Mr Karel Dillen was elected to EP in 1989, becoming the first MEP from Vlaams Blok, the Flemish national party. Joined Droites Européennes Gp; appointed mbr, Political Affairs Cmte and Cmte on Petitions. Mbr of Volksunie until 1970; founder of Vlaams National Party in 1977, and Vlaams Blok in 1979. Former mbr, Belgian Chamber of Deputies and senator. Worker for Renault. B Oct 16 1925.

Address: Colmastraat 3, 2100 Antwerpen-Deurne. Tel: (03) 321 84 39. Telefax: (02) 217 52 75.

DOMINGO SEGARRA, SRA TERESA
Spain, EUL (IU)

Sra Teresa Domingo Segarra, economist and university professor, was elected to EP in 1989, joining Cmte on Agriculture, Fisheries and Rural Development and also being appointed a vice-chair of Cmte on Women's Rights. B Apr 24 1953.

Address: Plaza de Honduras 5 P.29, 46021 Valencia.

DONNEA, FRANCOIS-XAVIER DE
Belgium, LDR (PRL)

Mr Francois-Xavier de Donnea was elected to EP in 1989, joining Cmte on Economic and Monetary Affairs and Industrial Policy. Appointed treasurer of LDR Gp. Mbr, Belgian Chamber of Deputies; professor at Univ of Louvain; communal councillor of Bruxelles. Minister of Defence and Minister for Region Bruxelloise, 1985-88; Secretary of State for Cooperation and Development, 1983-85. Coopted senator, 1981-85, being chmn, Senate finance cmte, 1982-83. Secretary-General of PRL, 1982-83. B Apr 29 1941.

Address: Avenue Louise 557, 1050 Bruxelles.

DONNELLY, ALAN
UK, Tyne and Wear, Soc (Lab)

Mr Alan Donnelly was elected MEP for this Euro seat in 1989 and joined EP Cmte on Economic and Monetary Affairs and Industrial Policy and Cmte on Institutional Affairs. Enlarged group of Labour MEPs elected him their secretary. National finance manager for the General Municipal and Boilermakers' Union since 1987; previously press liaison officer for union's regional secretary and regional finance and administrative officer. South Tyne cllr, 1980-83; sec/agent for Jarrow, 1975-80. Chmn, Trade Unionists for Labour finance cmte; director, Unity Trust Bank; mbr, Prince of Wales Venture management cmte. B Jul 1957; ed local Jarrow state schs.

Addresses: 1 South View, Jarrow. Tel: (091) 489 7643. 1 Shearwater-Souter Point, Whitburn, Tyne and Wear.

DOUSTE-BLAZY, PHILIPPE
France, EPP (Centre; UDF)

M. Philippe Douste-Blazy is president of l'ARCOL, an association for the prevention of cardio-vascular diseases; professor of cardiology and doctor of medicine. Elected to EP in 1989 on French Centre Party list headed by Mme Simone Veil; became mbr, Cmte on Environment, Public Health and Consumer Protection. Mayor of Lourdes (Haute-Pyrenees). B 1953.

*photograph
unavailable*

Address: 1 rue de Bagniere, 65100 Lourdes.

DÜHRKOP DÜHRKOP, SRA BARBARA
Spain, Soc (PSOE)

Sra Barbara Dührkop Dührkop was first elected to EP in 1987; re-elected 1989 and rejoined Cmte on Youth, Culture, Education, Information and Sport. Teacher. B Jul 27 1945.

Address: Bidebieta 2, Travesia Alondra, 5° D, 20009 San Sebastian. Tel: (43) 21 23 38

DURY, MME RAYMONDE
Belgium, Soc (PS)

Mme Raymonde Dury first became an MEP in 1982. A vice-chair of Socialist Gp after 1989 elections being leader of Belgian delegation; mbr, Political Affairs Cmte, Cmte on Institutional Affairs, and Cmte on Women's Rights, 1989- ; in outgoing Parliament was a vice-chair, Cmte on Petitions, and mbr, Cmtes on Social Affairs and Employment and on Rules of Procedure, Verification of Credentials and Immunities; former mbr, Cmte on Development and Cooperation. Press attache to Socialist Gp of EP, 1976-82. Sociologist. B Jul 22 1947.

Address: Parlement européen, Bureau 316, 97-113 rue Belliard, 1040 Bruxelles. Tel: (02) 234 21 11. Telefax: (02) 230 64 88.

DUVERGER, MAURICE
Italy, EUL (PCI)

M. Maurice Duverger successfully took advantage of the Italian law permitting citizens of other EC states to seek election in Italy; thus on Italian Communist list became MEP in 1989 and joined EP Cmte on Institutional Affairs. University professor; expert on constitutional law. Special adviser to President Mitterand. B Jun 5 1917

Address: 24 rue Fosses Saint Jacques, Paris. Tel: (1) 46 33 27 10.

ELLES, JAMES
UK, Oxford and Buckinghamshire, ED (C)

Mr James Elles became EDG spokesman on Cmte on External Economic Relations in 1989; first elected to EP in 1984; mbr, Budgets Cmte, 1984-89. Chmn, America-European Community Assocn European Parliamentary Cmte; founder, EC Baroque Orchestra; co-founder/patron, Thames Action and Resource Gp for Education and Training. Served in External Relations Division of EEC Commission, 1976-80, being the expert responsible for fisheries negotiations, 1976-77; participated in Tokyo Round multilateral trade negotiations in Gatt, 1977-80; Asst to Dep Director General of Agriculture, EEC Commission, 1980-83, with duties that included responsibility for food aid to Poland, 1980-82. B Sep 3 1949; ed Ashdown House; Eton; Edinburgh Univ.

Address: Conservative Centre, Church Street, Amersham. Tel: Amersham 21577. (01) 828 8477.

ELLIOTT, MICHAEL
UK, London West, Soc (Lab)

Mr Michael Elliott was first elected to EP in 1984 being mbr since then of EP Cmte on Youth, Culture, Education, Information and Sport; former whip of British Lab Gp of MEPs. Formerly a scientist in food industry. Contested Bedfordshire in first Euro elections in 1979, and Wembley South in 1970, 1966 and 1964 general elections. Mbr, Ealing BC, 1964-86 (former ldr of cl and chmn, ed cmte). B Jun 3 1932; ed Greenford GS; Brunel Coll of Tech. Mbr, Lab Coordinating Cmte, Co-op Pty, CND, Friends of the Earth, MSFU.

Address: 358 Oldfield Lane North, Greenford, Middlesex UB6 8PT. Tel: (01) 578 1303.

ELMALAN, MME MIREILLE
France, CG (PCF)

Mme Mireille Elmalan was elected MEP in 1989 and became mbr, Cmte on Social Affairs, Employment and Working Environment, and Cmte on Women's Rights. Clerk. Deputy mayor of Pierre-Benite (Rhone). On central cmte of PCF. B 1949.

Address: Comité Central du Parti Communiste Français, 2 place du Colonel Fabien, 75940 Paris Cedex 19.

EPHREMIDIS, VASSILIS
Greece, CG (SAP/Comm)

Mr Vassilis Ephremidis became MEP during 1979-84 Parliament being re-elected in 1984 and 1989. Became vice-chmn, Coalition des Gauches, after 1989 elections; was a vice-chmn, EP Communist and Allies Gp, in outgoing Parliament; mbr, Political Affairs Cmte, Institutional Affairs Cmte and Cmte on Rules of Procedure, Verification of Credentials and Immunities. Lawyer. Elected to Greek national assembly in 1950s; editor of *Avgi*, 1952-56. B Dec 31 1915. Has served on central cmte of his party.

Addresses: Leoforos Irakleiou 145, 142 31 New Ionia. Tel: (1) 252 21 91. Ithakis 41, 112 51 Athina. Tel: (1) 884 33 20.

ERNST DE LA GRAETE, MME BRIGITTE
Belgium, Verts (Ecolo)

Mme Brigitte Ernst de la Graete was elected to EP in 1989 and joined Cmtes on Economic and Monetary Affairs and Industrial Policy and on Women's Rights. Lawyer and sociologist. Local councillor at Liege, heading Ecolo gp; magistrate in Liege, 1983-88. Member of numerous associations connected with youth and environment. B Apr 23 1957.

photograph
unavailable

Address: 49 Thier de la Fontaine, 4000 Liege. Tel (041) 23 75 22.

ESCUDER CROFT, ARTURO
Spain, EPP (PP)

Señor Arturo Escuder Croft was nominated to EP in Jan 1986; elected for first time in 1987; re-elected 1989 and joined Cmte on Regional Policy and Regional Planning in 1989; former mbr, Cmte on Budgetary Control, on which he was ED Gp coordinator in outgoing Parliament; also former mbr, Cmte on External Economic Relations. Economist and lawyer, Universidad de Deusto. Former businessman and general manager of group of companies in food industry; former chmn, European Federation of Soft Drinks (CESDA); former mbr, World Health Organization's food additives cmte. President, Chamber of Commerce, Industry and Navigation of Santa Cruz de Tenerife; Counsellor, Cabildo de Tenerife, an organization of presentatives from all towns in Canary Islands; Vice-President, Santa Cruz Port Cl.
Address: Autopista Norte, Km 12, num. 59, Los Rodeos, La Laguna, Tenerife. Tel: (22) 25 75 03.

ESTGEN, NICOLAS
Luxembourg, EPP (PCS)

Mr Nicolas Estgen, formerly a teacher, has been an elected MEP since 1979; a Vice-President of EP, 1982-84; a vice-chmn in outgoing Parliament of EP Cmte on Rules of Procedure, Verification of Credentials and Immunities; former mbr, Political Affairs Cmte; mbr, Cmte on Youth, Culture, Education, the Media and Sport, 1989- . Connected with family and consumer organizations. At one time responsible for vocational training and secondary and higher technical education at education ministry of Duchy and later became an assistant government adviser. B Feb 28 1930.

Addresses: 3 rue du Curé, 1368 Luxembourg. Tel: 28 282. 1 rue P. Wigreux, Howald. Tel: 48 68 89.

149

EWING, MRS WINIFRED
UK, Highlands and Islands, ARC (SNP)

Mrs Winifred Ewing, President of the Scottish National Party since 1987; mbr of EP since 1975 being nominated MEP, 1975-79, and then first elected for this seat in 1979. Joined Arc-en-Ciel (Rainbow) Gp in 1989; remained on Cmte on Development and Co-operation, which she joined in 1987. A vice-chair, RDE Gp, 1979-89; chaired Cmte on Youth, Culture, Education, Information and Sport, 1984-87. Solicitor. Vice-pres, SNP, 1968-87; SNP MP for Moray and Nairn, 1974-79, and for Hamilton, 1967-70; contested Orkney and Shetland in 1983 general election. B Jul 10 1929. Mbr, exec cmte, Scottish Cl for Development and Industry, 1972- . Pres, Glasgow Bar Assocn, 1970-71.

Addresses: 52 Queen's Drive, Glasgow G42 8DD, Scotland. Tel: (041) 423 1765. Goodwill, 22 Kinnedder Street, Lossiemouth, Morayshire, Scotland.

FABIUS, LAURENT
France, Soc (PS)

M. Laurent Fabius, President of the French National Assembly and former Prime Minister, was elected to EP in 1989 and became mbr, Institutional Affairs Cmte. Deputy for Seine-Maritime; Deputy Mayor of Grand-Quevilly. B 1946.

Address: Hôtel de Lassay, 126 rue de l'Université, 75007 Paris. Tel: 47 05 30 10.

FALCONER, ALEXANDER
UK, Mid Scotland and Fife, Soc (Lab)

Mr Alexander Falconer was first elected to EP in 1984; mbr, Cmte on Legal Affairs and Citizens' Rights, 1989- ; Cmte on Economic and Monetary Affairs and Industrial Policy, 1984-89. B Apr 1 1940; ed St Joseph's Primary Sch; St John's Jnr Sch. Apprentice machine tool fitter; served 1959-68 in RN as stoker and leading stoker; with Min of Defence as an insulater at Rosyth Dockyard, 1969-84. Chmn, Fife Fed of Trades Cls. TGWU shop steward, 1970-84; lay delegate, nat negotiating cmte, 1973-84; political delegate, Lab Pty, 1977-84.

Address: 25 Church Street, Inverkeithing, Fife KY11 1LH, Scotland. Tel: (0383) 41 93 30. 22 Burnside Street, Rosyth, Fife KY11 2NX. Tel: (0383) 41 86 17.

FALQUI, ENRICO
Italy, Verts (Verde)

Sgr Enrico Falqui became elected MEP in 1989; joined Cmte on Agriculture, Fisheries and Rural Development. University lecturer. Regional councillor in Toscana. Founder of the Green list. B Aug 31 1946.

Address:

FANTINI, ANTONIO
Italy, EPP (DC)

Sgr Antonio Fantini, elected to EP in 1989, became mbr, Cmte on Transport and Tourism. Regional councillor, being chmn, region of Campania; former president, regional cl of Naples. B Jan 31 1936.

Address: Via Nicolardi 8 - P.co Orchidea, 80131 Napoli. Tel: (081) 743 01 28.

FANTUZZI, GIULIO
Italy, EUL (PCI)

Sgr Giulio Fantuzzi, engineer, was elected to EP in 1989. Joined Cmte on Agriculture, Fisheries and Rural Development. Mayor of Reggio Emilia. Vice-President of agricultural cooperative organization. B Sep 17 1950.

Address: Comune di Reggio Emilia, Piazzi Prampolini 1, 42100 - Reggio Emilia. Tel: (0522) 79 81.

FAYOT, BEN
Luxembourg, Soc (POSL)

Mr Ben Fayot, elected to EP in 1989 and mbr of Political Affairs Cmte, has been President of POSL, the Socialist Party of Luxembourg, since 1985. Mbr, Luxembourg Chamber of Deputies, 1984-89, and of communal council of Luxembourg since 1982. Professor at teacher training college. B Jun 25 1937.

Address: 36 bd de la Pétrusse, 2320 Luxembourg. Tel: 48 58 70 and 47 39 43 (bureau).

FERNÁNDEZ ALBOR, GERARDO
Spain, EPP (PP)

Señor Gerardo Fernández Albor, medical practitioner and surgeon; former President of Academy of Medicine and Surgery at Univ of Saint-Jacques-de-Compostelle. Became elected MEP in 1989; mbr, Cmte on Development and Cooperation. Former chmn, *Xubta* (regional govt), Galice; former deputy, regional assembly, Galice. B 1917.

Address: Alfredo Brañs, 16 Entlo., Santiago de Compostla, La Coruña.

FERNEX, MME SOLANGE
France, Verts (Verts)

Mme Solange Fernex was elected to EP in 1989 and became mbr, Cmte on Transport and Tourism. Secretary. Municipal councillor at Biederthal (Haut-Rhin). President of "Women for Peace" movement. Spokesperson for Les Verts; headed French list in 1979 European elections. B 1934.

Address: Biederthal, 68480 Ferette. Tel: 89 40 71 83.

FERRARA, GIULIANO
Italy, Soc (PSI)

Sgr Giuliano Ferrara became elected MEP in 1989 and joined EP Cmte on Legal Affairs and Citizens' Rights. Journalist. Former leader of Communist Party in Turin. B Jan 7 1952.

Address: c.o. Massimo di Nunzio, Via Bruxelles 53. 00198 Roma. Tel: (06) 811 96 96.

FERRER I CASALS, SRA CONCEPCIÓ
Spain, EPP (CiU)

Sra Concepció Ferrer i Casals was elected MEP in 1987; re-elected 1989 when she rejoined EP Cmte on Institutional Affairs; also mbr, Political Affairs Cmte. Professor of literature. Former mbr, Catalonian regional assembly; former secretary-general of UDC, the Democratic Union of Catalonia. Chairs Union of Christian-Democratic Women. B Jan 27 1938. Mbr, bureau, EPP Gp, as leader of groups Spanish delegation.

Addresses: Valencia, 246 Pral., 08017 Barcelona. Tel: (3) 215 55 66. Col.legi 51 5°A, 17600 Figueres (Girona). Tel: 50 12 92.

FERRI, ENRICO
Italy, Soc (PSDI)

Sgr Enrico Ferri, a former Minister for Public Works, was elected to EP in 1989 and became a vice-chmn, Cmte on Institutional Affairs, and mbr, bureau of Socialist Gp. University professor and magistrate; former mbr, Council of Magistrates and former president, National Association of Magistrates. B Feb 17 1942.

Address: Ministero dei Lavori Pubblici, Piazzale Porta Pia, 00198 Roma. Tel: (06) 85 30 97.

153

FINI, GIANFRANCO
Italy, NI (MSI-DN)

Sgr Gianfranco Fini, national secretary of the Italian Social Movement (MSI), was elected to EP in 1989 and joined Political Affairs Cmte. Mbr, Italian Chamber of Deputies. Journalist. B Jan 3 1952.

Address: MSI-DN, Via della Scrofa 30, 00186 Roma. Tel: (06) 654 51 26.

FITZGERALD, GENE
Ireland, RDE (FF)

Mr Gene Fitzgerald, a member of the Dail since the early 1970s, was first elected to the EP in 1984 and since then has been treasurer of RDE Gp. Mbr, Cmte on Regional Policy and Regional Planning, 1989- ; a vice-chmn, EP Cmte on Social Affairs and Employment, in outgoing Parliament; was also mbr, Cmte on Petitions. Minister of Labour, 1977-80; Minister for Finance and Public Service, 1980-81; President, EEC Council of Social Affairs Ministers, 1979; President, European Investment Bank, Jan to Jun 1981, B Aug 21 1932.

Address: 'Cloduv', 2 Melbourne Road, Bishopstown, Cork. Tel: (021) 544347.

FITZSIMONS, JIM
Ireland, RDE (FF)

Mr Jim Fitzsimons was elected to EP in 1984 and re-elected 1989 when he joined Cmte on Environment, Public Health and Consumer Protection and Cmte on Petitions. Has served on Cmte on Energy, Research and Technology. Irish Minister of State, Dept of Industry and Energy, Oct to Dec 1982; mbr of Dail since 1977. B Dec 16 1936.

Address: 'Ardsion', Dublin Road, Navan, Co. Meath, Tel: (046) 21540.

FLESCH, MME COLETTE
Luxembourg, LDR (PD)

Mme Colette Flesch, who has been both Minister and Opposition leader in her country, was re-elected to the EP in 1989. Became a vice-chair of LDR Gp and of Cmte on Budgets; also mbr, Cmtes on Budgetary Control and on Development and Cooperation which she formerly chaired. President, Parti democratique. Mbr of nominated EP from 1969; elected in 1979 but left in 1980; against elected MEP, 1984-85. Held office in Liberal Gp, 1970-80. Mbr, Chamber of Deputies, 1969-80 and 1984-89; Mayor of Luxembourg, 1970-80. Ministerial offices include foreign affairs, trade and cooperation, and justice. B Apr 6 1937; ed Wellesley Coll, Wellesley, Massachusetts; Fletcher School of Law and Diplomacy, Melford, Massachusetts. Administrator in secretariat of Council of EC, Brussels, 1964-69.
Address:11a bd Prince Henri, 1724 Luxembourg. Tel: 47 39 10.

FLORENZ, KARL-HEINZ
Germany, EPP (CDU)

Herr Karl-Heinz Florenz, farmer, was elected MEP in 1989 and became mbr, EP Cmte on Environment, Public Health and Consumer Protection. Municipal councillor; spokesman of CDU gp on Neukirchen-Vluyn cl; mbr, environment and agriculture consultative cmtes of CDU in Rhine-North Westphalia. B Oct 22 1947.

Address: Gut Gross-Opholt, 4133 Neukirchen-Vluyn.

FONTAINE, MME NICOLE
France, EPP (UDF-CDS)

Mme Nicole Fontaine was elected a Vice-President of EP in July 1989; formerly chaired the EPP Gp working party on political affairs. Elected MEP in 1984; mbr, Cmte on Youth, Culture, Education, the Media and Sport; former EPP spokesman on Cmte on Legal Affairs and Citizens' Rights; former mbr, Cmte on Women's Rights. Former Deputy Secretary-General, Catholic Education Secretariat. B Jan 16 1942. Doctorate in law; diploma in political science. Has served on Higher Cl of National Education and, from 1980, Economic and Social Cl.

Address: 13 rue Pierre Nicole, 75005 Paris. Tel: (1) 43 54 24 82.

FORD, GLYN
UK, Greater Manchester East, Soc (Lab)

Mr Glyn Ford was elected leader of enlarged Labour gp of MEPs immediately after 1989 Euro elections; senior vice-chmn, Socialist Gp, 1989- . First elected to EP 1984; mbr, Political Affairs Cmte, 1987- ; Cmte on Rules of Procedure, Verification of Credentials and Immunities, 1989- ; External Economic Relations Cmte, 1984-87; chmn, EP cmte of inquiry into growth of racism and fascism in Europe, 1984-86; vice-chmn, sub-cmte on security and disarmament, 1987-89. Contested Hazel Grove in 1987 general election. Senior Research Fellow, Manchester Univ, 1980-84; Hon Visiting Research Fellow since 1984; Visiting Professor, Tokyo Univ, 1983. B Jan 28 1950. Mbr, Tameside BC, 1978-86. Book reviewer.
Addresses: 3 Market Place, Ashton-under-Lyne, Lancashire OL6 7JD. Tel: (061) 344 3000. 149 Old Road, Ashton-under-Lyne, Lancashire OL6 9DA. Tel: (061) 330 9299.

FORLANI, ARNALDO
Italy, EPP (DC)

Sgr Arnaldo Forlani, former Italian Prime Minister and Minister and former President of the Council of Ministers, was elected to EP in 1989. Mbr, Italian Chamber of Deputies; lawyer; national secretary of DC party presiding over its national council; responsible for its information section. Former secretary-general, European Union of Christian Democrats. B Dec 8 1925; doctor of law.

Address: P. le SAchuman 15, 00144 Roma. Tel: (06) 677 51.

FORMIGONI, ROBERTO
Italy, EPP (DC)

Sgr Roberto Formigoni has been a Vice-President of EP since 1987; first elected MEP in 1984, and chaired Political Affairs Cmte, 1984-87; former mbr, Cmte on Youth, Culture, Education, Information and Sport. Graduate in philosophy; secondary school teacher; assistant university lecturer, 1971-73. Mbr, Chamber of Deputies. Former chmn and co-founder in 1976, *Movimento Popolare*, with aim to promote participation of Catholics in cultural, social and political activities by means of cooperatives, cultural centres and discussion groups. B Mar 3 1947.

Addresses: c.o. Mivimento Popolare, Via Copernico 7, 20125 Milano. Tel: (02) 60 66 41. Via Liberiana 21, 00185 Roma.

FORTE, MARIO
Italy, EPP (DC)

Sgr Mario Forte, lawyer, is a former Mayor of Naples. Elected MEP in 1989 and joined EP Cmte on Budgets. Local, provincial and regional official of DC. Mbr, Naples regional cl, and assessor. B Sep 22 1936; doctor of law.

Address: Via Sanfelice 20, 80129 Napoli. Tel: (081) 24 29 25.

FRIEDRICH, INGO
Germany, EPP (CSU)

Herr Ingo Friedrich, first elected to EP in 1979, is chmn of the European Medium and Small Business Union (EMSU). Mbr, EP Cmte on Economic and Monetary Affairs and Industrial Policy and a vice-chmn, Cmte on Petitions. Executive in electrical industyry from 1970; on staff of Institute for Politics and Communications, Univ of Erlangen-Nuremberg, 1967-70. Deputy chmn, CSU for Central Franconia region, 1977; CSU chmn, Weissenburg-Gunzenhausen district, from 1972. B Jan 24 1942.

Address: Albert-Schweitzer-Strasse 61, 8820 Gunzenhausen. Tel: (09831) 7447.

FUCHS, GÉRARD
France, Soc (PS)

M. Gérard Fuchs was re-elected to EP in 1989 and joined Cmte on Economic and Monetary Affairs and Industrial Policy, becoming a vice-chmn; also became mbr, Cmte on Institutional Affairs. Served as elected MEP, 1981-84, being mbr, Cmte on Development and Cooperation. Deputy Mayor, Blanc-Mesnil (Seine-Saint-Denis); regional councillor, d'Ile-de-France; national secretary, Socialist Party, responsible for European affairs and security; former Paris deputy. B May 18 1940.

Address: 10 rue de Solférino, 75007 Paris. Tel: 45 56 78 28.

FUNCK, HONOR
Germany, EPP (CDU)

Herr Honor Funck, agricultural engineer and farmer, was elected to EP in 1989 and became mbr of its Cmte on Agriculture, Fisheries and Rural Protection. Chmn, agriculture cmte, Bade-Wurftemberg CDU, and party spokesman on agriculture; chmn of a farmers' organization. Former mbr, Bundestag. B Jun 27 1930.

photograph
unavailable

Address: Schlossbezirk, 7959 Gutenzell. Tel: (07352) 2403.

GAIBISSO, GERARDO
Italy, EPP (DC)

Sgr Gerardo Gaibisso, journalist and director of federation of owner-farmers, was elected one of the EP's quaestors in July 1989. First became elected MEP 1984; mbr, Cmte on Environment, Public Health and Consumer Protection. Former mbr, Lazio regional Cl, and has been mbr, National Cl, Christian Democratic Party, and provincial cl of CISL (Italian Confederation of Workers' Trade Unions). Editor of Catholic trade union journal *Politica Sociale.* and periodical *La Zolla.* B May 30 1927.

Addresses: Via Moccia 76, 03100 Frosinone. Tel: (775) 85 00 26 or 85 53 22. Via Lecce 31, 03100 Frosinone. Tel: (775) 85 73 45.

GALLAND, YVES
France, LDR (Radical)

M. Yves Galland was elected a Vice-President of EP in July 1989. First elected to EP in 1979; re-elected 1984 but ceased being MEP; served on Cmte on Development and Cooperation; re-elected 1989 and rejoined Cmte on Development and Cooperation. Chmn, Radical Party. A Deputy Mayor of Paris and former Paris deputy. Company director. Has served as national secretary of UDF (Union for French Democracy). B Mar 8 1941.

Address: 36 rue Sainte Croix de la Bretonnerie, 75004 Paris. Tel: (1) 42 72 67 38.

GALLE, MARK
Belgium, Soc (SP)

Mr Mark Galle was elected to EP in 1989; became mbr, Cmte on Youth, Culture, Education, the Media and Sport; chmn, Cmte on Rules of Procedure, Verification of Credentials and Immunities; also mbr, bureau, Socialist Gp. Former minister in Belgian regional assembly. University professor. B Sep 11 1930.

Address: Wateringen 1, 9300 Aalst. Tel: (053) 78 70 70.

GALLENZI, GIULIO
Italy, EPP (DC)

Sgr Giulio Gallenzi was elected to EP in 1989; became mbr, Cmte on Economic and Monetary Affairs and Industrial Policy. Journalist. Vice-chmn, Rome regional council. B Nov 28 1931.

Address: Via Silvestri 204, 00135 Roma. Tel: (06) 625 75 04.

GALLO, MAX
France, Soc (PS)

M. Max Gallo, academic and journalist, was first elected to EP in 1984; re-elected 1989. Former Government spokesman; mbr, PS national cmte; Alpes-maritimes deputy, 1981. Holder of doctorate in contemporary history; former professor, Lycee de Nice. B Jan 7 1932.

Addresses: 17 rue de la Préfecture, 06000 Nice. Tel: 93 80 57 01. 5 place du Panthéon, 75005 Paris.

GANGOITI LLAGUNO, JUAN
Spain, NI (CN)

Señor Juan Gangoiti Llaguno was elected to EP in 1989 and joined Cmte on Youth, Culture, Education, the Media and Sport. Former deputy in Spanish Parliament and MEP, 1986-87. Was spokesman for Basque parliamentary gp in negotiations for Spanish membership of EC; former spokesman on agriculture and fruit cmtes. B Nov 5 1951; diploma on economic science and commerce.

Address: Heros 28, Bilbao.

GARAIKOETXEA URRIZA, JUAN CARLOS
Spain, ARC (EA)

Señor Juan Carlos Garaikoetxea Urriza was first elected MEP in 1987; after 1989 elections rejoined EP Cmte on Regional Policy and Regional Planning. President, regional Basque government, 1980-85; president of *Eusko Alkartasuna* (EA) Party. B Jun 2 1938.

Addresses: Avda. Baja Navarra 34, 31002 Pamplona. Tel: (48) 22 80 90. Eusko Alkartasuna, Plaza del Castillo 49 2°, 31001 Pamplona. Farrerias 9, 28004 San Sebastian.

GARCÍA, VASCO
Portugal, LDR (PSD)

Senhor Vasco García serves on EP Cmte on Agriculture, Fisheries and Rural Development. First elected to EP in 1987; re-elected 1989. University professor. Became a deputy in Portuguese national assembly, 1985. Deputy in regional assembly of Azores, 1980-84. B May 21 1939.

Addresses: Universidade dos Açores, 9500 Ponta Delgada, Açores. Tel: (096) 25 320. Bairro de Beléem 9, Estrada da Ribiera Grande, 9500 Ponta Delgada, Açores. Tel: (096) 32 449.

GARCÍA AMIGO, MANUEL
Spain, EPP (PP)

Señor Manuel García Amigo, Professor of Civil Law, Madrid Univ, became a nominated MEP in Jan 1986; first elected 1987. Mbr, Cmte on Legal Affairs and Citizens Rights; was ED Gp coordinator in outgoing Parliament. Has served as President, National Political Cl, Alianza Popular, 1982-84; Vice-President, Alianza Popular, 1980-82; from 1982, deputy for Zaragoza, Spanish Parliament; Vice-President, Constitutional Commission, Spanish Congress; Professor and Dean, Faculty of Political Science and Sociology, Complutense Univ, Madrid; Professor, Head of Civil Law Department, Univs of La Laguna (Canary Islands), Oviedo and Zaragoze. B Oct 2 1935.

Address: Paseo de la Castellana 129 8-C, 28046 Madrid. Tel: (1) 456 38 72.

GARCÍA ARIAS, SRA LUDIVINA
Spain, Soc (PSOE)

Sra Ludivina García Arias, a teacher, has been an MEP since 1986. After 1989 elections joined Cmte on Energy, Research and Technology. Former member, Spanish national Parliament. Teacher. Has served on EP Committees on Development and Cooperation and on Women's Rights. B Dec 13 1945.

Address: Carrera de San Jerónimo, 44-3° F, Madrid.

GASÒLIBA I BÖHM, CARLES-ALFRED
Spain, LDR (CiU)

Señor Carles-Alfred Gasòliba i Böhm became an MEP in 1986; after 1989 elections joined EP Cmte on Energy, Research and Technology and Cmte on Petitions; on Transport Cmte in outgoing Parliament. Economist. Former mbr, Spanish national Parliament. B Nov 22 1945.

Address: Valencia 231 1°, 08007 Barcelona. Tel: (3) 215 56 66. Taquigrafo Marti 10, Atico 2a, 08028 Barcelona. Tel: (3) 339 88 55.

GAWRONSKI, JAS
Italy, LDR (PRI)

Sgr Jas Gawronski, journalist, became an MEP in 1981 being re-elected 1984 and 1989. A vice-chmn, EP Cmte on Institutional Affairs, 1984-87, and since then, mbr of Political Affairs Cmte. B Feb 7 1936.

Address: Largo Fontanella Borghese 19, 00186 Roma. Tel: (06) 68 76 174.

GIANNAKOU-KOUTSIKOU, KA MARIETTA
Greece, EPP (ND)

Ka Marietta Giannakou-Koutsikou was elected to EP in 1984 and until 1989 was a vice-chair of Cmte on Women's Rights but is still mbr of cmte; also mbr, Cmte on Social Affairs, Employment and Work Environment. Mbr, bureau, EPP Gp as leader of Greek delegation. Mbr, executive, New Democracy. Doctor, neurologist and psychiatrist. Chaired EP cmte of inquiry into drugs problem. B Jun 5 1951; ed Athens Univ and in Belgium and England. Founder mbr, ONNED, the ND youth movement, and was general editor of its newspaper *Dimokratiki Proptoporia.* Founder mbr, Pan-Hellenic Union of Women Scientists.

Addresses: Rue Demertzi 10, 104 45 Athina. Tel: (1) 832 26 00 or 831 70 48. Voulis 41, 105 57 Athina. Tel: (1) 325 03 84.

GIL-ROBLES, JOSÉ MARÍA
Spain, EPP (PP)

Señor José María Gil-Robles, lawyer; official of Spanish Parliament and former university assistant professor. Elected to EP in 1989; mbr, Cmte on Youth, Culture, Education, the Media and Sport, and Cmte on Petitions. Mbr, cmte *"Pensee et Action"* of European Union of Christian Democrats. B Jun 17 1935.

Address: Velazquez 3, 20001 Madrid.

GIOVANNI, BIAGIO DE
Italy, EUL (PCI)

Sgr Biagio de Giovanni, university professor, was elected to EP in 1989. He became mbr, Cmte on Youth, Culture, Education, the Media and Sport and Cmte on Institutional Affairs. B Dec 21 1931.

Address: Via d'Isernia 57, 80100 Napoli. Tel: (081) 761 20 31.

GISCARD D'ESTAING, VALÉRY
France, LDR (UDF-PR)

M. Valéry Giscard d'Estaing, former President of France, was elected to EP in 1989 when he headed the UDF-RPR list from which 26 became MEPs. Elected leader of Liberal and Democratic Reformist Gp (LDR). Leader of UDF Party. Chairs Foreign Affairs Cmte of National Assembly; deputy for Puy-de-Dome; President of regional council of Auvergne. B Feb 2 1926.

Address: 19 rue Francois 1er, 75000 Paris.

GIUDICE, CALOGERO LO
Italy, EPP (DC)

Sgr Calogero Lo Giudice, university professor specialising in agriculture and rural studies, is chmn of the region of Sicily and chairs parliamentary gp in Sicilian regional assembly. Elected to EP in 1989 and joined Cmtes on Budgets and Budgetary Control. Mbr, national cl, Italian Confederation of Cooperatives; formerly provincial and regional coordinator. B Jun 16 1938.

Address: Via Pergusa - Pal. Marzuolo, 94100 Enna. Tel: (0935) 249 34.

GLINNE, ERNEST
Belgium, Soc (PS)

Mr Ernest Glinne, first elected to EP in 1979, was chmn of Socialist Gp, 1979-84, a vice-chmn, 1984-87, and mbr of its bureau, 1987-89. Elected an EP quaestor in 1984 and re-elected 1989 when he also joined Cmte on Social Affairs, Employment and Working Environment. Ws a gp vice-chmn in nominated EP which he joined in 1968. Mbr, Belgian Parliament, as deputy for Charleroi, 1961-84. Former Minister of Employment and Labour. B Mar 30 1931; graduate in political, administrative and diplomatic science. Burgomaster of Courcelles, 1965-79.

Address: 1 square Salvador Allende, 6180 Courcelles. Tel: (071) 45 30 66.

GOLLNISCH, BRUNO
France, DR (FN)

M.Bruno Gollnisch, doctor of international law and professor of Japanese at university of Lyon, was elected to EP in 1989. Joined Cmte on Legal Affairs and Citizen's Rights and Cmte on Rules of Procedure, Verification of Credentials and Immunities. Mbr, Rhone-Alpes regional council; former deputy for Rhone. B Jan 28 1950.

Address: 18 Boulevard de l'Europe, 69110 Saint-Foy-Les-Lyon.

GOMES, FERNANDO SANTOS
Portugal, Soc (PS)

Senhor Fernando Santos Gomes became an MEP in 1988 and was chairman of the EP Cmte on Social Affairs and Employment until 1989; now on Cmte on Regional Policy and Regional Planning. Chaired municipal council of Vila do Conde, 1974-81. Elected to Portuguese national assembly in 1979. Former Secretary of State. B Apr 13 1946.

Addresses: Av. do Ferrol 374, 4480 Vila do Conde. Tel: (52) 63 34 78. R. Arco do Carvalhão 211-6° A, 1300 Lisboa. Tel: (1) 68 70 72.

GORIA, GIOVANNI
Italy, EPP (DC)

Sgr Giovanni Goria was elected to EP in 1989 and became chmn of the Political Affairs Cmte in July 1989, and also mbr, bureau, EPP Gp. Mbr, Italian Chamber of Deputies; former Prime Minister and minister; former President of Cl of Ministers. Was responsible for economic department of DC Party. B Jul 30 1943; doctor of economic science.

Address: Corso Alfieri 310, 14100 Asti. Tel: (0141) 324 31.

GÖRLACH, WILLI
Germany, Soc (SDP)

Herr Willi Görlach, teacher, was elected to EP in 1989 and appointed to Cmte on Agriculture, Fisheries and Rural Development. Former mbr of and Minister for Agriculture and the Environment, Hesse regional assembly. B Dec 17 1940.

Address: Oberpforte 2, 6308 Butzbach 5. Tel: (06033) 60292.

GRAEFE ZU BARINGDORF, FRIEDRICH-WILHELM
Germany, ARC (GRÜNE)

Herr Friedrich-Wilhelm Graefe zu Baringdorf was first elected to EP in 1984 and was a vice-chmn of Cmte on Agriculture, Fisheries and Food. Was a co-chmn of ARC Gp; later resigned; re-elected 1989 and reappointed vice-chmn of Cmte on Agriculture, Fisheries and Rural Development. Teacher and farmer. Was member, Evangelical Young Farmers of Westphalian/Lippisch Young Farmers. Took leading role in formulating alternative agricultural policy. Part of his farm has been turned over to organic farming. B Nov 29 1942.

Address: Am Berningshof 2, 4905 Spenge, Tel: (05225) 1744.

GREEN, MS PAULINE
UK, London North, Soc (Lab)

Ms Pauline Green won this seat in 1989 and became mbr, EP Cmte on Environment, Public Health and Consumer Protection. She was assistant parliamentary secretary, Co-operative Union Ltd, responsible for European affairs. Coordinated Co-op Union campaign to persuade EC Commission and Parliament of need for food hygiene legislation as integral part of 1992 programme. B Dec 8 1948; ed John Kelly Sec Mod Girls Sch, Brent; Open Univ; LSE. School governor and trustee. Ex-chair, Chipping Barnet and constituency Lab Pty sec; currently asst CLP sec. Usdaw; Nat Assocn of Co-op Officials.

Address:8 Normandy Avenue, Barnet EN5 2JA, Herts. Tel (01) 449 4885.

GREMETZ, MAXIMÉ
France, CG (PCF)

M. Maximé Gremetz was first elected to EP in 1979; re-elected 1984, served on Cmte on Legal Affairs and Citizens Rights, but ceased membership during the Parliament being re-elected 1989. Now on Cmte on External Economic Relations. Mbr, National Assembly for the Somme, 1978-81; county councillor for Somme. Has served as secretary, Central Cmte of French Communist Party; is mbr of its political bureau. Metal worker. B Sep 3 1940.

Address: 31 rue J.P. Timbaud, 93700 Drancy.

GRÖNER, FRAU LIESELOTTE
Germany, Soc (SDP)

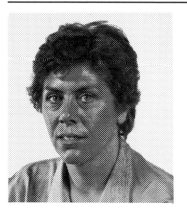

Frau Lieselotte (Lissy) Gröner, secretary and housewife, has held several posts in SPD organization. Elected to EP in 1989 and joined Cmte on Youth, Culture, Education, the Media and Sport. B May 31 1954.

Address: Parkstrasse 15, 8530 Naustadt/Aisch.

GRUND, FRAU JOHANNA-CHRISTINA
Germany, DR (Repub)

Frau Johanna-Christina Grund, journalist, was elected to EP in 1989 and joined Cmte on Legal Affairs and Citizens' Rights and Cmte on Women's Rights. Vice-President of Republican Party. B 1934.

Address: Jennerstrasse 6, 8262 Altotting.

GUCHT, KAREL DE
Belgium, LDR (PVV)

Mr Karel de Gucht has been an MEP since May 1980. Mbr, Cmte on Legal Affairs and Citizen's Rights and Cmte on Institutional Affairs; former mbr, Political Affairs Cmte. National Vice-President of PVV; national chmn, Young PVV, 1977-79. Lawyer. Held public office in Lebbbeke, 1982-88. B Jan 27 1954.

Address: Hoogstraat 9, 9290 Berlare. Tel: (052) 42 53 86. Telefax: (052) 42 53 88.

GUIDOLIN, FRANCESCO
Italy, EPP (DC)

Sgr Francesco Guidolin chairs regional council of Venice. Journalist; syndicates for CISL, the Italian Confederation of Workers' Trade Unions. Elected to EP in 1989; mbr, Cmte on Environment, Public Health and Consumer Protection. B Mar 24 1923.

Address: Via Cadorna 7, 36100 Vicenza.

167

GUILLAUME, FRANÇOIS
France, RDE (RPR)

M.François Guillaume, a former Franch Minister of Agriculture, was elected to EP in 1989 and became mbr, Cmte on Agriculture, Fisheries and Rural Development. Farmer. Former president, economic and social council for Lorraine. B 1932.

*photograph
unavailable*

Address: Ville-en-Vernoism 54210 St Nicolas de Port.

GUTIÉRREZ DIAZ, ANTONI
Spain, EUL (IU)

Señor Antoni Gutiérrez Diaz, an elected MEP since 1987, rejoined EP Cmte on Regional Policy and Regional Planning after 1989 elections. Also on Cmte on Petitions. Vice-chmn, EUL Gp. Doctor. Secretary-General, Catalonia Socialist Party, 1977-81 and 1982-86. Former mbr, Spanish national Parliament; mbr, regional government of Catalonia, 1977-80. B Jan 19 1929.

Addresses: Ciutat n° 7, Comité Central PSUC, Barcelona. Tel: (3) 302 74 40. Balmes n° 349 2° 4°, Barcelona. Tel: (3) 417 33 62.

HABSBURG, OTTO
Germany, EPP (CSU)

Herr Otto Habsburg was first elected to EP in 1979; became EPP Gp spokesman on Political Affairs Cmte, remaining on cmte after 1989 elections. President, International Pan-European Union. Mbr, French Academy for Moral and Political Science, the Portuguese Cultural Academy and the Spanish Royal Academy for Moral and Political Science. President, International Cl of European Documentation and Information Centre, 1953-60, subsequently honorary President. B Nov 20 1912.

Addresses: Hindenburgstrasse 15, 8134 Pöcking. Tel: (08157) 7015. Paneuropa Büro, Karlstrasse 57, 8000 Munchen 2. Tel: (089) 55 46 83.

HÄNSCH, KLAUS
GERMANY, Soc (SPD)

Herr Klaus Hänsch is a vice-chmn of Socialist Gp in EP; and been chairman of EP delegation for relations with the United States. First elected to the EP in 1979 serving on the EP Political Affairs Cmte since and was a cmte vice-chairman, 1984-87; remained on cmte after 1989 elections; also mbr, Cmte on Institutional Affairs. Editor and former senior civil servant, North Rhine-Westphalia Ministry for Science and Research. Press adviser. Has chaired Mettman local SPD; holds several offices in party. B Dec 15 1938.

Addresses: Sperberweg 12, 4006 Erkrath. Tel: (0211) 246860. Europaabgeordnetenburo, Kavalleriestrasse 22/V, 4000 Dusseldorf 1. Tel: (0211) 132912.

HAPPART, JOSÉ
Belgium, Soc (PS)

Mr José Happart was first elected to EP in 1984 and since then has served on the Cmte on Agriculture, Fisheries and Rural Development; mbr, Cmte on Petitions, 1989- ; former mbr, Cmte on Regional Policy and Regional Planning. Former Mayor of Furons. Founder President of movement *Wallonie region d'Europe*. Agricultural engineer; active in farming organization. B Mar 14 1947.

Addresses: 23 En Feronstrée, 4000 Liege. Tel: (041) 23 06 69. 63a Rullen, 3792 Fouron-Saint-Pierre. Tel: (041) 81 06 56. 68 76 56.

HARRISON, LYNDON
UK, Cheshire West, Soc (Lab)

Mr Lyndon Harrison gained this Euro seat for Lab in 1989. He joined EP Cmte on Regional Policy and Regional Planning and became a vice-chmn of Cmte on Rules of Procedure, Verification of Credentials and Immunities. Student union manager; vice-chmn of North West Tourist Board. Mbr, Cheshire CC, 1982 and 1984-89, being chmn, Libraries and Countryside Cmtes, 1984-89. Nalgo and Co-op Pty. B Sep 28 1947; ed Warwick, Sussex and Keele Univs.

Addresses: 28 Gladstone Road, Chester CH1 4BZ. Tel: (0244) 37 56 26. 2 Stanley Street, Chester CH1 2LR. Tel: (0244) 438 26.

169

HEMELDONCK, MEVR MARIJKE VAN
Belgium, Soc (SP)

Mevr Marijke van Hemeldonck became an MEP in 1982; re-elected 1984 and 1989. Mbr, Cmte on Eco nomic and Monetary Affairs and Industrial Policy; has also served on Cmte on Women's Rights; former mbr, Cmte on Budgetary Control and Cmte on Environment, Public Health and Consumer Protection. Former civil servant, Bruxelloise region, and in national Ministry of Education. Expert on issues affecting employment of women, serving on various cmtes. B Dec 23 1931.

Address: Sterreplein 3, 1050 Brussel. Tel: (02) 648 78 18.

HERMAN, FERNAND
Belgium, EPP (PSC)

Mr Fernand Herman was first elected to EP in 1979; mbr, Cmte on Economic and Monetary Affairs and Industrial Policy and Cmte on Institutional Affairs; former mbr, Cmte on Rules of Procedure, Verification of Credentials and Immunities. Vice-chmn, PSC. Was Secretary-General, Cercles populaires europeens (European people's movement). Minister for Economic Affairs, 1975-77; Senator for Brussels, 1977-78, and deputy for Brussels, 1978-79. Director, National Society for Investment (SNI), 1964-75. B Jan 23 1932; doctor of law and degree in economics at Catholic Univ of Louvain.

Address: 28 rue Franklin, 1040 Bruxelles. Tel: (02) 735 87 91. Telefax: (02) 736 56 45.

HERMANS, MEVR ANNA
Belgium, EPP (CVP)

Mevr Anna Hermans, elected to EP in 1989, became mbr, Cmte on Youth, Culture, Education, the Media and Sport and Cmte on Women's Rights. Professor at the Catholic Univ of Louvain. Former Secretary-General, *Katholieke Arbeidersvrouwen* (KAV), the Catholic League of Women Workers; also chaired Belgian council for emancipation and Belgian development cl. B Sep 23 1944.

Address: Oude Baan 47, 3070 Boutersem. Tel: (016) 73 42 12.

HERSANT, ROBERT
France, LDR (UDF)

M. Robert Hersant, first elected to EP in 1984, is chmn and director-general of *Le Figaro*; founder president of Hersant press gp and, since 1972, Vice-President, National French Press Federation. Oise deputy, 1956-57; Mayor of Ravenel, 1953-59, and Liancourt, 1967-74; county councillor, 1954-73. B Jan 31 1920.

Addresses: "Le Figaro". 37, rue du Louvre, 75002 Paris. Tel: (1) 42 33 44 00. 32 rue du Calvaire, 92210 Saint-Cloud.

HERZOG, PHILIPPE
France, CG (PCF)

M. Philippe Herzog, university professor, was elected to EP in 1989; joined Cmte on Economic and Monetary Affairs and Industrial Policy. Mbr, political bureau of PCF; also Economic and Social Council. B 1940.

Address: Comité Central du Parti Communiste Français, 2 place du Colonel Fabien, 75940 Paris Cedex 19.

HINDLEY, MICHAEL
UK, Lancashire East, Soc (Lab)

Mr Michael Hindley was elected to the EP in 1984. Has served as coordinator of Socialist Gp on trade matters; former mbr of gp bureau; a vice-chmn, EP External Economic Relations Cmte, 1984-87, and still a cmte mbr. B Apr 11 1947; ed Clitheroe Royal GS; London and Lancaster Univs; Free Univ of West Berlin. Was a teacher in Poland and East Germany; at time of election in 1984 was tutor at Trade Union Study Centre, Blackburn. Mbr, Hyndburn DC, 1979-84 (ldr of cl, 1981-84). Contested Blackpool North in 1983 general election. GMB.

Addresses: ELCA Research, Old Municipal Offices, Bury Road, Haslingden BB4 5PG. Tel: (0706) 830013. Telefax: (0706) 83 05 36. 27 Commercial Road, Great Harwood, Lancashire BB6 7HX. Tel: (0254) 887017.

HOFF, FRAU MAGDALENE
Germany, Soc (SPD)

Frau Magdalene Hoff is a member of the EP Cmte on Economic and Monetary Affairs and Industrial Policy; former mbr, Cmte on Budgets. First elected to EP in 1979. Member, federal executive of SPD. Civil engineer and lecturer on industrial safety and accident prevention. B Dec 29 1940. Has served on Hagen Federation of SPD and on Hagen Municipal Council.

Address: Riegestrasse 8, 5800 Hagen. Tel: (02331) 76333. Telex: 823 132 euro d. Telefax: (02331) 7 08 54.

HOLZFUSS, MARTIN
Germany, LDR (FDP)

Herr Martin Holzfuss. former major-general, was elected to EP in 1989 and became mbr, Cmtes on Budgets and on Budgetary Control. B Dec 24 1925.

Address: Eschbacher Weg 30, 6308 Butzbach-Maibach.

HOON, GEOFFREY
UK, Derbyshire, Soc (Lab)

Mr Geoffrey Hoon, a barrister, was elected to the EP in 1984. Mbr, EP Legal Affairs and Citizens' Rights Cmte, being Lab gp spokesman, 1984- ; a former vice-chmn, Verification of Credentials Cmte. B Dec 6 1953; ed Jesus Coll, Cambridge. Lab Pty agent in Leeds for both Westminster and European elections in 1979. Worked in local furniture factory before reading law at Cambridge. Lecturer in law, Leeds Univ, 1972-82; Visiting Professor of Law, Sch of Law, Louisville Univ, Kentucky, 1979-80. TGWU.

Address: 5 Hawthorn Avenue, Breaston, Derbyshire DE7 3BL. Tel: (033) 172238.

HOPPENSTEDT, KARSTEN
Germany, EPP (CDU)

Herr Karsten Hoppenstedt, veterinary surgeon, was elected to EP in 1989; mbr, Cmte on Economic and Monetary Affairs and Industrial Policy. Former Mayor of Burgwedel; deputy district prefect in 'Land' of Hanover. B 1937.

Address: Gartenstrasse 16, 3006 Burgwedel 1.

HORY, JEAN-FRANÇOIS
France, Soc (PS)

M.Jean-François Hory was elected to EP in 1989 and joined Cmte on Budgets. Town councillor at Venarey-les-Laumes (Cotes-d'Or); former deputy for Mayotte. B 1949.

Address: 1bis, place de Saussaiens, 75008 Paris.

HOWELL, PAUL
UK, Norfolk, ED (C)

Mr Paul Howell became EDG (Conservative) spokesman on Cmte on Agriculture, Fisheries and Rural Development in 1989; previously on cmte, 1979-84. First elected to EP in 1979; EDG spokesman on EP Cmte on Youth, Culture, Education, Information and Sport, 1984-87; vice-chmn, EEC-Comecon delegation, 1984-87. Farmer. B Jan 17 1951; ed Gresham's Sch, Holt; St Edmund Hall, Oxford. Pres, Cl, Centre for Euro Ed, 1985- . Desk officer for agriculture, Europe, and prices and consumer affairs, Cons Research Dept, 1973-75; political adviser to Minister of Agriculture to Feb 1974, and to shadow Minister of Agriculture and shadow Minister for Prices and Consumer Affairs, 1974-75.

Address: The White House Farm, Bradenham Road, Scarning, East Dereham, Norfolk NR20 3EY. Tel: (036 287) 239.

HUGHES, STEPHEN
UK, Durham, Soc (Lab)

Mr Stephen Hughes was first elected to EP in 1984; on its Environment, Public Health and Consumer Protection Cmte, 1984-89; mbr, Cmte on Social Affairs, Employment and Working Environment, 1989- ; chmn, Euro all-pty inter-gp on peace and nuclear disarmament. Was local govt officer. Former research assistant to MEP; former chmn of a local cl. Sec, Chester-le-Street and N Durham CLPs, 1982-84, and exec mbr, Northern Reg Lab Pty. B Aug 19 1952; ed St Bede's Sch, Lanchester; Newcastle Poly. GMB; vice-chmn, Sedgefield District Cl Branch, 1982-84.

Addresses: County Hall, Room 4/74, Durham DH1 5UR. Tel: (091) 384 9371. 79 Greenbank Road, Darlington, DL3 6EN. Tel: (0325) 480975.

HUME, JOHN
UK, Northern Ireland, Soc (SDLP)

Mr John Hume has been leader of the SDLP since 1979; deputy leader, 1970-79; founder mbr. Teacher. Won Westminster (UK) seat of Foyle in 1983 general election; contested Londonderry, Oct 1974. B Jan 18 1937; ed St Columb's Coll, Londonderry; St Patrick's Coll, Maynooth. Elected mbr, European Parliament, 1979- , serving since then on bureau of Socialist Group; mbr, Cmte on Regional Policy and Regional Planning, 1989- , having formerly served on it; ACP/EEC Jt Assembly, 1979- ; former mbr, Institutional Affairs Cmte. MP for Foyle, N Ireland Parliament, 1969-73. Elected for Londonderry to NI Assembly, 1973-75; NI Constitutional Convention, 1975-76; NI Assembly, 1982-86. Mbr, NI Forum, 1983-84. Minister for Commerce in NI power sharing executive, 1974.
Address: 14 Strand Road, Derry, Northern Ireland. Tel: (504) 265340.

IACONO, FRANCO
Italy, Soc (PSI)

Sgr Franco Iacono was elected to EP in 1989 and was appointed to Cmte on Transport and Tourism. Former president, Naples Regional Cl; regional assessor. B Feb 4 1942.

Address: Via Zappino, 80075 Forio Isola d'Ischia (NA). Tel: (081) 99 74 06.

IMBENI, RENZO
Italy, EUL (PCI)

Sgr Renzo Imbeni, the Mayor of Bologna, was elected to EP in 1989 and joined Cmte on Environment, Public Health and Consumer Protection. Trade unionist. Mbr of central cmte and management caucus of Italian Communist Party. B Oct 12 1944.

Address: Comune di Bologna, Piazza Maggiore 6, 40121 Bologna. Tel: (051) 27 38 91.

INGLEWOOD, LORD
UK, Cumbria and Lancashire North, ED (C)

Lord Inglewood became EDG spokesman on EP Cmte on Legal Affairs and Citizens' Rights after his election as MEP in 1989 as Mr Richard Vane, shortly before the death of his father. Farmer, chartered surveyor and barrister. Contested Durham in 1984 Euro election; Houghton and Washington in 1983 general election. Pres, Penrith and the Border Cons Assocn, 1986-87. Mbr, Lake District Special Planning Bd, 1984- (chmn, development control cmte, 1985-); NW Water Authority, 1987- (being on its regional land drainage cmte, 1985-); steering gp, W Cumbria Groundwork Trust, 1986- . B Jul 31 1951. Mbr, Country Landowners' Assocn Parly and Legal Cmte; Historic Houses Assocn tax cmte; court, Lancaster Univ; central cmte, Carlisle Cathedral Appeal; standing cmte, Cumbria Countryside Conference.
Address: Hutton in the Forest, Penrith, Cumbria CA11 9TY. Tel: (08534) 500.

IODICE, ANTONIO
Italy, EPP (DC)

Sgr Antonio Iodice, first elected to EP in 1984, joined Cmte on Economic and Monetary Affairs and Industrial Policy after 1989 elections; became a vice-chmn of EPP Gp; former mbr, Political Affairs Cmte. Was lecturer in institutes of higher education; national councillor of teachers' trade union, SNALS. Former provincial Secretary of Democrazia Cristiana for Naples; has served on DC regional cmte for Campania. Municipal councillor, 1973-78. Began political career in "Italian Youth for Catholic Action" movement and in early 1960s was its diocesan president, later becoming its regional secretary. B Oct 28 1941; diploma in political science.

Addresses: Piazza Bovio 14, 80133 Napoli. Via G Ferraris 2, 80014 Giugliano (Napoli). Tel: (081) 89 42 339 or 89 44 601.

IVERSEN, JOHN
Denmark, EUL (SF)

Mr John Iversen became an MEP on Jan 1 1985 then being given his party's second seat in the EP taken when the MEP representing Greenland departed after its vote to leave the EC. Teacher. Upon re-election in 1989, he rejoined the EP Cmte on Environment, Public Health and Consumer Protection, and was appointed a vice-chmn; also mbr, Cmte on Budgetary Control, and treasurer of the EUL Gp. Has held leading appointments in Socialist People's Party. B Jan 4 1954.

Address: Skaering Hedevej 190, 8250 EGA. Tel: (86) 22 65 67.

IZQUIERDO ROJO, SRA MARÍA
Spain, Soc (PSOE)

Sra María Izquierdo Rojo, a member of the Spanish national Parliament and Secretary of State for the regions (1982), was elected to EP in 1989. University professor. B Nov 13 1946.

Address: Murillo 15, Colmenar Viejo, Madrid.

JACKSON, MRS CAROLINE
UK, Wiltshire, ED (C)

Mrs Caroline Jackson became EDG (Conservative) spokesman on environment in 1989. Elected MEP since 1984; mbr, EDG bureau, 1987- . On EP Cmte on Environment, Public Health and Consumer Protection since 1984; EP Cmte on Institutional Affairs, 1984-87; ex-mbr, EP Cmte on Women's Rights. Director, Peugeot Talbot (UK) Ltd, 1987- . Head, London office, EDG, 1979-84; with Secretariat of Cons Gp, European Parliament, Luxembourg, 1974-76. Contested Birmingham Erdington in Feb 1974 election. B Nov 5 1946. Mbr, Nat Consumer Cl, 1982-84; British Nat Cmte for European Year of the Environment, 1987-88.

Addresses: 74 Carlisle Mansions, Carlisle Place, London SW1P 1HZ. Tel: (01) 222 2160. New House, Hanney Road, Southmoor, Abingdon, Oxon OX13 5HR. Tel: (0865) 821243.

JACKSON, CHRISTOPHER
UK, Kent East, ED (C)

Mr Christopher Jackson was elected Deputy Leader of ED (Conservative) Gp in Sep 1989; Cons spokesman on agriculture, 1987-89; EDG and Cons spokesman on overseas aid and development and cooperation, 1981-87; rejoined Cmte on Development and Cooperation, 1989; mbr, EDG bureau, 1984-89. First elected to EP in 1979; mbr, EP inter-group on animal welfare; rapporteur-general, ACP-EEC Jt Assembly, 1985-86. Director of corporate development, Spillers Ltd, 1974-80. Contested East Ham South, 1970 general election, and Northampton North, Feb 1974. Underwriting mbr, Lloyds, 1985- ; company director. B May 24 1935. Pres, Kent Hotels and Restaurants Assocn; vice-pres, Assocn of District Cls; Assocn of Local Cls. Mbr, cl, Centre for European Agricultural Studies, Wye Coll, 1981-87.
Address: 8 Wellmeade Drive, Sevenoaks, Kent TN13 1PL. Tel: (0732) 456688.

JACOBSEN, ERHARD
Denmark, EPP (CD)

Mr Erhard Jacobsen was an elected MEP, 1979-87; MEP again since 1988; mbr of nominated Parliament, 1973-79. Chmn of Centre Democrats Party; mbr of the Folketing,, the Danish Parliament, since 1953. former Minister of Economic Coordination; former Mayor of Gladsaxe. Was Social Democrat but broke away in 1973 to form the new party. Chmn, European Movement in Denmark, 1964-73. B Feb 25 1917.

Addresses: Folketinget, Christianborg, 1240 Koben-havn K. Tel: (01) 11 66 00 - 4214. Telefax: (01) 14 54 20. Sovej 27, 2880 Bagsvaerd. Tel: (02) 98 01 70.

JANSSEN VAN RAAY, JAMES
Netherlands, EPP (CDA)

Mr James Janssen van Raay is serving on the Cmte on Legal Affairs and Citizens' Rights; also mbr, EP Cmte on Rules of Procedure, Verification of Credentials and Immunities. Elected MEP, 1979-84, and since 1986. Lawyer and public prosecutor. B Jun 1 1932. President, International Federation of Professional Footballers.

Addresses: Postbus 4402, 3006 AK Rotterdam. Tel: (010) 413 34 11. Mecklenburglaan 14, 3062 BJ Rotterdam. Tel: (010) 452 74 57. Grineweg 88, 3055 Rotterdam. Tel: (010) 461 58 99. Fax: (010) 418 23 90.

JENSEN, FRU KIRSTEN
Denmark, Soc (S)

Fru Kirsten Jensen, journalist, was elected to EP in 1989 and became mbr, Cmte on Environment, Public Health and Consumer Protection. B Mar 3 1961.

Address: Vesterbrogade 104 4. th., 1620 Kobenhavn V.

JEPSEN, FRU MARIE
Denmark, ED (KF)

Fru Marie Jepsen was elected to EP in 1984; re-elected 1989 and became mbr, EP Political Affairs Cmte. Danish deputy chmn of ED Gp and mbr of bureau from 1987; former mbr, Cmte on Agriculture, Fisheries and Food. Mbr, Silkeborg City Cl, 1978-84; elected to Aarhus County Cl, 1982; on board of Aarhus Theatre and Tourist Association of Silkeborg; mbr, executive, Danish Conservative Party, 1986. Chmn, Teacher Training College of Silkeborg. BMar 27 1940.

Address: Hattenaesvaenget 10, 8600 Silkeborg. Tel: (06) 84 62 10. Telefax: (86) 84 62 10.

JOANNY-SCHLECHT, MME CLAIRE
France, Verts (Verts)

Mme Claire Joanny-Schlecht, water supply engineer, was elected to EP in 1989; joined Cmte on Transport and Tourism. Militant in Friends of the Earth movement in Dunkirk in 1970s and elected town councillor there in 1983 on egology list, gaining 9.3% of the vote, but had to resign soon afterwards for professional reasons. Later she moved to Le Havre where she fought against the Honfleur bridge project. B 1951.

Address: 127 Bd de Strasbourg, 76600 Le Havre.

JUNKER, FRAU KARIN
Germany, Soc (SDP)

Frau Karin Junker was elected to EP in 1989 and joined Cmte on External Economic Relations. Journalist; official with Geldrnkirchen Council. Holds posts in several party bodies. B Dec 24 1940.

Address: Josefstrasse 25, 4650 Gelsenkirchen. Tel: (0209) 29049.

JUPPÉ, ALAIN
France, RDE (RPR)

M.Alain Juppé, a Paris deputy and Deputy Mayor of Paris, was elected to EP in 1989, becoming mbr, Cmte on Institutional Affairs and Cmte on Regional Policy and Regional Planning. Former minister in charge of budget; Secretary General of RPR party; Inspector of Finance. B Aug 15 1945.

Address: 19-21 avenue de Villepreux, 92420 Vaucresson. Tel: (1) 47 01 08 63.

KELLETT-BOWMAN, EDWARD
UK, Hampshire Central, ED (C)

Mr Edward Kellett-Bowman, business and management consultant, MEP for Lancashire East, 1979-84, was elected for this seat at by-election in December 1988 following the death of Mr Basil de Ferranti. Mbr, EP Cmte on Economic and Monetary Affairs and Industrial Policy, 1988-89 and after 1989 elections became EDG spokesman on Cmte on Budgetary Control and mbr, Cmte on Budgets. Contested Pontefract in 1959 general election. B Feb 25 1931. Husband of Dame Elaine Kellett-Bowman, Cons MP for Lancaster and former MEP for Cumbria. Served on five local authorities in London, 1957-74. In pharmaceutical management, 1955-72, having his own consultancy since. Fellow, BIM. Freeman, City of London.
Addresses: 4a Desborough Road, Eastleigh, Hampshire SO5 5NX. Tel: (0703) 617219, or (01) 734 4902. Naishes Barn, Newnham, Basingstoke, Hampshire RG27 9AF. Tel: (0256) 726103.

KEPPELHOFF-WIECHERT, FRAU HEDWIG
Germany, EPP (CDU)

Frau Hedwig Keppelhoff-Wiechert is chair of Deutscher Landfrauenverband, the German federation of women farmers; vice-chair of women farmers' cmte of Comite des Organisations Professionels Agricoles de la CEE (COPA). Elected to EP 1989 and became mbr, Cmte on Agriculture, Fisheries and Rural Protection. B May 31 1939.

photograph unavailable

Address: Coesfelder Strasse 104, 4282 Velen.

KILLILEA, MARK
Ireland, RDE (FF)

Mr Mark Killilea, former farmer, became an MEP in 1987 being re-elected in 1989; mbr since 1987, EP Cmte on Agriculture, Fisheries and Rural Development, and appointed a cmte vice-chmn in 1989; mbr, Cmte on Women's Rights, 1989- . Dail deputy for Galway West, 1981-82 and Galway East, 1977-81. Minister of State, Dept of Posts and Telegraphs, 1979-81. Senator, Labour panel, 1982-87 and 1969-77. B Sep 1939; ed St Jarlath's Coll, Tuam, Co. Galway.

Address: Caherhugh House, Belclare, Tuam., Co. Galway. Tel: (093) 55414. Telefax: (093) 55386

KLEPSCH, EGON
Germany, EPP (CDU)

Herr Egon Klepsch has been leader of the European People's Party (Christian Democratic) Gp since 1984, a position he held 1979-82 and in the nominated EP, 1977-79. A Vice-President of EP, 1982-84; mbr since 1977 being first elected in 1979. Serves on Political Affairs Cmte and the Security and Disarmament Sub-cmte. CDU mbr of Bundestag, 1965-80; former mbr, assemblies of Cl of Europe, WEU and Nato. B Jan 30 1930. PhD. Former lecturer on international politics. President, European Union of Young Christian Democrats, 1964-70.

Address: Pastor Busenbender Strasse 14, 5400 Koblenz-Guls. Tel: (0261) 40 38 73.

KÖHLER, HEINZ
Germany, Soc (SDP)

Herr Heinz Köhler, lawyer, was elected to EP in 1989; joined Cmte on Regional Policy and Regional Planning. Local councillor; holds various party posts. B May 12 1942.

photograph unavailable

Address: Burgstaller Weg 7, 8610 Mitwitz. Tel: (09266) 1566.

KÖHLER, KLAUS-PETER
Germany, DR (Repub)

Herr Klaus-Peter Köhler, detective, was elected to EP in 1989; became mbr, Cmte on Environment, Public Health and Consumers. Party chmn at Baden Wurttemberg. B 1943.

Address: Verdistrasse 20, 7920 Heidenheim an der Brenz.

KOFOED, NIELS ANKER
Denmark, LDR (V)

Mr Niels Anker Kofoed, former Danish Minister of Agriculture and Fishing, was elected to EP in 1989. He was elected a Vice-President of the Parliament and joined Cmte on Agriculture, Fisheries and Rural Development. Farmer; mbr of Folketing (Danish Parliament); former MEP. B Feb 21 1929.

Address: Knarregård, Ibskeyvej 25, 3730 Nekso.

181

KOSTOPOULIS, SOTIRIS
Greece, Soc (PASOK)

Mr Sotiris Kostopoulis, journalist, was elected MEP in 1989 becoming mbr, Cmte on Youth Culture, Education, the Media and Sport, and Cmte on Women's Rights. Sits on central cmte of PASOK. B 1943.

photograph unavailable

Address: Filadelfias 37, 161 21 Kessariani.

KRIEPS, ROBERT
Luxembourg, Soc (POSL)

Mr Robert Krieps became elected MEP in 1989 and joined Cmte on Youth, Culture, Education, the Media and Sport, being one of its vice-chmn; also a vice-chmn of Socialist Gp. Mbr, Luxembourg Chamber of Deputies, 1969-74 and 1979-84. Minister of Education, Justice and Cultural Affairs, 1974-79, and Minister of Justice, Cultural Affairs and Environment, 1984-89. Former president, POSL, Luxembourg's Socialist Party. Lawyer; former head of law course at Univs of Nancy and Bruxelles, B Oct 16 1922.

Address: 25 rue Giselbert, 1627 Luxembourg. Tel: 44 08 27.

LACAZE, JEANNOU
France, LDR (UDF-RPR)

M. Jeannou Lacaze, French Army general and former Army Chief of Staff, was elected to EP in 1989 on UDF-RPR list and joined Liberal and Democratic Gp. Became mbr, Political Affairs Cmte. B 1924.

Address: 148 rue de Longchamp, 75116 Paris.

LAGAKOS, EFSTATHIOS
Greece, EPP (ND)

Mr Efstathios Lagakos was elected to EP in 1989; mbr, EP Cmte on Development and Cooperation; jt vice-chmn, EPP working gp on political affairs, 1989- . Former Greek permanent representative to Nato; former ambassador, now honorary ambassador. B 1921; graduate in law.

Address: Kapsali 7, 106 74 Athenes.

LAGORIO, LELIO
Italy, Soc (PSI)

Sgr Lelio Lagorio was elected to the EP in 1989 when he joined the Cmte on Energy, Research and Technology. A vice-chmn of Socialist Gp and leader of Italian delegation. Lawyer and journalist. Former Mayor of Firenza and President, regional council of Tuscany. At various times has been Minister, mbr and president of defence cmte of Chamber of Deputies. B Nov 9 1925.

Address:

LALOR, PATRICK J.
Ireland, RDE (FF)

Mr Patrick (Paddy) Lalor, first elected an MEP in 1979, was a Vice-President of EP, 1982-87; on EP Cmte on Budgets, 1987-89; Mbr, Political Affairs Cmte, and Cmte on Rules of Procedure, Verification of Credentials and Immunities, 1989- ; elected a quaestor in July 1989; previously quaestor, 1979-82. A vice-chmn, RDE Gp since 1979. Minister for Defence and Govt Chief Whip, 1977-79. Mbr, Dail, 1961-81; Minister for Industry and Commerce, 1970-73; Minister for Posts and Telegraphs, 1969-70. Opposition chief whip, 1973-77. B Jul 21 1926.

Address: Main Street, Abbeyleix, Portlaoise, Co. Laois. Tel: (502) 31206.

183

LAMASSOURE, ALAIN
France, LDR (UDF-Clubs P et R))

M. **Alain Lamassoure,** member of French National Assembly and UDF spokesman, was elected to EP in 1989. Joined Cmte on Budgets and Cmte on Budgetary Control. Deputy for Pyrenees-Atlantiques; leading official of Clubs Perspectives et Realites. B 1944.

Address: 6 Villa E. Lindet, 75015 Paris.

LAMBRIAS, PANAYOTIS
Greece, EPP (ND)

Mr **Panayotis Lambrias,** journalist, lawyer and former Secretary-General, Greek National Tourist Office, was first elected to EP in 1984. In outgoing Parliament was vice-chmn of EPP Gp responsible for internal questions and communications. Mbr, Cmtes on Regional Policy and Regional Planning and on Petitions. Mbr of Parliament and Secretary of State attached to President's Office, 1974-77; Secretary of State for Tourism, 1977-81. Writes for many newspapers; director since inception of *Mesimvrini.* Translated and supplemented Unesco's three-volume dictionary of social sciences. Responsible for Greek edition of General de Gaulle's memoirs and Greek edition of Time-Life Science Library.

Addresses: Neophytou Vamva 10, 106 71 Athina. Tel: (1) 72 30 489. Vas. Sofias 7, 106 71 Athina. Tel: (1) 36 41 611.

LANE, PATRICK
Ireland, RDE (FF)

Mr **Patrick (Paddy) Lane,** farmer, former Army officer, was elected to EP in 1989 and joined Cmte on Agriculture, Fisheries and Rural Development. A former President of the Irish Farmers' Association. Mbr, Economic and Social Cmte. Irish rugby international cap. B Sep 7 1934

Address: Quinpool, Parteen, Clare. Tel: (061) 52299.

LANGER, ALEXANDER
Italy, Verts (Verde)

Herr Alexander Langer, teacher, university professor, translator, journalist and one of founders of Green political movement in Italy, was elected to EP in 1989, becoming co-president of the Green Gp - *Les Verts* - and joining Political Affairs Cmte and Cmte on Rules of Procedure, Verification of Credentials and Immunities. Mbr, Trentine Regional Cl. On South Tyrol Regional Cl, 1978-81 and 1983-88. A director of League for the Environment. Since 1960s has tried to unite linguistic groups of Alto Adige and since 1970s has contributed to providing a valid inter-ethnic alternative to German/Italian problems in the South Tyrol.

Address: c.o. Lista Verde Alternativa, Via Crispi 9, 39100 Bolzano. Tel: (0471) 99 30 15.

LANGES, HORST
Germany, EPP (CDU)

Herr Horst Langes chairs the EPP Gp working party on budget and agricultural affairs; mbr of gp bureau. First elected MEP in 1979; mbr, Cmte on Budgets and Cmte on Budgetary Control. Former headmaster. Mbr, Rhineland Palatinate 'Land' Assembly, 1967-69; Secretary of State to Rhineland-Palatinate Ministry of Culture, Education and Religious Affairs, 1974-79; mbr, Trier municipal cl from 1960; Trier executive and federal cmte of CDU. B Dec 2 1928.

Addresses: Bonhofferstrasse 32, 5500 Trier. Tel: (0651) 31659. CDU-Geschäftsstelle, Kaiserstrasse 24, 5500 Trier. Tel: (0651) 48434.

LANNOYE, PAUL
Belgium, Verts (Ecolo)

Mr Paul Lannoye, research scientist at University of Namur, was elected to EP in 1989 and joined Cmte on Energy, Research and Technology, being appointed one of its vice-chmn. Senator since 1988. Federal secretary of Ecolo, 1981-87, except for 1984; local councillor, Namur, from 1982 and except since he became senator. Founder mbr, Friends of the Earth, 1975, and of Ecolo, 1980. B Jun 22 1939. Included in his list of hobbies is: *Amateur de bon vin (Bordeaux).*

Addresses: Rue Basse-Marcelle 28, 5000 Namur. Tel: (081) 22 78 71. Telefax: (081) 23 06 03. 81 rue des Nobles, 5003 Saint-Marc (Namur). Tel: (081) 73 21 17.

LARIVE, MEVR JESSICA
Netherlands, LDR (VVD)

Mevr Jessica Larive joined EP Cmte on Energy, Research and Technology after 1989 elections; also on Cmte on Women's Rights; served on EP Cmte on Social Affairs and Employment and Cmte on Women's Rights in the outgoing Parliament. First elected to EP in 1984. International civil servant, 1973-78, and then on staff of EP Liberal and Democratic Gp, 1979-84. B Nov 24 1945.

Address: 30, Avenue Ernest Cambier, 1030 Bruxelles. Tel: (2) 734 85 66.

LARONI, NEREO
Italy, Soc (PSI)

Sgr Nereo Laroni, former Mayor of Venice, was elected to EP in 1989; joined Cmte on Youth, Culture, Education, the Media and Sport. Local assessor. Teacher. B Sep 2 1942.

Address: Via Monviso, 23/3, 30030 Favaro Veneto (VE). Tel: (041) 63 46 71.

LATAILLADE, PIERRE
France, RDE (RPR)

M. Pierre Lataillade became an MEP in March 1986; re-elected 1989; a vice-chmn, EP Cmte on Economic and Monetary Affairs and Industrial Policy in outgoing Parliament and still a mbr of cmte. Mbr of bureau of RDE Gp. Mayor of d'Arcachon; former deputy for Gironde. B Apr 27 1933.

Addresses: Maire d'Arcachon, 33120 Arcachon. Tel: 56 83 17 20. 10 avenue Général Mangin, 33115 Pyla-sur-Mer. Tel: 56 22 58 82.

LE CHEVALLIER, JEAN-MARIE
France, DR (FN)

M. Jean-Marie Le Chevallier was first elected to EP in 1984 being M. Le Pen's principal private secretary. Mbr, EP Cmte on Social Affairs, Employment and Working Environment. Former mbr, Economic and Social Cl. Municipal councillor, Toulon; former deputy for Var. Appointments: Director general, Rennes Chamber of Commerce and Industry, 1965-76; administrator, Pinault-Investments Society. B Nov 22 1936.

Addresses: Spen-NPC, 25 avenue Marceau, 75116 Paris. L'Oiseau de Feu, Rue Henri Poincaré, 83000 Toulon.

LEHIDEUX, MME MARTINE
France, DR (FN)

Mme Martine Lehideux was first elected to EP in 1984; re-elected 1989. A vice-chair of DR Gp in outgoing Parliament; mbr, EP Cmte on Development and Cooperation; former mbr, Cmte on Women's Rights. Has served on National Front central cmte. Chairs National Circle of European Women. B May 27 1933.

Address: 20 rue Camille Périer, 78400 Chatou. Tel: (1) 39 52 10 47 or 46 02 40 21 (bureau).

LEMMER, GERD
Germany, EPP (CDU)

Herr Gerd Lemmer, first elected to EP in 1979, is mbr, Cmte on External Economic Relations; has also served on Cmte on Development and Cooperation. State Secretary to Federal Ministry for Refugees and War Victims and later in Federal Ministry for Posts and Telecommunications, 1967-69. Industrialist. Mbr, Remscheid municipal authority, 1952-75 (First Burgomaster, 1961-63); N Rhine-Westphalia 'Land' assembly, 1958-75, being 'Land' minister for federal affairs, 1962-66. B Sep 13 1925.

Addresses: c.o. Fried. Krupp GmbH, Altendorterstrasse 103, 4300 Essen 1. Tel: (0201) 188 2072/73. Fax: (0201) 188 4100. Hindemithstrasse 28, 5630 Remscheid. Tel: (02191) 72316.

LENZ, FRAU MARLENE
Germany, EPP (CDU)

Frau Marlene Lenz chairs the EPP women's section. She chaired the EP Cmte on Women's Rights, 1984-87, and since then has remained a mbr of the cmte; also serving on Political Affairs Cmte and its sub-cmte on human rights. A vice-chair in 1979-84 Parliament of cmte of inquiry into situation of women in Europe. First elected to EP in 1979. Became a vice-president of the European Women's Union in 1977, having been executive mbr, 1975-77. Translator; former EC Commission official. B Jul 4 1932; ed Heidelburg Univ. General secretary, European Women's Union, 1967-71; adviser to external relations office, CDU federal headquarters, 1972-75. Rapporteur to Bundestag cmte of inquiry on women and society.

Address: Burgstrasse 102, 5300 Bonn 2. Tel: (0228) 31 38 45.

LE PEN, JEAN-MARIE
France, DR (FN)

M. Jean-Marie Le Pen, former French presidential candidate has been president of the National Front since 1972. First elected to EP in 1984 and since then has chaired the group, Droites Européenes. Became mbr, EP Cmte on Agriculture, Fisheries and Rural Development in 1989 when he unsuccessfully stood for Presidency of EP; former mbr, Cmte on Institutional Affairs. B Jun 20 1928; ed Jesuit college of Saint-Francois Xavier, Vannes, and Lorient grammar school. Licentiate of laws. Paratroop officer, Indo-China, 1954. Seine deputy (independent), 1958-62.

Address: 8 Parc de Montretout, 92210 Saint Cloud. Tel: (1) 46 02 40 21.

LIMA, SALVATORE
Italy, EPP (DC)

Sgr Salvatore Lima was first elected to EP in 1979. Mbr, Cmte on Rules of Procedure, Verification of Credentials and Immunities; former mbr, Cmte on Environment. Deputy director, Bank of Sicily; graduate in law. Mbr, Italian Chamber of Deputies, 1968-79; several times Under Secretary of State for Finance and for the Budget; Mayor of Palermo; Commissioner Extraordinary of Sicilian Agrarian Reform Office, 1962-63; secretary, Palermo Province DC Party, 1961-68. B Jan 23 1928.

Address: Via Danae 19, 90149 Palermo (Valdesi). Tel: (091) 45 45 61.

LINKOHR, ROLF
Germany, Soc (SDP)

Herr Rolf Linkohr, a physicist, serves on the EP Cmte on Energy, Research and Technology. First elected an MEP in 1979. A vice-chairman, EP delegation for relations with Central America and Contadora Gp. Chairman of Stuttgart SPD from 1977, mbr since 1972. B Apr 11 1941.

Address: Asangstrasse 219a, 7000 Stuttgart 61. Tel: (0711) 324945.

LIVANOS, DIONYSSIOS
Greece, Soc (PASOK)

Mr Dionyssios Livanos, lawyer, was elected MEP in 1989 and joined Cmte on Agriculture, Fisheries and Rural Development. Former mbr, national Parliament. Publisher and editor. B 1934.

photograph unavailable

Address: Lykavittou 1a, 106 72 Athenes.

LLORCA VILAPLANA, SRA CARMEN
Spain, EPP (PP)

Sra Carmen Llorca Vilaplana was nominated as MEP in Jan 1986; first elected 1987; re-elected 1989; vice-chair, EP Cmte on Women's Rights, 1989- ; on cmte previously as ED Gp coordinator; also mbr, Cmte on Environment, Public Health and Consumer Protection. Elected to Cortes in 1982 and MP for Madrid; president, cmte on parliamentary control of Spanish TV; mbr, Cl of Administration of Spanish TV (RTVE), 1980-83. Professor of Contemporary World History, Complutense Univ; journalist and author; first woman President, Madrid Athenaeum; Vice-President, Spain-Israel Friendship Association. B Nov 29 1921.

Address: c/Luchana 17, 28010 Madrid. Tel: (1) 445 78 93/90.

LOMAS, ALFRED
UK, London North East, Soc (Lab).

Mr Alfred Lomas, was leader of British Labour Gp in EP, 1985-87; has also been deputy ldr; mbr, EP Cmte on Development and Cooperation, and Cmte on Budgetary Control; former mbr, Political Affairs Cmte. First elected to EP in 1979. Sec, London Co-operative Political Cmte, 1965-79, and mbr, London regional exec of Lab Pty. Railway signalman, 1951-59; Lab Pty sec/agent, 1959-65. B Apr 30 1928; ed St Paul's Elementary Sch, Stockport; various further ed establishments. Vice-pres, Inst for Workers' Control; British Peace Assembly; Waltham Forest Community Relations Cl. Director, Theatre Royal, Stratford. Author of *The Common Market - Why we should keep out.*

Addresses: Essex House, Room 12, 3rd Floor, 375-7 High Street, Stratford, London E15 4QZ. Tel: (01) 519 8114. 23 Hatcliffe Close, London SE3. Tel: (01) 852 5433.

LOPES PORTO, MANUEL
Portugal, LDR (PSD)

Senhor Manuel Lopes Porto was elected to EP in 1989 and became mbr, Cmte on External Economic Relations. Economist; chmn, National Cl for the Central Plan. University professor, having attended Oxford and Coimbra Univs. B Jun 1943.

Address: Rue Henriques Sêco 32-1°, 3000 Coimbra.

LUCAS PIRES, FRANCISCO
Portugal, EPP (CDS)

Senhor Francisco Lucas Pires, a former Vice-President of the EP, has been an MEP since 1986; first elected 1987. After 1989 elections became chmn of EPP Gp working party on political affairs and joined EPP bureau being leader of Portuguese delegation. Mbr, Cmte on Regional Policy and Regional Planning and Cmte on Petitions; former mbr, Budgets Cmte. University professor; lawyer. Former Minister, former mbr, Cl of State and former chmn of CDS. B Sep 15 1944.

Address: Rua Julieta Ferrao Lote E. 4. dto, 1600 Lisboa. Tel: (1) 76 71 53.

LULLING, MME ASTRID
Luxembourg, EPP (PCS)

Mme Astrid Lulling was elected to EP in 1989 and was appointed to its Cmte on Economic and Monetary Affairs and Industrial Policy; served in nominated Parliament, 1965-74. Was in Luxembourg Chamber of Deputies, 1965-89; former mbr, North Atlantic Assembly and Benelux interparliamentary cl. Chairs European Centre of International Cl of Women and Luxembourg cmte of working women; mbr, national cl of women. Burgomaster of commune of Schifflange, 1970-85, and Schifflange communal councillor. B Jun 11 1929.

Address: 28 Gringe Wee, 3878 Schifflange. Tel: 54 82 56.

LUSTER, RUDOLF
Germany, EPP (CDU)

Herr Rudolf Luster, former mbr of the Bundestag, is leader of the EPP Gp German delegation and mbr of gp bureau; MEP since 1978, being first elected 1979. A vice-chmn of EP Legal Cmte until 1984; now on Cmte on Institutional Affairs and Cmte on Development and Cooperation. Barrister and notary. Berlin city councillor, 1950-51; mbr, Berlin Parliament, 1967-76. For many years mbr, CDU executive, 'Land' of Berlin and district chmn in Berlin-Steglitz. B Jan 20 1921.

Addresses: Platz der Republik, Reichstagsgebäude, 1000 Berlin 21. Tel: (030) 39 77 437. Holbeinstrasse 60. 1000 Berlin 45.

LÜTTGE, GÜNTER
Germany, Soc (SDP)

Herr Günter Lüttge became elected MEP in 1989 and joined EP Cmte on Transport and Tourism. Mayor of Ihlow; mbr, regional government of Mieder-Saxony. Teacher. B Jul 8 1938.

Address: Martin-Buber-Weg 14, 2965 Simonswolde-Ihlow.

MADELIN, ALAIN
France, LDR (UDF-RPR)

M.Alain Madelin, former French Minister for Industry, for Posts and Telecommunications and for Tourism, was elected to EP in 1989; became a vice-chmn of Cmte on Economic and Monetary Affairs and Industrial Policy. Lawyer; Secretary-General of Republican Party (PR). Mbr, French national assembly as deputy for Ille-et-Vilaine; regional councillor for Bretagne (Britanny) and chmn, regional cl's finance cmte; Redon town councillor. B 1946.

Address: Institute Euro 92, 21 avenue d'Iena, 75016 Paris.

MAGNANI NOYA, SIGNORA MARIA
Italy, Soc (PSI)

Signora Maria Magnani Noya, lawyer, was elected to EP in 1989 and became mbr, Cmte on Development and Cooperation and EP mbr of ACP/EC Assembly. Mayor of Turin. Former mbr, Italian Chamber of Deoputies; former Under Secretary of State for Health and local councillor. B Oct 24 1931.

*photograph
unavailable*

Address: Comune di Torino, Piazza Palazzo Città, 1, 10100 Torino. Tel: (011) 57 65 30 00.

MAHER, THOMAS
Ireland, LDR (Ind)

Mr Thomas Maher, first elected to EP in 1979, became a vice-chmn of the LDR Gp and until 1987 was one of the Parliament's quaestors. In outgoing Parliament was a jt vice-chmn, EP Cmte on Regional Policy and Regional Planning, and was reappointed in July 1989; former mbr, Cmte on Agriculture, Fisheries and Food. Farmer; President, Irish Farmers' Assocn, 1967-76; former President, Irish Agricultural Organization Society, and of General Cmte for Agricultural Cooperation in EC. Mbr, Economic and Social Cmte of EC, 1973-78. B Apr 29 1922.

Addresses: Castlemoyle, Boherlahen, Cashel, Co. Tipperary. Tel: (0504) 41106. Ladyswell Street, Cashel, Co. Tipperary. Tel: (062) 61320/61248.

MAIBAUM, FRAU GEPA
Germany, Soc (SDP)

Frau Gepa Maibaum was elected to EP in 1989 and joined Cmte on Regional Policy and Regional Planning and Cmte on Women's Rights. Councillor and Mayor of Cologne; leader of local SPD. B Dec 21 1935.

Address: Marderallee 11, 5000 Koln 40. Tel: (02234) 7 61 63.

MAIJ-WEGGEN, MEVR (HANJA) JOHANNA
Netherlands, EPP (CDA)

Mevr Johanna Maij-Weggen, an elected MEP since 1979, is vice-chair of EPP Gp with responsibility for international relations and links with Christian Democrat international and European organizations; mbr, EP Cmtes on Environment, Public Health and Consumer Protection and on Women's Rights; former mbr, Cmte on Social Affairs and Employment. Nurse and teacher. Has held various posts in ARP (Anti-Revolutionary Party) and CDA; was mbr, organization cmte and the ARVC/CDA Women's Advisory Gp and of executive, Dutch Women's Council. Mbr, Dutch Govt delegation, 32nd UN General Assembly, New York, 1977. B Dec 29 1943; attended AZVU nurses school, Amstelveen; studied social pedagogy at Amsterdam Municipal Univ.

Address: Aquariuslaan 53, 5632 BB Eindhoven. Tel: (040) 41 63 10.

MALANGRÉ, KURT
Germany, EPP (CDU)

Herr Kurt Malangré, elected to the EP in 1979, was a vice-chmn of the EP Cmte on Rules of Procedure, Verification of Credentials and Immunities, on which he still serves; also mbr, EP Cmte on Legal Affairs and Citizens Rights; former mbr, Cmte on Petitions. Became chmn of Aachen regional cl in 1976; Burgomaster of Aachen, 1971-73, and Chief Burgomaster since 1973. Joined Aachen municipal assembly in 1969, becoming political gp chmn in 1970. B Sep 18 1934. Lawyer.

Address: Wilhelmstrasse 2, 5100 Aachen. Tel: (0241) 72 517 or 47 22 02 or 320 02 (Büro).

193

MALÉNE, CHRISTIAN DE LA
France, RDE (RPR)

M. Christian de la Maléne was re-elected chmn of the RDE (European Democratic Alliance) Gp (previously DEP) in 1989, having led it since 1984; elected chmn of DEP (European Progressive Democrats) in 1979, a position he held in outgoing nominated Parliament. Mbr, Cmte on Transport and Tourism, 1989- ; former mbr, Cmte on Legal Affairs and Citizens' Rights. Deputy 1958-77; former State Secretary for Information; former Minister for Scientific Research. Senator for Paris from 1977 and city councillor and First Assistant to Mayor of Paris. B Dec 5 1920.

Addresses: Hôtel de Ville, 75196 Paris RP. Tel: 42 76 57 21. 4 av. la Criolla, 92150 Suresnes.

MALFA, GIORGIO LA
Italy, LDR (PRI-PLI-Fed)

Sgr Giorgio La Malfa, mbr of Italian Chamber of Deputies, was elected to EP in 1989. Former minister; journalist and university professor. Secretary-General of Italian Republican Party (PRI). B Oct 13 1939.

Address: Partito Repubblicano Italiano, Piazzi dei Caprettari 70, 00186 Roma. Tel: (06) 654 46 41.

MALHURET, CLAUDE
France, LDR (UDF-RPR)

M. Claude Malhuret, doctor and former director of *Médecins sans frontières*, was elected to EP in 1989; mbr, Political Affairs Cmte, 1989- . Former Secretary of State for Human Rights; Mayor of Vichy (Allier); national secretary of Republican Party. B 1950.

Address: Hôtel de Ville, 03200 Vichy.

MARCK, POL
Belgium, EPP (CVP)

Mr Pol Marck, became an MEP in 1981; re-elected 1984 and 1989. President of Belgian Agricultural and Horticultural Marketing Board. Mbr, EP Cmte on Agriculture, Fisheries and Food, on which he has chaired working party for monitoring dairy quotas; also mbr, Cmte on Budgetary Control. Was deputy secretary, Belgian farmers' union, 1957-81. Lawyer; professor at Catholic University of Louvain, from 1964. Has served on national bureau of CVP. B Dec 6 1930.

Address: Schoonzichtlaan 46, 3009 Winksele-Herent. Tel: (016) 48 83 91.

MARINHO, LUIS
Portugal, Soc (PS)

Senhor Luis Marinho was first elected to EP in 1987; serves on Cmte on Legal Affairs and Citizens' Rights; former mbr, Cmtes on Budgets and on Petitions. Deputy, Portuguese national assembly, 1976-86. Lawyer. B Jun 5 1949.

Address: Rua António Feliciano de Castiho, 111 D-9° Dt°, 3000 Coimbra. Tel: (39) 71 66 93.

MARLEIX, ALAIN
France, RDE (RPR)

M. Alain Marleix became an MEP quite early during the 1984-89 Parliament; re-elected in 1989; mbr, Cmte on Transport and Tourism; former mbr, Cmte on External Economic Relations. Journalist. Conseiller general, Cantal. B Jan 2 1946.

Addresses: RPR, 123 rue de Lille, 75007 Paris. Tel: (1) 45 50 32 19. Molompize, 15500 Massias. Tel: 71 73 60 27.

195

MARQUES MENDES, ANTÓNIO
Portugal, LDR (PSD)

Senhor António Marques Mendes was first elected to EP in 1987; re-elected 1989; mbr, Cmtes on Social Affairs, Employment and Working Environment, 1989- ; Cmte on Petitions, 1989- . Chmn, municipal council of Fafe, 1973-74. Elected deputy to Portuguese national assembly in 1976, 1983 and 1985.B Mar 30 1934.

Address: Aroes de S. Romão, Lugar do A, 4820 Fafe. Tel: 49 13 98.

MARTIN, DAVID
UK, Lothians, Soc (Lab)

Mr David Martin was elected a Vice-President of EP in July 1989; joined EP Cmte on Regional Policy and Regional Planning and Cmte on Institutional Affairs. Leader, British Labour Gp of MEPs, 1987-88; first elected to EP 1984; a vice-chmn, EP Budgetary Control Cmte, 1984-87; mbr, EP Cmte on Rules of Procedure, the Verification of Credentials and Immunities, 1987-89; former mbr, Budgets Cmte. Mbr, Lothian Regional Cl, 1982-84; vice-pres, Nat Playbus Assocn, 1985- . B Aug 26 1954. Director, St Andrews Animal Fund, 1986- ; mbr, bd of governors, Road Industry Training Bd, Livingston Multi-Occupational Training Ed Centre, 1985- ; cmte, Scottish Soc for Prevention of Vivisection, 1985- . TGWU.
Address: Ruskin House, 15 Windsor Street, Edinburgh EH7 5LA. Tel: (031) 557 0936. Telefax: (031) 557 5671. 7 Mortenhall Park Gardens, Edinburgh EH17 8SL. Tel: (031) 664 9178.

MARTIN, MME SIMONE
France, LDR (UDF/RPR)

Mme Simone Martin was first elected MEP in 1979. After 1989 elections, rejoined Cmte on Agriculture, Fisheries and Rural Development; in outgoing Parliament was also on Cmte on Environment, Public Health and Consumer Protection. Local councillor at Saint Dizier. Mbr of several agricultural organizations; has held office as President, Young Farmers Departmental Centre, Haute-Marne; vice-chair, Young Farmers National Centre; general secretary, Haute-Marne Chamber of Agriculture; chair, EDE (departmental stock farming board) of Haute-Marne; has served on regional economic and social cmte of Champagne Ardenne. B Apr 14 1943.

Addresses: Thonnance Les Moulins, 52230 Poissons. Tel: 25 95 52 90. Residence Cigny Val d'Ornel, Entrée 2, Appartement 19, 52100 Saint Dizier. Tel: 25 05 75 86.

MATTINA, VINCENZO
Italy, Soc (PSI)

Sgr Vincenzo Mattina, first elected to EP in 1984, was a vice-chmn of Socialist Gp in outgoing Parliament; elected treasurer of gp after 1989 elections; mbr, Cmte on Economic and Monetary Affairs and Industrial Policy. Graduate in jurisprudence. Has held important offices in trade union movement since 1960, serving on executive of PSI with special responsibilities for professional workers' section of party. Chmn, Centre for Research into Economic of Labour. Secretary General (from 1980), Federation of Italian Trade Unions. Mbr, Chamber of Deputies, 1983- . B Jul 29 1940.

Addresses: Via G De Calvi 6, 00151 Roma. Tel: (06) 534 69 25 or 537 92 56. Salita dei Trecento 9, 84034 Padula (SA).

MAYER, MME SYLVIE
France, CG (PCF)

Mme Sylvie Mayer, scientific research worker with special responsibility nationally for environment problems, was elected MEP in 1989 and joined Cmte on Budgetary Control. B Oct 13 1946.

Address: 52 rue Pierre Riquet, 29200 Brest.

MAZZONE, ANTONIO
Italy, NI (MSI-DN)

Sgr Antonio Mazzone was elected to EP in 1989 joining Cmte on Legal Affairs and Citizens' Rights and Cmte on Rules of Procedure, Verification of Credentials and Immunities. Mbr, Chamber of Deputies. Former MSI regional official and councillor in Campania. B Dec 19 1934.

Address:

197

McCARTIN, JOHN JOSEPH
Ireland, EPP (FG)

Mr John Joseph McCartin leads the Irish delegation within the EPP Gp and is mbr, bureau of EPP Gp. First elected to EP in 1979; joined Cmte on Agriculture, Fisheries and Rural Development in 1989; was a vice-chmn of EP Cmte on Social Affairs and Employment from 1984; served on it and Transport Cmte in outgoing Parliament. Farmer and company director. Mbr, Dail, since 1981; senator, 1973-81 (Vice-President of Senate, 1977-81). B Apr 24 1939. Elected to Leitrum County Cl in 1967; has served on General Cl of Cmtes of Agriculture (chmn, 1970-72); and North Western Health Board.

Address: Mullyaster, Newtowngore, Carrick-on-Shannon, Co. Leitrum. Tel: (049) 33490 (home); (049) 33395 (office).

McCUBBIN, HENRY
UK, Scotland North East, Soc (Lab)

Mr Henry McCubbin, film and television cameraman, won this Euro seat for Labour in 1989 and joined EP Cmte on Agriculture, Fisheries and Rural Development. Mbr, general cl, Association of Cinematograph, Television and Allied Technicians, holding union offices as branch and shop chairman and branch secretary; author of union response to proposed European media legislation; has worked in several EEC states. Chmn and former treasurer, Hillhead CLP; also chmn and treasurer of local Dundee branch. B Jul 15 1942; ed Open Univ. Mbr, Campaign for Press and Broadcasting Freedom.

Address: 28 Holly Road, Dundee DD5 2LZ. Tel: (0382) 76046.

McGOWAN, MICHAEL
UK, Leeds, Soc (Lab)

Mr Michael McGowan, first elected to EP in 1984, was chmn of EP Cmte on Development and 1987-89; mbr since 1984 and is still on it. Also chaired African Caribbean Pacific/EEC jt cmte. Cooperative employment development officer with Kirklees Cl until elected MEP. B May 19 1940; ed Heckmondwike GS; Leicester Univ. Former lecturer and BBC journalist. Contested Brighouse and Spenborough in 1979 general election, and Ripon, 1966. Former mbr, Leeds City Cl; West Riding CC; mbr, Spenborough BC, 1962-65. NUJ and TGWU.

Addresses: Civic Hall, Leeds LS1 1UR. Tel: 462839. 3 Grosvenor Terrace, Otley, W Yorkshire LS21 1HJ. Tel: (0943) 462864.

McINTOSH, MISS ANNE
UK, Essex North East, ED (C)

Miss Anne McIntosh, political adviser, was elected to the EP in 1989 and became EDG (Conservative) spokesman on Cmte on Procedure, Verification of Credentials and Immunities; also mbr, Cmte on Transport and Tourism. Contested Workington in 1987 general election. Worked for European Democratic Gp in EP, 1983-89. B Sep 20 1954; ed Harrogate Coll; Edinburgh Univ; Aarhus Univ, Denmark. Admitted to Faculty of Advocates in 1982; practised European law in Community Law Office, Brussels, 1982-83.

Address: 17 Gardenfields, Stebbing, Essex CM6 3RG. Tel: (0371) 867 05.

McMAHON, HUGH
UK, Strathclyde West, Soc (Lab)

Mr Hugh McMahon was first elected to EP in 1984; mbr, Cmte on Youth, Culture, Education, Information and Sport, 1984-87; Cmte on Budgetary Control, 1987-89; Cmte on Social Affairs, Employment and Working Environment, 1989- ; Cmte on Budgetary Control, 1989- . Worked as teacher in various Scottish HS and Acads, 1962-84, being asst head teacher, Ravenspark Acad, Irvine, 1972-84. Contested Angus North and Mearns in 1979 general election. Mbr, Scottish exec, Lab Pty, 1980-83. Chmn, Scottish Cl, Fabian Soc, 1979-84; Socialist Ed Assocn of Scotland, 1978-82; Ardrossan Lab Pty, 1973-82; N Ayrshire CLP, 1975-80. B Jun 17 1938; ed Ardrossan Acad; Glasgow Univ; Jordanhill Coll of Ed. GMB.

Address: 6 Whitlees Court, Ardrossan KA22 1PA. Tel: (0294) 66692. 250 Seedhill, Paisley PA1. Tel: (041) 889 9990.

McMILLAN-SCOTT, EDWARD
UK, York, ED (C)

Mr Edward McMillan-Scott, an elected MEP since 1984, joined EP Cmte on Transport and Tourism in 1989 as EDG spokesman; mbr, Cmte on Youth, Culture, Education, Information and Sport, 1984-89; and spokesman on that cmte, 1987-89; mbr, Budgets Cmte, 1985-87; vice-chmn, 1979 Cmte of Cons MEP backbenchers, 1988- . Nat coordinator, 1992 Club, 1987- ; mbr, gen cl, Cons Gp for Europe, 1987- ; vice-pres, Yorks and Humbs Dev Assocn, 1987- . Public relations executive and parly consultant, 1976-84, and research assistant to two MEPs; political adviser to Falkland Islands Govt, London Office, 1983-84; tour director in Europe, Scandinavia, Africa and USSR, 1968-75. B Aug 15 1949. Mbr, court, York Univ.
Addresses: Wick House Farm, Wick, Pershore, Worcestershire. Tel: (0386) 552366. 109 Town Street, Old Malton, North Yorkshire, YO17 0HD. Tel: (0653) 693277.

MEDINA ORTEGA, MANUEL
Spain, Soc (PSOE)

Señor Manuel Medina Ortega was a vice-chairman of EP Committee on Legal Affairs and Citizens Rights in the outgoing Parliament; remained mbr of cmte in new Parliament. Became MEP in 1986; first elected 1987. Former member, Spanish national Parliment. University professor. B Dec 15 1935.

Addresses: Congreso de los Diputados, Fernanflor s/n, Madrid. Tel: (1) 429 51 93, Uga (Yaiza), Lanzarote, Islas Canarias. Tel: (28) 83 00 63.

MEGAHY, THOMAS
UK, Yorkshire South West, Soc (Lab)

Mr Thomas Megahy was a Vice-President of the European Parliament, 1987-89. MEP since 1979; mbr, Social Affairs and Employment Cmte, 1984- ; ldr, British Lab Gp of MEPs, 1984-85, and dep ldr, 1985-87; has served on Cmtes on Legal Affairs and Institutional Affairs, and was a vice-chmn, EP Cmte on Verification of Credentials. Vice-Pres, AMA, 1979- ; Yorks and Humberside Development Assocn, 1981- . Lecturer, Park Lane Coll, Leeds, 1965-79; Huddersfield Tech Coll, 1960-65; Rotherham Coll of Tech, 1956-59. Railway signalman, 1950-53. B Jul 16 1929. Ldr, Kirklees MBC, 1973-76; opposition ldr, 1976-78; mbr, Mirfield UDC, 1963-74. TGWU.

Addresses: 3 Burton Street, Wakefield, West Yorkshire WF1 2DD. Tel: (0924) 382396. 6 Lady Heton Grove, Mirfield, West Yorkshire WF14 9DY. Tel: (0924) 492680.

MEGRET, BRUNO
France, DR (FN)

M. Bruno Megret, civil engineer, is former National Assembly deputy for l'Isere. Elected to EP in 1989 and became mbr, Cmte on Economic and Monetary Affairs and Industrial Policy. B Apr 4 1949.

Address: 10 rue de Navarre, 75007 Paris.

MELANDRI, EUGENIO
Italy, Verts (DP)

Padre Eugenio Melandri was elected to EP in 1989; joined Cmte on Cooperation and Development. Was missionary at Xavier Mission from 1969; ordained priest 1974. Studied sociology at Trentino Univ, and in 1979 was asked to become a director of the journal *Missione Oggi* (Mission Today). Leader of "Cmte against the Merchants of Death", he has opposed international trade in arms; mbr, Ecclesiastical Cmte against Hunger. B Sep 21 1948.

Address: c.o. Democrazia Proletaria; Via Farini 62, 00185 Roma. Tel (06) 481 73 42-3-4.

MELIS, MARIO
Italy, ARC (VV-PSDA)

Sgr Mario Melis, of the Sardinian Action Party and former president of regional government of Sardinia, was elected to EP in 1989, joining Cmte on Regional Policy and Regional Planning. Lawyer. Former senator and mbr, Italian Chamber of Deputies. B Jun 10 1921.

Address: Viale Ciusa 97, 09100 Cagliari. Tel: (070) 27 22 50.

MENDES BOTA, JOSÉ
Portugal, LDR (PSD)

Senhor José Mendes Bota, economist, became elected MEP in 1989 and joined EP Cmte on Development and Cooperation. Mbr, Portuguese national Parliament from 1979; elected President of the council at Loule in 1982. B Aug 4 1955.

Address: Estacão de Loulé, 8100 Loule.

MENRAD, WINFRIED
Germany, EPP (CDU)

Herr Winfried Menrad, professor, heads a department at the School of Economics at Schwabisch-Hall. Chmn, CDA (*Rassemblement des employes democrates-chretiens*), North Wurtemberg. Elected to EP 1989; joined Cmte on Social Affairs and Employment and Working Environment. Mbr, CDU metalworkers' board for European questions. B Feb 10 1939.

*photograph
unavailable*

Address: Sudetenweg 55, 7178 Schwäbisch Hall. Tel: (0791) 5 31 66.

MERZ, FRIEDRICH
Germany, EPP (CDU)

Herr Friedrich Merz, elected MEP in 1989, joined EP Cmte on Economic and Monetary Affairs and Industrial Policy. Lawyer to the Chemical Industry Association of Germany. Serves on environment consultative cmte of Rhine-North Westphalia CDU. B Nov 11 1955.

*photograph
unavailable*

Address: Am Alfterhof 2, 5300 Bonn 1.

METTEN, ALMAN
Netherlands, Soc (PvdA)

Mr Alman Metten is a mbr of the EP Cmte on Economic and Monetary Affairs and Industrial Policy. First elected an MEP in 1984. Sociologist; taught in University of Amsterdam. Has held various posts in trade union movement. B Oct 9 1948.

Address: Loggerhof 179, 1034 CG Amsterdam. Tel: (020) 33 15 42.

MICHELINI, ALBERTO
Italy, EPP (DC)

Sgr Alberto Michelini, Italian television (RAI-TV) journalist and mbr of Chamber of Deputies, was elected to EP in 1984 and re-elected 1989; mbr, Political Affairs Cmte, 1989- ; former mbr, Cmte on Development and Cooperation. B Jul 25 1941; graduate in law. Began in cultural programmes on Italian television in 1968 and from 1970 with television news in Italy and abroad as a special correspondent. Then was responsible for various studio broadcasts.

Address: Piazzi S. Salvatore in Lauro 15, 00186 Roma.

MIHR, KARL-HEINRICH
Germany, Soc (SDP)

Herr, Karl-Heinrich Mihr rejoined the EP Cmte on Economic and Monetary Affairs and Industrial Policy after the 1989 elections. Has served as a vice-chairman of EP delegation to Austria. Became MEP in Jan 1980, being re-elected in 1984 and 1989. Was metal worker at VW factory in Kassel becoming full-time chairman of works council in 1972, and member of the general works council of Volkswagen AG Germany and of the supervisory board of the Volkswagen group. Mbr, SPD Federal Council; chaired SPD group on Gudensberg Municipal Council. B Jul 22 1935.

Address: Schwerinerweg 4, 3505 Gudensberg. Tel: (05603) 2830.

MIRANDA DA SILVA, JOAQUIM
Portugal, CG (PCP)

Senhor Joaquim Miranda Da Silva serves on the Cmte on Bugets. MEP since Jan 1986; first elected in 1987; re-elected 1989. Mbr, Central Cmte of PCP. Deputy in Portuguese national assembly, 1980-86. B Sep 7 1950.

Addresses: Travessa do Marçal 12 2., 7300 Portalegre. Tel: 22 632. Sala 208, Rua Soeiro Pereira Gomes 1, 1699 Lisboa Codex.

MIRANDA DE LAGE, SRA ANA
Spain, Soc (PSOE)

Sra Ana Miranda de Lage has been an MEP since 1986; first elected 1987. After 1989 elections joined Cmte on External Economic Relations; former mbr, Cmte on Legal Affairs and Citizens' Rights. Party administrator. B May 8 1946.

Address: c/Paseo Arriola 53 - 2° B, 20008 San Sebastian. Tel: (43) 21 35 83.

MONNIER-BESOMBES, GÉRARD
France, Verts (Verts)

M.Gérard Monnier-Besombes, scientist specialising in marine ecology, was elected to EP in 1989 and joined Cmte on Environment, Public Health and Consumer Protection; also a vice-chmn, Cmte on Petitions. Mbr, national cl, inter-regional organization of Les Verts (CNIR). Long time active mbr of Friends of the Earth. B 1953.

Address: 9 rue de la Grande Armée, 13001 Marseille. Tel: 91 50 31 76.

MONTERO ZABALA, JOSÉ MARÍA
Spain, NI (HB)

Señor José María Montero Zabala was first elected MEP in 1987 and served on Cmte on Legal Affairs and Citizens' Rights; after 1989 elections joined Cmte on Regional Policy and Regional Planning. Lawyer. B Apr 24 1954.

Addresses: Bidebarrieta 3-3°E, 48005 Bilbao, Vizcaya. Tel: (94) 415 92 97. Elorduigoitia n° 8-3°, Mungia, Vizcaya. Tel: (94) 674 30 31.

MOORHOUSE, JAMES
UK, London South and Surrey East, ED (C)

Mr James Moorhouse became a vice-chmn of EP Cmte on External Economic Relations in 1989 having been EDG spokesman on subject, 1984-87; spokesman on Transport Cmte, 1987-89; previously spokesman, 1979-84. First elected to EP 1979; chmn, EP delegation to N Europe and Nordic Cl, 1979-84. Director, Project Development International, 1985- ; consultant, 1980-84; gp environmental affairs adviser, Rio Tinto Zinc Corporation, 1973-80; previously with Shell, 1953-73. Contested St Pancras North in 1966 and 1970 general elections. B Jan 1 1924. Mbr, ICC Commission on Environment, 1978- ; exec cmte, Field Studies Cl, 1975-81; board of International Centre for Industry and the Environment, 1975-82. Chartered engineer.
Addresses: 14 Buckingham Palace Road, London SW1 0QP. Tel: (01) 828 3153/4. Telex: 89 55 788. Jordan Cottage, 18 Orbel Street, London SW11 3NZ. Tel: (01) 228 8080.

MORÁN LÓPEZ, FERNANDO
Spain, Soc (PSOE)

Señor Fernando Morán López first became an MEP in 1987; re-elected 1989 and rejoined Political Affairs Cmte on which he was serving in outgoing Parliament. Mbr, bureau, Socialist Gp, 1989- . Has served as diplomat, senator and deputy in Spanish national Parliament. Minister for Foreign Affairs, 1982-85; Spanish Ambassador to United Nations, 1985-87. B Mar 25 1926.

Address: Casa de la Reina pral. 2, San Lorenzo de El Escorial, Madrid. Tel: (93) 980 41 98.

MORETTI, LUIGI
Italy, ARC (Lega-L)

Sgr Luigi Moretti, sponsor and founder of the Lombady Regional Party (Lega Lombarda), was elected to EP in 1989 and became mbr, Cmte on External Economic Relations. Mbr, Lombardy regional council. B Jun 6 1944.

Address: c.o. Lega Lombarda, Piazza Massari 2, 20125 Milano. Tel: (02) 607 03 79.

MORODO LEONCIO, RAUL
Spain, LDR (CDS)

Señor Raul Morodo Leoncio became elected MEP in 1987; after 1989 elections rejoined Political Affairs Cmte. Former Spanish ambassador to Unesco and rector of International University of Menendez y Pelayo. B Jan 9 1935.

Addresses: Eduardo Dato 21, Madrid. Tel: (1) 410 08 30. Fortuny 14, Madrid. Tel: (1) 419 75 18.

MORRIS, DAVID
UK, Mid and West Wales, Soc (Lab)

Mr David Morris was first elected to EP in 1984. Mbr, Cmte on Agriculture, Fisheries and Food (senior vice-chmn of fisheries sub-cmte), 1984-88; Cmte on Regional Policy and Regional Planning, 1988-89; Cmte on Development and Cooperation, 1989- . Contested Brecon and Radnor in 1983 general election; former Newport county borough cllr. B Jan 28 1930; ed Central Sch, Llanelli; Ruskin Coll, Oxford; Univ Coll, Swansea; Theological Coll, Aberystwyth. Worked as labourer in a foundry; then minister of religion in Mid-Wales and Newport, Presbyterian Church of Wales, 1958-62; educational adviser with Gwent CC, 1974-84. Chmn, Welsh region, Socialist Health Assocn. TGWU.

Address: 65 Harlech Crescent, Swansea. Tel: (0792) 206968.

MOTTOLA, GIUSEPPE
Italy, EPP (DC)

Sgr Giuseppe Mottola, journalist; director of Italian Confederation of Farmers' Unions and of Chamber of Commerce. Chmn, research institute of tobacco industry. Elected to EP in 1989 and joined Cmte on Agriculture, Fisheries and Rural Development. Regional councillor. B Apr 20 1936.

Address: Via Ponti Rossi 188, 80131 Napoli. Tel: (081) 751 12 66.

MÜLLER, GERD
Germany, EPP (CSU)

Herr Gerd Müller, elected MEP in 1989, became mbr, Cmte on Transport and Tourism. Former senior civil servant of "Land" of Bavaria; chmn, "Junge Union" of Bavaria; mbr, CSU central cmte. B Aug 25 1955.

Address: Schulstrasse 22, 8989 Deisenhausen-Unterbleichen.

MÜNCH, WERNER
Germany, EPP (CDU)

Herr Werner Münch was first elected to EP in 1984. Served on Cmte on Energy, Research and Technology, and then joined Cmte on Youth, Culture, Education, Information and Sport, being EPP spokesman in outgoing Parliament; still on that cmte. Doctorate in philosophy; lecturer at Catholic Technical College of North Germany. Mbr, CDU federal cultural cmte, since 1980. B Sep 25 1940.

Addresses: Brinkstrasse 27, 3842 Lohne (Oldenburg). Tel: (04442) 6878. Telefax: (04442) 71739. Zur Tonkuhle 15, 2842 Lohn (Oldenburg). Tel: (04442) 3879.

MUNTINGH, HEMMO
Netherlands, Soc (PvdA)

Mr Hemmo Muntingh, first elected to the EP in 1979, has been serving on the Cmte on Environment, Public Health and Consumer Protection; stayed on cmte after 1989 elections. Has also served as chmn of the *Fondation Européene pour L'Environnement*; was secretary of *Landelijke Vereniging tot Behoud van de Waddenzee*. Business economist with special interest in conservation. B Dec 30 1938; studied through Free Univ of Amsterdam.

Address: Zonderwansreed 1, 9079 PJ St Jacobiparochie. Tel: (05189) 16 73. Telefax: (05189) 12 30.

MUSCARDINI, SIGNORA CHRISTIANA
Italy, NI (MSI-DN)

Signora Christiana Muscardini was elected to EP in 1989 and became mbr, Cmte on Environment, Public Health and Consumer Protection. Journalist. Former mbr, Chamber of Deputies; local councillor. On central cmte of MSI. B Nov 6 1948.

Address:

NAPOLETANO, SIGNORA PASQUALINA
Italy, EUL (PCI)

Signora Pasqualina Napoletano, teacher, was elected to EP in 1989 and joined Cmte on Development and Cooperation and Cmte on Women's Rights; also mbr of ACP-EC Assembly. Mbr, central cmte of Italian Communist Party. Regional councillor, Lazio. B Sep 28 1949.

Address: Piazza Dante 12, 00185 Roma. Tel: (06) 731 04 31.

NAPOLITANO, GIORGIO
Italy, EUL (PCI)

Sgr Giorgio Napolitano was elected to EP in 1989, joining Cmte on Political Affairs. Mbr, Italian Chamber of Deputies where he was leader of Communist Gp. Mbr, central cmte and management body of Italian Communist Party; responsible for political strategy of party. B Jun 29 1925.

Address: Direzione PCI, Via delle Botteghe Oscure 4, 00186 Roma. Tel: (06) 678 42 82.

NAVARRO VELASCO, ANTONIO
Spain, EPP (PP)

Señor Antonio Navarro Velasco, nominated to EP in Jan 1986, was elected in 1987 and re-elected 1989. Mbr, Cmte on Agriculture, Fisheries and Food, being ED Gp coordinator in outgoing Parliament; remained on cmte after 1989 elections. Deputy chmn, International Wheat Cl, 1981-82; chmn of its executive cmte, 1979-80. Mbr of Cortes for Malaga; secretary, Alianza Popular political cl and on national executive. Appointments include Doctor in agricultural engineering and specialist in forestry, Univ of Pisa; consultant engineer, Grasa Institute of Seville; director of oil plant, Marchena, 1965-69; agricultural counsellor, Spanish Embassy, London, 1973-81. B Sep 1 1936.

Addresses: Paseo de Recoletos 14 - 2°, 28001 Madrid. Tel: 275 83 25. Finca "La Sabina", c/Mirador 2, Olvera, Cadiz. Tel: (6) 13 12 22.

NEUBAUER, HARALD
Germany, DR (Repub)

Herr Harald Neubauer, journalist, was elected to EP in 1989; became mbr, Cmte on External Economic Relations. Party chairman in Bavaria. B 1951.

Address: Schleissheimer Strasse 186, 8000 München 40.

NEWENS, STANLEY
UK, London Central, Soc (Lab)

Mr Stanley Newens was deputy leader, British Lab Gp of MEPs, 1988-89; chmn of gp, 1985-87; elected MEP since 1984; mbr, EP Political Affairs Cmte, 1984-89; Cmte on Agriculture, Fisheries and Rural Development, 1989- . Former teacher and miner. Lab MP for Epping, 1964-70, and Harlow, 1974-83; contested Harlow in 1987 general election. Chmn, Liberation (formerly Movement for Colonial Freedom), 1967- ; Tribune Gp of Lab MPs, 1982-83; Eastern Area gp of Lab MPs, 1974-83; PLP foreign and Commonwealth affairs gp, 1982-83. Director, London Co-op Soc, 1971-77, and pres, 1977-81. Vice-chmn, Eastern Regional Lab Pty; Lab Action for Peace. Sec, Harlow Cl for Voluntary Service, 1983-84. B Feb 4 1930; ed Buckhurst Hill County HS; Univ Coll, London; Westminster Coll of Ed. NUT.
Address: The Leys, 18 Park Hill, Harlow, Essex CM17 0AE. Tel: (0279) 20108.

NEWMAN, EDWARD
UK, Greater Manchester Central, Soc (Lab)

Mr Edward Newman, first elected to EP in 1984, joined EP Cmte on Budgets in 1989 and also Cmte on Petitions; mbr, Regional Policy and Regional Planning Cmte, 1984-89, being a vice-chmn, 1984-87; has also served on Women's Rights Cmte. Treas, British Lab Gp of MEPs, 1988-89. Worked as a semi-skilled manual worker in light engineering and cable-making and then as a postal worker in Manchester. B May 14 1953. Mbr, Manchester City Cl, 1979-85. UCW, being senior rep in Manchester amalgamated branch.

Addresses: Deansgate House, 274 Deansgate, Manchester M3 4HF. Tel: (061) 834 3849. 19 Sibson Road, Manchester M21 1NH. Tel: (061) 881 9641.

NEWTON DUNN, WILLIAM
UK, Lincolnshire, ED (C)

Mr William Newton Dunn became a vice-chmn of EP Cmte on Budgets in 1989 when he also joined Cmtes on Political Affairs and on Petitions. Mbr, Transport Cmte, 1984-89 (Cons spokesman, 1984-87); spokesman on cmte on Rules of Procedure, Verification of Credentials and Immunities, 1987-89. First elected to EP 1979; mbr, bureau, ED Gp, 1987- ; chmn, 1979 Cmte of Cons backbench MEPs, 1983-87; representative for Gibraltar. With Fisons Ltd (Fertilizer Division) 1974-79, being purchasing controller. B Oct 3 1941; ed Marlborough Coll; the Sorbonne, Paris; Gonville and Caius Coll, Cambridge; INSEAD Business Sch, Fontainebleau. Contested Carmarthen in Feb 1974 general election and Cardiff West in Oct 74 election.
Addresses: 42 Lanchester Road, London N6 4TA. Tel: (01) 883 2527. 10 Church Lane, Navenby, Lincoln LN5 0EG. Tel: Lincoln 810812.

NIANIAS, DIMITRIOS
Greece, RDE (DI-ANA)

Mr Dimitrios Nianias, university professor, was elected MEP in 1989 and joined Cmte on Social Affairs, Employment and Working Environment. Former mbr, Greek national Parliament and former Minister for Press, Information and Culture. B 1923. Became vice-chairman of RDE Group.

Address: Kleomenous 39a, 106 76 Athenes.

NICHOLSON, JAMES
UK, Northern Ireland, EPP (OUP)

Mr James Nicholson, farmer, was elected to the EP in 1989. Became UK's sole representative in EPP Gp, joining gp bureau; mbr, Cmte on Regional Policy and Regional Planning, 1989-. Westminster Official Ulster Unionist MP for Newry and Armagh, 1983-86, losing it in the by-election forced by the Unionist protest at the Anglo-Irish Agreement. B Jan 29 1945; ed Aghavilly Primary Sch. OUP Assembly mbr, 1982-86; OUP mbr, Armagh DC, 1976- .

Address: 147 Keady Road, Ballyards, Armagh BT60 3AE. Tel: (0861) 523307. Telefax: (0861) 523307.

NIELSEN, FRU TOVE
Denmark, LDR (V)

Fru Tove Nielsen, an elected MEP since 1979, was a vice-chmn of Liberal and Democratic Gp (LDR) at EP, 1979-89. Mbr, Cmte on Social Affairs, Employment and Working Environment, 1989- ; former mbr, Cmte on Economic and Monetary Affairs and Industrial Policy. Vice-chmn, EP-Israel interparliamentary delegation, in outgoing Parliament. Minister of Education, 1973-75; consultant to Danish Employers' Association. Teacher. Mbr, Danish Parliament (Folketing) 1972-73 and 1975-77. President, Nordic Cl for Adult Education, from 1975. B Apr 8 1941.

Address: Kokkedalsvej 5 B, Postbox 139, 2970 Horsholm. Tel: (42) 57 00 65.

NORDMANN, JEAN-THOMAS
France, LDR (UDF-Rad)

M. Jean-Thomas Nordmann, Paris councillor since 1983, was first elected to EP in 1984; mbr, Cmte on Development and Cooperation. Vice-chmn, Radical Party; former chmn, Young Radicals. Former technical adviser to various government ministries, including departments of education, environment and trade. Author of publications on French history and literature in 19th and 20th centuries and works on history of radicalism. B Feb 16 1946.

Addresses: Parti Radical, 1 place de Valois, 75001 Paris. Tel: (1) 42 61 56 32. 14 rue Pirandello, 75013 Paris. Tel: (1) 47 07 58 70.

OCCHETTO, ACHILLE
Italy, EUL (PCI)

Sgr Achille Occhetto, Secretary-General of Italian Communist Party, was elected to EP in 1989. Publisher. Mbr, Italian Chamber of Deputies. B Mar 3 1936.

Address: Direzione PCI, Via delle Botteghe Oscure 4, 00186 Roma. Tel: (06) 671 11.

ODDY, MS CHRISTINE
UK, Midlands Central, Soc (Lab)

Ms Christine Oddy won this Euro seat for Labour in 1989 and joined EP Cmte on Legal Affairs and Citizens' Rights. Solicitor, lecturer in law, specialising in trade union and employment law, EEC law and comparative law. Worked in general secretariat, European Commission, 1980, and in a law firm in Paris in 1982. Governor, City of London Poly; mbr, Haldane Soc of Socialist Lawyers; Industrial Law Soc. B Sep 20 1955; ed Stoke Park GS, Coventry; Univ Coll, London; Inst of European Studies, Brussels; Birkbeck Coll, London. NATFHE being branch sec, 1985-89, and mbr, reg exec cmte, 1987-88. Mbr, Poly Standing Advisory Panel, 1986- . In 1987 visited US on NATFHE Walter Page scholarship and in 1985 visited France on Cl of Europe scholarship to investigate women's employment rights.

Address: 33 Longfellow Road, Coventry CV2 5HD.

O'HAGAN, LORD
UK, Devon, ED (C)

Lord O'Hagan was first elected for this Euro seat in 1979; an Independent mbr of nominated EP, 1973-75. Mbr, EP Social Affairs and Employment Cmte, and after 1989 elections became ED (Conservative) spokesman on it; former mbr, Political Affairs Cmte and Legal Affairs Cmte; former deputy chief whip, ED Gp; mbr, ED Gp bureau, 1980-82. Front bench spokesman in House of Lords for Conservatives, 1977-79, on the EEC, transport and environment. B Sep 6 1945; ed Eton; New Coll, Oxford.

Address: 12 Lyndhurst Road, Exeter, Devon EX2 4PA. Tel: (0392) 410532.

OLIVA GARCÍA, FRANCISCO
Spain, Soc (PSOE)

Señor Francisco Oliva García has been an MEP since 1986. After 1989 elections rejoined EP Cmte on Regional Planning and Regional Policy on which he served in outgoing Parliament. Lawyer and former civil servant. Former mbr, Spanish national Parliament. B Nov 24 1946.

Address: c/Puccini no 14, Puerto de la Torre, Malaga.

ONUR, FRAU LEYLA
Germany, Soc (SDP)

Frau Leyla Onur, vocational training teacher, was elected to EP in 1989; became mbr, Cmte on Regional Policy and Regional Planning. Mayor of Braunschweig; office holder in party organization. B Jan 8 1945.

Address: Georg-Westermann-Allee 61, 3300 Braunschweig.

OOMEN-RUIJTEN, MEVR MARIA
Netherlands, EPP (CDA)

Mevr Maria Oomen-Ruijten, elected to EP in 1989, became mbr, Cmte on Social Affairs, Employment and Working Environment. Has held various appointments in CDA; mbr, Dutch Second Chamber, since 1981, and mbr of parliamentary gp bureau. Public relations consultant; specialist on environment, consumer protection and social affairs. B Sep 6 1950.

Address: Julianalaan 55, 6051 As Maasbracht.

OOSTLANDER, ARIE
Netherlands, EPP (CDA)

Mr Arie Oostlander, psychologist, is scientific collaborator at the Free Univ of Amsterdam; chairs CDA scientific institute; director, Fondation A. Kuypers. Elected to EP in 1989; joined EP Cmte on Youth, Culture, Education, the Media and Sport. Mbr, CDA bureau. B Mar 28 1936.

Address: De Wielewaal 12, 2761 XZ Zevenhuizen. Tel: (01802) 2315.

OREJA AGUIRRE, MARCELINO
Spain, EPP (PP)

Señor Marcelino Oreja Aguirre was elected to EP in 1989, becoming a vice-chmn of EPP Gp and chmn of Cmte on Institutional Affairs. Vice-President of Parti Popular. Secretary-General of Cl of Europe, 1984-89. Former national deputy and senator; Minister for Foreign Affairs, 1976-80, and ambassador; Govt delegate to Basque area of Spain, 1980-82. Doctor of law; diplomat; senator for Roi. B Feb 13 1935.

Address: Genova 13 7°, 28004 Madrid.

ORTIZ CLIMENT, LEOPOLDO
Spain, EPP (PP)

Señor Leopoldo Ortiz Climent, agricultural engineer and fruit and vegetable exporter, was elected to EP in 1989 and joined Cmte on Agriculture, Fisheries and Rural Development. Director-general of Spanish cmte on the export of citrus fruits; mbr, EC consultative cmte on farm structures; Spanish cmtes on agriculture and relations with Nato. B 1942.

Address: Bachillaer 7 1°, 46021 Valenzia.

OUTRIVE, LODE VAN
Belgium, Soc (SP)

Mr Lode van Outrive, university professor, was elected to EP in 1989 and became mbr, Cmte on Legal Affairs and Citizens' Rights. B Jan 18 1932. Doctor of law, political and social sciences.

photograph unavailable

Address: Van Couwenhovelaan 28, 3009 Herent. Tel: (016) 48 84 58.

PACHECO HERRERA, PEDRO
Spain, ARC (PA)

Señor Pedro Pacheco Herrera was elected to EP in 1989 and joined Cmte on Agriculture, Fisheries and Rural Development. Mayor of Jerez de la Frontera since 1979 and President, Andalucia Regional Party. B Apr 2 1949.

Address: Santo Domingo 8 5°F, 11402 Jerez de la Frontera Cadiz.

PACK, FRAU DORIS
Germany, EPP (CDU)

Frau Doris Pack, at the time of her election to EP in 1989, was a mbr of the Bundestag and of the assemblies of Cl of Europe and WEU; party speaker on European policy. Became mbr of Cmtes on Regional Policy and Regional Planning and on Women's Rights; jt vice-chair, EPP working gp on social affairs, 1989- . Headmistress. Vice-chair, Saar branch, European Movement. B Mar 18 1943.

Address: An der Weissen Eiche 1, 6601 Bübingen.

215

PAGOROPOULOS, DIMITRIOS
Greece, Soc (PASOK)

Mr Dimitrios Pagoropoulos, lawyer, was elected to EP in 1989. Joined Cmte on Social Affairs, Employment and Working Environment and became a vice-chmn of Cmte on Petitions. Mbr, administrative council of the Bar; chairman of special cmte of inquiry (1989) into financial irregularities. B Jan 30 1931.

Address: Har. Trikoupi 46, 106 80 Athenes. Tel: 362 00 52/361 77 40.

PAISLEY, THE REV IAN
UK, Northern Ireland, NI (DUP)

The Rev Ian Paisley, leader, Democratic Unionist Party; MP for Antrim N since 1970. Resigned seat in 1985 in protest at Anglo-Irish Agreement and retained it in 1986 by-election. Elected MEP in 1979; mbr, Cmte on Social Affairs, Employment and Working Environment, 1989- ; former mbr, Political Affairs Cmte. Mbr, N Ireland Assembly, 1982-86. Minister of Martyrs Memorial Free Presbyterian Church, Belfast, 1946- . Hon director, Voice Newspapers Ltd and Protestant Telegraph Ltd. Sat as Prot U MP, 1970-74. B Apr 6 1926. Ordained 1946. Won Bannside in 1970; Stormont MP until 1972; ldr of opposition, Stormont, and chmn, PASC, 1971-72. Dem U mbr for N Antrim of NI Assembly, 1973-75, and UUUC mbr, NI Constitutional Convention, 1975-76.

Address: The Parsonage, 17 Cyprus Avenue, Belfast BT5 5NT. Tel: 655694.

PANNELLA, MARCO
Italy, NI (PLI/PRI)

Sgr Marco Pannella was first elected to EP in 1979; former vice-chmn, Cmte on Institutional Affairs; now mbr, Political Affairs Cmte and Cmte on Social Affairs, Employment and Working Environment; former mbr, Cmte on Development and Cooperation. Journalist. Elected to Italian Parliament 1976; former chmn, parliamentary gp of Partito Radicale. One of party's founders; former Secretary General. Has chaired League of Conscientious Objectors since 1973. B May 2 1930; degree in jurisprudence.

Address: Gruppo Parlamentare Radicale, Camera dei Deputati, Via Uffici del Vicario 21, 00186 Roma. Tel: (06) 67 17 92 97.

PAPAYANNAKIS, MIHAIL
Greece, EUL (SAP/Comm)

Mr Mihail Papayannakis, economics journalist, was elected to EP in 1989 on Greek Communist Alliance list SAP (Synaspismos). Joined Cmte on Social Affairs, Employment and Working Environment and was appointed a vice-chmn; also mbr, Cmte on Economic and Monetary Affairs and Industrial Policy. Mbr, executive cmte of Hellenic Left (EAR).

Address: Evridikis 3-5, 176 71 Kallithea.

PAPOUTSIS, CHRISTOS
Greece, Soc (PASOK)

Mr Christos Papoutsis, a former vice-chmn of Socialist Gp and leader of its Greek delegation, became an MEP in 1984; re-elected 1989. Economist. Mbr, EP Cmte on Budgets and Cmte on Budgetary Control; in outgoing Parliament was a vice-chmn, EP-Canada interparliamentary delegation. B Apr 11 1953. Mbr, Pasok's central cmte; former mbr, National Cl for Higher Education.

Address: Sokratous 59, 155 62 Holargos. Tel: (1) 65 32 962.

PARTSCH, KARL
Germany, Verts (Grüne)

Herr Karl Partsch, biologist and ecologist, became elected MEP in 1989 and joined Cmte on Environment, Public Health and Consumer Protection. Only West German on list of honour of UN environment organization. After last war, went into fishing industry; developed wide interest in ecological issues. Specialised in new methods to protect mountain forests from damage by avalanches. B 1922.

Address: Nr 25, 8972 Ofterschwang. Tel: (08321) 3504.

PASTY, JEAN-CLAUDE
France, RDE (RPR)

M. Jean-Claude Pasty was first elected to EP in 1984; a vice-chmn, Cmte on Budgets, 1987-89 and mbr of cmte since 1984; also mbr, Cmte on Budgetary Control; a vice-chmn, RDE Gp, 1989- . Civil administrator; conseiller general, Creuse; conseiller regional, Limousin. Creuse deputy (RPR), 1978-81; national secretary of RPR. Deputy head, policy division, then head of research division, FORMA (agricultural markets guidance and regularization fund), 1965-67; technical adviser in private office of Robert Boulin (Minister of Agriculture), Bernard Pons (Secretary of State for Agriculture) and Jacques Chirac (Minister of Agriculture), 1968-73. Director of social affairs, Ministry of Agriculture, 1973-78. B Jun 15 1937.

Addresses: 12 Sente de la Folie, 92420 Vaucresson. Tel: (1) 47 41 14 33. Résidence Notre Dame, Rue André Desmoulins, 23000 Gueret. Tel: 55 52 93 25.

PATTERSON, BEN
UK, Kent West, ED (C)

Mr Ben Patterson was EDG spokesman on economic and monetary affairs and industrial policy, 1984-89, and is still serving on that EP cmte; spokesman on social affairs and employment, 1981-84; former mbr, EP cmte on Rules of Procedure, Verification of Credentials and Immunities. First elected to EP in 1979. Deputy Head of London office of EP, 1974-79. Contested Wrexham, 1970 general election. B Apr 21 1939; ed Westminster Sch; Trinity Coll, Cambridge; LSE. Journalist and company director. Mbr, Hammersmith BC, 1968-71. Founder mbr, Cons Gp for Europe; mbr, CPC nat advisory cmte, 1982-85. Lecturer, Swinton Cons Coll, 1961-65; editor, *CPC Monthly Report*, 1965-74.

Address: Elm Hill House, Hawkhurst, Kent TN18 4XU. Tel: (0580) 753260.

PEDERSEN, KLAUS RISKAER
Denmark, LDR (V)

Mr Klaus Riskaer Pedersen, company managing director, was elected to EP in 1989; became mbr, Cmte on Economic and Monetary Affairs and Industrial Policy. B Apr 22 1956.

Addresses: c.o. Accumulator Invest A/S, Amaliegade 45, 1256 Kobenhavn K. Tel: (33) 32 46 00. Telefax: (33) 93 46 11. Vedbaek Strandvej 322, 2950 Vedbaek. Tel: (42) 89 44 22.

PEIJS, MEVR KARLA
Netherlands, EPP (CDA)

Mevr Karla Peijs, professor of economic science at Utrecht, has had various responsibilities within the CDA at centre and local level; secretary to DC executive. Mbr, provincial state govt, Utrecht. Elected to EP in 1989; mbr, Cmte on External Economic Relations. B Sep 1 1944.

Address: Achtersloot 53, 3401 NS Ijsselstein.

PENDERS, JEAN
Netherlands, EPP (CDA)

Mr Jean Penders, an elected MEP since 1979, is a mbr of the EP Cmte on Political Affairs. Mbr, bureau of the EPP Gp, and leader of its Netherlands delegation. On staff of Scientific Cl for Govt policy, 1976-79; worked at Ministry of Foreign Affairs, 1968-72; Permanent Secretary to KVP, Second Chamber Parliamentary Pty, 1972-76. B Apr 5 1939; holds doctorate in history (Nijmegen).

Address: Voorburgseweg 11, 2264 AC Leidschendam. Tel: (70) 27 86 91.

PEREIRA, VIRGILIO
Portugal, LDR (PSD)

Senhor Virgilio Pereira was a vice-chmn of the EP Cmte on Environment, Public Health and Consumer Protection; remained on cmte after 1989 elections. Former mbr, Cmte on Petitions; has been on EP-South America interparliamentary delegation. Became MEP in 1987; re-elected 1989. Deputy in Portuguese national Assembly, 1983-85; Mayor of Funchal, 1974-83. B Jan 11 1941.

Address: Rua Silvestre Quintine de Freitas 11D, 9000 Funchal, Madeira. Tel: 30 201.

PÉREZ ROYO, FERNANDO
Spain, EUL (IU)

Señor Fernando Pérez Royo was elected a Vice-President of EP in July 1989. First elected MEP in 1987 and after 1989 elections he rejoined Political Affairs Cmte. Lawyer. Former mbr, Spanish national Parliament. B Jan 25 1943.

Address: Grupo Parlamentario IU-CA, Reyes Catolicos 15-6a, 41001 Sevilla.

PERGOLA, ANTONINO LA
Italy, Soc (PSI)

Sgr Antonino la Pergola was elected to EP in 1989 and became chmn of Cmte on Energy, Research and Technology. Former Italian Minister for European Affairs; former President of the Constitutional Court. University lecturer; journalist. B Nov 13 1931.

Address: Via Bracciano 46, 00189 Roma. Tel: (06) 376 77 34.

PERREAU DE PINNINCK DOMENECH, CARLOS
Spain, NI (R-Mateos)

Señor Carlos Perreau de Pinninck Domenech was elected to EP in 1989 on list of group seeking election of Spanish businessman, Mr Ruiz-Mateos. Joined Cmte on Budgets and Cmte on Petitions. Lawyer and businessman. B Mar 5 1953.

Address: Velazquez 10, 28001 Madrid.

PERSCHAU, HARTMUT
Germany, EPP (CDU)

Herr Hartmut Perschau, elected to EP in 1989, joined Cmte on Development and Cooperation. Former army major. Mbr and Christian Democrat leader of "Land" of Hamburg. B Mar 28 1942.

Address: Fontenay-Allee 9, 2000 Hamburg 36.

PERY, MME NICOLE
France, Soc (PS)

Mme Nicole Pery was re-elected Senior Vice-President of EP in 1989, an appointment she had held 1987-89; first became a Vice-President in July 1984. On bureau of Socialist Gp. First elected MEP in 1979; mbr, Cmte on Development and Cooperation; former mbr, Cmte on Youth, Culture, Education, Information and Sport. Former PS federal secretary for women's rights and national cmte mbr. Regional councillor d'Aquitaine; municipal councillor, Bayonne (Pyrenees-Atlantiques); deputy mayor, Ciboure. B May 15 1943.

Address: Villa "Xori-Kanta", 40 rue Massy, 64500 Ciboure. Tel: 59 47 28 92 or 59 47 87 50.

PESMAZOGLOU, IOANNIS
Greece, EPP (ND)

Mr Ioannis Pesmazoglou was an elected MEP, 1981-84; re-elected 1989 and joined EP Political Affairs Cmte. Mbr, Greek Parliament, for Athens, 1974-81 and 1985-89. Minister of Finance in first govt after fall of dictatorship, Jul to Oct 1974. President, Society for Study of Greek Problems, 1971-72 when he was exiled. Arrested and detained in solitary confinement 1973. President, Party of Democratic Socialism (KO.DI.SO), 1979-84. B Mar 1 1918; Univ of Athens; St John's Coll, Cambridge (Hon Fellow, 1988). Lecturer and professor, Athens Univ, 1950-70. Deputy Govenor, Bank of Greece, 1960-67.

Address: Neofytou Vamva 6, 106 74 Athenes. Tel: 7212458.

221

PETER, HELWIN
Germany, Soc (SDP)

Herr Helwin Peter, trade union leader, became mbr of EP in 1989 election; joined Cmte on Social Affairs, Employment and Working Environment. Former mbr, Bundestag. B Jul 18 1941.

Address: Fliederstrasse 3, 6692 Oberthal.

PETERS, JOHANNES WILHELM
Germany, Soc (SDP)

Herr Johannes Wilhelm Peters, a miner, was elected a Vice-President of EP in July 1989; was first elected to EP in 1979; a vice-chairman, EP Cmte on Social Affairs and Employment, until 1984; still a member of cmte and also mbr of EP Cmte on Rules of Procedure, the Verification of Credentials and Immunities. Secretary, with responsibility for training, Mine and Energy Workers Union, 1961-73. Head of housing administration for Westphalia of Neue Heimst Building Society, 1973-79. Mbr, West Westphalian District Executive Cmte of SPD; Dortmund City Cl, 1969-79.

Senftenbergstrasse, 4600 Dortmund 14. Tel: (0231) 230374. SPD Bezirksbüro Westliches Westfalen, Brüderweg 10-12, 4600 Dortmund 1. Tel: (0231) 527781.

PICCOLI, CESARE DE
Italy, EUL (PCI)

Sgr Cesare de Piccoli became elected MEP in 1989 joining EP Cmte on Economic and Monetary Affairs and Industrial Policy. Deputy Mayor of Venice; regional councillor. Mbr, central cmte of Italian Communist Party. B Jan 25 1946.

Address: Comune di Venezia, 30100 Venezia. Tel: (041) 522 36 65.

PIERMONT, FRAU DOROTHEE
Germany, Verts (Grüne)

Frau Dorothee Piermont was an elected MEP, 1984-87; re-elected 1989 when she rejoined Political Affairs Cmte. Former antiquarian bookseller from Bonn specialising in French books. Graduate in Romanist studies; university lecturer. Lived several years in Italy and France, among her occupations being lecturer in German politics and contemporary history in Paris. Was worker for independent socialists (PSU) in France and the movement for women's rights. On return to Germany, active in peace activities of Greens. More recently campaigned against extremist right parties in Europe. B Feb 27 1943.

Addresses: Europagruppe Die Grunen, Bundeshaus HT, D-5300 Bonn 1. Tel: (0228) 16 91 98. Postfach 21 02 32, D 5300 Bonn 2. Tel: (0228) 18 73; (0228) 16 91 98.

PIERROS, FILIPPOS
Greece, EPP (ND)

Mr Filippos Pierros, elected to EP 1989, joined EP Energy, Research and Technology Cmte. Legal adviser in the Human Rights Section of United Nations at Geneva. Doctor of law. B 1957.

Address: Mavromichali 124, 114 72 Athenes.

PIMENTA, CARLOS
Portugal, LDR (PSD)

Senhor Carlos Pimenta became an MEP in 1987; re-elected 1989. Mbr, EP Cmtes on Environment, Public Health and Consumer Protection, and on Institutional Affairs, 1989- ; former mbr, Cmte on External Economic Relations. Became deputy in Portuguese national Assembly in 1985; former Secretary of State. Electronics engineer. B May 7 1955.

Address: Av. Almirante Gago Coutinho, 38-5° Esq°, 1700 Lisboa. Tel: (1) 80 06 04.

PINXTEN, KAREL
Belgium, EPP (CVP)

Mr Karel Pinxten, economist, was elected to EP in 1989; joined Cmte on Economic and Monetary Affairs and Industrial Policy. Mayor of Overpelt; serves in cabinet of Minister of Finances; mbr, national bureau of CVP. B July 19 1952; graduate in economic science; master of philosophy in economics.

Address: Koningstraat 27, 3583 Overpelt. Tel: (011) 64 71 20.

PIQUET, RENÉ-EMILE
France, CG (PCF)

M. René-Emile Piquet, first elected an MEP in 1979, became chairman of the Coalition des Gauches Gp after the 1989 elections; a vice-chmn of Communist and Allies Gp in outgoing Parliament; mbr, Cmte on Agriculture, Fisheries and Rural Development, 1989- ; former mbr, Political Affairs Cmte. Former metal worker. Mbr, PCF political bureau, having been secretary, central cmte, French Communist Party. B Oct 23 1932.

Addresses: Comité Central du Parti Communiste Français, 2 place du Colonel Fabien, 75940 Paris Cedex 19. Tel: (1) 42 38 66 55. 1 allée Marc St Saëns, 31100 Toulouse. Tel: 61 44 12 13.

PIRKL, FRITZ
Germany, EPP (CSU)

Herr Fritz Pirkl is head of the CSU delegation in the EPP Gp and mbr of EPP Gp bureau. First elected MEP in 1984, being mbr, Cmte on Development and Co-operation; also mbr, Political Affairs Cmte, 1989- . Former Bavarian "Land" Minister for Labour and former member of the Landtag. Former civil servant. Founder in 1967 and later chmn, Hanns Seidel Foundation. Mbr, CSU central cmte. B Aug 13 1925.

Addresses: Hanns-Seidel-Stiftung, Lazarettstrasse 19, 8000 München 19. Tel: (089) 125 83 20.

PISONI, FERRUCCIO
Italy, EPP (DC)

Sgr Ferruccio Pisoni has been an MEP since 1984; also mbr, nominated Parliament, 1972-79. Former Under Secretary of State at Italian Ministry of Agriculture, and in outgoing Parliament was on Cmte on Agriculture, Fisheries and Food; mbr, Cmte on Social Affairs, Employment and Working Environment, 1989- . Chmn, EPP Gp working party on social matters, 1989- , and on EPP Gp bureau. Elected to Chamber of Deputies in 1968; was vice-chmn of EEC-Greek joint cmte which prepared way for Greek entry to EC. Has chaired Italian Association of Catholic Primary School Teachers of Trento province. B Aug 6 1936.

Address: Federcantine, via Conciliazione 1, 00193 Roma. Tel: (06) 6569370. Vicolo della Cervara 1/1, 38100 Trento.

PISONI, NINO
Italy, EPP (DC)

Sgr Nino Pisoni was elected to EP in 1984; re-elected 1989; mbr, Cmte on Agriculture, Fisheries and Rural Development. Farmers' union official; expert on economic and agricultural problems. Former mbr, Lombardy regional executive; has acted as DC national advisor and been Mayor of Bernate Ticino. Mbr, board of Milan Chamber of Commerce, 1961-82. Director of wine growers' association in Milan. Former teacher. B May 5 1927.

Addresses: Via Santa Tecla 4, 20122 Milano. Tel: (02) 805 23 16. Via Monterosa 3, 20015 Parabiago (Milano). Tel: (0331) 55 24 03.

PLANAS PUCHADES, LUIS
Spain, Soc (PSOE)

Señor Luis Planas Puchades has been MEP since 1986; served on Political Affairs Cmte in outgoing Parliament, being a vice-chmn, and rejoined it after 1989 elections. Former Government inspector of works and social security. Former mbr, Spanish national Parliament. B Nov 20 1952.

Address: Calle Ximénez de Quesada 17, 14004 Cordoba. Tel: (57) 41 25 15.

225

PLUMB, LORD
UK, Cotswolds, ED (C)

Lord Plumb was President of the European Parliament, 1987-89; leader, European Democratic (Conservative) Group, 1982-87; chmn, EP Agriculture Cmte, 1979-82, and rejoined cmte in July 1989; mbr, Transport Cmte, 1984-87. Formerly Sir Henry Plumb, being made life peer in 1987. Elected to EP in 1979. Pres, NFU, 1970-79; dep pres, 1966-69. Chmn, British Agricultural Cl, 1975-79. Pres, *Comité des Organisations Professionels Agricoles de la CEE* (COPA), 1975-77; International Fed of Agricultural Producers, 1979-82; chmn, International Agricultural Training Programme, 1987- . Non-executive director, United Biscuits, Lloyds Bank and Fisons. Mbr, Cl, CBI; Animal Health Trust. B Mar 27 1925. Pres, Nat Fed of Young Farmers' Clubs, 1976- . Liveryman, Farmers' Company. Dep Lieut of Warwickshire 1977.
Address: Maxstoke, Coleshill, Birmingham. Tel: (0675) 63133.

POETTERING, HANS-GERT
Germany, EPP (CDU)

Herr Hans-Gert Poettering, a lawyer, was first elected MEP in 1979; mbr, EP Political Affairs Cmte, and became chmn of sub-cmte on Security and Disarmament; previously on Cmte on Regional Policy and Regional Planning. On staff of CDU/CSU Bundestag gp, 1976-79; personal adviser to deputy gp chmn, Dr Burkhard Ritz. B Sep 15 1945. Doctorate in philosophy and law. District chmn, Osnabruck "Land" "Junge Union", 1974-76. From 1974, chmn of Bersenbruck municipal CDU and mbr, Osnabruck 'Land' CDU district executive. From 1976, mbr, Osnabruck-Emsland CDU executive; and 'Junge Union' Lower Saxony 'Land' executive.

Address: Sophienstrasse 8, 4505 Bad Iburg. Tel: (0541) 57060 (Dienst), (05403) 4855 (privat).

POLLACK, MS ANITA
UK, London South West, Soc (Lab)

Ms Anita Pollack gained this seat for Labour in 1989 having contested it in the 1984 Euro elections; joined EP Cmte on Environment, Public Health and Consumer Protection, and Cmte on Women's Rights. Contested Woking in 1987 general election. Political researcher; former book editor. Party service includes being exec mbr, Greater London Lab Pty; vice-chair, Newham NE CLP; nat exec mbr, Labour Co-ordinating Cmte. B Jun 3 1946; ed City of London Poly; Birkbeck Coll, London Univ. MSFU and TGWU.

Address: 139 Windsor Road, London E7 0RA. Tel: (01) 471 1637.

POMPIDOU, ALAIN
France, RDE (RPR)

M.Alain Pompidou, professor of medicine and son of the former President of France, was elected to EP in 1989; became mbr, Cmte on Energy, Research and Technology. B 1942.

Address: 25 rue Saint-Louis en l'Ile, 75004 Paris.

PONS GRAU, JOSEP ENRIQUE
Spain, Soc (PSOE)

Señor Josep Enrique Pons Grau became an MEP in 1986 and was a vice-chmn of Cmte on External Economic Relations in outgoing Parliament; after 1989 elections joined Cmte on Development and Cooperation. University professor of history and geography. Mbr, Spanish national Parliament. B Jun 19 1948.

Address: c/Jurista n° 11 pt 6, 46001 Valencia.Tel: 331 89 80.

PORRAZZINI, GIACOMO
Italy, EUL (PCI)

Sgr Giacomo Porrazzini was elected to EP in 1989 and joined Cmte on Energy, Research and Technology and Cmte on Transport and Tourism. Mayor of Terni. Mbr, national assembly of Italian regional councils. B Jan 28 1941.

Address: Comune di Terni - Palazzo Spada, Piazza Europa, 05100 Terni. Tel: (0744) 54 95 40-1.

PRAG, DEREK
UK, Hertfordshire, ED (C)

Mr Derek Prag was first elected to EP in 1979; mbr since of Institutional Affairs Cmte being EDG spokesman, 1982-84 and 1987-89, when he was appointed senior cmte vice-chmn; mbr, Cmte on Environment, Public Health and Consumer Protection, 1989- . Political spokesman for EDG, 1984-87; chmn, EP all-pty disablement gp, 1980- ; dep chmn, cmte of inquiry into rise of Facism and Racism in Europe, 1984-85. Chmn, London Europe Society. ECSC and then EEC Commission civil servant, 1955-73, being head of Commission's Information Office in London, 1965-73. Had consultancy on Euro affairs, 1973-79. Previously economic journalist with Reuters and editor of *Financial Times* Business Letter from Europe. B Aug 6 1923.
Address: Pine Hill, 47 New Road, Digswell, Welwyn, Herts AL6 0AQ. Tel: (043871) 2999. Telex: 82 65 42 TELTEX G (Prag). Facsimile: (043871) 5247.

PRICE, PETER
UK, London South East, ED (C)

Mr Peter Price, solicitor, became chmn of EP Cmte on Budgetary Control in July 1989; mbr, EDG bureau, from Sep 1989; EDG spokesman on Budgets Cmte, 1987-89; previously served on Legal Affairs and Citizens' Rights Cmte (being gp spokesman, 1984-87), Budgetary Control Cmte (vice-chmn, 1979-84) and Cmte on Verification of Credentials. Mbr, ACP/EEC Jt Assembly, 1981- ; cl, European Movement, 1971-81. Elected for London SE in 1984; MEP for Lancashire West, 1979-84. Vice-chmn, Cons Gp for Europe, 1979-81. B Feb 19 1942; ed Worcester Royal GS; Aberdare Boys' GS; Southampton Univ; Coll of Law, Guildford. Contested Caerphilly, 1970 general election, Aberdare 1964 and 1966. Vice-pres, Llangollen International Eisteddfod, 1981- .
Addresses: 60 Marlings Park Avenue, Chislehurst, Kent BR7 6RD. Tel: (0689) 20681. Fax: (0689) 890622. 37 Heol St. Denys, Cardiff CF4 5RU. Tel: (0222) 761792.

PROUT, CHRISTOPHER
UK, Shropshire and Stafford, ED (C)

Mr Christopher Prout QC became Leader of European Democratic (Conservative) Gp in 1987; mbr, Cmtes on Institutional Affairs, on Rules of Procedure, Verification of Credentials and Immunities, and on Regional Policy and Regional Planning, 1989- ; Gp chief whip, 1983-87; deputy whip, 1979-82; chmn, EP Cmte on Electoral Disputes, 1982-83; chmn, EP Cmte on Legal Affairs, 1987. First elected MEP for this seat in 1979. Leverhulme Fellow and Lecturer in Law, Sussex Univ, 1969-79; Staff Mbr, World Bank Gp, Washington DC, 1966-69; English Speaking Union Fellow, Columbia Univ, 1963-64. Reserve officer (Major) with 16/5th Lancers, 1974-82, and 3rd Armoured Division, 1982- . B Jan 1 1942; ed Sevenoaks Sch; Manchester Univ; Queen's Coll, Oxford; Middle Temple.

Address: 5 Oakfield Road, Shrewsbury, Shropshire SY3 8AA. Tel: (063083) 218.

PUERTA GUTIÉRREZ, ALONSO
Spain, CG (IU)

Señor Alonso Puerta Gutiérrez became elected MEP in 1987 and was a vice-chmn of EP Cmte on Transport in outgoing Parliament; after 1989 elections joined Cmte on Environment, Public Health and Consumer Protection and Cmte on Institutional Affairs. Civil engineer. Secretary-General, Socialist Action Party; municipal councillor of Madrid. Has served in Spanish national Parliament. B Mar 24 1944.

Addresses: Espoz y Mina 5-1°, 28012 Madrid. Tel: (1) 473 73 76. Avda. Albufera 133-135, 28038 Madrid. Tel: (1) 477 01 05.

PUNSET I CASALS, EDUARDO
Spain, LDR (CDS)

Señor Eduardo Punset i Casals, elected MEP since 1987, rejoined Cmte on Economic and Monetary Affairs and Industrial Policy after 1989 elecitions; also on Cmte on Petitions. Economist; formerly with International Monetary Fund. Minister with special responsibility for relations with EC, 1980-81; former mbr, Spanish national Parliament and regional Parliament of Catalonia. B Nov 20 1936.

Addresses: Instituto de Empresa, Calle Maria de Molina 13-15, 28006 Madrid. Tel: (1) 262 81 00-08-09. Rigel 11, Aravaca, Madrid. Tel: (!) 207 91 51.

PUTTEN, MEVR MAARTJE VAN
Netherlands, Soc (PvdA)

Mevr Maartje van Putten, social worker, was elected to EP in 1989 and joined Cmte on Development and Cooperation. President, national movement for road safety. B Jul 5 1951.

Address: Roemer Visscherstraat 21, 1054 EV Amsterdam. Tel: (020) 12 81 55.

229

QUISTHOUDT-ROWOHL, FRAU GODELIEVE
Germany, EPP (CDU)

Frau Godelieve Quisthoudt-Rowohl was elected MEP in 1989; joined EP Cmte on Energy, Research and Technology. Former professor (physics and chemistry) at Univ of Louvain, Belgium; Head of Institute of Applied Linguistics, Hildesheim, since 1979. B Jun 18 1947; degree in chemistry.

Address: Lisztstrasse 9, 3200 Hildesheim.

QUISTORP, FRAU EVA-MARIA
Germany, Verts (Grüne)

Frau Eva-Maria Quistorp, theologian, was unemployed until her election to EP in 1989 when she joined Cmte on Environment, Public Health and Consumer Protection. Mbr, national executive, Die Grunen, 1986-88. Was joint organiser of Women's Peace March to Paris, Geneva, Vienna and Santiago de Compostela. B 1945.

Address: Babelsbergerstrasse 46, 1000 Berlin 31. Tel: (030) 86 15 848.

RAFFARIN, JEAN-PIERRE
France, LDR (UDF-PR)

M.Jean-Pierre Raffarin, local councillor and leader of Poitou-Charentes Regional Council, was elected to EP in 1989 and joined Cmte on Regional Policy and Regional Planning. Consultant. B 1948.

Address: Hôtel de la Région, 86021 Poitiers Cedex.

RAGGIO, ANDREA
Italy, EUL (PCI)

Sgr Andrea Raggio, first elected to EP in 1984, is mbr, Cmte on Regional Policy and Regional Planning; also on bureau of European United Left Gp; former mbr, Cmte on Social Affairs and Employment. Elected an EP quaestor in July 1989. Former chmn, regional council for Sardinia; led PCI gp on council; mbr, central cmte of party. Administrator. B Nov 30 1929.

Address: Via del Pozzetto 8, 09100 Cagliari. Tel: (070) 37 41 64.

RAMÍREZ HEREDIA, JUAN DE DIOS
Spain, Soc (PSOE)

Señor Juan de Dios Ramírez Heredia, an MEP since 1986, joined Cmte on Legal Affairs and Citizens' Rights after his re-election in 1989; on Cmte on Youth, Culture, Education, Information and Sport in outgoing Parliament. Teacher. Former mbr, Spanish national Parliament and parliamentary Assembly of Cl of Europe. B Jun 29 1942.

Address: Carretera Cabo de Gata 2 3°, 04007 Almeria.

RANDZIO-PLATH, FRAU CHRISTA
Germany, Soc (SDP)

Frau Christa Randzio-Plath, lawyer and writer, was elected to EP in 1989 and became mbr, Cmte on External Economic Relations. Adviser to finance department, Hamburg Cl. Vice-President, International Union of Socialist Women. B Oct 29 1940.

*photograph
unavailable*

Address: Abgeordnetenbüro, Grosse Backerstrasse 2, 2000 Hamburg 1. Tel: (040) 36 43 95.

231

RAUTI, GIUSEPPE
Italy, NI (MSI-DN)

Sgr Giuseppe Rauti, assistant secretary of Italian Social Movement (MSI), was elected to EP in 1989. Became mbr, Cmte on Development and Cooperation. Mbr, Italian Chamber of Deputies. Journalist. B Nov 19 1926.

Address: MSI-DN, Via della Scrofa 30, 00186 Roma. Tel: (06) 31 04 61.

RAWLINGS, MISS PATRICIA
UK, Essex South West, ED (C)

Miss Patricia Rawlings was elected to EP in 1989 and speaks for ED (Conservative) Gp on Cmte on Women's Rights; also mbr, Cmte on Youth, Culture, Education, the Media and Sport, 1989- . Contested Doncaster Central in 1987 general election and Sheffield Central, 1983. Mbr, Conservative Women's National Cmte, 1984- . Chaired London branch of British Red Cross Society, resigning in 1988, having been mbr since 1964; awarded Nat Badge of Honour in 1981 for services to nursing. Special adviser to Mr David Trippier, wen Under Secretary of State for Environment; formerly with textile company, specializing in exports and public relations. Mbr, Peace through Nato Cl; Video Classification Cl; Royal Inst of International Affairs; European Union of Women. B Jan 27 1939.

Address: 87 Eaton Square, London SW1W 9AG. Tel: (01) 235 0870.

READ, MS IMELDA (MEL)
UK, Leicester, Soc (Lab)

Ms Imelda (Mel) Read was elected to EP in 1989 and joined Cmte on Economic and Monetary Affairs and Industrial Policy and Cmte on Women's Rights. Employment officer for Nottingham Community Relations Cl, previously laboratory technician, Plessey Telecommunications. Contested Leicestershire North West in 1983 general election and Melton in 1979. Former lecturer and researcher at Trent Poly; has served on nat exec cl, ASTMS, now MSFU. B Jan 8 1939; ed Bishopshalt GS; Nottingham Univ. Mbr, TUC Women's Advisory Cmte, and chairs regional TUC Women's Cmte.

Address: 27 Ashfield Road, Stoneygate, Leicester LE2 1LB. Tel: (0533) 704770.

RÉDING, MME VIVIANE
Luxembourg, EPP (PCS)

Mme Viviane Réding was elected to EP in 1989 and became chair of Petitions Cmte and mbr, Political Affairs Cmte; also on bureau of EPP Gp. Journalist. Mbr, Luxembourg Chamber of Deputies, 1979-89; national council of women; cmte of working women; chairs PCS women's section and Christian Democrat gp in North Atlantic Assembly. Communal councillor for Ville d'Esch-sur-Alzette. Former mbr, Benelux interparliamentary consultative council. B Apr 27 1951.

Address: 94 rue Emile Mayrisch, 4240 Esch-sur-Alzette. Tel: 55 60 98.

REGGE, TULLIO
Italy, EUL (PCI)

Sgr Tullio Regge, professor of physics, was elected to EP in 1989 and became mbr, Cmte on Energy, Research and Technology. Mbr of several scientific bodies. B Jul 11 1931.

Address: c.o. Federazione PCI, Piazza Castello 9, 10123 Torino. Tel: (011) 552 41.

REYMANN, MARC
France, EPP (UDF/RPR)

M.Marc Reymann, elected to EP in 1989, is National Assembly deputy for Bas-Rhin and a Strasbourg municipal councillor; director of vocational training centre. Lawyer specializing in family law. Mbr, EP Cmte on Legal Affairs and Citizens' Rights, 1989- . B 1937.

Address: 17 rue de Verdun, 67000 Strasbourg.

RINSCHE, GÜNTER
Germany, EPP (CDU)

Herr Günter Rinsche, economist, is mbr of EP Cmte on Energy, Research and Technology, and Cmte on Rules of Procedure, Verification of Credentials and Immunities; chmn, EP-SE Asian states interparliamentary delegation. First elected MEP in 1979; ldr, German delegation in EPP gp and mbr, bureau, EPP Gp. Mbr, Bundestag, 1965-72; former mbr, North Rhine-Westphalia "Land" assembly, being CDU gp spokesman on economic affairs. He has been Chief Burgomaster of Hamm; on North Rhine-Westphalia "Europa Union" "Land" executive and German Cl of European Movement; chaired planning cmte, Institute for International Solidarity; on executive of Konrad Adenauer Foundation; and president, North Rhine-Westphalia convention of municipal authorities. B Jul 13 1930; doctorate in political science. *Address: Feldgarten 15, 4700 Hamm 1. Tel: (02381) 52330.*

ROBLES PIQUER, CARLOS
Spain, EPP (PP)

Señor Carlos Robles Piquer has been MEP since Jan 1986; first elected 1987; re-elected 1989; mbr, Political Affairs Cmte and Cmte on Energy, Research and Technology. Diplomat, senator representing Grupo Popular, and mbr, Madrid Assembly. At Spanish Embassy, Bogota, 1955-59; consul, Nador, Morrocco, 1959-62; secretary, Spanish Embassy, London, 1962; Ambassador to Libya and Chad, 1973; Rome and La Valetta, 1976. Secretary of State for Foreign Affairs, 1979. Was Managing Director of Information and then of Popular Culture and Entertainment, 1962-69; Minister for Education and Science, 1975-76. Managing director, Spanish Public Radio and TV Network, 1981-82; President, Inst of Ibero-American Cooperation, 1982. B Oct 13 1925.
Addresses: c/Genova 13, 28004 Madrid. Tel: (1) 410 29 78. Calle Monte Alto 42, 28023 Madrid. Tel: (1) 715 50 95.

ROGALLA, DIETER
Germany, Soc (SDP)

Herr Dieter Rogalla became an MEP in 1981; re-elected in 1984 when he was appointed chairman of the EP Cmte on Verification of Credentials until 1987; still a cmte mbr; also on Cmte on Economic and Monetary Affairs and Industrial Policy. Re-elected 1989. Lawyer. On staff of European Commission, 1961-81. Mbr, management cmte of Steinfurt SPD. B Aug 20 1927.

Addresses: SPD Europa Büro, Harpener Hellweg 152, 4630 Bochum 1. Tel: (0234) 23 38 97. Gildestrasse 9, 4418 Nordwalde. Tel: (02573) 3112.

ROMEOS, GEORGIOS
Greece, Soc (PASOK)

Mr Georgios Romeos, economist and journalist, was elected to EP in 1984. A Vice-President of EP, 1987-89, and re-elected Vice-President in July 1989; on bureau of Socialist Gp. Mbr, Political Affairs Cmte, 1989- ; former mbr, Cmte on Agriculture, Fisheries and Food. Former Director General, Greek radio and television service. B Dec 21 1934.

Addresses: Omirou 13, 154 51 N Psychiko. Tel: (1) 647 34 31.

ROMERA I ALCÀZAR, DOMÈNEC
Spain, EPP (PP)

Señor Domènec Romera i Alcàzar was nominated to EP in 1986 and first elected 1987. Mbr, Cmte on Transport and Tourism. On executive of Alianza Popular in Cataluna; mbr, Cataluna regional assembly. Former senator. Director-General, Official International Trade Fair, Barcelona; adviser to various companies and banks; President, Maritime Mediterranean; mbr, General Cl of Savings Banks and Old Age Pensions; mbr, consultative cl, Barcelona Chamber of Commerce.

Addresses: Déu i Mata 150, 08029 Barcelona. (3) 239 19 81. Escoles Pies 84, 08017 Barcelona. Tel: (3) 247 54 37.

RONN, FRU JOANNA
Denmark, Soc (S)

Fru Joanna Ronn, who became elected MEP in 1989, was appointed to Cmte on Social Affairs, Employment and Working Environment. Social worker. Former mbr, Folketing (Danish Parliament). B Feb 20 1947.

Address: Tommerupvang 16, 2770 Kastrup. Tel: (32) 52 20 88.

235

ROSMINI, FRÉDÉRIC
France, Soc (PS)

M. Frédéric Rosmini, director of social economics organization, was elected to EP in 1989 and joined Cmte on Regional Policy and Regional Planning. Mbr, Provence-Alpes-Cote d'Azure Regional Council; on executive bureau of PS; treasurer of federation of Bouches-du-Rhone. B 1940.

*photograph
unavailable*

Address: 21 rue Paulet, 13008 Marseille. Tel: 91 71 84 58.

ROSSETTI, GIORGIO
Italy, EUL (PCI)

Sgr Giorgio Rossetti was first elected to EP in 1984; re-elected 1989; mbr, Cmte on External Economic Relations. Journalist. Mbr, central cmte of PCI and has served as regional secretary of PCI in Friuli Venezia-Giula area. Regional councillor, Friuli Venezia-Giula; former Trieste councillor. B Aug 24 1938.

Addresses: Comitato Regionale di Triests PCI, Via Capitolina 3, 34131 Triests. Tel: (040) 744046/7. Via S Spiridione 7, 34112 Triests. (040) 639896.

ROSSA, PROINSIAS DE
Ireland, CG (WP)

Mr Proinsias de Rossa was elected to EP in 1989 and became a vice-chmn, Cmte on Regional Policy and Regional Planning. Vice-chmn and treasurer, Coalition des Gauches Gp, 1989- . First elected to Dail in 1982 when he won Dublin North West. Mbr, Cmte on Procedure and Privileges, since 1987; Dublin City Cl, 1985- ; Eastern Health Board, 1985- ; Irish TGWU; Community Development Movement; CND; Nicaragua Support Gp. B May 5 1940; ed Coll of Technology, Kevin Street, Dublin. Formerly in fruit and vegetable business.

Addresses: Linster House, Kildare Street, Dublin 2. Tel: (01) 766554. Telefax: 789119. 39 Pinewood Crescent, Dublin 11. Tel: (01) 425644.

236

ROTH, FRAU CLAUDIA
Germany, Verts (Grüne)

Frau Claudia Roth, press spokesman for Greens in Bundestag since 1985, was elected to EP in 1989, joining Cmte on Youth, Culture, Education, the Media and Sport; became a joint vice-chair of Verts Gp. Began career in political drama in Swabian State Theatre in 1974. Later, at Buhnen Dortmund and with Hoffman Comic Theatre, associated with politically orientated rock band *Ton steine scherben*; took part in tour of pop groups in Greens electioneering. Says not all press releases recognised as "hits" but party has climbed political charts and has own popular "covers". B.1955

Address: An der Steinbrücke 19, D-5300 Bonn 1. Tel: (0228) 66 60 13; (0228) 16 54 39.

ROTH-BEHRENDT, FRAU DAGMAR
Germany, Soc (SDP)

Frau Dagmar Roth-Behrendt became elected MEP in 1989 and joined EP Cmte on Environment, Public Health and Consumers; was also appointed a vice-chair of Cmte on Women's Rights. Lawyer working in Berlin. B Feb 21 1953.

Address: Weinmeisterhornweg 39, 1000 Berlin 20.

ROTHE, FRAU MECHTILD
Germany, Soc (SDP)

Frau Mechtild Rothe was first elected to the EP in 1984 and has served on the Cmte on Agriculture, Fisheries and Food which she rejoined after 1989 elections; has also been vice-chair of EP/Cyprus delegation. Teacher. Mbr, SPD Federal Council and of town council of Bad Lippspringe. B Aug 10 1947.

Addresses: Europabüro, Am Steintor 2, 4792 Bad Lippspringe. Tel: (05252) 51888. Karlstrasse 5, 4792 Bad Lippspringe. Tel: (05252) 51617.

ROTHLEY, WILLI
Germany, Soc (SDP)

Herr Willi Rothley, a lawyer, was first elected to the EP in 1984; re-elected 1989. He serves on the Cmte on Institutional Affairs, and after the 1989 elections, he was also appointed one of the vice-chairmen of the Cmte on Legal Affairs and Citizens' Rights. Former mbr, Rheinland-Pfalz regional assembly; deputy state chairman of SDP and holder of other party posts. B Dec 15 1943.

Addresses: Ringstrasse 29, 6760 Rochenhausen. Tel: (06361) 693-694. Im Gothental 31, 6760 Rockenhausen. Terl: (06361) 8443.

ROUMELIOTIS, PANAYOTIS
Greece, Soc (PASOK)

Mr Panayotis Roumeliotis, university professor, was elected to EP in 1989 and joined Cmte on Economic and Monetary Affairs and Industrial Policy. Former Greek Minister of Trade and Finance and special adviser to former Prime Minister Papandreou.

Address:Z. Moreas 64, 152 31 Halandri.

ROVSING, CHRISTIAN
Denmark, ED (KF)

Mr Christian Rovsing was elected to EP in 1989 and became mbr, Cmte on Energy, Research and Technology. Engineer, general manager and computer expert. Former mbr, Copenhagan county cl. B Nov 2 1936.

Address: Berlingsbakke 16 C, 2920 Charlottenlund. Tel: (31) 64 40 44. Telefax: (31) 64 49 41.

RUBERT DE VENTÓS, XAVIER
Spain, Soc (PSOE)

Señor Xavier Rubert de Ventós has been an MEP since 1986 and after re-election in 1989 he rejoined Cmte on Development and Cooperation on which he served in outgoing Parliament. Teacher and writer. Former mbr, Spanish national Parliament. B Sep 1 1939.

Address: Carrasco i Formiguera 21, 08017 Barcelona. Tel: (3) 203 90 61.

RUFFINI, MARIO
Italy, EPP (DC)

Sgr Mario Ruffini was elected to EP in 1989; appointed to Cmte on Energy, Research and Technology. Lombardie regional councillor responsible for department of industry and crafts; chairs *Comunita montana* of l'Alto Sebino and serves on national cl of Union of Mountain Communes. B Apr 15 1937.

photograph unavailable

Address: Via Nazionale 2, 24062 Costa Volpino (BG). Tel: (035) 97 05 38.

RUIZ-GIMÉNEZ AGUILAR, SRA GUADALUPE
Spain, LDR (CDS)

Sra Guadalupe Ruiz-Giménez Aguilar was elected to EP in 1989 joining Cmte on Development and Cooperiation and Cmte on Women's Rights. University professor. Secretary-General of Spanish/Amercian research association. B Aug 10 1947.

Addresses: Claudio Coello 86 4° derecha, 28006 Madrid. Tel: 577 06 40/42/43/44. Telefax: 276 30 70. Avda. de los Madronos 19 3°F, 28043 Madrid. Tel: 200 72 92.

239

RUIZ-MATEOS, JOSÉ MARÍA
Spain, NI (R-Mateos)

Señor José María Ruiz-Mateos, businessman, financier, founder and former owner of RUMASA (Ruiz-Mateos SA), an important holding company in Spain, was elected to EP in 1989. Joined Cmte on Economic and Monetary Affairs and Industrial Policy. He contested European elections in his campaign refutting charges being brought against him. B Apr 11 1931.

Address:

RUPO, ELIO DI
Belgium, Soc (PS)

Mr Elio di Rupo was elected to EP in 1989. Mbr, Belgian Chamber of Deputies since 1987 being on parliamentary cmtes on finance and justice; local councillor at Mons. Doctor of science; an inspector-general for energy, Walloon region; attache and then chef de cabinet, Walloon region, for budget and energy, 1982-85. Has served on inter-ministerial committees on nuclear security, gas and electricity. B Jul 18 1951.

Address: 11 rue du 11 Novembre, 7000 Mons. Tel: (065) 35 20 33. Telefax: (065) 36 04 79.

SABY, HENRI
France, Soc (PS)

M. Henri Saby, engineer, became an MEP in 1981; after 1989 elections appointed chmn of EP Cmte on Development and Cooperation, and mbr, Cmte on Budgetary Control; a vice-chmn of Socialist Gp, 1984-89; former mbr, Political Affairs Cmte. Political posts: Socialist Party steering cmte 1974 (vice-chmn, 1979-81); executive bureau, Socialist Party federation of Haute-Garonne (first secretary, 1977-80); steering cmte, National Federation; former president, Haute-Garonne federation of elected socialists and republicans; Mayor of Ayguesvives (Haute-Garonne) and Midi-Pyrenees regional councillor. Former mbr, directory, National Centre of Scientific Research (CNRS). B Aug 8 1933; ed Toulouse Univ.

Address: Rte de St Leon, Ayguesvives, 31450 Montgiscard. Tel: 61 81 92 95.

SAINJON, ANDRÉ
France, Soc (PS)

M.André Sainjon, former Secretary General of French Metalworkers Union, was elected to EP in 1989; became mbr, Cmte on External Economic Relations. Turner. Former mbr, central cmte of Communist Party (PCF).

Address: Irise, 6 Cité Paradis, 75010 Paris. Tel: 48 00 00 34.

SAKELLARIOU, JANNIS
Germany, Soc (SDP)

Herr Jannis Sakellariou, first elected to EP in 1984, is on the Cmte on Regional Policy and Regional Planning. Engineer and economist. Scientific director of German army academy in Munich. Spokesman for Munich Young Socialists, 1972-74, becoming deputy chairman, local SDP, Sendlingnen; holder of various party posts. B Nov 12 1939.

Address: Dieburger Strasse 240, 6100 Darmstadt. Tel: (06151) 714240-26221.

SALEMA, SRA MARIA MARGARIDA
Portugal, LDR (PSD)

Sra Maria Margarida Salema, who was elected to the EP in 1989, joined the Cmtes on Legal Affairs and Citizens' Rights, on Women's Rights, and on Rules of Procedure, Verification of Credentials and Immunities. Lawyer; university teacher. Elected mbr, Portuguese national Parliament in 1980, 1983, 1985 and 1987. B Jan 19 1954.

Address: Bairro do Alcaide, Lote 25 R/C Dto, 2750 Cascais

SÄLZER, BERNHARD
Germany, EPP (CDU)

Herr Bernhard Sälzer, civil engineer; lecturer at Darmsdtadt College of Technology; former mbr of Hesse Landtag. First elected to EP in 1979, serving on Cmte on Energy, Research and Technology, being one of its vice-chmn since 1984. Has served as a vice-chmn, EP-Japan interparliamentary delegation. Vice-chmn, European Affairs Advisory Cmte of Bundestag, jointly composed of mbrs of National and European Parliaments. Has also served as Mayor of Marburg; CDU gp chmn, Darmstadt City Cl, 1968-76. B Sep 4 1940.

Address: Dieburger Strasse 240, 6100 Darmstadt. Tel: (06151) 71240 - 26221.

SALISCH, FRAU HEINKE
Germany, Soc (SDP)

Frau Heinke Salisch was first elected to the EP in 1979 and has served since then on the Cmte on Social Affairs, Employment and Working Environment, being one of its vice-chmn 1984-87; rejoined cmte after 1989 elections; also mbr of EP Cmte on Women's Rights. Interpreter. B Aug 14 1941. Became mbr, Karlsruhe Municipal Council, in 1971.

Address: Sonntagstrasse 2, 7500 Karlsruhe 1. Tel: (0721) 818888.

SAMLAND, DETLEV
Germany, Soc (SDP)

Herr Detlev Samland was elected to EP in 1989; appointed to Cmte on Budgets. Planning engineer; former director of advertising agency. Mbr of party council; spokesman for Young Socialists. B May 1 1953.

Address: Holunderweg 35a, 4300 Essen 1. Tel: (0201) 41 10 59.

SANDBAEK, FRU ULLA
Denmark, ARC (Folkebevaegelsen mod EF)

Fru Ulla Sandbaek, elected MEP in 1989, became mbr, Cmte on Social Affairs, Employment and Working Environment. Minister in Danish State Church. B Apr 1 1943.

Address: Gongehusvej 288, 2970 Horsholm.

SANTOS, SRA MARIA
Portugal, Verts (Os Verdes)

Sra Maria Santos was elected to EP in 1989 and elected co-chair of new Green gp *Les Verts*; unsuccessful Green candidate in election for presidency, July 1989; mbr, EP Cmte on Development and Cooperation. Deputy in Portuguese national Parliament, 1985-89, serving on environment, culture, human rights and women's rights committees; chaired Green parliamentary gp, 1987-89.; Mbr, executive committee of Os Verdes since 1983. University lecturer. B Aug 25 1952. Her mandate as co-chair is to last for 15 months.

Addresses: c/o Os Verdes, Av. Torredo Bolem 8, PG 1400 Lisboa. Tel: (01) 617 046. Quinta da Horta, N°22-1°E, 2800 Almada.

SANZ FERNÁNDEZ, FRANCISCO JAVIER
Spain, Soc (PSOE)

Señor Francisco Javier Sanz Fernández, an MEP since 1986, rejoined EP Cmte on Energy, Research and Technology after 1989 elections. Agricultural engineer; university professor. Former mbr, Spanish national Parliament. B Jan 13 1949.

Address: Pza. José María Orense 5 30a, 46022 Valencia. Tel: (6) 372 77 88.

SAPENA GRANELL, ENRIQUE
Spain, Soc (PSOE)

Señor Enrique Sapena Granell, an MEP since 1986, rejoined the EP Cmte on Transport and Tourism after the 1989 elections. Engineer. Former senator and deputy, Spanish national Parliament. B Jan 17 1939.

Address: c/San Vicente 163 8° 15a, 46007 Valencia. Tel: (6) 341 20 14.

SARIDAKIS, GEORGIOS
Greece, EPP (ND)

Mr Georgios Saridakis became an MEP in 1984 and re-elected 1989. A vice-chmn, EPP Gp. Mbr, EP Cmte on Agriculture, Fisheries and Rural Development, 1989- ; a former vice-chmn, EP Cmte on Legal Affairs and Citizens' Rights. Former Deputy Govenor, Greek Industrial Development Bank. B Jul 17 1938; graduate in economics and politics and in maritime and aviation law.

Addresses: J.R. Collon 53, 1200 Bruxelles. Vassilissis Sofias 10, 106 71 Athina. Tel: (1) 72 19 682.

SARLIS, PAVLOS
Greece, EPP (ND)

Mr Pavlos Sarlis, lawyer, is a former Greek deputy and former mbr, Greek delegation to Assembly of Cl of Europe. Former Secretary-General, Ministry of Merchant Marine. Elected MEP in 1989 and joined EP Cmte on Transport and Tourism. B 1932.

Address: Karaiskou 117, 185 35 Pireas.

SBOARINA, GABRIELE
Italy, EPP (DC)

Sgr Gabriele Sboarina was elected to EP in 1989; mbr, Cmte on Economic and Monetary Affairs and Industrial Policy. Mayor of Verona. Former Italian deputy; former secretary, Verona section of Christian Democrat party. B Mar 24 1935; doctor of economic science.

Address: Via G.C. Camozzini 20, 37126 Verona. Tel: (045) 91 24 43.

SCHINZEL, DIETER
Germany, Soc (SDP)

Herr Dieter Schinzel serves on the EP Cmte on Energy, Research and Technology; previously on Cmte on Economic and Monetary Affairs. Elected MEP since 1979. B Nov 14 1942. Chairman of Aachen SPD from 1976. Mbr, Aachen Municipal Cl, 1972-75; of Bundestag, 1972-76. Head of a North Rhine-Westphalian Land social welfare organization, 1977-79.

Addresses: Europa-Büro, Bahnofstrasse 23, 5100 Aachen. Tel: (0241) 35171, (0241) 39393. Kirchrather Strasse 34, 5100 Aachen. Tel: (0241) 82001.

SCHLEE, EMIL
Germany, DR (Repub)

Herr Emil Schlee, former senior civil servant, was elected to EP in 1989. Appointed to Cmte on Energy, Research and Technology. Party chairman in Schleswig-Holstein. B 1922.

Address: Danziger Strasse 4, 2313 Raisdorf.

SCHLEICHER, FRAU URSULA
Germany, EPP (CSU)

Frau Ursula Schleicher was appointed a vice-chair of EP Cmte on Environment, Public Health and Consumer Protection in 1984, and reappointed after 1989 elections; first elected to EP in 1979 when she joined environment cmte. Mbr, Bundestag, 1972-80; chaired Bundestag cmte on problems of women and society. CSU adviser on women's rights, 1965-75; formerly chaired European Union of Women. Has served as praesidium mbr, German Cl of European Movement, and been deputy federal chmn, German Catholic Workers' Movement. President, "Pan-European Union", *Unterfranken*. B May 15 1933. Harpist.

Addresses: Bundeshaus, 5300 Bonn 1. Tel: (0228) 167745. Backoffenstrasse 6, 8750 Aschaffenburg. Tel: (06021) 92901.

SCHMID, GERHARD
Germany, Soc (SDP)

Herr Gerhard Schmid has been an elected MEP since 1979. Mbr, EP Cmte on Environment, Public Health and Consumer Protection; previously on Cmte on Energy, Research and Technology. Jt vice-chairman, EP/Gulf States delegation. Mbr, Niederbayern-Oberpfalz SPD district executive; district chairman, Young Socialists, 1972-75; mbr, SPD district management in Lower Bavaria-Upper Palatinate from 1975. B May 5 1946. Chemist; research fellow; staff of Institute of Biochemistry, Regensburg.

Addresses: Richard Wagner Strasse 4, 8400 Regensburg. Tel: (0941) 793801 and 57945. Telex: 065747. Altdorfstrasse 13a, 8400 Regensburg. Tel: (0941)26619.

SCHMIDBAUER, FRAU BARBARA
Germany, Soc (SDP)

Frau Barbara Schmidbauer became an MEP during the last Parliament and was re-elected to EP in 1989 when she joined Cmtes on Development and Cooperation and on Petitions; previously on Cmtes on External Economic Relations and on Women's Rights. Housewife. Former mbr, Darmstadt cl; mbr of party cl. B Nov 15 1937.

Addresses: Heidelberger Landstrasse 77B, 6100 Darmstadt 13. Tel: (06151) 53 72 06. Europabüro SPD-Hessen-Sud, Fischerfeldstrasse 7-11, 6000 Frankfurt 1. Tel: (069) 28 56 72.

SCHODRUCH, HANS-GÜNTER
Germany, DR (Repub)

Herr Hans-Günter Schodruch, lawyer, was elected MEP in 1989 and joined EP Cmtes on Transport and Tourism and on Budgetary Control. Party chairman in North Rhine Westphalia. B 1926.

Address: Römerstrasse 49, 5200 Siegburg.

SCHÖNHUBER, FRANZ
Germany, DR (Repub)

Herr Franz Schönhuber, writer and journalist and chairman of German Republican Party, was elected to EP in 1989; became mbr, Political Affairs Cmte. B 1923.

Address: Knöbelstrasse 28, 8000 München 22.

SCHWARTZENBERG, LÉON
France, Soc (PS)

M.Léon Schwartzenberg, professor of medicine and specialist in treatment of cancer, was elected to EP in 1989 and became mbr, Cmte on Environment, Public Health and Consumer Protection. Former minister with responsibility for health. B 1923.

Address: Hôpital Paul Brousse, 12 av P. Vaillant Couturier, 94800 Villejuif.

SCOTT-HOPKINS, SIR JAMES
UK, Hereford and Worcester, ED (C)

Sir James Scott-Hopkins became a vice-chmn of EP Cmte on Environment, Public Health and Consumer Protection after 1989 elections. Leader, ED (Conservative) Gp, 1979-82, since when mbr, EP Political Affairs Cmte (a vice-chmn, 1984-86) and then Budgets Cmte (a vice-chmn, 1986-89). Nominated mbr of EP, 1973-79; first elected 1979. Deputy ldr, Conservative Gp, 1974-79, and a Vice-President of EP, 1976-79. MP for West Derbyshire, 1967-79, and for North Cornwall, 1959-66; Parliamentary Secretary, Ministry of Agriculture, Fisheries and Food, 1962-64. Farmer. B Nov 29 1921; ed Eton; New Coll Oxford; Emmanuel Coll, Cambridge.

Address: Bicknor House, English Bicknor, Coleford, West Gloucestershire GL16 7PF. Tel: (0594) 60234. SW1. Tel: (01) 828 4481.

SEAL, BARRY
UK, Yorkshire West, Soc (Lab)

Mr Barry Seal was leader of British Labour Gp of MEPs, 1988-89, being a vice-chmn of the Socialist Gp; previously mbr of gp bureau; former chief whip of Lab gp; chmn, EP Cmte on Economic and Monetary Affairs and Industrial Policy, 1984-87; a vice-chmn of that cmte, 1987-89 and still a mbr of cmte; former vice-chmn, Cmte on External Economic Relations. Senior then principal lecturer, Huddersfield Poly, 1971-79; consultant on computers. Contested Harrogate, Oct 1974 general election. Mbr, Bradford City Cl, 1971-74; Bradford MDC, 1973-79, being ldr, Lab gp, 1976-79. B Oct 28 1937. Laboratory asst and then chemical engineer, ICI Ltd, 1958-64; development engineer and later divisional chemical engineer, Murex Ltd, 1964-68; senior engineer, BOC International, 1968-71.

Address: City Hall, Bradford, West Yorkshire BD1 1HY. Tel: (0274) 752091 and (0274) 726288.

SELIGMAN, MADRON
UK, Sussex West, ED (C)

Mr Madron Seligman, elected MEP since 1979, became EDG spokesman in 1989 on EP Cmte on Energy, Research and Technology; a former cmte vice-chmn. Chairs EP Intergroup on Animal Welfare; vice-pres, European Energy Foundation. Chmn, Incinerator Co, Eaton Socon, 1960- ; director, APV Gp, 1951-84 (the APV engineering company was founded by his father, a metallurgist); former director, St Regis International. B Nov 10 1918; ed Rokeby Sch, Wimbledon; Harrow; Balliol Coll, Oxford (Pres of Union, 1940). During Second World War served as major in 6th Armoured Division Signals in Africa, Italy and Austria. Mbr of British Olympic skiing squad in 1948. Mbr, Royal Inst of International Affairs, Royal Thames Yacht Club, MCC.

Address: Micklepage House, Nuthurst RH13 6RG. Tel: (0403891) 533. Telefax: (0403891) 1010.

SIERRA BARDAJI, MATEOS
Spain, Soc (PSOE)

Señor Mateos Sierra Bardaji, farmer, rejoined EP Cmte on Agriculture, Fisheries and Rural development after 1989 elections; first became MEP in 1986 and first elected 1987. Former senator. B Dec 30 1936.

Addresses: Avda. Madrid 41 8° C, Fraga, Huesca. Tel: (74) 47 15 33. Infanta Mercedes 105 5° E, Madrid.

SIMÉONI, MAX
France, ARC (Verts/UPC)

M.Max Siméoni, hospital doctor, is Secretary-General of UPC, the Corsican People movement, and represents movement regionally. Town councillor at Bastia and mbr, Corsican regional council. Elected to EP in 1989 and was appointed a vice-chmn of Cmte on Youth, Culture, Education, the Media and Sport. B 1929.

Address: Union di U Populu corsu, 19 boulevard De Gaulle, 20200 Bastia, Corse.

SIMMONDS, RICHARD
UK, Wight and Hampshire East, ED (C)

Mr Richard Simmonds was MEP for Midlands West, 1979-84; first elected for this seat, 1984. Mbr, EP Cmte on Budgets and EDG spokesman, 1989- ; Cmte on Agriculture, Fisheries and Food, 1984-89; spokesman on Budgetary Control Cmte, 1984-87, and on youth and education, 1982-84. PPS to Sir James Scott-Hopkins, Leader of EDG, 1979-82; British Cons whip, 1987- . Farmer - free range poultry; consultant surveyor. B Aug 2 1944; ed Trinity Coll, Glenalmond. Mbr, Berkshire CC, 1973-79, being chmn of four cmtes. Personal asst to Mr Edward Heath, 1973-75; Nat YC vice-chmn, 1973-75. Chmn, governors, Berkshire Coll of Agriculture, 1979- . Founding Pres, Mounted Games Assocn of UK.
Addresses: Woodlands Farm, Cookham Dean, Maidenhead, Berkshire SL6 9PJ. Tel: Marlow 4684 (office). Telefax: (062) 889 8128. Dyars, Cookham Dean, Maidenhead, Berkshire. Tel: Marlow 3269.

SIMONS, FRAU BARBARA
Germany, Soc (SDP)

Frau Barbara Simons, a teacher, is a mbr of the EP Cmte on Development and Cooperation, being first elected to EP in 1984 and re-elected 1989. Head of department, Hanover adult education centre. Mbr, SDP executive, Lower Saxony. B Jun 16 1929.

Addresses: Europabüro, Odeonstrasse 15-16, 3000 Hannover 1. Tel: (0511) 16740. Löwenstrasse 11, 3000 Hannover 1. Tel: (0511) 851934.

SIMPSON, ANTHONY
UK, Northamptonshire, ED (C)

Mr Anthony Simpson, barrister, first elected to EP in 1979, was re-elected one of the Parliament's quaestors in July 1989; previously a quaestor, 1979-87; joined Cmte on Legal Affairs and Citizens' Rights in 1989. EDG spokesman on and mbr of Cmte on Development and Cooperation, and of ACP Joint Assembly, 1987-89; mbr, EDG bureau, 1987-88. Worked in legal service of European Commission in Brussels, 1975-79. Contested Leicester West in both 1974 general elections. B Oct 28 1935; ed Rugby; Magdalene Coll, Cambridge. Common Market Law Editor, Current Law, 1965-72. In Brussels was chmn of European Democrat Forum; vice-pres (1980-) and cmte mbr (1976-78), British Cons Assocn, Belgium. Mbr, Oadby UDC, 1968-71.
Addresses: Avenue Michel-Ange 57, 1040 Bruxelles. Tel: 736 42 19. Bassets, Great Glen, Leicestershire LE8 0GQ. Tel: (053) 759 2386.

SIMPSON, BRIAN
UK, Cheshire East, Soc (Lab)

Mr Brian Simpson, teacher, won this Euro seat in 1989 and became mbr, EP Cmte on Transport and Tourism, and Cmte on Petitions. Chairs Warrington South constituency Lab Pty. Merseyside cty cllr, 1981-86, serving on Merseyside Police Authority and being deputy chair, Liverpool Airport, 1981-86. Mbr, Warrington BC, 1987- , and exec mbr, Warrington Co-op Pty. NAS/UWT being Liverpool exec mbr, 1986-87. B Feb 6 1953; ed local state schs; W Midlands Coll of Ed.

Address: 28 Walkers Lane, Penketh, Warrington WA5 2PA. Tel: (0925) 728093.

SISO CRUELLAS, JOAQUIN
Spain, EPP (PP)

Señor Joaquin Siso Cruellas was elected MEP in 1989 and joined Cmte on Economic and Monetary Affairs and Industrial Policy. Water and forest engineer; architect; former deputy; former director of programme of Minister of Planning and Development. Spokesman for executive Cmte of Alianza Popular.

Address: Ciruelos 3, Urb. Monteprincipe, 28023 Boadilla Del Monte, Madrid.

SMITH, ALEX
UK, Scotland South, Soc (Lab)

Mr Alex (Sandy) Smith, gardener, gained this Euro seat for Labour in 1989 and became mbr, EP Cmte on Regional Policy and Regional Planning. . He chaired Cunninghame South Labour Party, 1983-87, and was constituency trade union liaison officer, 1986-88. TGWU, being mbr of union's regional and public services and political cmtes; was convenor of shop stewards cmte. Chmn, Irvine and District Trades Cl; Cunninghame Campaign Against the Poll Tax. B Dec 2 1943; ed Irving Royal Acad.

Address: 35 Kersland Foot, Girdle Toll, Irvine KA11 1BP, Scotland. Tel: (0294) 216704.

SMITH, LLEWELLYN
UK, South East Wales, Soc (Lab)

Mr Llewellyn Smith was first elected to EP in 1984; since then has served on its Cmte on Energy, Research and Technology; has also been on Cmte on Economic and Monetary Affairs and Industrial Policy. Former labourer with Pilkington Glass and George Wimpey, builders; then computer operator with British Steel Corporation; tutor-organizer, Workers' Educational Assocn. B Apr 16 1944; ed Cardiff Univ. Former chmn, Abertillery CLP and exec mbr, Welsh Lab Pty. Vice-pres, Anti-Apartheid Wales. TGWU.

Address: The European Office, NUM Building, Hillside, Crumlin, Gwent. NP1 4QB. Tel: (0495) 249111. The Mount Uplands, Newbridge, Gwent NP1 4RH. Tel: (0495) 245487.

SONNEVELD, JAN
Netherlands, EPP (CDA)

Mr Jan Sonneveld, elected to EP in 1989, became mbr, Cmte on Agriculture, Fisheries and Rural Development. Has been an attache at the Dutch Embassy in Washington. Agricultural engineer specialising in the environment. B May 13 1933.

Addresses: Prinses Mariannelaan 42, 2275 BH Voorburg. Tel: (070) 87 66 19. Marktstraat 36, 7642 Am Wierden. Tel: (05496) 713 76.

SPECIALE, ROBERTO
Italy, EUL (PCI)

Sgr Roberto Speciale was elected to EP in 1989, joining Cmte on Economic and Monetary Affairs and Industrial Policy. Mbr of bureau of European United Left Gp; central cmte and national directorate of PCI. Regional councillor in Liguria. B Aug 3 1943.

Address:

SPENCER, TOM
UK, Surrey West, ED (C)

Mr Tom Spencer, Associate Dean, Templeton Coll, Oxford, was elected for this Euro seat in 1989 and joined EP Cmte on Agriculture, Fisheries and Rural Development; MEP for Derbyshire, 1979-84, when he was defeated there. ED spokesman on social affairs and employment, 1079-81, and on external economic relations, 1982-84. B Apr 10 1948; ed Nautical Coll, Pangbourne; Southampton Univ. With Peat, Marwick, Mitchell and Co, 1972-75; assistant to director, Britain-in-Europe Campaign, 1975; with J Walter Thompson and Co, 1975-79. Mbr, cl, European Movement, 1968-75; chmn, European Union of Cons and Christian Democratic Students, 1971-73.

Address: Thornfalcon House, Northchapel, West Sussex GU28 9HP. Tel: (042878) 756.

SPERONI, FRANCESCO
Italy, ARC (Lega-L)

Sgr Francesco Speroni, a pilot with Alitalia airline, was elected to EP in 1989. Appointed a vice-chairman of the Cmte on Legal Affairs and Citizens' Rights also became mbr, Cmte on Institutional Affairs. Provincial secretary in Milan for Lega Lombarda. Local councillor. B Oct 4 1946.

Address:

STAES, PAUL
Belgium, Verts (Agalev)

Mr Paul Staes was first elected to the EP in 1984 representing the Danish People's Movement against membership of EC. He joined the ARC (Rainbow) Gp and in the outgoing Parliament was one of the four co-chmn; now in Green Gp; joined Cmte on Regional Policy and Regional Planning in 1989; former mbr, Cmte on Energy, Research and Technology. Former journalist with *Standaard/ Nieuwsblad*; regular contributor to ecological and other publications. Executive mbr, League for a Better Environment, the World Wildlife Fund (Flanders section) and Flemish Forestry Association. B Dec 3 1945; studied in UK and Germany at Stonyhurst Coll and Goethe Inst.

Addresses: Grote Singel 11, 2120 Schoten. Tel: (03) 658 49 71.

STAMOULIS, IOANNIS
Greece, Soc (PASOK)

Mr Ioannis Stamoulis, lawyer specialising in European Community law. Elected to EP in 1989 and became mbr of Cmte on Transport and Tourism and Cmte on Rules of Procedure, Verification of Credentials and Immunities.

Address: Akadimias 42, 106 72 Athenes.

STAUFFENBERG, FRANZ LUDWIG GRAF VON
Germany, EPP (CSU)

Herr Franz Ludwig Graf von Stauffenberg, first elected to EP in 1984, was appointed chmn of EP Cmte on Legal Affairs and Citizens' Rights after 1989 elections; a vice-chmn, Cmte on Institutional Affairs, 1987-89, and mbr of cmte, 1984-89. Former mbr of Bundestag. Deputy chmn, German Youth Union, 1969-73. Vice-chmn, Europa Union Deutschland; also served on CSU state executive. B May 4 1938. Mbr, bureau, EPP Group.

Addresses: 8601 Kirchlauter. Tel: (09536) 222. Bundeshaus, 5300 Bonn 1. Tel: (0228) 163254.

STAVROU, KONSTANTINOS
Greece, EPP (ND)

Mr Konstantinos Stavrou, former Greek ambassador to OECD, has been an MEP since 1984. A vice-chmn, EP Cmte on External Economic Relations, 1989- ; mbr, Cmte on Rules of Procedure, Verification of Credentials and Immunities, 1989- ; former mbr, Cmte on Agriculture, Fisheries and Food (chaired sub-cmte on fisheries). Former finance and trade adviser to Greek Government. B Jul 20 1928. Doctorate in economics and graduate in law.

Addresses: 264B av. de Tervueren, 1150 Bruxelles. Xenias 3, 115 27 Athina. Tel: (1) 721 61 77.

STEVENS, JOHN
UK, Thames Valley, ED (C)

Mr John Stevens was elected for this Euro seat in 1989 and became mbr, EP Cmte on Economic and Monetary Affairs and Industrial Policy. . A director of Morgan Grenfell International, merchant bankers, since 1986; foreign exchange bond trader in France, Germany and Italy, 1977-1980, when he joined Morgan Grenfell; presently responsible for securities trading in European capital markets. Contested Rotherham in 1987 general election. Mbr, nat cl, European Movement, 1981-82. B May 23 1955; ed privately in America; Winchester Coll; Magdalen Coll, Oxford; Rome Univ.

Address: 15 St James's Place, London SW1A 1NW. Tel: (01) 493 8111.

STEVENSON, GEORGE
UK, Staffordshire East, Soc (Lab)

Mr George Stevenson, bus driver, 1966-84, was first elected to EP in 1984 serving on Cmte on Transport until 1987. Mbr, Cmte on Budgets, 1987-89; Cmte on Agriculture, Fisheries and Rural Development, 1989- . Chmn, Lab gp of MEPs, 1987-88; vice-pres, South Asia EP delegation. Mbr, Stoke-on-Trent City Cl, 1972-86; Staffs CC, 1981-85. Mbr, TGWU, since 1964, being branch shop steward, 1968-84, and chmn, 1975-81. Transport driver, 1964-66; miner, 1957-64; pottery caster, 1953-57. B Aug 30 1938; ed Uttoxeter Rd Primary Sch; Queensberry Rd Sec Sch, Stoke-on-Trent.

Addresses: Euro Constituency Office, Pioneer House, 76/80 Lonsdale Street, Stoke-on-Trent ST4 4DP. Tel: (0782) 414232. 56 Canberra Crescent, Meir Park, Stoke-on-Trent ST3 7RA. Tel: (0782) 39 34 96.

STEWART, KENNETH
UK, Merseyside West, Soc (Lab)

Mr Kenneth Stewart was first elected to EP in 1984. Mbr, EP Cmte on Transport and Tourism, 1987- ; EP Cmte on Social Affairs and Employment, 1984-87; Liverpool City Cl since 1964 (former chmn of housing and consumer protection cmtes); also on Merseyside CC (former dep chmn). Joiner, mbr of Ucatt, the building trade union. B Jul 28 1925. Former chmn and sec, Liverpool West Derby Lab Pty; former shop steward; ex-sergeant, Parachute Regiment.

Address: 62 Ballantyne Road, Liverpool L13 9AL. Tel: (051) 256 7782.

STEWART-CLARK, SIR JACK
UK, Sussex East, ED (C)

Sir Jack Stewart-Clark, MEP for this seat since 1979, became EDG spokesman on Cmte on Youth, Culture, Education, the Media and Sport in 1989. Treasurer, ED Gp, since 1979. Mbr, EP Cmte on Economic and Monetary Affairs and Industrial Policy, 1987-89. Non-exec director, Low and Bonar plc; A T Kearney Ltd; Pioneer Concrete Holdings Ltd; managing director, Pye of Cambridge Ltd, 1975-79; Philips Electrical Ltd, London, 1971-75; J A Carp's Garenfabrieken, Holland, 1967-69; J and P Coats, Pakistan, Ltd, 1961-67; with J and P Coats Ltd, 1952-69. Contested Aberdeen North in 1959 election. B Sep 17 1929. Pres, Conference of Regions of North West Europe; Supervisory Bd, Euro Inst for Security, 1984-86; director and trustee, Euro Centre for Work and Society.
Address: Puckstye House, Holtye Commons, nr Cowden, Kent TN8 7EL. Tel: (0342) 850285. Telefax: (032) 850789.

255

SUAREZ GONZÁLEZ, FERNANDO
Spain, EPP (PP)

Señor Fernando Suarez González was first elected MEP in 1987; mbr, Cmte on Social Affairs, Employment and Work Environment. Professor of Labour Law at Universidad Nacional de Educacion a Distancia; was director of major colleges; Director-General, Spanish Institute for Emigration. Has served as Technical Secretary General to Presidency, Minister of Labour and third Vice-President of Government; was mbr of Constituent Cortes; appointed representative of the King during Spanish constitutional reform. Chmn, Ibero-American Academy of Labour Law. Mbr of Parliament, Alianza Popular, for Madrid. Spanish vice-chmn of ED Gp until 1989. B Aug 10 1933.

Address: Genova 13, 28004 Madrid. Tel: (1) 410 11 43.

TARADASH, MARCO
Italy, Verts (Anti-Pro)

Sgr Marco Taradash is secretary and coordinator of the movement to de-criminalise drug offences. Elected to EP in 1989, joined Green Gp and became mbr, Cmte on Youth, Culture, Education, the Media and Sport, and Cmte on Rules of Procedure, Verification of Credentials and Immunities. Journalist. B May 19 1950.

Address: c.o. Radio Radicale, Via Principe Amedeo 2, 00185 Roma. Tel: (06) 46 05 41-2-3.

TAURAN, JACQUES
France, DR (FN)

M.Jacques Tauran, editor, was elected to EP in 1989; mbr, Cmte on Transport and Tourism. Former mbr, Economic and Social Cl. B May 7 1930.

Address: Puy-de-Mont, 87700 Aixe-sur-Vienne.

TAZDAIT, MME DJIDA
France, Verts (Verts)

Mme Djida Tazdait was elected to EP in 1989 becoming mbr, Cmte on Legal Affairs and Citizens' Rights. Director of audio-visual programmes; chairs Association of Young Arabs of Lyons and District. B 1957.

Address: 5 rue de la Platrière, 69001 Lyon. Tel: 78 27 44 03.

TELKÄMPER, WILFRIED
Germany, Verts (Grüne)

Herr Wilfried Telkämper became an MEP during the 1984-89 Parliament; re-elected 1989 and in July 1989 was elected a Vice-President of EP; mbr, EP Cmte on Development and Cooperation. Arc-en-Ciel spokesman in outgoing Parliament. Teacher. Came into politics through youth movements including Evangelic Youth Movement and Young Socialists. Became a voluntary worker with information centre for Third World in Freiburg and editor of their journal; also broadcaster with Free Radio station *Dreyeckland*. B Jan 16 1953.

Address: Elsa-Brändströmstrasse 31, 7800 Freiburg. Tel: (0761) 44 22 99.

THAREAU, BERNARD
France, Soc (PS)

M. Bernard Thareau, farmer, has been an MEP since 1981, serving on Cmte on Agriculture, Fisheries and Rural Development. Has served as Socialist Party assistant national secretary for agriculture; vice-president, National Centre for Young Farmers (CNJA), 1966-70; president, National Porcine Federation, and administrator, National Federation of Farmers' Unions (FNSEA), 1969-77. B Sep 2 1936.

Addresses: Parti Socialiste Français, 10 rue de Solferino, 75007 Paris. Tel: (1) 45 50 34 35. La Milsonnière, La Rouxiere, 44370 Varades. Tel: 40 96 95 68.

257

THEATO, FRAU DIEMUT
Germany, EPP (CDU)

Frau Diemut Theato became an MEP in October 1987; re-elected 1989. Mbr, EP Cmte on Budgets and Cmte on Budgetary Control. B Apr 13 1937; translator and conference organiser. Holds office in regional party organizarions.

Address: Wiesenweg 21, 6903 Neckargemünd-Waldhilsbach. Tel: (06223) 3477.

TINDEMANS, LEO
Belgium, EPP (CVP)

Mr Leo Tindemans was first elected to EP in 1979 but resigned in 1980; re-elected to EP in 1989. Former Prime Minister of Belgium and former Minister for External Relations. Honorary president, being founder and former chmn, of European People's Party; former chmn and secretary-general, European Union of Christian Democrats (EUCD); chmn, Christelijke Volkspartij (CVP). Leader of Belgian delegation on EPP Gp and mbr, bureau, of gp, 1989- ; mbr, Political Affairs Cmte and Cmte on Development and Cooperation; co-President, African, Caribbean, Pacific - EC Assembly, 1989- . B Apr 16 1922. National secretary, Christian People's Party, 1958-65; Burgomaster of Edegem, 1965-76. Held many ministerial offices during 1970s and 1980s.

Address: Verbertlei 24, 2520 Edegem.

TITLEY, GARY
UK, Greater Manchester West, Soc (Lab)

Mr Gary Titley was elected to the EP in 1989 and was immediately elected whip of the enlarged group of British Labour MEPs. Became mbr, Cmte on External Economic Relations. Campaign manager from 1987-89 to Mr John Bird, Labour MEP for Midlands West, and from 1984-87 to his predecessor, the late Mr Terry Pitt. Contested Dudley West in 1987 general election and Bromsgrove, 1983. Director, W Midlands Enterprise Bd; chmn, West Midlands Co-operative Finance Co. B Jan 19 1950; ed York Univ. Mbr, W Midlands CC, 1981-86 (vice-chmn, economic development cmte and consumer services cmte); was also chmn, Black Country Co-operative Development Agency and of Wolverhampton Consumer Panel. Chmn, Halesowen and Stourbridge CLP, 1981-83. TGWU.

Address: 20 Glendale Close, Halesowen B63 3LD. Tel: (021) 550 5489.

TOMLINSON, JOHN
UK, Birmingham West, Soc (Lab)

Mr John Tomlinson joined bureau of Socialist Gp after 1989 elections; appointed rapporteur on 1990 EC budget being mbr of Cmtes on Budgets and Budgetary Control on which he was previously gp and Labour gp spokesman. Dep Ldr, British Labour Gp of MEPs, 1987-88; Chief Whip, Socialist Gp, 1985-89. First elected to EP in 1984. MP for Meriden, 1974-79, being PPS to the then Mr Harold Wilson, Prime Minister, 1975-76; Parly Under Secretary of State for Foreign and Commonwealth Affairs, 1976-79, and Parly Sec, Ministry of Overseas Development, 1977-79. Contested Warwicks North, 1983. Lecturer in industrial relations and management and later Head of Social Studies, Solihull Coll of Tech, 1979-84. B Aug 1 1939. *Addresses: 42 Bridge St, Walsall WS1 1JQ. Tel: (0922) 22586. Telefax: (0922) 724923. 23 Meriden Road, Hampton in Arden, West Midlands B92 0BS. Tel: (06755) 2689.*

TONGUE, MS CAROLE
UK, London East, Soc (Lab)

Ms Carole Tongue was elected deputy leader of enlarged group of British Labour MEPs in June 1989. First elected to EP 1984; mbr, EP Cmte on Economic and Monetary Affairs and Industrial Policy, 1989- ; Cmte on Environment, Public Health and Consumer Protection, 1984-89; former mbr, Cmte on Women's Rights. Admin assistant/secretary, Socialist Gp, EP, 1980-84; Robert Schuman scholarship for research in social affairs with EP, 1979-80; courier/guide in France with Sunsites Ltd, 1978-79; asst editor, *Laboratory Practice*, 1977-78. B Oct 14 1955; ed state sch in Harold Wood; Brentwood County HS; Loughborough Univ. Vice-Pres, Socialist Environmental and Resources Assocn; AMA; Labour Action for Peace; mbr, Quaker Cl of European Affairs. Apex.

Address: 84 Endsleigh Gardens, Ilford, Essex IG1 3EG. Tel: (01) 514 0198. Telefax: 553 4764.

TOPMANN, GÜNTER
Germany, Soc (SDP)

Herr Günter Topmann, a retired senior police officer, was first elected to EP in 1984 and he has served on the Cmte on Transport and Tourism since then and been a vice-chairman since 1987 being re-appointed after 1989 elections. Mayor of Altenahr. Mbr, Bundestag, until 1983. B May 7 1934. Trained cobbler.

Addresses: SPD-Europabüro, Breitenfeld 1b, 5880 Lüdenscheid. Tel: (02351) 6535. Graf-Engelbert-Strasse 24, 5990 Altena. Tel: (02352) 24123.

TORRES COUTO, JOSÉ MANUEL
Portugàl, Soc (PS)

Senhor José Manuel Torres Couto, Secretary-General of the trade union UGT since 1978, was elected to EP in 1989, joining Cmte on Social Affairs, Employment and Working Environment. Deputy in Portuguese national Parliament since 1987. Mbr, executive cmte, International Confederation of Free Trade Unions (CISL), and executive cmte of European Confederation of Trade Unions (CES). B Feb 1 1947.

Address: Av. Afonso III, 23-5° C, 1900 Lisboa.

TRAUTMANN, MME CATHERINE
France, Soc (PS)

Mme Catherine Trautmann became Mayor of Strasbourg (Bas-Rhin) in March 1989 and in June 1989, second on the Socialist list headed by M Laurent Fabius, ws elected to EP which at present holds its plenary sessions in Strasbourg. Joined Political Affairs Cmte. Mbr, municipal council since 1983; deputy for Bas-Rhin, 1986-88; in May 1988 became Secretary of State at Ministry of Social Affairs in first Rocard Government, with responsibility for the aged and handicapped. Since 1988, has chaired interdepartmental cmte to counter drug addiction. Theologian. B Jan 15 1951.

Address: Hôtel de Ville, 9 rue Brulée, 67000 Strasbourg. Tel: 88 32 99 03.

TRIVELLI, RENZO
Italy, EUL (PCI)

Sgr Renzo Trivelli was first elected to EP in 1984; re-elected 1989. Mbr, Cmte on Development and Co-operation. On central Cmte of PCI. B May 3 1925.

Addresses: Direzione PCI, Via delle Botteghe Oscure 4, 00186 Roma. Tel: (06) 6711. Piazza Vincenzo Ceresi 23, 00100 Roma. Tel: (06) 5379851.

TSIMAS, KONSTANTINOS
Greece, Soc (PASOK)

Mr **Konstantinos Tsimas** was elected to EP in 1989, joining Cmte on External Economic Relations. Mbr, central cmte of PASOK. Former Secretary-General of Ministry of Interior and former head of the National Information Service. B 1936.

Address: Aetideon 19, 155 61 Holargos.

TURNER, AMÉDÉE
UL, Suffolk, ED (C)

Mr **Amédée Turner, QC,** patent barrister and author, joined EP Cmte on Development and Cooperation in 1989. First elected to EP in 1979. EDG spokesman on Cmte on Energy, Research and Technology, 1984-89; a vice-chmn, EP Legal Affairs Cmte, 1979-84; mbr, Economic and Monetary Cmte, 1979-84; Transport Cmte, 1981-84; EEC/ACP jt assembly, 1980-. B Mar 26 1929. Called to Bar (Inner Temple) 1954; practised patent bar, 1955-57; Associate, Kenyon and Kenyon, patent attorneys, New York, 1957-60; returned to London practice, 1960. Contested Norwich North in 1970, 1966 and 1964 general elections.

Addresses: 3 Montrose Place, London SW1X 7DU. Tel: (01) 235 3191. 1 Essex Court, The Temple, London EC4Y 9AR. Tel: (01) 583 8290. The Barn, Westleton, Saxmundham, Suffolk IP17 3AN. Tel: (072) 873 235.

UKEIWÉ, DICK
France, RDE (RPR)

M.Dick Ukeiwé, senator for Nouvelle-Caledonie, was elected to EP in 1989 and joined Cmte on Development and Cooperation. Became mbr, bureau, RDE Gp. Co-founder of Association for New Caledonia in France. B 1928.

Address: Palais de Luxembourg, 15 rue de Vaugirard, 75006 Paris.

261

VALENT, SIGNORA DACIA
Italy, EUL (PCI)

Signora Dacia Valent was elected to EP in 1989 and joined Cmte on Legal Affairs and Citizens' Rights. Mbr, Italian state police force and anti-Mafia organization. B Feb 12 1963.

Address: Via S. Martino 29, 33100 Udine. Tel: (0432) 50 06 28.

VALVERDE LOPEZ, JOSÉ LUIS
Spain, EPP (PP)

Señor José Luis Valverde Lopez, Professor of History of Pharmacy and Pharmaceutical Legislation at Univ of Granada, was elected to EP in 1987; re-elected 1989. Mbr, Cmte on Institutional Affairs, on which he was a vice-chmn in outgoing Parliament; and mbr, Cmte on Environment, Public Health and Consumer Protection. Author of numerous works on history of Spanish pharmacy; executive director of magazine *Pharmaceutica*; mbr, International Academy of History of Pharmacy. B Aug 11 1940.

Addresses: Departamento de Farmacia y Tecnologia, Universidad de Granada, 18001 Granada. Tel: 27 25 89. Severa Ochoa 13 7°b, 18001 Granada. Tel: 27 23 54.

VANDEMEULEBROUCKE, JAAK
Belgium, ARC (VU)

Mr Jaak Vandemeulebroucke was a vice-chmn of the EP Cmte on Regional Policy and Regional Planning, 1987-89; mbr, Cmte on Youth, Culture, Education, the Media and Sport, and Cmte on Rules of Procedure, Verification of Credentials and Immunities, 1989- ; former mbr, Cmte on Environment, Public Health and Consumer Protection. A co-chmn of ARC (Rainbow) Gp in outgoing Parliament; reappointed after 1989 elections. Became an MEP in 1981. Former teacher. Mbr of his party's bureau since 1973. Mbr, Chamber of Representatives, 1974-77; Deputy Chef de Cabinet to Secretary of State Anciaux. B May 27 1943. Communal councillor at Ostend from 1970.

Address: Anjelierenlaan 25, 8400 Oostende. Tel: (059) 800428.

VAYSSADE, MME MARIE-CLAUDE
France, Soc (PS)

Mme Marie-Claude Vayssade was first elected to EP in 1979; chmn, EP Legal Affairs and Citizens' Rights Cmte, 1984-87, vice-chmn since 1987, being reappointed after 1989 elections; also mbr, Cmte on Women's Rights. Head of Workers' Education Centre, Institute of Labour, Univ of Nancy II, 1968-69. Party appointments: federal executive cmte, PS; federal bureau, Meurthe-et-Moselle Socialist Party; mbr, Unified Socialist Party, 1967-74, when she joined Socialist Party. B Aug 8 1936; graduate in law.

Address: 78 rue du Marèchal Oudinot, 54000 Nancy. Tel: 83 56 16 72.

VÁZQUEZ FOUZ, JOSÉ
Spain, Soc (PSOE)

Señor José Vázquez Fouz has been an MEP since 1986; first elected 1987. Former civil servant with special responsibility for agriculture. After 1989 elections he rejoined Cmte on Agriculture, Fisheries and Rural Development. Former mbr, Spanish national Parliament. A Spanish representative to Cl of Europe. B Dec 19 1944.

Address: c/Salvador Moreno 23-1° izq, 36001 Pontevedra.

VECCHI, LUCIANO
Italy, EUL (PCI)

Sgr Luciano Vecchi became elected MEP in 1989 joining EP Cmte on Development and Cooperation and Cmte on Rules of Procedure, Verification of Credentials and Immunities. Mbr, national cmte, Federation of Young Communists. B Aug 19 1961.

Address:

VEIL, MME SIMONE
France, LDR (UDF/RPR)

Mme Simone Veil was leader of the Liberal and Democratic Reformist Group (LDR), 1984-89. First elected to EP in 1979, being its President, 1979-82, and then chaired its Legal Affairs Cmte until 1984; after 1989 elections joined Cmte on Environment, Public Health and Consumer Protection. Appointed Minister of Public Health in 1974, becoming Minister of Public Health and Family Affairs in 1978, resigning in 1979. B Jul 13 1927; qualified in law at Institut d'Etudes Politiques in Paris. Joined prisons service, Ministry of Justice, 1957, specializing in probation and rehabilitation. Appointed Secretary-General of Conseil Superieur de la Magistrature (Supreme Court of Judiciary) in 1970.

Address: 11 place Vauban, 75007 Paris. Tel: (1) 45510968.

VELZEN, WILLEM VAN
Netherlands, Soc (PvdA)

Mr Willem van Velzen, teacher, was elected to EP in 1989; became a vice-chmn of Political Affairs Cmte. National secretary of PvdA. B May 13 1938.

Address: Botterwijnseweg 11, 1272 EG Huizen. Tel: (02152) 542 09.

VERBEEK, HERMAN
Netherlands, ARC (CPN)

Mr Herman Verbeek was elected an MEP in 1984 but left in 1986; elected again in 1989 and joined Cmte on Agriculture, Fisheries and Rural Development; former mbr, Cmte on Development and Cooperation. Author, theologian and priest. Former leader of Radical Party. B May 17 1936.

Address: Nieuwe St Janstraat 29, 9711 VC Groningen. Tel: (050) 13 57 59.

VERDE I ALDEA, JOSEP
Spain, Soc (PSOE)

Señor Josep Verde i Aldea, MEP since 1986, rejoined EP Political Affairs Cmte after 1989 elections. Appointed a vice-chmn of Socialist Gp. Lawyer. Former mbr, Spanish national Parliament and Vice-President, Parliamentary Assembly of Cl of Europe. B Nov 3 1928.

Addresses: Enric Granados 95 3° 1a, 08008 Barcelona. Tel: (3) 218 22 70. PSC-PSOE, c/Nicaragua 75, 08029 Barcelona. Tel: (3) 321 90 16. Telex: 50 463.

VERHAGEN, MAXIME
Netherlands, EPP (CDA)

Mr Maxime Verhagen, elected to EP in 1989, joined Cmte on Development and Cooperation. Adviser on European affairs to CDA Gp in Dutch Second Chamber. B Sep 14 1956. Historian.

Address: Mr F. Bordewijklaan 15, 2343 KS Oegstgeest. Tel: (071) 17 65 20.

VERNIER, JACQUES
France, RDE (RPR)

M. Jacques Vernier, Mayor of Douai (Nord) and regional councillor since 1983, was first elected MEP in 1984; re-elected 1989; mbr, Cmte on Environment, Public Health and Consumer Protection. Polytechnician and mining engineer. Assistant general secretary, Seine-Normandy Basin Agency, 1972-74; director, Agence de l'Eau Nord-Artois-Picardie, 1974-83. Founder chmn, Douai Consumers' Association, 1978-83; chmn, Douai Housing Aid Association, 1976-83. Author, *The Battle of the Environment*, 1971. B Jul 3 1944.

Addresses: Mairie de Douai, 59500 Douai. Tel: 27 87 26 63. 162 quai de Petit Bail, 59500 Douai. Tel: 29 97 82 02.

VERTEMATI, LUIGI
Italy, Soc (PSI)

Sgr Luigi Vertemati was elected to EP in 1989. Became mbr, Cmte on Budgets.

Address:

VERWAERDE, YVES
France, LDR (PR)

M.Yves Verwaerde was elected to EP in 1989, joining Cmte on Energy, Research and Technology. Paris councillor and regional councillor for Ile-de-France. B 1947.

Address: 105 rue de l'Université, 75007 Paris.

VISENTINI, BRUNO
Italy, LDR (PRI-PLI-Fed)

Sgr Bruno Visentini, President of Italian Republic Party (PRI), was elected to EP in 1989 and joined Cmte on Economic and Monetary Affairs and Industrial Policy. Senator and former minister. Lawyer. B Aug 1 1914.

Address: Senato della Repubblica, Piazza Madama, 00186 Roma. Tel: (06) 670 61.

VISSER, BEN
Netherlands, Soc (PvdA)

Mr **Ben Visser** was first elected an MEP in 1984 and since then been a mbr of EP Cmte on Transport and Tourism, rejoining cmte after 1989 elections. At the time of his selection he was a mbr of Gelderland provincial council. Accountant. B Feb 6 1934.

Address: Huygenslaan 22, 6824 JH Arnhem. Tel: (085) 42 15 01.

VITTINGHOFF, KURT
Germany, Soc (SDP)

Herr **Kurt Vittinghoff** was first elected to the EP in 1984; re-elected 1989 when he rejoined Cmte on Environment, Public Health and Consumer Protection. Cabinet maker. Former general secretary, IG-metal trade union; mbr of SPD federal study group on employee problems. B Jan 9 1928.

Addresses: c.o. IG Metall, Salinenstrasse 37, 6550 Bad Kreuznach. Tel: (0671) 30021. Kolberger Strasse 6, 6550 Bad Kreuznach, Tel: (0671) 64843.

VITTO, LORENZO DE
Italy, EPP (DC)

Sgr Lorenzo de Vitto, elected to EP in 1989, joined the Cmte on Social Affairs, Employment and Working Environment and was appointed one of its vice-chairmen; also mbr, Cmte on Petitions. Regional official and mbr, national council of DC. Regional and provincial government councillor. Lawyer. B Oct 13 1925.

Address: Via Sepe, 83054 S. Angelo dei Lombardi (AV). Tel: (0827) 232 20.

VOHRER, MANFRED
Germany, LDR (FDP)

Herr Manfred Vohrer, diplomat and former head of an environmental institute, was elected to EP in 1989 and joined Cmte on Environment, Public Health and Consumers. Former mbr of Bundestag. B Jun 21 1941.

Address: Hörhalde 1, 7816 Münstertal/Schwarzwald.

VRIES, GIJS DE
Netherlands, LDR (VVD)

Mr Gijs de Vries was first elected to EP in 1984; re-elected in 1989 and joined Cmte on External Economic Relations; former mbr, Cmte on Economic and Monetary Affairs and Industrial Policy. On staff of university of Leidnen; was local councillor. B Feb 22 1956.

Address: Postbus 11613, 2502 AP 's-Gravenhage. Tel: (070) 647 447.

VRING, THOMAS VON DER
Germany, Soc (SDP)

Herr Thomas von der Vring became chmn of EP Cmte on Budgets after 1989 elections; was on cmte in outgoing Parliament; first elected to EP in 1979, since when he has also served on EP Cmte on Regional Policy and Regional Planning. B May 27 1937. University lecturer and former Rector of University of Bremen. Deputy federal chmn, Young Socialists, 1964-70; mbr, Bremen executive, SPD, from 1974, and holder of other posts in party organization.

Address: Meissener Strasse 7, 2800 Bremen. Tel: (0421) 351557.

WAAL, LEEN VAN DER
Netherlands, NI (SGP)

Mr Leen van der Waal is a mbr of the EP Cmte on Transport and Tourism. First elected to EP in 1984. Engineer; formerly manager of a transport company and oil businesses. Mbr of cmte of Reform Church in Holland. B Sep 23 1928.

Address: Lagendijk 60, 2981 EM Ridderberk. Tel: (01804) 25064.

WAECHTER, ANTOINE
France, Verts (Verts)

M. Antoine Waechter, presidential election candidate in 1988, was elected to EP in 1989 and was appointed chmn, Cmte on Regional Policy and Regional Planning. Ecological engineer; spokesman for Les Verts; regional councillor in Alsace since 1986 and town councillor at Mulhouse (Haut-Rhin) since March 1989. At founding of ecological/political movement in Alsace in 1973. B 1949.

Address: 10 avenue de Lattre, 68100 Mulhouse. Tel: 89 66 00 20.

WALTER, GERD
Germany, Soc (SDP)

Herr Gerd Walter, first elected to EP in 1979, has been serving on the Political Affairs Cmte; also mbr of bureau of Socialist Gp since 1984 being leader of the SPD MEPs. Chmn, Schleswig-Holstein regional SPD cmte and former chmn of its Young Socialists. B Apr 24 1949; graduate in political science. Journalist and further education lecturer.

Address: SPD-Landesverband, Europabüro, 28-30 Kleiner Kuhberg, 2300 Kiel 1. Tel: (0431) 90606-22-20.

269

WEBER, FRAU BEATE
Germany, Soc (SDP)

Frau Beate Weber chaired the EP Cmte on Environment, Public Health and Consumer Protection, 1987-89, and after 1989 elections remained on cmte. First elected MEP in 1979, she became a vice-chairman of the environment cmte being reappointed in 1984. Chair, SPD Federal Council; mbr, Heidelburg municipal council, since 1975. B Dec 12 1943. Teacher.

Address: Sickingenstrasse 1, 6900 Heidelberg. Tel: (06221) 33626.

WECHMAR, RÜDIGER VON
Germany, LDR (FDP)

Herr Rüdiger von Wechmar, elected to EP in 1989, unsuccessfully contested Presidency in July 1989; became mbr, Institutional Affairs Cmte. Since 1988, German representative of United Service Organizations (USO), Washington; Ambassador to Britain, 1983-88; President, 35th General Assembly of UN and Ambassador to Italy, 1980-81; Ambassador to UN, 1974-81. Former diplomatic correspondent in Bonn, Strasbourg and Moscow; press consul, Consulate General, New York, 1958-63. Deputy chief of press and information and spokesman of Federal German Government and Secretary of State, 1969-74. Born Nov 15 1923.

Address: Hiltensperger Strasse 15, 8000 München 40.

WELSH, MICHAEL
UK, Lancashire Central, ED (C)

Mr Michael Welsh was first elected to EP 1979; mbr and Cons coordinator on Political Affair Cmte, 1987-89, and still mbr of cmte; chmn, EP Social Affairs and Employment Cmte, 1984-87. EDG spokesman on external trade, 1980-82, and on economic and monetary affairs, 1982-84. Director, Initial plc. With Levi Strauss and Co Europe Ltd, 1969-79, being director of market development, 1976-79; general manager, Channel Road Services Ltd, 1966-69. B May 22 1942; ed Betteshanger Sch, Deal; Dover Coll; Lincoln Coll, Oxford.

Address: Watercrook, 181 Town Lane, Whittle-le-Woods, nr Chorley, Lancashire PR6 8AG. Tel: (02572) 76992.

WEST, NORMAN
UK, Yorkshire South, Soc, (Lab)

Mr Norman West was first elected to EP 1984; mbr since then of Cmte on Energy, Research and Technology. Miner. B Nov 26 1935; ed Worsboro C of E Sch and Holgate GS, Barnsley; Sheffield Univ. Former mbr, South Yorks CC (chmn, highways cmte and anti-nuclear working pty); has been vice-chair of county Lab Pty and chairs Barnsley West and Penistone CLP. NUM.

Addresses: County Treasurer's Department, Second Floor, Regent Street, Barnsley S70 2DX. Tel: (0226) 200738. 43 Coronation Drive, Birdwell, Barnsley S10 5RJ. Tel: (0226) 287464.

WETTIG, KLAUS
Germany, Soc (SDP)

Herr Klaus Wettig was first elected to EP in 1979. After 1989 elections jpined Cmtes on Economic and Monetary Affairs and Industrial Policy and Cmte on Budgetary Control; former mbr, Cmte on Agriculture, Fisheries and Food. Treasurer of Socialist Gp until 1984. Chmn, Hanover Young Socialists, 1969-70; mbr, SPD bureau, Hanover, from 1970. Compositor. B Aug 15 1940.

Address: Rohnsterrassen 6, 3400 Göttingen. Tel: (0551) 58 150.

WHITE, IAN
UK, Bristol, Soc (Lab)

Mr Ian White, criminal lawyer with Bristol practice, won this Euro seat in 1989; contested Wansdyke in 1987 general election. Became mbr, EP Political Affairs Cmte, 1989- . B Apr 8 1945; ed Merrywood GS, Bristol. Mbr, Society of Lab Lawyers; Lab Campaign for Criminal Justice; CND; Avon Wildlife Trust; Legal Action Gp; TGWU; Co-op Pty. Panel mbr for representation before mental health tribunals.

Address: 22 Park Road, Thornbury, Bristol BS12 1HN. Tel: (0454) 415207.

WIJSENBEEK, FLORUS
Netherlands, LDR (VVD)

Mr Florus Wijsenbeek, former secretary general of the Federation of European Liberals, was first elected to EP in 1984; re-elected 1989. Mbr, Cmte on Transport and Tourism; a vice-chmn, Cmte on Rules of Procedure, the Verification of Credentials and Immunities. Has also served on EP Cmte on Legal Affairs and Citizens' Rights. Head of personal cabinet of Mr Cornelius Berkhouwer during his Presidency of the EP, 1973-75. Former mbr, legal service of European Commission.

Addresses: Postbus 11581, 2502 AN 's-Gravenhage. Tel: (070) 647447. Telefax: (070) 647001. J van Oldenbarneveltlaan 71, 2582 NK 's-Gravenhage, Tel: (070) 551284.

WILSON, JOSEPH
UK, Wales North, Soc (Lab)

Mr Anthony Joseph (Joe) Wilson won this Euro seat in 1989 and joined Cmte on Social Affairs, Employment and Working Environment. Contested Montgomery in 1983 general election. Lecturer in physical education at NE Wales Inst, Wrexham. Chaired Wrexham/Maelor District Lab Pty, 1973-88; vice-chmn, Cmte of Welsh District Cls, 1987-89; Wrexham CLP. Mbr, Wrexham/Maelor BC, for 12 years, being convenor of Lab gp; Wrexham Trades Cl, 1977-, being education officer, 1977-86. B Jul 1937; ed local state schs; Loughborough Coll; Univ of Wales. NATFHE.

Address: 79 Ruabon Road, Wrexham LL13 7PU. Tel: (0978) 352808.

WOGAU, KARL VON
Germany, EPP (CDU)

Herr Karl von Wogau, commercial lawyer, was first elected to the EP in 1979; mbr, Cmte on Economic and Monetary Affairs and Industrial Policy; bureau of EPP Gp. Chairs EPP Gp working party on economic policy. Political activities in "Junge Union" and CDU since 1964, holding office in several regional party organizations. Worked for Europa Union. B Jul 18 1941.

Address: Leo-Wohleb-Strasse 6, Postfach 5540, 7800 Freiburg/Breisgau. Tel: (0761) 218 08 41. Telex 772828 bawis d. Telefax 0761/218 08 21.

WOLTJER, EISSO P.
Netherlands, Soc (PvdA)

Mr Eisso P Woltjer, an MEP since 1979, is a long serving member of the EP Cmte on Agriculture, Fisheries and Rural Development. A vice-chairman of Socialist Gp leader of Netherlands delegation. Was member of teaching staff at Deventer Agricultural College. Mbr, Limburg Provincial Council, 1978-79. B Jan 9 1942; studied at Wageningen Agricultural College.

Address: Bergkwartier 10, 5801 PS Venray. Tel: (04780) 84324.

WURTZ, FRANCIS
France, CG (PCF)

M. Francis Wurtz was a vice-chmn, EP Cmte on Development and Cooperation, 1984-89, and is still mbr of cmte; former mbr, Cmte on Energy, Research and Technology. First elected MEP in 1979. Has served on central cmte, French Communist Party. B Jan 3 1948. Former secretary, Bas-Rhin Federation of French Communist Party and of Strasbourg "new university".

Address: 27 rue des Serruriers, 67000 Strasbourg. Tel: 88 32 42 69.

WYNN, TERRY
UK, Merseyside East, Soc (Lab)

Mr Terence (Terry) Wynn was elected to the EP in 1989 and became a vice-chmn of Cmte on Budgetary Control; also mbr, Cmte on Development and Cooperation. A training adviser in shipbuilding industry; formerly marine engineer in Merchant Navy. Mbr, Wigan MBC, 1979- . Vice-chmn, Westhoughton CLP, 1975-80; founder mbr and chmn, Wigan Co-op Pty. B Jun 27 1946; ed Leigh Coll; Riversdale Coll, Liverpool; Liverpool Poly; Salford Univ. Methodist local preacher; youth club ldr. MSFU.

Address: 34 Holden Brook Close, Leigh WN7 2HL, Lancashire. Tel: (0942) 607327.

ZAIDI, MME NORA
France, Soc (PS)

Mme Nora Zaidi, a student, was elected to EP in 1989, joining Cmte on Youth, Culture, Education, the Media and Sport. Organiser of SOS racism movement at Montbeliard. B 1965.

Address: Bureau de Mme Rossignol, Assemblée Nationale, 126 rue de l'Université, 75007 Paris.

ZARGES, AXEL
Germany, EPP (CDU)

Herr Axel Zarges, lawyer and notary, has been an elected MEP since 1984; serves on EP Cmte on External Economic Relations. Became vice-chmn, European Union of Germany and of German Cl of the European Movement, and chmn, European Union of Hesse. B Oct 7 1932.

Addresses: Ob. Königstrasse 47, 3500 Kassel. Tel: (0561) 12477-79. Rieckstrasse 10a, 3500 Kassel. Tel: (0561) 40 34 67.

ZELLER, ADRIEN
France, EPP (Centre; UDF-CDS)

M.Adrien Zeller, Mayor of Saverne, was elected to EP in 1989 on French Centre Party list headed by Mme Simone Veil; leader, French delegation on EPP Gp and mbr of bureau; mbr, EP Cmte on Social Affairs, Employment and the Working Environment; a vice-chmn, Cmte on Rules of Procedure, Verification of Credentials and Immunities. Deputy for Bas-Rhin; was Secretary of State for Social Affairs; former regional councillor in Alsace; former MEP. Agricultural engineer; held post of principal administrator with EC Commission. B 1940.

Address: 23 rue Erckmann-Chatrian, 67700 Saverne.

Thatcherism sets tone for Euro manifestos

By Philip Webster
Chief Political Correspondent of *The Times*

On September 20, 1988, Margaret Thatcher went to Bruges in Belgium and delivered a speech which was to have momentous repercussions for Britain's relations with her European partners and for the history of the Community over the years that followed.

Setting her face against moves towards economic and monetary union, the Prime Minister warned against the folly of trying to fit independent nations into "some sort of Identikit European personality."

It would be highly damaging to try to suppress nationhood and concentrate power at the centre of a European conglomerate, she said. "We have not successfully rolled back the frontiers of the state in Britain only to see them reimposed at a European level with a European superstate exercising a new dominance from Brussels."

Mrs Thatcher's uncompromising rejection of proposals for European integration and apparent insistence on a Thatcherite future for Europe was to set the tone for the way the political parties in Britain presented themselves to the electorate in the third direct election to the European Parliament.

For it had the effect of polarizing attitudes within and between the parties about the future of Europe.

The impact of that speech, and others in the same vein, was to be seen in the programmes that the main political parties in Britain put to the electorate in the third direct elections to the European Parliament on June 15, 1989.

In many ways it was the roles reversal election. The Conservative Party's manifesto, despite the efforts of the strong European wing of the party to tone down what they saw as its anti-Community sentiments, captured much of the spirit of Bruges.

The Labour Party, who as recently as 1983 had gone to the country on a pledge to withdraw from the European Community, produced a document which spoke enthusiastically of Labour's wish to work constructively and in harmony with Britain's partners in Europe.

The Tories, traditionally pro-European and internationalist, found themselves in danger of being cast in a negative, little Englander role. Labour, traditionally more introspective and doubtful about the Community, found itself campaigning on a proposition that it was more truly European than Mrs Thatcher's Conservatives.

Britain's third party, the Social and Liberal Democrats, again left no doubt in the voters' minds that it was the most strongly pro-European of them all. In a manifesto which differed little in substance from that of the European Parliament's Liberal and Democratic group, the SLD called for Britain to take her place in the dynamic mainstream of the Community.

The Conservative Party

Deep divisions within the Conservative Party over the future of the European Community meant that its manifesto for the elections needed to be drafted with high skill and extreme sensitivity.

Mrs Thatcher gave the task to one of her ministers blessed with a comfortable degree of both. Mr Christopher Patten, then the Minister for Overseas Development and one of Mrs Thatcher's speechwriters for many years, successfully squared the circle of avoiding the worst excesses of Europeanism while making clear that the Government would not accept some of the wilder dreams of the European federalists. Mr Patten was soon to enter the Cabinet as Secretary of State for the Environment.

The 62-page manifesto, *Leading Europe into the 1990s,* portrayed the Community not as a narrow, inward looking club but as a partnership of independent, sovereign countries aimed at securing the prosperity of their peoples.

The manifesto endorsed the "when the time is ripe" formula for entry into the exchange rate mechanism of the European Monetary System, but firmly opposed the vision of monetary and economic union envisaged in the controversial Delors report. It also opposed the social charter, abolition of frontier controls and harmonization of value added tax.

Mrs Thatcher asserted in a foreword: "We are leading Europe into the 1990s on a Conservative agenda. Only the Conservatives can be trusted to safeguard the achievements of the last decade and to rise to the challenge of the next.

"That means keeping Europe committed to the economics of freedom and enterprise. And it means taking a practical, constructive approach to new problems, like the threat to Europe's environment and the world. We believe in a Europe of independent sovereign states cooperating freely, in a climate of economic liberty, for our common good.

"We believe in a Europe committed firmly to the defence of the West. We believe in a Europe whose industries are more competitive, whose economies are more open and prosperous, and whose people have greater choice and freedom. We believe in a Europe whose nations need not sacrifice their uniqueness, but can build together to enhance the quality of life of all their citizens."

The detailed proposals were:

Enterprise and the single market: Mrs Thatcher's deep opposition to full implementation of the Delors report on monetary union, which envisaged a staged move towards the creation of a single European currency and central bank, was strongly expressed in the manifesto.

It said: "Full economic and monetary union would involve a fundamental transfer of sovereignty. It would require new European institutions to administer a common currency and decide interest rates, and a considerable degree of central control over budgetary policy.

"The Delors report as taken as a whole implies nothing less than the creation of a federal Europe. Such ideas go way beyond what is realistic or desirable in the foreseeable future.

"Indeed, to think in these terms is not only unrealistic but damaging, for it distracts political attention and energy from the Community's central current task - completing the single market of 1992."

The Conservatives offered voters a package of Customs reforms in their manifesto. They said they planned to raise from £250 to £1,000 the value of goods that could be bought by travellers to the EC without incurring domestic VAT. In addition travellers who had bought goods in non-EC countries would have their VAT exemption limit raised from about £30 to £250.

The Conservative Government, it said, wanted to move in the long run towards the total abolition of such import taxes aimed at ending the discrepancy between high British car prices and lower ones on the Continent.

It proposed the removal of all tariffs on imports from less developed countries, meaning an end to the Community's system of 10 per cent blanket import tariffs alleviated by exemptions under the generalized system of preferences.This should give a boost to the hard pressed primary producers in developing countries.

The manifesto rejected the European Commission's plans for tax harmonization. "We do not believe that compulsory harmonization or approximation of indirect tax rates within the Community, whether of VAT or excise duties, is necessary for the succcssful operation of the single market.

"As the United States proves, it is possible to retain control of such taxes at the state level without artificially distorting internal trade.

"To the extent that significant divergences exist, market forces will help iron them out so long as firms and individuals can import and export freely.

"Conservatives believe that tax harmonization should be a market-led process, and that fiscal frontiers can be abolished without such harmonization being compulsory.

"We have repeatedly made clear our intention to retain zero-rating on food, domestic fuel and power, and children's shoes and clothing. We stand by that pledge. We shall honour it."

The Conservatives, it promised, would take the single market programme forward to include: The complete liberalization of financial services; the elimination of the remaining delays and bureaucracy at frontiers; free competition in public purchasing within the Community; further liberalisation of continental air travel and bus and coach services; a common system for patents and other intellectual property.

Rejecting the social charter it stated:

"We believe that each country should be left to frame its own laws on social and industrial relations according to national experience and requirements. These are not matters which cut across European competition, European free trade or the interests of European consumers.

"Accordingly, we oppose any legislation which might unnecessarily inhibit the free flow of labour or investment in the Community by establishing extra burdens on business.

"We do not believe in the rigid imposition on every European company of mandatory worker participation. Of course employees should be encouraged to have a stake in the firm for which they work; but obligatory participation is as nonsensical as compulsory volunteering. The idea of mandatory participation is rooted in a class conscious idea of industry, which has less and less meaning in the modern world."

International: Nato is the other channel of Britain's contribution to Europe, said the manifesto. It was the "sturdy determination" of Western Europe and the United States that had brought about the INF treaty and the reduction in Soviet force superiority.

Europe should try to speak as one on the great international issues of the day. When it did; it counted as more than one nation alone. But Europe stretched across the boundaries of the EC, encompassing those lying behind the Iron Curtain. No European could be content while the Berlin Wall stood to divide their nations. The manifesto warned against giving the American allies the impression of "wanting the benefits of peace on the cheap." It said that as Europe grew wealthier it must do more for its own defence.

Calling for a "war-free Europe" the Conservatives pledged modernisation of Britain's nuclear deterrent, and the updating of Nato nuclear forces. While Europe needed to defend itself militarily, it must not become a trade fortress. The single market should be a step towards greater trade liberalisation across the world.

Pollution and quality of life: The manifesto committed Britain to work with EC and other countries to counter threats to the environment. Farmers, it said, had the crucial part to play in maintaining the British countryside and allowing it to be enjoyed by all - not as a museum but as a living community. Therefore Britain could press for greater use of environmentally sensitive areas and of set-aside of redundant agricultural land to protect the natural habitat. It promised to ensure that Commission proposals on pesticides and nitrates were "relevant and sensible" and that the rules applied equally to all member states. It would seek to change the CAP to strike a better balance between agriculture and conservation.

The manifesto promised the consumer the highest degree of sensible protection over food standards, better labelling and realistic rules on plant and animal health. It backed a permanent ban on seal-hunting and the development of alternatives to experiments on live animals.

While defending its record on river quality, it said it wanted to do better by setting new goals with firm timetables for implementation. It promised tough new controls on the quality of drinking water, £1 billion over four years for improving sewage treatment and disposal and stricter controls on dangerous industrial effluents. Bathing water standards off the beaches would meet "relevant EC standards." The manifesto included a firm commitment to nuclear power, while working for the highest standards of safety including waste disposal. There would be even tighter controls on the shipping and dumping of hazardous waste.

Budgetary reform: The Conservatives had saved the country £5 billion since 1985 from the reforms of the EC budget, the manifesto claimed. Legally binding limits had been imposed in the CAP, cutting its growth from 10 per cent a year to a projected 2 per cent.

"Reforming the CAP makes sense for farmers as well as for taxpayers and consumers - it is the best way to ensure the continued success of British agriculture in what is bound to become an ever more competitive market place."

The manifesto recognised the difficulties facing farmers, saying that the Government had improved their position by securing regular adjustments in the green pound. It had also helped by achieving an agreement to phase out completely by 1992 the so-called monetary compensatory amounts, resulting from divergences between the green pound and real exchange rates.

The manifesto promises better value for money from the CAP; a bigger role for market forces in determining farm prices; a greater emphasis on the interests of the consumer; making farm price intervention a safety net, not an alternative market; a crackdown on fraud and a reduction in waste and efficiency; strict application of agricultural stabilisers; encouraging farmers to match output to consumer demands and to develop other sources of income; better enforcement of Community rules on illegal fishing and close monitoring of fish stocks and the finances of fishermen.

The revival of Britain: The manifesto stated that Britain had breathed new life into its partnership with its neighbours. It underlined the Tory commitment to Europe: "Our present and future lies with them."

The Conservatives concluded their appeal thus: "Only the narrowest of margins - 15 seats - gives the Conservatives and our allies a majority over the left in the European Parliament. That is why these European elections matter so much. They will make a difference to the way we can stand up for Britain's interests and the way we can protect and enhance Europe's.

"There are many things that we once did on our own that we now willingly do with our European partners. We cooperate with them because that is the way we do things better - for example, protect our environment and increase our trade.

"With the creation of the single market European cooperation takes a significant step forward. We will be making something new — opening up fresh opportunities, setting ourselves and our partners unfamiliar challenges.

"To make the best of these opportunities, to rise to these challenges, we need a like-minded team at Westminster and at Strasbourg - inspired by the same convictions, committed to the same principles of enterprise, freedom and choice."

The Labour Party

Labour's 1989 Euro manifesto marked Neil Kinnock's success in six years as party leader in reversing his party's attitude to the Community.

The party's 1984 general election manifesto declared that the next Labour Government would be bound to find continued membership "a most serious obstacle." Withdrawal was therefore the right policy for Britain.

Five years later, Labour declared that it wanted Britain to take full advantage of working with "our European partners." Indeed, a main theme of its campaign throughout was that Labour was more constructively European in intent and spirit than Mrs Thatcher. In the document, Labour committed itself to making the single market work and accused the Conservatives of failing to prepare Britain for 1992. It urged reform of the CAP and higher environmental standards while opposing full scale monetary union and harmonizing of VAT rates, Tory policies both.

Labour also shared the Tory caution about joining the exchange rate mechanism of the European monetary system, suggesting, although not quite in so many words, that Labour would join when the time was right.

The main issue of difference between Tory and Labour was the so-called social dimension.

Labour enthusiastically backed the European Commission's plan to lay down for all member states a social charter on worker participation and industrial relationships. Labour's aim was clearly to present itself as the better European, a task helped by some of Mrs Thatcher's statements the previous year, particularly the Bruges speech, and the intepretation of them as anti-European. There was help as well because of the divisions within the Tory ranks over Mrs Thatcher's attitudes.

So Labour's document, *Meeting the Challenge in Europe,* set the seal on Labour's final conversion to support for the European Community after a history of bitter feuding on the issue.

Calling for the use of Europe's combined strength to tackle common problems, it concentrated on attacking the Government for failing to prepare Britain adequately for the single European market in 1992.

It described Margaret Thatcher as being "out of sympathy with the European agenda." It focussed less sharply on solely European issues than the Tory document and instead based its main appeal on its comprehensive policy review launched the previous month.

On the future of Europe the line was not too dissimilar from Mrs Thatcher's. The document said: "We see the path to future progress as being one of closer and closer cooperation rather than an attempt to create a United States of Europe."

Labour said the Community in 1992 should not become a fortress Europe closed to the goods of outside producers and the party objected to the creation of a centralized tier of government in Brussels.

Neil Kinnock, in a foreword, said that Labour wanted to use the combined strength of Europe to meet common problems like the threat to the environment, and saw an urgent need for more investment in education, training and research and development.

He accused the Conservatives of blocking or delaying the operation of every progressive Community measure "no matter how it would raise standards of environmental improvement, trading conditions or education provision."

Attacking the Conservatives, he said: "For them the future is in deregulation without social obligation. To them Western Europe must only be a barrier-free trade group without any cooperative responsibilities. To them Europe must only be a market, not a community." He called for the collective strength of the Community to be used to encourage change in the wider world but promised: "We will retain in our own Parliament the rights of determination on issues that are of direct and important national interest."

Labour's key proposals were:

Economy: It stated that the European Monetary System, as at present constituted, suffered from too great an emphasis on deflationary measures as a means of achieving monetary targets, "and substantial changes would therefore be required before we could take sterling into the exchange rate mechanism."

It added: "We do not at present see any advantage in trying to create a full-scale monetary union."

Mr Kinnock explained that a Labour Government would not contemplate entering the ERM until there were proper arrangements for financial support during the transitional period, an expanded role for the social and regional funds in the EC, an agreed EC growth strategy and until Britain was able to join at a "competitive rate."

It called for fundamental reform of the Community budget, saying: "Labour wants a great improvement in the balance between expenditure on the structural funds and expenditure on agriculture. Furthermore, we do not accept the argument put forward by the Commission, for the need to harmonize VAT rates or for the ending of zero rating."

Social Charter: The manifesto stated that Labour was enthusiastically committed to the proposals for a social Europe - a "European Community where workplaces are safe and workers are well trained, fully consulted and properly rewarded throughout the course of their working lives, and a Europe where the role and contribution of women is properly recognized."

The document explained that Labour supported the Community proposals for employees' statutory rights to negotiate and participate with management. "We support a legal right for workers to be informed about major changes in their company. We will back proposals on extending rights to part-time workers, which will greatly improve the position of many women workers. We will end the Tory opposition to the directive on rights for temporary workers. We will lift the Tory imposed veto on directives covering such issues as the use of dangerous substances, protection against biological agents at work, requirements for work with visual display units, and equal treatment for men and women in statutory and occupational social security schemes."

European rights: Labour would strengthen the law to require positive action to promote equal rights for women. It wanted to establish a range of childcare services providing for the education, welfare and care of children under five and for older children out of school. "We also aim to help families with the real costs of bringing up children, by providing better child and maternity benefits."

Labour would provide millions of carers, mostly women, who looked after elderly and infirm relatives, with an extended invalid care allowance backed with help from high quality community health and care services. Labour would establish statutory rights to minimum pay and rights to equal pay for full and part-time workers. It wanted to extend opportunities for women in work by introducing accessible training that would enable them to update and improve their skills.

Industry: Labour would press for Europe-wide policies for industry including the development of a coherent strategy to build industries capable of competing with the Americans and Japanese. It called for cooperation between governments to ensure that multinational companies were not able to play one country off against another; more cooperative efforts at European level to improve scientific and technological research; a new priority for investment and training, backed by more money from the social fund; and new programmes of investment to improve the infrastructure like public transport and telecommunications.

Environment: Labour is committed to a programme to improve the environment and proposed an environmental protection executive independent of government to implement and monitor standards. "We want to see the quality of drinking water raised and our beaches cleaned up. We want to cut back atmospheric pollution dramatically and reduce the threat from global warming. We want to tackle litter-strewn streets and noisy neighbourhoods and ban the trade in hazardous wastes. We will ensure that our housing and transport policies make a major contribution to improving the environment in which people live. We will help councils to clean up the local environment, institute research programmes to find solutions to current problems amd predict future problems, and introduce a major programme of energy conservation."

Agriculture: Labour proposed a system based on countryside management agreements designed to channel support to farmers most in need. It proposed a shift of emphasis from agricultural policy to food policy, intending to change the nature of the Ministry of Agriculture and to establish a Food Standards Agency. The CAP was still "desperately expensive, highly wasteful and environmentally damaging."

The Challenge of 1992: British industry was said by Labour to be "dangerously ill-prepared for the competitive world of the 1990s" when North Sea oil would no longer be such an advantage. There was a huge skill gap between Britain and her competitors who had invested more in training, research and new technology. Britain was steadily losing its share of world markets. Unless something was done after 1992 "jobs and investment will drain away from Britain to the more prosperous parts of Europe" and more and more industries would be sold to the highest bidder. "On present form 1992 will be a disaster for Britain rather than an opportunity."

Labour would set up a body called British Technology Enterprise to work with industry to develop hi-tech firms. It proposed a new national programme for science, a stronger Department of Trade and Industry and a tough new policy on mergers, with bidders having to prove that the merger was in the public interest. Labour would boost regional policy by "devolving economic power from Whitehall to new elected national and regional assemblies."

The Social and Liberal Democratic Party

Once again, after the 1989 European elections, Britain's main centre party was left ruing the fact that its overtly pro-European stance had counted for little when the votes were cast. The Social and Liberal Democrats, formed a year before from the amalgamation of the old Liberal Party and the old Social Democratic Party, again failed to win a seat and, despite its obvious environmental credentials, suffered the ignominy of finishing behind the Green Party in terms of the share of the vote cast.

The SLD, short title the Democrats, probably did not suffer because of its Europeanism. Rather, the European elections came before it had recovered from the trauma of its painful birth and the parting of the ways with Dr David Owen who, always opposed to the merger, kept his SDP in existence as a separate party when the SLD was formed.

Under its new leader, Paddy Ashdown, the SLD unashamedly presented itself to the electorate as the only party fully committed to the ideal of a federal, democratic European Union.

It told the nation in its *Manifesto for a People's Europe*: "For too long our country has been shut off from the rest of the world by the insular chauvinism of the two old parties. Through missing, time and time again, opportunities for full participation in the activities of the European Community, we have lost chances to boost our economy and expand consumer choice, improve our approach to environmental protection and social justice, and use our and our partners' voice to promote peace and prosperity on a global scale."

It said: "Working together with our Liberal and Democrat allies in every Community nation we pledge ourselves to fight for you in Europe by fighting for the European ideal. Tories and Labour cannot do this: Mrs Thatcher is unique not only in missing the European train but announcing in advance that she intends to miss it; and Conservatives and Labour stand together as one in opposing the development of democracy and the people's voice in the Community."

The Democrats made their appeal on the following central policies:

Economy and completion of the single market: Stating that the establishment of a European central bank in London building on British financial expertise is clearly desirable, the SLD said it would not happen if the Government maintained its "blinkered" opposition to the proposals for economic and monetary union, which was risking the development of a two-speed Europe with Britain left behind in the slow lane.

It therefore called for:

● Immediate British entry into the exchange rate mechanism of the European Monetary System, providing much-needed exchange rate stability without resort to excessively high interest rates.

● A unified approach to monetary policy, including moves towards the establishment of a European central bank, committed to the objective of non-inflationary sustainable growth, leading to the eventual creation of a common European currency and full economic union.

● The development of a Community economic strategy, promoting investment in industry, ensuring adequate supplies of skilled labour, and stimulating innovation in private enterprise.

In order to take full advantage of the single market, the SLD proposed:

● Agreement on Community-wide high minimum standards of consumer and environmental protection and health and safety regulations.

● Real freedom of movement between Community nations, including a passport union and the abolition of routine border controls.

● Greater coordination between Community police forces to fight crime and drug-trafficking.

● An effective competition policy examining mergers and takeovers in a strategic European context.

● Community control over state subsidies to "lame duck" industries.

● Gradual tax "approximation" over time - tax uniformity was unnecessary and undesirable, it said.

Environment: The Community, it said, as shown by its calls for more rigorous controls over vehicle exhausts and higher standards of water purity, was a far more effective defender of health and environment than the British Prime Minister.

The aim must be to build an economy and society that was environmentally sustainable. The SLD called for: Reduction of pollution to levels which avoid harm to human health; an immediate ban on the discharge of untreated effluents into the sea; establishment of a Community environmental early warning unit to which the effects of chronic pollution or environmental accidents would be reported.

It also called for: An urgent increase in funding for development of renewable sources of energy; top priority for energy conservation; drastic reduction of environmentally damaging emissions from fossil-fuelled power stations; phasing out of dependence on nuclear fission power as fast as possible.

It proposed incentives to farmers to adopt less intensive systems to protect the environment, reduce water pollution and soil erosion.

Political development: The SLD proposed policies to strengthen democratic control over the powers that have already left Westminster, and over the anonymous economic forces which national governments alone can no longer control.

It called for: Euro MPs to be elected by a common system based on PR; the appointment of individual members of the Commission to be subject to European Parliament veto; powers for the Parliament to pass legislation agreed with the Commission should the Council fail to adopt or reject the measure within a specified time; ending of secret meetings of the Council; extension of majority voting in the Council of Ministers to areas of environmental and social policy currently subject to the veto.

Social Justice: The SLD called for the regional and social dimensions of the Community to be given equal priority with the 1992 programme to ensure that all

European citizens share in the prosperity and the jobs that the single market will create.

It proposed: The doubling of the social and regional development funds over the next four years; making Community spending truly additional to national and local funding; a Community "working women's charter" settling out entitlements to training for women entering the labour market and protection against discrimination.

International: The SLD called for a strengthening of European cooperation in defence policy, through establishing a strong European pillar within Nato and injecting a sense of purpose and dynamism into the Western European Union; a common policy for defence procurement; the imposition by the Community of mandatory sanctions against South Africa; the Community to work together within the United Nations and Nato to play a part in improving relations between East, West and Central Europe.

The Green Party

After the Green Party's astonishing rise to third place in the 1989 elections one of the big questions in British politics was : "What do they stand for?" People knew that the party's basic stance was the care and protection of the earth and its species. But what else were the Greens offering to the British people? The Conservatives and the Social and Liberal Democrats, who appeared to have suffered most at the hands of the Greens, consoled themselves with the thought that the electorate, if it really understood the Green party's defence and economic policies, would not vote for it at a general election.

Whatever the truth of that, the Greens' rise spurred its political opponents into action on the environmental front. Old "green" policies were dusted off; there was immediate talk of "green" ministers and shadow ministers being appointed.

The Greens in Britain stood on a Europe-wide platform agreed with their colleagues in 14 other countries. That ultimately seeks a Europe of autonomous regions without any borders, with local production for local needs using energy-saving non-polluting methods.

Its manifesto *Don't let your world turn grey* called for the maximum self-reliance of the regions of Europe, with an emphasis on the production of local goods for local needs, and on human effort rather than a dependence on ever more complex technology. "This does not mean a return to the handloom or customs posts at every county boundary; it simply means that each region would be encouraged to develop a varied and sustainable local economy which would enable it to survive even in difficult times. Trading between regions would be an essential supplement to local production, but would not be seen as the only way to trade, as it is at present."

The Greens called for a Europe without military alliances, a policy plank its opponents began highlighting from the moment the size of the Green vote began to become apparent on the night the votes were counted, and predicted eventual failure for the 1992 single market. It said that the concept of ever-expanding consumption within a free-for-all European marketplace was profoundly unecological, unsustainable, and doomed to fail. "The demands of the world economy will inevitably overwhelm calls for a fair internal market. With an end to monetary barriers, wealth will migrate even more quickly to those areas which are already wealthy, while the peripheral areas will continue to be fed grudgingly with money for inappropriate projects like wall-to-wall holiday apartments and nuclear waste dumps.

The manifesto said: "Our guiding principle is that no authority be held at a higher level than is absolutely necessary." They called for environmental taxes on goods and resources, a shift to renewable sources of energy, revitalization of water networks, organic farming and more flexible working. They proposed a halt to the dumping of all human, industrial and nuclear waste at sea, with all nations policing waters to a 12-mile limit.

The manifesto called for a long-term food supply strategy, replacing farm and distribution policies with those that promoted health and quality over profit, and legislation against unrestricted economic growth, the development of extensive energy conservation programmes, a ban on ozone damaging gases, an end to the reprocessing of nuclear waste. The Greens opposed the Community as it is, seeking a

Europe of regions and an enlarged European Confederation. They supported greater powers for the Parliament over the Commission and the Council of Ministers.

Its defence policy is set out thus: "The Green Party is concerned that the distinctions between the EEC and Nato have become blurred. Although EEC citizens have not been consulted, preparations have already been made for a fully nuclear-capable European Army. All European green parties are committed to a Europe free from nuclear, biological and chemical weapons. At a time when the United States and the USSR are negotiating weapons reductions and European public opinion is clearly supportive of moves towards lasting peace, we think it is disgraceful that a new European military superpower is being created with no democratic mandate."

The Greens also proposed steps to reduce the size of the European population in order to achieve a sustainable economy. "Encouraging people to limit the number of children they have need not involve repression; what is needed is accurate information about population, appropriate education, and easy access to safe and pleasant birth control materials. Because Europe is the most densely populated continent in the world, we believe that it is irresponsible for national governments to call for an increase in birth rates under any circumstances. The Green Party would like to see a programme to reduce European birth rates. Only then will we have a moral right to encourage poorer countries to do likewise."

The Social Democratic Party

The European elections of 1989 were the first that the SDP, headed by Dr David Owen, had failed to fight as a national party. A squeeze on finances meant a scaling down of activities with only 16 candidates standing in the Euro poll.

But its manifesto *In Europe for Good* maintained the former Social Democratic Party's enthusiastic support for the European Community without endorsing the federal vision of their former partners, the Social and Liberal Democrats.

The SDP criticized Labour for using Europe as a stick with which to beat Mrs Thatcher; the Prime Minister for seeing Europe as "an idea to ridicule, an institution to browbeat;" and the SLD for wanting a federated United States of Europe, "something as unrealistic as it is unwanted by the British people."

It stated: "The European Community is a coalition of governments and by failing to accept this concept Mrs Thatcher's Government has made Britain no more than a grudging player in someone else's game.

"Our nation is suffering from this stubborn insularity. There will be a European system of central banks, but it could be in Frankfurt, not London. There will be a "social Europe" but it may not take full account of British social needs. There will be a single market in Europe, but our companies may not gain fully from it. Narrow minded nationalism in Europe is a betrayal of British interests.

The SDP put forward the main themes of a programme for Europe as follows:

Security: Experience in two world wars demonstrated the dangers of a divided Europe, the manifesto stated. In the Second World War it stood alone until the Japanese attacked the United States at Pearl Harbor. That served as a warning against relying on the US nuclear guarantee in perpetuity. As long as the Soviet Union had nuclear weapons, Britain and France should keep their deterrents.

Democracy: The SDP existed to change the basis of British democracy. "Our democratic system was once the most respected in the world. It is now no longer admired. We are the most centralised European country. Our voting system is distorted and unfair, our Government unrepresentative and the absence of a Bill of Rights is a grave omission. Only within a more sensitive, responsive, and proportional democracy will our people's wish to preserve and conserve their environment be properly reflected."

Prosperity: The SDP championed the creation of a social market in Britain, encouraging profit and enterprise while building a sound social foundation. This was the best way to prepare for a vigorous single market by 1992. "We believe in Green Growth combining affordable public expenditure to deal with environmental concerns and the principle that the polluter pays. Our goal is a country in which the market serves the consumer, responding to individual choice.

"The SDP does not see Europe as a harnessed giant, outwardly domineering and

283

inwardly demanding uniformity. We desire an open self-assured society that is centralized where necessary and close to the citizens where possible.

"The SDP does not want to see our country squander the opportunity to increase our security, democracy and prosperity. That is what the European Community of sovereign states offers us. We are now in Europe permanently. We must ensure we are in Europe for good."

The European People's Party

Ardent advocacy of the goal of ultimate European union formed the basis of the appeal to the European electorate of the European People's Party, the party of the Christian Democrats within the Community and which attracted its first UK representative - from Northern Ireland - after the 1989 elections.

"Our goal is the United States of Europe, " said the introduction to its manifesto *On the People's Side.* "Only a Europe which speaks with one voice can bring its whole weight to its political and economic responsibilities in the world and make its contribution to overcoming the division of Europe. Only a united Europe can protect its natural environment and rehabilitate it. Only a European Community which comes together to form a security union can in the long term guarantee peace, justice and freedom in Europe, be an equal partner in the Atlantic Alliance and be a factor for peace in the world. Only a strong and self-confident Europe is capable of meeting its commitments to the people of the third world."

In easily the most aggressively pro-European manifesto on offer in 1989, it said: "The European People's Party sees it as its historical duty to push forward with the unification of Europe and to bring this process to its conclusion. Therefore our most important future task is the further development of the European Community to a political union, to a socially responsible economic and monetary union and to a security union."

In pursuit of its objective of the progressive realisation of the United States of Europe, with a government responsible to the democratically-elected European Parliament and given all the powers of law-making and control of the administration, the EPP demanded:

Continuation of the reforms of the Single European Act to strengthen the Parliament in its authority and rights. The Parliament, with the Council fo Ministers, must be part of a joint legislative procedure.

That the Commission should increasingly undertake the duties of a government and concentrate on problems which national governments could not cope with individually.

That the Community be given its own powers on taxation, although this must not lead to an increase in the overall burden of taxation in the Community. Decision-making on taxation would be transferred to the budget authority, namely the Parliament and the Council of Ministers. It said, nevertheless, that the financing of the Community must respect the financial autonomy both of the member states and the Community.

That the Parliament draw up a new draft treaty for European Union containing those proposals. National parliaments and governments would ratify the treaty and the acceptance of such a constitution by the parliaments and governments of a majority of the member states would lead to a situation where the more reluctant governments "will not be able to stand aside from the construction of European union." It went on: "Only a decisive step, not influenced by those who wish to prevent unity, can move the opponents of union towards sensible compromise."

The completion of the internal market, with the removal of frontiers for people, goods, services and capital provided the essential basis.

It proposed a Europe which would give European citizens the chance to live, work and study in other countries when the frontier posts had been taken away. There should be a Europe of the citizens, in which there was a real right to security. The Community must improve its common policy for dealing with terrorism, crime and drug trafficking.

The road to European union favoured by the EPP was similar to that propounded in the contentious report from M Jacques Delors, president of the Commission - harmonisation of the powers of supervision of central banks, creation of a European currency union, and then the creation of a European central bank.

Confederation of European Socialist Parties (The Socialist Group)

The British Labour Party happily endorsed the majority of the text of the Socialist Group's manifesto for the European elections.

But on the key issues of parliamentary control and sovereignty it was at variance with its sister parties.

Labour declined to go along with an important passage of the Socialist manifesto calling for a big increase in the powers of the European Parliament.

Extracts which Labour did not accept included the following: It stated that the 1992 objectives would demand big changes in the EEC. "The creation of the internal market is leading to a profound restructuring of economic power. Accordingly it is necessary to reinforce the machinery of democratic control so as to ensure that vested interests do not accumulate excessive power at the expense of the citizens and their elected representatives. It is a matter of absolute priority to complete the legal framework and strengthen the institutions in such a way that the Community authorities will be able to defend the public interest."

It said that as the volume and pace of decision making in the Community had increased in the run-up to 1992, faults in the Community'a democratic processes had emerged. "Unfortunately the loss of control on the part of the national parliament has not been offset by a parallel increase in the responsibilities of the European Parliament. The touchstone of Community democracy is respect for parliamentary democracy as the system which, with most certainty, safeguards the rule of law and the rights of citizens."

It said that "no area of EC policy should be exempt from parliamentary control and the European Parliament must play a key role in the democratic control of the Community and the Community decision-making process."

It said that the European Parliament rendered the Single European Act possible by means of the 1984 draft treaty on European union. "It now has the duty and responsibility of laying the foundation, on a democratic basis, of the next step forward."

The Socialists set the following objectives for the work of the next European Parliament: Strengthening of the power and democratic legitimacy of the Commission; progressive achievement of a system of full co-decision-making between the Parliament and the Council of Ministers, together with an extension of majority voting in the Council; increased participation by the Parliament on decisions affecting the Community budget.

In other respects, the document was fully supported by Labour. It set the creation of employment as its highest priority. It said the Community must guarantee to the more than 16 million people without work the right to work at a time when its wealth was increasing. "We must gurantee equality of rights and opportunities for men, women and young people."

It said that European monetary cohesion over the last 10 years or so had found partial expression only in the European Monetary System, which should be tranformed to improve its operations.

It said the EMS must not be an end in itself; it was an instrument for ensuring better exchange rate stability, but it must also allow the introduction of expansionist non-inflationary economic policies.

"The aim of the EMS could be achieved by integrating the European currencies that are not yet part of the exchange rate system, but this would have to be in such a way as to take account of the different economic conditions within individual countries and must be accompanied by measures to prevent financial disruption."

On defence the Socialists said: "The system of nuclear deterrence is an element of the military security system in Europe. Our long term aim is still to overcome the system of mutual deterrence by arms reductions and by reducing antagonisms within a peaceful European and world order. As long as nuclear weapons exist they should only be instruments for deterrence, never for war-fighting. We are committed, however, to reducing the scale and impact of that component. In particular we wish to reach the situation where conventional stability enables both alliances to abolish all non-strategic nuclear weapons."

The European Commission

The present European Commission took office on January 6 1989 under the Presidency, for a second four year term, of M. Jacques Delors of France. For the first time, women commissioners were appointed. The portfolios of the Commissioners are as follows:

Jacques Delors (France), President - Secretariat General, Legal Services, Monetary Affairs, Spokesman's Service, Joint Interpreting and Conference Service, Think Tank, Security Office.

Frans Andriessen (Netherlands) - External relations and trade policy, cooperation with other European countries.

Henning Christophersen (Denmark) - Economic and financial affairs, coordination of structural instruments, statistical office.

Manuel Marin (Spain) - Cooperation and development (Lome), fisheries.

Filippo Maria Pandolfi (Italy) - Research and science, telecommunications, information technology and innovation, joint research centre.

Martin Bangemann (West Germany) - Internal market and industrial affairs, relations with the European Parliament.

Sir Leon Brittan (United Kingdom) - Competition policy, financial institutions.

Carlo Ripa Di Meana (Italy) - Environment, nuclear safety, civil protection.

Antonio Cardoso E Cunha (Portugal) - Personnel and administration, energy, Euratom supply agency, policy on small and medium sized enterprises, tourism, social economy.

Abel Matutes (Spain) - Mediterranean policy, relations with Latin America, North-South relations.

Peter Schmidhuber (West Germany) - Budget, financial control.

Mme Christiane Scrivener (France) - Taxation, customs union, obligatory levies (fiscal or social levies).

Bruce Millan (United Kingdom) - Regional policy.

Jean Dondelinger (Luxembourg) - Audio-visual policy, cultural affairs, information and communication policy, Citizens' Europe, Office for Official Publications.

Ray MacSharry (Ireland) - Agriculture, rural development.

Karel Van Miert (Belgium) - Transport, credit, investments and financial instruments, consumer protection.

Mrs Vasso Papandreou (Greece) - Social affairs and employment, education and training, human resources.

M. Jacques Delors has been President of the European Commission since January 1985; Economics, Finance and Budget Minister in governments formed by M Pierre Mauroy, 1981-84; MEP (Socialist list), 1979-81, and chaired EP Cmte on Economic and Monetary Affairs; became member of central committee of Socialist Party, in 1979; national coordinator for international economic relations of the party, 1976-79. Former adviser to Prime Minister on social and cultural affairs; has served on General Council of Banque de France; associate professor of business management at University of Paris-Dauphine. B Jul 20 1925.

Mr Frans Andriessen became a Commssioner in Feb 1981 with responsibilities for relations with European Parliament and competition policy; from Jan 1985 a Vice-President of Commission, handling agriculture. Dutch Minister for Finance 1977-79; became mbr, First Chamber of the of the States-General (Senate), in 1980; mbr of Second Chamber, 1967-77 (President, KVP Gp, 1971-77), and of Utrecht Provincial States 1958-67. B Apr 2 1929; degree in law at State Univ of Utrecht; from 1954-72 discharged various duties at Catholioc Institute for Housing.

Mr Henning Christophersen became a Vice-President of Commission in charge of the EC budget in Jan 1985. Mbr of Folketing (Danish Parliament) from 1971; Minister for Foreign Affairs, 1978-79, and Deputy Prime Minister and Minister for Finance, 1982-84; Chmn of Cl of Economic and Finance Ministers during Danish EC Presidency in second half of 1982. Acting national chmn of Liberal Party 1977 and chmn, 1978; chmn Liberal Party parliamentary gp, 1979-82. Mbr, Nordic Cl, 1981-82. B Nov 8 1939; graduated in economics from Copenhagen Univ. Economics reporter for weekly newspaper *Weekendavisen*, 1971-78.

Mr Manuel Marin became a Vice-President of the Commission in Jan 1986. Elected Spanish Deputy (Socialist mbr for Ciudad Real in southern Spain) in three general elections becoming mbr, Foreign Affairs and Defence Cmtes; mbr of consultative assembly of Cl of Europe, and of European Parliament - Spanish Cortes Joint Cmte. Was PSOE (Spanish Workers Socialist Party) spokesman on foreign affairs cmte of Cortes Generales. State Secretary for Relation with European Communities, 1982-85. B Oct 21 1949; law degree from Madrid Univ; a master's degree in Community law from Univ of Nancy; diploma in European Studies, Coll of Europe, Bruges, where he has also lectured.

Sgr Filippo Maria Pandolfi, aged 61 when he became a Commissioner in Jan 1989, was a Christian Democrat deputy in the Italian Parliament in 1968. Business connections with publishing. Under Secretary of State at Ministry of Finance, 1974-786 aand from 1976-88 was successively minister of finance, treasury, industry and agriculture.

Herr Martin Bengemann, lawyer and mbr of Free Democratic Party (Liberal), was German Federal Minister for Economic Affairs, 1984-88, becoming a Commissioner and a Vice-President in Jan 1989. Federal president of his party, 1985-88. Lawyer. Former mbr of Bundestag; MEP 1973-84, being chmn, Liberal and Democratic Gp, 1979-84 and deputy chmn, 1975-79, in nominated EP. B Nov 15 1934.

Sir Leon Brittan, QC, a UK Commissioner and one its its Vice-Presidents from Jan 1989, became Secretary of State for Trade and Industry in 1985; resigned in 1986 during controversy over the future of the Westland helicopter company. Barrister; former company director and consultant. Home Secretary, 1983-85; Chief Secretary to the Treasury with seat in Cabinet, 1981-83; Minister of State, Home Office, 1979-81. Cons MP for Richmond (Yorks), 1983-88; MP for Cleveland and Whitby, Feb 1974-1983. B Sep 25 1939; ed Haberdashers' Aske's Sch; Trinity Coll, Cambridge (Pres of Union, 1960); Yale Univ. Bencher, Inner Temple, since 1983.

Sgr Carlo Ripa Di Meana, journalist, joined the EC Commission in Jan 1985. Was Italian Socialist Party MEP 1979-84, serving on Cmte on Transport and Political Affairs Cmte. Was in Communist Party but left it to join Socialists in 1958. In 1970 was elected a Lombardy regional councillor. Chaired FUSIE, an Italian press federation. Chmn, Biennial International Exhibition of Modern Art in Venice, 1974-79; has also served on board of La Scala in Milan. Led international section of Italian Socialist Party, 1979-80. In 1983 he became President of the Institute for International Economic Co-operation and Development Problems. B Aug 15 1929.

Senhor Cardoso e Cunha, who became a Commissioner in 1986, has held Portuguese Govt posts of Secretary of State for Foreign Trade in 1978, Secretary of State for Industry, 1979; and Minister of Agriculture and Fisheries, 1980-81. Elected Social Democrat MP in general elections of 1979, 1980 and 1985. B Jan 28 1934. Chemical and industrial engineer. Lived in Angola, 1965-77, where he was managing director of group of private companies; had seat in Angola Legislative Assembly. In Portugal became director of mining, industrial and civil construction companies.

Señor Abel Matutes became a Commissioner in 1986 following a business career that included directorships of a bank, hotel chain and holding company; deputy chmn, Ibiza and Formentera Tourist Board, 1964-79; Mayor of Ibiza, 1970-71. Senator for Ibiza and Formentera, elected in 1977 and re-elected in 1979 elections; Alianza Popujlar deputy for Balearic Islands, elected in 1982; Popular Gp spokesman fr Congress of Deputies' Economics and Finance Cmte. Party posts held include chmn of Alianca Popular's national electoral and economic and finance cmtes, and deputy national chmn of party.

Herr Peter Schmidhuber became an EC Commissioner in Sep 1987. From 1978, mbr of Bundesrat (Federal Upper House of Parliament), Bavarian Parliament, Bavarian Minister of State for Federal Affairs and Federal Govt representative of Bavarian Free State. From 1965-69 and 1972-78, mbr of Bundestag (Federal Lower House of Parliament), Cl of Europe and WEU. B Dec 15 1931; lawyer; mbr of CSU and has held various party offices.

Mme Christiane Scrivener, businesswoman, was Secretary of State for Consumer Affairs during the presidency of M. Giscard d'Estaing, 1976-78. MEP 1979-88, serving on Cmtes on Budgets and Budgetary Control; rapporteur EC budget, 1984. Was asst general secretary, Republican Party; adviser to chmn of agency for technical, industrial and economic cooperation. Former Electricite de France administrator. A vice-chair of Kangaroo Gp. Joined Commission in Jan 1989. B Sep 1 1925; ed Paris Univ; Springfield Univ, Massachusetts; Harvard Business Sch.

Mr Bruce Millan, a UK Commissioner from Jan 1989, was Labour's Secretary of State for Scotland from 1976-79, and in Opposition its chief spokesman on Scotland from 1979-83. Mbr, shadow Cabinet, 1981-83; Minister of State for Scotland, responsible for Scottish Economic Planning Department, 1974-76; an Opposition spokesman on Scotland, 1973-74, and on industry, 1970-73; Under Secretary of State for Scotland, 1966-70; Under Secretary of State for Defence for the RAF, 1964-66. MP for Glasgow, Govan, 1983-86, and for Glasgow, Craigton, 1959-83; contested that seat, 1955, and West Renfrewshire, 1951. Chartered accountant. Was parly adviser, Inst of Chartered Accountants of Scotland. B Oct 5 1927; ed Harris Acad, Dundee. Mbr, Cl of Europe and WEU, 1984-88. Sponsored as MP by trade union Apex.

Mr Jean Dondelinger was Luxembourg's deputy permanent representative in Brussels 1961-70 and its permanent representastive, as Ambassador, 1970-84 when he became Secretary-General of Luxembourg's Ministry of Foreign Affairs. Chaired negotiating group on Single European Act and was vice-chmn of international conference on satellite television frequencies. In 1984, became chmn of Warehouse Service Agency. A Commissioner from Jan 1989. B Jul 4 1930; lawyer; studied at St Antony's Coll, Oxford.

Mr Ray McSharry, a Commissioner from Jan 1989, was President of the Cl of Budget Ministers when Ireland had the Presidency of EC in 1979; was MEP 1984-87 when he became Minister of Finance and Public Affairs. Was vice-chmn in EP of RDE Gp. Mbr, Dail, from 1969; Minister of State, Department of Finance, 1977-79; Minister for Agriculture, 1979-81; Deputy Prime Minister and Minister for Finance, Mar to Dec 1982. Former mbr, national executive, FF, and former party treasurer. Governor, Bank of European Investment, 1982. B Apr 1938; ed Summerholl Coll, Sligo.

Mr Karel van Miert, who joined the Commission in Jan 1989, served on the staffs of EC Commissioners Mansholt and Simonet. Lectured at Free Univ, Brussels. MEP from 1979-85; served on Cmtes on Political Affairs and Institutional Affairs. Held office as vice-chmn of Socialist International, from 1986; vice-chmn, EC Socialist Parties, 1978-80; also chaired BSP (Belgische Socialistische Partij) Flemish Socialists until 1988. Former university teacher. B Jan 17 1942.

Mrs Vasso Papandreou, a Commissioner from Jan 1989, was Greek Deputy Minister of Commerce in 1988; Deputy Minister of Industry, Energy and Technology, 1986-87; State Secretary for Industry, Energy and Technology, 1985-86; director of organization for small and medium-sized businesses, 1981-85, and also lectureред on economics; mbr, administrative cl, Commercial Bank of Greece, 1982-85. On Central Cmte of PASOK from 1984 and on its executive bureau, 1984-88. B Dec 9 1944; ed Arthens School of Science, Economics and Commerce; London and Reading Univs. Lectured on economics at Exeter Univ, 1971-73 and did research at Oxford, 1973-74.

European Commission offices are at:

Belgium
Archimedesstraat 73, 1040 Brussels. Tel: 235 11 11. Telex: 266 57 COMINF B. Telecopy: 235 01 66.

Denmark
Hojbrohus, Ostergade 61, Postbox 144, 1004 Kobenhavn K. Tel: 14 41 40. Telex: 16402 COMEUR DK. Telecopy: 11 12 03.

France
61 rue des Belles-Feuilles, 75782 Paris Cedex 16. Tel: 45 01 58 85. Telex: Paris 611 01 019 F COMEUR. Telecopy: 47 27 26 07. The Marseille sub-office is at: CMCI/Bureau 320, 2 rue Henri Barbusse, F-13241 Marseille CEDEX 01. Tel: 91 46 00. Telex: 402 538 EURMA. Telecopy: 90 98 07.

West Germany
Zitelmannstrasse 22, 5300 Bonn. Tel: 23 80 41. Telex: 886648 EUROP D. Telecopy: 23 80 48. The Berlin sub-office is at: Kurfurstebdamm 102, 1000 Berlin 31. Tel: 892 40 28. Telex: 184015 EUROP D. Telecopy 892 20 59. The München sub-office is at: Erhardstrasse 27, 8000 München. Tel: 202 10 11. Telex: 52 18 135. Telecopy: 202 10 15.

Greece
2 Vassilissis Sofias, PO Box 11002, Athina 10674. Tel: 724 39 82. Telex: 219324 ECAT GR. Telecopy: 722 37 15.

Ireland
39 Molesworth Street, Dublin 2. Tel: 71 22 44. Telex: 93 827 EUCO EI. Telecopy: 71 26 57.

Italy
Via Poli 29, 00187 Roma, Tel: 678 97 22. Telex: 610184 EUROMA I. Telecopy: 679 16 58. Milano sub-office is at: Corso Magenta 61, 20123 Milano. Tel: 80 15 05/6/7/8. Telex: 316002 EURMIL I. Telecopy: 481 85 43.

Luxembourg
Batiment Jean Monnet, Rue Alcide De Gasperi, 2920 Luxembourg. Tel: 430 11. Telex: 3423/3446/3476 COMEUR LU. Telecopy: 4301 4433.

The Netherlands
Lange Voohout 29, Den Haag. Tel: 46 93 26. Telex: 31094 EURCO NL. Telecopy: 64 66 19.

Portugal
Centre Européen Jean Monnet, 56 rua do Salitre, 1200 Lisboa. Tel: 154 11 44. Telex: 0404/18810 COMEUR P. Telecopy: 155 43 97.

Spain
Calle de Serrano 41, 5a planta. Madrid 1. Tel: 435 17 00/435 15 28. Telex: 46818 OIPE E. Telecopy: 276 03 87.

Switzerland
Case postale 195, 37-39 rue de Vermont, 1211 Geneve 20. Tel: 34 97 50. Telex: 28261 et 28262 ECOM CH. Telecopy: 34 23 31.

United Kingdom
8 Storey's Gate, London SW1P 3AT. Tel: (01) 222 8122. Telex: 23208 EURUK G. Telecopy: 222 0900. The Belfast (Northern Ireland) sub-office is at: Windsor House, 9/15 Bedford Street, Belfast BT2 7EG. Tel: (0232) 240708. Telex: 74117 CECBEL G. Telecopy: 24 82 41. The Cardiff (Wales) sub-office is at: 4 Cathedral Road, Cardiff CF1 9SG. Tel: (0222) 371631. Telex: 497727 EUROPA G. Telecopy: 39 54 89. The Edinburgh (Scotland) sub-office is at: 7 Alva Street, Edinburgh EH2 4PH. Tel: (031) 225 2058. Telex: 727420 EUEDING. Telecopy: 26 41 05.

Presidents of the European Parliament
Common Assembly of the European Coal and Steel Community

Henri Spaak (Belgium, Soc)	Sep 11 1952 to May 11 1954
Alcide de Gasperi (Italy, CD)	May 11 1954 to Aug 18 1954

(On Mr de Gasperi's death, Jean Fohrman, Luxembourg, Soc, assumed the office but not the title of President from Aug 19 1954 to Nov 29 1954 until a successor could be elected.)

Giuseppe Pella (Italy, CD)	Nov 29 1954 to Nov 27 1956
Hans Furler (Germany, CD)	Nov 27 1956 to Mar 19 1958

European Parliament (Nominated MEPs)

Robert Schuman (France, CD)	Mar 19 1958 to Mar 28 1960
Hans Furler (Germany, CD)	Mar 28 1960 to Mar 27 1962
Gaetano Martino (Italy, LD)	Mar 27 1962 to Mar 21 1964
Jean Duvieusart (Belgium, CD)	Mar 21 1964 to Sep 24 1965
Victor Leemans (Belgium, CD)	Sep 24 1965 to Mar 7 1966
Alain Poher (France, CD)	Mar 6 1966 to Mar 12 1969
Mario Scelba (Italy, CD)	Mar 12 1969 to Mar 9 1971
Walter Behrendt (Germany, Soc)	Mar 9 1971 to Mar 13 1973
Cornelis Berkhouwer (Netherlands, LD)	Mar 13 1973 to Mar 11 1975
Georges Spenale (France, Soc)	Mar 11 1975 to Mar 8 1977
Emilio Columbo (Italy, EPP)	Mar 8 1977 to Jul 17 1979

European Parliament (Elected MEPs)

Simone Veil (France, LD)	Jul 17 1979 to Jan 18 1982
Pieter Dankert (Netherlands, Soc)	Jan 20 1982 to Jul 24 1984
Pierre Pflimlin (France, EPP)	Jul 24 1984 to Jan 20 1987
Lord Plumb (United Kingdom, ED)	Jan 20 1987 to Jul 25 1989
Enrique Barón Crespo (Spain, Soc)	Jul 25 1989 to

The bureau of the Parliament consists of the President and Vice-Presidents and the enlarged bureau consists of those appointees plus the political group leaders. The five quaestors, elected to look after MEPs interests sit in on the meetings of the enlarged bureau which arranges the Parliament's agenda and supervises all its activities.

European Parliament Information Offices

The European Parliament holds its plenary sessions at the Palais de l'Europe, Strasbourg (Tel: 88/374001). The European Parliament's secretariat is based at the Centre européen, Plateau du Kirchberg, Luxembourg (Tel: 4300 1) and the Parliament has a block of offices at 97-113, rue Belliard, B-10040 Brussels (Tel: 234 2111). The Secretariats of the political groups and an increasing number of EP staff are based in Brussels and MEPs can be contacted there, especially during committee sessions. The President of the Parliament has offices in each of the three centres of activity.

Information offices of the European Parliament are in:

Athens (Greece) Tel:	
2, avenue Vassilissis Sophias, 10674 Athenes	1/723 34 21
Bonn (West Germany)	
Bonn Center, Bundeskanzlerplatz, 5300 Bonn 1	0228/23 10 01
Bruxelles (Belgium)	
89-91 rue Belliard - 1040 Bruxelles	2/234 21 11
The Hague (The Netherlands)	
Lange Voorhout 27A-2514EB's Gravenhage	70/62 49 31
Dublin (Eire)	
43 Molesworth Street - Dublin 2	1/71 91 00
Copenhagen (Denmark)	
Borsen, 1217 Kobenhavn K	1/14 33 77
London (United Kingdom)	
2 Queen Anne's Gate - London SW1H 9AA	01/222 0411
	Fax: 01/222 2713
	Telex: 894160 EP-LDNG

The London Information Office also contains the offices of the European Democratic (Conservative) Group - Tel: (01) 222 1720 - and the British Labour Group - Tel: (01) 222 2719.

Paris (France)	
288 Bd St. Germain, 75007 Paris	1/45 550 34 11
Rome (Italy)	
Via IV Novembre 149 - 00187 Roma	6/679 06 18 or 6/679 05 07
Madrid (Spain)	
Fanan Flor 4, 28014 Madrid.	Tel: (1) 429 33 52
Lisbon (Portugal)	
Rua do Salitre 56-60, 1200 Lisboa.	Tel: (1) 54 11 44/54 14 49